AMERICAN LABOR

*FROM CONSPIRACY
TO
COLLECTIVE BARGAINING*

THE GOVERNMENT IN
LABOR DISPUTES

Edwin Emil Witte

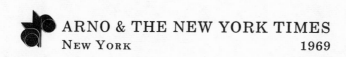
ARNO & THE NEW YORK TIMES
NEW YORK   1969

Reprint edition 1969 by Arno Press, Inc.

Library of Congress Catalog Card No. 70–89770

Reprinted from a copy in
The New York State Library

Manufactured in the United States of America

THE GOVERNMENT IN LABOR DISPUTES

THE GOVERNMENT
IN
LABOR DISPUTES

BY
EDWIN E. WITTE

*Chief, Wisconsin Legislative Reference Library, and Lecturer,
University of Wisconsin*

FIRST EDITION

McGRAW-HILL BOOK COMPANY, INC.

NEW YORK AND LONDON

1932

THE MAPLE PRESS COMPANY, YORK, PA.

To

JOHN R. COMMONS
Teacher—Counselor—Friend

PREFACE

Injunctions in labor disputes have been a subject of much controversy for a generation. Relief from injunctions is organized labor's foremost legislative demand and the principal objective of its non-partisan political campaigns. On no other issue is labor so united; conservatives and radicals alike regard injunctions as an outrage and in strongest terms denounce the courts which issue them. Employers, holding opposite views, feel as keenly.

The strife over injunctions has obscured for the public the fact that this is not the only phase of governmental policy in labor disputes which is in controversy. The "injunction question" as it exists today is much more extensive than the legal process known as the injunction. In the minds of trade unionists, the "abuse of injunctions" includes the numerous criminal prosecutions growing out of labor disputes—in fact, all of labor's grievances against the law. Employers use the term as broadly, connecting injunctions with the entire problem of law enforcement and the protection of their legal rights.

The controversy over injunctions has produced a considerable literature, including contributions by many qualified and disinterested scholars. Most of these have been written by professors of law and have dealt exclusively with legal problems. Recently have been made a number of excellent studies of the actual practice in injunction cases and of other economic and social aspects of the law of labor disputes. All of these studies, however, are monographic in character, none presenting a complete statement of the "injunction question."

This is the aim of this book. It seeks to give a complete account of the role of the government in labor disputes in the United States and of all related problems. It deals with both the law and the activities in this field of every branch of the federal and state governments. Written for the general public, its purpose is to present the facts in such manner that well-informed readers can grasp the complicated questions which are at issue. Although decisions, statutes, and legal theories are discussed, it is an economic, rather than a legal, treatise. Throughout, the emphasis is upon the problems of social policy which are involved. In this, the aim is not to gain converts for any particular program, but to arouse interest in these problems and to give all material facts essential to sound public action.

The writer has followed all developments in this field for more than twenty years. In these years a vast amount of material has been collected from every available source, of which only small portions have heretofore been made public.

The author is neither a trade unionist nor an employer and has received no subsidy from any source for this study. Literally hundreds of trade unionists, employers, judges, clerks of courts, and attorneys, however, have rendered assistance in furnishing information and records relating to concrete cases, in response to inquiries or in connection with field studies. While this is an exceedingly controversial subject, the contending parties and the public officials concerned have, with rare exceptions, been very cooperative and, while they cannot here be named, the author is deeply indebted to all who has thus assisted him in his studies. He also acknowledges his indebtedness to the prior studies in this field.

The inspiration for this study came from Dr. John R. Commons, who has been the author's adviser thoughout the preparation of this book and has read the entire manuscript. Professor W. H. Kiekhofer and Dr. Anna Campbell Davis of the Economics Department and Professor William G. Rice, Jr., of the Law School of the University of Wisconsin and Professor Felix Frankfurter of the Harvard Law School also read the manuscript and offered many helpful suggestions.

The writer is under great obligations to his secretary, Miss Alice Kelly, whose services were invaluable in all phases of the writing stage of this book. Finally, he is indebted to his wife, to whose patient insistence the completion of this study is mainly due.

EDWIN E. WITTE.

MADISON, WISCONSIN,
   October, 1931.

CONTENTS

THE GOVERNMENT IN LABOR DISPUTES

CHAPTER I

THE PUBLIC'S STAKE

COST OF STRIKES

Strikes undoubtedly are the most spectacular of all phenomena in present-day industrial relations, and to the average person they seem the most important. In fact, people who are not directly connected with industry are apt to think of labor problems only when strikes occur.

This is, of course, an uninformed and exaggerated view. That strikes are not the most important aspect of labor problems is brought out vividly by comparing estimates of the losses occasioned by strikes with the cost of accidents, sickness, and unemployment. The National Association of Manufacturers, an organization not likely to underestimate the losses resulting from strikes, has reported that the cost of strikes in the ten-year period 1916–1925 reached the total of $12,982,048,000, of which $46,000,000 fell on employers, $1,804,000,000 on employees, and $10,682,000,000 on the general public.[1] Great as is this total, it does not approach that resulting from industrial accidents, which has been variously estimated at from $3,000,000,000 to $5,000,000,000 per year; or sickness among wage earners, which costs employers, employees, and the public even more. As for unemployment, even in prosperous years the number of men idle because they cannot find employment far exceeds that of workmen on strike. Only once (in 1919) were as many as 2.5

---

[1] Nat. Assoc. of Mfrs., *Convention Proc.*, 136 (1926). For an estimate which places the cost of strikes at a much larger figure, see the booklet "The High Cost of Strikes," by Marshall Olds, published by G. P. Putnam's Sons, New York (1921).

1

per cent of the whole number of working people in this country involved in strikes.[1] In contrast, above 6,000,000 were unemployed in January, 1931, according to Secretary of Commerce Lamont, and this does not include those working part time.

Complete or exact figures upon the cost of strikes are not obtainable.[2] For the period 1906–1913 there are no strike statistics, and for more recent years the number of strikes and the number of men involved are the only data available. Only estimates of the loss resulting from strikes can be given and these must needs ignore many factors which should be considered: whether or not the strikers would have had employment except for the strike; the money they earn in other industries; the improved conditions which they may win; the higher prices manufacturers often get through strikes for their products; and many others.[3]

Nevertheless, strikes, while not the greatest, are an important, source of industrial waste. The largest number of strikes in any year occurred in 1917, when there were 4,450. The maximum number of workingmen directly involved was in 1919, when the total was 4,160,348. More than 1,000,000 workingmen were

---

[1] James J. Davis, Secretary of Labor, in 22 *Monthly Labor Rev.* 15 (1926).

[2] Prior to 1906, the U. S. Commissioner of Labor gathered strike statistics through field agents and included these in four of his annual reports, the last of which was the *Twenty-first Annual Report: Strikes and Lockouts* (1906), which summarizes the earlier reports and gives statistics of strikes for each year from 1881 to 1905. Thereafter, there is a gap until 1914, when the U. S. Bureau of Labor Statistics began gathering strike statistics through news reports, supplemented by correspondence. These are not so complete as the statistics for earlier years and since 1926 take account only of strikes involving six or more employees. The strike statistics collected are published currently in the *Monthly Labor Review* and after the close of the year are brought together in an annual summary, which includes comparisons with prior years. The most recent of these is the article Strikes and Lockouts in the United States, 1916–1929, in 30 *Monthly Labor Rev.* 1328–1338 (June, 1930).

[3] Peculiarly, the years of great coal strikes have generally been years in which the coal miners worked an unusually large number of days. With an average of below two hundred days of work in the bituminous fields per year, the miners can strike for nearly a hundred days and yet work and earn as much during the year as when they do not strike.

For a more complete discussion of the cost of strikes, see the article by Edson L. Whitney on this subject in 11 *Monthly Labor Rev.* 583–600 (September, 1920).

engaged in strikes in each year from 1916 to 1922, inclusive. Since 1922, there has been a marked decrease both in the number of strikes and in the number of workingmen involved, with 1928 showing the lowest total number of strikes—629; and 1929, the smallest number of strikers—230,463. This is less than 1 per cent of all wage earners, but, even so, a conservative estimate of the wage loss alone runs into the millions, and this, of course, is only a small part of the total cost. Strikes in one industry often compel shutdowns and lay-offs in other industries; many strikes cause great inconvenience and even suffering to the general public. T. N. Carver has advanced the thesis that strikes necessarily result in higher prices and that the public is always the loser, no matter who wins.[1] This is an extreme view, but it is at least partially true.

And there are still other items of cost. Strikes often result in loss of life and destruction of property. Almost invariably, they engender a vast amount of bitterness and leave sore spots that are not healed for years. At best, strikes represent a breakdown in the functioning of existing industrial machinery. This is usually later repaired, but often at the cost of lasting resentment. Fundamentally an effect rather than a cause of industrial ills, strikes frequently aggravate the situation and make a solution more difficult.

LABOR DISPUTES WHICH DO NOT RESULT IN STRIKES

Even this is not the entire story. While strikes and labor disputes are usually regarded as synonymous terms, the latter is the more inclusive. Labor disputes are disagreements between employers and employees over the terms of the employment contract, which may result in strikes but more commonly do not. Most labor disputes are amicably adjusted, but many of them, unfortunately, leave unsatisfied grievances, which are none the less serious because they do not lead to strikes.

Smoldering discontent may exist for a long time without coming to a head. Such discontent is reflected in decreased efficiency and an increased cost of production. Even strikes may be preferable, clearing a surcharged atmosphere and affording a

---

[1] "The Present Economic Revolution in the United States," pp. 140–164 (1925).

basis for a fresh start. Many an industry which has had no strikes for years nevertheless has anything but satisfactory industrial relations.

Labor disputes are not necessarily an evil. Human progress has ever been marked by conflict. It is not to be expected that employers and employees will ever be in entire agreement as to the share of each in the common product. But although conflict is natural and not wholly bad, it exacts its toll even when suppressed dissatisfaction takes the place of open revolt.

PROBLEM NOT SOLVED

The marked decrease in the number of strikes since 1922 has resulted in a widespread belief that the problem which they represent is gradually being solved. Beyond question, there was genuine progress toward more harmonious industrial relations in the decade of the twenties. This was a decade of rising wages and of greatly increased attention by employers to the human side of industry. New techniques for dealing with labor have been developed, unquestionably superior to the older, harsher methods. Until the present depression came, an entirely new attitude toward labor seemed to be developing among employers, based on the philosophy that business enterprises are conducted for the benefit of employees no less than for the stockholders, and the belief that high wages are the best guarantee of prosperity.

Another factor contributing to the decrease in the number of strikes was the weak position of the unions and the unfavorable condition of the labor market. Throughout the decade, the labor market has been distinctly an employers' market, with a surplus of labor at all times. This was a period of continued and accelerated concentration in industry.[1] The individual *entrepreneur* and the partnership have almost disappeared in manufacturing, and by 1927, 45 per cent of the assets of all corporations were held by the two hundred largest corporations of the country. The merger and chain movements have apparently been too much for the labor unions to cope with. Since the World War

---

[1] Interesting discussions of this development and its effects upon the labor movement are the papers by Gardiner C. Means, The Large Corporation in American Economic Life, and Myron H. Watkins, Trustification and Economic Theory, in 21 *Proc. Amer. Econ. Assoc.*, 10–43, 60–63 (1931).

they have been distinctly on the defensive, no more than holding their own and even losing some ground. Today, the labor unions of the country have a million members less than in 1920 and embrace only one-fifth of all wage earners, excluding agricultural laborers.[1]

The solid front of the employers, their more enlightened policy, their welfare work, and their company unions, the surplus in the labor market, and the weak position of the labor unions all operated to keep down the number of strikes in the last decade. What has happened during the present depression, however, suggests that the pendulum may soon swing the other way. The widespread wage cuts demonstrate that the philosophy of high wages has not yet really been accepted by American industry. Many employers who attended President Hoover's conference and applauded his appeal to keep up the wage level went home and cut wages in their own plants. Numerous industrial welfare plans have been scrapped and company unions have lost much of their attraction. The employers have so much the upper hand that little resistance on the part of labor is to be expected; but when conditions improve, unless employers show much more industrial statesmanship than is now apparent, a great increase in labor troubles is to be expected.

Nor is the weak position of the unions a favorable factor. Most strikes occur in organized industries, but there are also strikes among the unorganized; and these strikes are likely to be the most violent. When workingmen are unable to gain their ends by peaceful means, the temptation to resort to violence becomes very strong. It is not true, as represented by a recent popular writer,[2] that violence in labor disputes is a relatively new phenomenon, nor even that there has been more violence in strikes recently than formerly. But the labor racketeer is new and organized violence far more prevalent than formerly. Weak unions are likely to be radical unions, and strikes against wage cuts peculiarly violent.

------

[1] HUNT, EDWARD EYRE, "An Audit of America," pp. 81–83, McGraw-Hill Book Company, Inc., New York (1930). Unions affiliated with the American Federation of Labor had 4,078,740 members in 1920; 2,865,799 in 1924; and 2,961,096 in 1930.

[2] ADAMIC, LOUIS, "Dynamite," The Viking Press, New York (1931).

THE GOVERNMENT'S ROLE

The government as the representative of the general public cannot remain indifferent to strikes. The waste and suffering which they entail and, still more, the menace to the public peace which they so often involve compel government to take cognizance of strikes and in many cases to interfere actively. No government ever has adopted a complete hands-off policy in labor disputes. The extent to which government should interfere in labor disputes is debatable, but some degree of governmental intervention is necessary and inevitable.

The legislative, executive, and judicial branches of the government have all perforce had to interest themselves in labor disputes. The federal Congress and the several state legislatures have enacted laws which set forth some of the rules which the contestants must observe. The executive and administrative departments of both the state and federal governments have sought to preserve law and order—not always very effectively—in labor disputes and have also endeavored to prevent and adjust such troubles. Most important, however, has been the role of the judiciary in labor disputes. As the situation has developed, the courts have exercised not only the strictly judicial function of interpreting and applying the law in concrete cases but also have made the law, or most of it. Upon the courts likewise has fallen much of the burden of law enforcement.

DISCONTENT WITH GOVERNMENTAL ACTION

Every phase of governmental intervention in labor disputes has come in for a great deal of criticism. There are few interested parties or students who are altogether satisfied with the manner in which the several governments in this country have dealt with labor disputes, and it is difficult to find anything to which we can point with pride in our handling of labor troubles. There is little reason to believe that governmental action has had much to do with the decrease in strikes. Former Secretary of Labor Davis claims that the United States has relatively the smallest number of strikes of any country.[1] This may be true of the last few years, but can we be sure that there will not be more strikes

---

[1] Speech on the bituminous coal situation, to the American Mining Congress, Dec. 10, 1925, reprinted in 22 *Monthly Labor Rev.* 8–16 (1926).

again in the near future? And even six hundred strikes a year and a quarter million workmen directly involved constitute quite a problem.

With regard to law and order in strikes, our record is distinctly worse than in the matter of the number of strikes. The fact is that there is probably no other country in which violence is so common. Nearly all strikes of importance lead to clashes between strikers and strike sympathizers on the one hand and strike breakers and guards and spies furnished by detective agencies on the other. Assaults, bombings, and even murders are all too frequent. Why this state of affairs exists will be discussed in Chap. IX, and it will there be shown that by no means the entire responsibility falls upon labor. Here, the only point made is that, unfortunately, violence is very prevalent in labor disputes in this country and greatly increases their seriousness.

A further undeniable fact is the discontent of labor over what it believes to be the unfair course and attitude of the courts in labor disputes. This is one of the principal causes of industrial unrest. Upon the "injunction question," there are no radicals or conservatives in the labor movement; labor is 100 per cent opposed to the injunction and critical of the courts. The most conservative of labor leaders have been the most extreme in their denunciation of the attitude of the courts in labor disputes. A statement of labor's view, which is typical of many hundreds of others that might be cited, is that given in the report of the Executive Committee of the American Federation of Labor to the convention of the Federation in 1922, which was unanimously approved by that convention:

In the great industrial struggle of the past year, as in former years, employers have found our courts ever ready and willing to throw the forces of the state on the side of capital and against that of labor . . . Considered from every point, and in the light of a valid and most extensive experience, the injunction process, as used by the courts of our land in industrial disputes, is not an instrument of equity but a weapon of oppression. Through its unwarranted uses and flagrant abuses, the courts of equity have become the courts of the rich, the protectors of property and property rights, and have disregarded the human aspirations and personal rights of the workers . . . In cases dealing with disputes between business men and organizations of labor, the courts clearly establish the fact that in similar cases, there is one rule for workers and another rule for employers.

Nor has labor alone been critical of the existing situation. Employers have often condemned the pusillanimity of police and executive officers in their handling of labor difficulties and the legislature for deliberate toadying to labor. At times they have even expressed dissatisfaction with the judges. In the "Recommendations to the United States Commission on Industrial Relations of the American Anti-boycott Association" in 1914, this occurs:

Even in the federal courts, the wind blows from a different quarter than is popularly believed . . . Courts also show a notable aptitude and inclination to avoid the issues in important and well-presented cases, thereby leaving present and future litigants in a state of uncertainty . . . Other judges make strenuous efforts to settle such cases or try to pass the responsibility over to some associate.

In similar vein, *Law and Labor*, the organ of the League for Industrial Rights, the successor of the American Anti-boycott Association, said, in reviewing John P. Frey's book "The Labor Injunction," a criticism of injunctions in labor disputes by a labor leader:

If Mr. Frey will take the trouble to examine the records, he will find the number of contempt cases involving parties to industrial disputes remarkably few, and he will find that the courts lean over backward in their care to avoid a judgment of contempt when there may be any shadow of doubt concerning the facts of the case.[1]

Numerous criticisms have come also from leaders of the bench and bar and from men prominent in public life. In perhaps no other field of law are dissents so frequent as in cases arising in connection with labor disputes, and there is a considerable diversity with regard to the law as interpreted in different jurisdictions. Many of our most eminent jurists and legal scholars have severely condemned the present law and procedure governing the use of injunctions in labor disputes, if not in their entirety, then in some major phase thereof. Among these, mention will here be made only of the late S. J. Gregory, a president of the American Bar Association; Dean William Draper Lewis, now director of the American Law Institute; former United States Senator George

[1] 4 *Law and Labor* 317 (1922).

W. Pepper of Pennsylvania; and Justices Holmes, Clarke, and Brandeis of the U. S. Supreme Court. Former President Taft once said:

Government of the relations between capital and labor by injunction is a solecism. It is an absurdity. Injunctions in labor disputes are merely the emergency brakes for rare use and in case of a sudden danger. Frequent application of them would shake to pieces the whole machine. They should be availed of only when the soviet policy of a selfish aggregation of men pushes society against the wall into a desperate situation.[1]

Holding diametrically opposite views, but likewise dissatisfied with the existing law, are many who believe that we have not gone far enough in this country in placing restrictions upon labor disputes. Compulsory arbitration has had many able advocates, and there have been numerous proposals in legislatures and elsewhere to make it easier to sue labor unions, to compel labor unions to incorporate, and to place still further restrictions upon what labor may do in labor disputes.

The general public knows little about this subject and hardly realizes that it presents any problem. Members of Congress and of state legislatures, the executive and judicial officers, and the political leaders of the country, however, not only know that the relation of government to labor disputes presents a serious public question but are constantly confronted with this problem in one phase or another. Antiinjunction bills are introduced in every session of Congress and of most state legislatures. Political platforms very often include "injunction planks," and this controversy is something of an issue in all presidential and many congressional elections. In 1928 both the Republican and Democratic parties pledged correction of the abuses which have grown up in connection with the issuance of injunctions in labor disputes. Strikes causing great public inconvenience, riots and acts of violence in labor troubles, and requests for the use of the troops or the militia for the suppression of such disturbances are among the most difficult problems which perplex Presidents and governors. And as for the courts, while in absolute number

---

[1] From an interview published in the *Philadelphia Public Ledger*, Nov. 20, 1919, quoted in the U. S. Senate Hearings on "Limiting Injunctions in Labor Disputes," p. 38 (1928).

labor cases constitute but a small percentage of all cases, judges recognize that these cases are among the most difficult coming before them, arousing more feeling than any other class of litigation and entering often into their campaigns for reelection.

In view of these several aspects of this problem and the widely differing views as to how it should be met, it is timely to inquire: What are the present methods and machinery of governmental intervention? What is the law applicable, and how does it work out? To these questions the succeeding chapters of this book are devoted, and while they do not pretend to give a complete and final answer, they seek to bring together the known facts in a manner intelligible to the average citizen.

Bibliographical Note

Strikes—what they mean to the community and what governmental action should be taken in regard to them—are discussed in every general treatise on labor problems. The best single book on the subject is John A. Fitch, "The Causes of Industrial Unrest," Harper & Brothers, New York (1924). E. T. Hiller, "The Strike: A Study in Collective Action," University of Chicago Press, Chicago (1929), is a sociological study of strikes. The "Report on the Steel Strike of 1919" by the Commission of Inquiry of the Interchurch World Movement, published by Harcourt, Brace & Company, New York (1920), is an account of a particular strike, which is very suggestive upon all problems involved in strikes.

Boycotts are dealt with in Leo Wolman, "The Boycott in American Trade Unions," Johns Hopkins Press, Baltimore (1916); and Harry W. Laidler, "Boycotts and the Labor Struggle," John Lane Co., New York (1913).

Upon the questionable methods used by employers to fight labor, Sidney Howard, The Labor Spy, A Survey of Industrial Espionage, *New Republic* (1924), is very suggestive. On the other side, the following attacks upon organized labor may be consulted: "Violence in Labor Disputes," Cleveland Chamber of Commerce (1916); "A History of Organized Felony and Folly: The Record of Union Labor in Crime and Economics," reprint of articles published in the *Wall Street Journal* (1923); G. L. Hostetter and Thomas Q. Beasley, "It's a Racket," Les Quin Book Co., Chicago (1929); John Landesco, Organized Crime in Chicago, in *Illinois Crime Survey*, pp. 960–975 (1929); Louis Adamic, "Dynamite," The Viking Press, New York (1931).

For criticisms of the present methods of governmental interference in labor disputes emanating from organized labor, almost any issue of any labor periodical or the proceedings of any labor convention may be consulted. Particularly valuable in this connection are the *Proceedings* of the annual conventions of the American Federation of Labor and almost monthly editorials along this line in the *American Federationist*, the official organ of the American Federation of Labor. Good statements of labor's position also occur in John P. Frey, "The Labor Injunction," Equity Publishing Co., Cincinnati (1922); and in William Green, "Labor and Injunctions," a pamphlet published by the American Federation of Labor in 1927. A good secondary article on this subject is David E. Lilienthal, Labor and the Courts, in the *New Republic*, pp. 314–316, May 16, 1923.

For appraisals of the existing situation from the employers' point of view consult: "Some Recommendations Submitted to the United States Commission on Industrial Relations by the American Boycott Association" (1914), and "Proposed Legislation on Public Policy and Industrial Warfare submitted to the Industrial Conference," League of Industrial Rights (1919), both of which are obtainable from this league, which has its headquarters in New York.

CHAPTER II

COURT DECISIONS

What workingmen may and may not do in labor disputes is set forth principally in the decisions of the courts in labor cases. These decisions have been modified only to a minor degree by statutes. It is the purpose of this chapter to summarize these decisions and to present in language intelligible to laymen the conclusions reached by the courts upon the legality of labor's activities in industrial disputes.[1]

LABOR UNIONS

First, the labor unions themselves. As to their right to exist, all courts agree. The permanent combinations known as "trade unions" or as "labor unions," embracing both national and local unions, state federations, and city centrals, are everywhere regarded as lawful organizations. In a few of the early unreported cases in this country, all labor combinations were regarded as unlawful, but, at least since Commonwealth v. Hunt,[2] unions have been regarded as lawful *per se*. In only two decisions since, neither of them by a court of final jurisdiction, have "regular" labor unions been held unlawful, and one of these was reversed upon appeal.[3]

Very different from that of the regular unions is the status of revolutionary unions, such as the communist organizations and the Industrial Workers of the World. These have come under the ban of the antisyndicalism laws now on the statute

---

[1] The law upon what employers may and may not do is discussed in Chap. IX.

[2] 4 Metcalf 111 (Mass. 1842).

[3] Kealy v. Faulkner, 18 (Ohio) Sup. and C. P. Dec. 498 (1908); Hitchman Coal and Coke Co. v. Mitchell, 206 Fed. 512 (1912), reversed in 245 U. S. 229. Labor unions were also most scathingly condemned in Lake Erie and W. R. R. Co. v. Bailey, 61 Fed. 494 (1893) and in A. L. Reed Co. v. Whitman, 3 *Law and Labor* 236 (1921), but in neither of these cases did the courts go so far as to hold the unions to be unlawful.

books of twenty-two states and territories, which laws have been sustained by the courts wherever they have been tested. Under these statutes, mere membership in the I. W. W. has been held to be an offense punishable by imprisonment.[1] Affiliation with this organization has been held ground for the refusal of citizenship to an alien, for the cancellation of a certificate of naturalization, and for the deportation of an alien.[2]

Antisyndicalism laws have never been applied to unions affiliated with the American Federation of Labor, to the railroad unions, nor to any of the non-communistic independent unions. The courts have consistently maintained that governing authorities may forbid public employees to belong to labor unions,[3] but even unions of public employees have not been regarded as unlawful or membership therein as punishable.

Labor unions are not only lawful organizations, but they are institutions favored and protected by statutes. Many states have enacted laws to protect union labels, union cards, and union funds[4]; and in many states the property of labor unions, or at least that of their meeting places, is exempted from taxation.

Despite such governmental favors, labor unions are not in any sense public or quasi-public organizations. They possess no governmental powers, and membership is entirely voluntary. In short, the legal status of unions is practically identical with

---

[1] For Washington decisions to this effect, see State v. Lowery, 177 Pac. 355, 104 Wash. 520 (1918); State v. Hennessy, 195 Pac. 211, 114 Wash. 351 (1921); People v. Steelik, 203 Pac. 78, 187 Cal. 361 (1921); People v. Roe, 209 Pac. 381, 58 Cal. App. 690 (1922); People v. La Rue, 216 Pac. 627, 62 Cal. App. 276 (1923); People v. Thornton, 219 Pac. 1020, 63 Cal. App. 724 (1923); People v. Wagner, 225 Pac. 464, 65 Cal. App. 704 (1924); People v. Cox, 226 Pac. 14, 66 Cal. App. 287 (1924); People v. Johansen, 226 Pac. 634, 66 Cal. App. 343 (1924); People v. Powell, 236 Pac. 311, 71 Cal. App. 500 (1925).

[2] *In re* Olson, 4 F. (2nd) 417 (1925); U. S. v. Swelgin, 254 Fed. 884 (1919); *ex parte* Bernat, 255 Fed. 429 (1918).

[3] People *ex rel.* v. City of Chicago, 278 Ill. 318, 116 N. E. 158 (1917); McNatt v. Lawther, 223 S. W. 503 (Tex. Civ. App. 1920); San Antonio Fire Fighters v. Bell, 223 S. W. 506 (Tex. Civ. App. 1920); Hutchinson v. Magee, 278 Pa. 119, 122 Atl. 234 (1923); Seattle High School Chapter v. Sharples, 10 *Law and Labor* 212 (Super. Ct. Wash. 1928).

[4] *Cf.* Chap. IV, pp. 80–81.

that of fraternal organizations. They cannot be compelled to admit anyone to membership; and the expulsion of members is not reviewable in the courts as long as the procedure is fair and conforms to the union constitution and by-laws.[1] Similarly, the courts will not interfere in the relations between local and international unions, except to enforce the union constitution. Unions may "settle disputes between the members on questions of policy, discipline, or internal government, so long as the government of the society is fairly and honestly administered in conformity with its laws and the laws of the land, and no property or civil rights are involved."[2]

TRADE AGREEMENTS

Passing from the internal to the outside relationships of labor unions discloses a vastly different court policy. Instead of the hands-off attitude which the courts have pursued toward internal union quarrels, practically all dealings of unions with outsiders have come under their close scrutiny and many activities have been condemned.

Collective bargaining, the prime objective of all unions, however, has generally been regarded as not only a lawful, but a praiseworthy activity.

Trade agreements, the fruition of collective bargaining, have usually come before the courts in suits by individual workmen who accepted employment assuming themselves covered by an unexpired trade agreement only to have the employer later claim otherwise. The disposition of these cases has given the courts little difficulty, the generally accepted view

---

[1] Mayer v. Journeymen Stone Cutters Assoc., 47 N. J. Eq. 519, 20 Atl. 492 (1890); Simmons v. Berry, 210 App. Div. 90, 205 N. Y. S. 204 (1924); Frank v. National Alliance, 89 N. J. L. 380, 99 Atl. 134 (1916); Pratt v. Amalgamated Assoc., 50 Utah 472, 167 Pac. 830 (1917); Crisler v. Grum, 115 Neb. 375, 213 N. W. 366 (1927); Havens v. King, 224 N. Y. S. 193 (1927); Agrippino v. Perrotti, 169 N. E. 793 (Mass. 1930). *Contra:* Grand International Brotherhood v. Green, 210 Ala. 496, 98 S. 569 (1923).

[2] Stivers v. Blethen, 124 Wash. 473, 215 Pac. 7 (1923). For a complete discussion of the law governing the relations between unions and their members and between national and local unions and of the fundamental questions of public policy involved, see Zechariah Chafee, The Internal Affairs of Associations Not for Profit, in 43 *Harvard Law Rev.* 993–1029 (1930).

being that where employers have concluded trade agreements, the terms thereof are understood to be incorporated in every contract which they make with workmen of the class covered, unless expressly negatived. In reaching this conclusion, however, there has been considerable diversity, some courts regarding the trade agreement as a mere usage, others as an enforcible contract.

The first theory is the older. This is well stated in a Kentucky case:

A labor union, as such, engages in no business enterprise. It has not the power and does not undertake to supply employers with workmen. It does not, and cannot, bind its members to a service for a definite, or any, period of time, or even to accept the wages and regulations which it might have induced an employer to adopt in the conduct of his business . . . It (the trade agreement) is just what it, on its face, purports to be, and nothing more . . . It is . . . not a contract . . . It comes squarely within the definition of usage . . . "an established method of dealing, adopted in a particular place, or by those engaged in a particular vocation or trade, which acquires legal force, because people make contracts with reference to it."[1]

While this conception of the legal nature of trade agreements is not without support even now, the tendency in recent years has been to treat them as contracts. Damages have seldom if ever been recovered by either party against the other for breaches of trade agreements, but there are numerous instances of injunctions allowed to compel observance.[2]

---

[1] Hudson v. Cincinnati, etc., Co., 152 Ky. 711, 154 S. W. 47 (1913). To the same effect are Burnetta v. Marceline Coal Co., 180 Mo. 241, 79 S. W. 136 (1906); and Barnes v. Berry, 157 Fed. 883 (1908).

[2] Gulla v. Burton, 164 App. Div. 293, 149 N. Y. S. 952 (1914); Tracey v. Osborne, 226 Mass, 25, 114 N. E. 959 (1917); Burgess v. Ga., etc., R. R. Co., 148 Ga. 415, 96 S. E. 864 (1918); Mastell v. Salo, 140 Ark. 408, 215 S. W. 583 (1919); Moody v. Model Window Glass Co., 145 Ark. 197, 224 S. W. 436 (1920); Nederlandsch, etc., v. Stevedores, 265 Fed. 397 (1920); Kinloch Telephone Co. v. Local Union, 265 Fed. 312, 275 Fed. 241 (1920–21); Schlesinger v. Quinto, 201 App. Div. 485, 194 N. Y. S. 401 (1922); Leveranz v. Cleveland Brewing Co., 24 (Ohio) N. P. N. S. 193 (1922); Maisel v. Sigman, 205 N. Y. S. 807 (1924); Pearlman v. Millman 7 *Law and Labor* 286 (Mass. 1925); Cross Mountain Co. v. Ault, 9 S. W. (2nd) 692 (Tenn. 1928); Gary v. Central of Ga. Ry., 141 S. E. 819 (Ga. 1928); Weber v. Nasser, 286 Pac. 1074 (Cal. App. 1930).

For a complete discussion of the legal status of trade agreements, both in the United States and abroad, see the article by William G. Rice, Jr.,

Whether this tendency is advantageous to labor or to society is debatable. William B. Wilson, in his report as Secretary of Labor in 1921, argued vigorously that the policy of regarding trade agreements as contracts would result in discouraging their use.[1] Further, the recognition of trade agreements as contracts is almost certain to result in increased scrutiny of their provisions by the courts. Heretofore, they have been challenged in only a few cases, but if they are to be enforced by the courts, it would seem inevitable that it must be inquired whether they were obtained under duress and whether they are consistent with public policy.[2] This spells increased judicial control of industrial relations—a prospect which dulls labor's enthusiasm for the recent decisions in which contract-breaking employers have been ordered to comply with trade agreements which they had signed.

Collective Labor Agreements, 14 *Harvard Law Rev.* 572–608 (1931). See also R. F. Fuchs, Collective Labor Agreements in American Law, 10 *St. Louis Law Rev.* 1 (1925).

[1] This same view has been expressed on many occasions by Dr. John R. Commons.

[2] There are already several cases in which the courts have passed upon the legality of trade agreements providing for a closed shop.

Such trade agreements were held lawful in Stone Cleaning, etc., Union v. Russell, 77 N. Y. S. 1049 (1902); Jacobs v. Cohen, 183 N. Y. 207, 76 N. E. 5 (1905); Mills v. U. S. Printing Co., 91 N. Y. S. 185 (1904); Kissam v. Printing Co., 199 N. Y. 76, 92 N. E. 214 (1909); National Fireproofing Co. v. Mason Builders, 169 Fed. 259 (1909); Cusumano v. Schlesinger, 152 N. Y. S., 1081 (1915); Tracey v. Osborne, 226 Mass. 25, 114 N. E. 959 (1917); Shinsky v. O'Neil, 232 Mass. 99, 121 N. E. 790 (1919); Reihing v. Local Union, 94 N. J. L. 240, 109 Atl. 367 (1920); Uden v. Schaefer, 110 Wash. 391, 188 Pac. 395 (1920); Ryan v. Hayes, 243 Mass. 168, 137 N. E. 344 (1922); Des Moines City R. Co. v. Amalgamated Assoc., 204 Ia. 1195, 213 N. W. 264 (1927). Preferential agreements have been held legal in Hoban v. Dempsey, 217 Mass. 166, 104 N. E. 717 (1914) and in Underwood v. R. R. Co., 178 S. W. 38 (Tex. Civ. Appeals, 1915). To the contrary are the following decisions in which closed-shop agreements were held to be unlawful as creating a monopoly: Connors v. Connolly, 86 Conn. 641, 86 Atl. 600 (1913); Baldwin Lumber Co. v. Teamsters, 91 N. J. Eq. 240, 109 Atl. 147 (1920); Goyette v. Watson, 245 Mass. 577, 140 N. E. 285 (1923); Overland Publishing Co. v. H. S. Crocker Co., 193 Cal. 109, 222 Pac. 812 (1924); Polk v. Cleveland R. Co., 20 Ohio App. 317 (1925). In Folsom Engraving Co. v. McNeil, 235 Mass. 269, 126 N. E. 479 (1920), a preferential agreement was held unlawful for the same reason.

On the other hand, this development tends to bring American law into line with the generally accepted notion of the nature of trade agreements the world over. Everywhere in continental Europe and also in Australasia, trade agreements are treated as enforcible contracts. Their breach renders the guilty parties liable to damages and in some countries even to criminal prosecution. Individual agreements conflicting with collective agreements are forbidden in France. In Austria and Germany, such agreements may by administrative orders be applied to employers who were not parties thereto. None of the American decisions approaches these European statutes, but they have in recent years been giving increased sanction to trade agreements. And while there are drawbacks to labor, this development should put at rest for all time the argument that employers have no security in dealing with labor unions because trade agreements are unenforcible.

STRIKES: GENERAL PRINCIPLES

The most important of the methods used by labor combinations to secure trade agreements and to effect their other purposes is the strike. While organized labor regards the strike as a measure of last resort, to be used only when all other methods fail, it has always been uncompromisingly opposed to any restriction of the right to strike. Unionists regard striking as a fundamental right guaranteed by the Constitution, particularly by the thirteenth amendment, which prohibits slavery and involuntary servitude.

This is not the conception of the courts. There is only one state (California) in which all strikes, regardless of their purpose, are accounted lawful.[1] There are many statements in the decisions of courts in other states, particularly in earlier cases, to the effect that all strikes are lawful,[2] but when these decisions

---

[1] For a clear statement of the position of the California courts, see Parkinson Co. v. Building Trades Council, 154 Cal. 581, 98 Pac. 1027 (1908).

[2] A typical statement of this kind occurs in Albro J. Newton Co. v. Erickson, 126 N. Y. S. 949, 951 (1911):

"A strike is a combination to quit work; and a strike can never in and of itself be illegal. It does not need to be justified. The absolute right to quit work, which necessarily exists in a free constitutional government construed on individualistic principles, is guaranteed by our Constitution,

are analyzed, it will be found that they turn upon the meaning of the term "strike." As used in these cases, it covers only the quitting of work collectively.[1] As usually understood, it embraces not only the collective quitting of work but the antecedent agreement among the workmen to quit work unless their demands are met. It also carries with it the idea that the quitting of work is but temporary, that the workmen intend to return after an agreement has been reached with their employer upon the matters in dispute. So, in its ordinary usage, the term "strike" includes the entire plan to bring the employer to terms, of which the collective quitting of work is but a part.

Courts which say that the workingman has a right to strike for any or no reason usually mean that the quitting of work may not be prohibited by injunction. Quitting work is not always lawful. It is mutiny for a seaman to quit work while a vessel is at sea, and it is a criminal offense for train crews to abandon a train at a time and under circumstances endangering human life.[2] Similarly, it is unlawful for workmen to quit before the expiration of their contracts, and they are liable for any resulting damages. The courts, however, will never issue an order requiring workmen to perform a contract of employment. If the services are unique, as those of a famous actress or a great baseball player, they will enjoin the person under contract from

---

and cannot be abridged by legislative, executive, or judicial power. Whatever the workmen may legally do, they may announce their intention of doing, and such announcement, even if called a threat, is not illegal."

[1] That the strike embraces something more than the quitting of work and the combination to quit work is implied in the strike advertising laws of many states, which provide that employers in advertising for labor must mention the fact that a strike is in progress if this is the case. These laws have given rise to many close questions, when employers claimed that strikes had ended while the unions claimed that they were still in progress. In these cases, the courts have generally adopted the view that a strike continues until the employer has a full contingent of new employees and the plant produces its normal output. Wisconsin by statute (Stat. 1927, s. 103.43 [1a]), however, has defined a strike so as to make the question whether it is still on turn upon whether the union has or has not given up the struggle.

[2] Until the La Follette Seamen's Act of 1915, seamen were not allowed to quit work even in port before the expiration of their contracts: Robertson v. Baldwin, 165 U. S. 275, 17 Sup. Ct. 326 (1897). For a case in which the abandonment of a train was held a criminal offense, see Clements v. U. S., 297 Fed. 206 (1924), 266 U. S. 605, 45 Sup. Ct. 92 (1924).

working for anyone else but, even in such a situation, do not specifically direct the employee to fulfill the contract.

This does not mean that strikes (using this term in its ordinary sense) are always lawful, as is illustrated by the change made by the Circuit Court of Appeals in the injunction which figured in the oft-cited case of Arthur v. Oakes.[1] The original injunction in that case enjoined the employees of the Northern Pacific Railroad "from so quitting the service of the said receivers, with or without notice, as to cripple the property, or prevent or hinder the operation of the said railroad." The Circuit Court of Appeals modified this particular clause so that it prohibited the employees only "from conspiring or combining to quit, with or without notice, the service of said receivers with the object and intent of crippling the property . . . or embarrassing the operation of said railroads." While courts will not enjoin workmen from quitting work, they will in proper cases prohibit them from combining to quit work. They will, moreover, do everything possible to hinder the workmen from making a success of an unlawful strike, short of ordering them to continue at work. In many recent cases, the courts have even enjoined workmen from "striking," using this term in its usual, broad meaning.

Strikes, then, are not always lawful. On the contrary, everywhere except in California, the legality of strikes depends upon the purpose for which they are conducted. As stated by the U. S. Supreme Court in Dorchy v. Kansas,[2] "neither the common law nor the fourteenth amendment confers the absolute right to strike"; and "a strike may be illegal because of its purpose, however orderly the manner in which it is conducted."

The general principles applied to determine whether the purpose of a strike is lawful or unlawful have been stated by the Massachusetts Supreme Court:

Whether the purpose for which a strike is instituted is or is not a legal justification for it is a question of law to be decided by the court. To justify interference with the rights of others the strikers must in good faith strike for a purpose which the court decides to be a legal justifica-

---

[1] 11 C. C. A. 209, 63 Fed. 310 (1894).
[2] 272 U. S. 306, 47 Sup. Ct. 86 (1926).

tion for such interference . . . A strike is not a strike for a legal purpose because the strikers struck in good faith for a purpose which they thought was a sufficient justification for a strike. As we have said already, to make the strike a legal strike, the purpose of the strike must be one which the court as a matter of law decides is a legal purpose of a strike, and the strikers must have acted in good faith in striking for such a purpose.[1]

LAWFUL AND UNLAWFUL STRIKES

The application of these general principles governing the legality of strikes is to be found literally in hundreds of decisions. It is not possible in brief space to consider all of these cases, nor to state precisely what strikes are lawful and unlawful in each of the several states. Despite the large number of strike cases, the supreme courts of most states have not passed upon many of the purposes for which strikes are undertaken. There is, however, relatively little contradiction, and a decision in one state is very likely to serve as precedent in another.

Cases in which strikes have been held to be lawful are far less frequent than cases in which strikes have been held unlawful. This, in part at least, is due to the fact that the legality of strikes is taken for granted, the question before the court concerning only the legality of acts done in furtherance of the strike. Strikes are more frequently undertaken for increased wages or reduced hours than for any other cause, and such strikes are everywhere accounted lawful.[2] Even strikes to compel out-of-town contractors to pay the higher wage scale of their home communities on such outside work are lawful.[3]

As a general rule, strikes in which the central purpose of the strikers is to secure additional work are also lawful. Yet in

---

[1] De Minico v. Craig, 207 Mass. 593, 94 N. E. 317 (1911).

[2] OAKES, E. S., " Organized Labor and Industrial Conflicts," Secs. 263 and 266, with the long list of cases cited in the footnotes to these sections.

[3] N. J. Painting Co. v. Painters, 96 N. J. Eq. 632, 126 Atl. 399 (1924); Douglas v. Mallette, 7 Law and Labor 304 (Superior Ct. R. I. 1925); Barker Painting Co. v. Local 734, 12 F. (2nd) 945 (1926), review refused upon ground that issue had become moot question, in 34 F. (2nd) 3, 280 U. S. 550, 50 Sup. Ct. 88 (1930); Barker Painting Co. v. Brotherhood of Painters, etc., 23 F. (2nd) 743 (1927), writ of certiorari denied in this case by the U. S. Supreme Court in 276 U. S. 631, 48 Sup. Ct. 324 (1928). Contra: Hass v. Local Union 26, 300 Fed. 894 (1924); Barker Painting Co. v. Brotherhood, 15 F. (2nd) 16 (1926).

concrete situations there are nearly as many cases in which strikes
having this central purpose have been condemned as unlawful.
Strikes have been sustained in which the strikers sought to
force the employment of more men on machines or to limit the
number of apprentices, and in some cases where the employer
attempted to have his work done in outside shops by sub-
contractors.[1] On the other hand, strikes to prohibit an employer
from working on the job himself[2] have invariably been
held illegal, and there are cases condemning strikes to compel
employers to continue manufacturing operations, or to make
them hire more men at given operations than they choose to
employ.[3]

Many other varieties of strike have been condemned as
unlawful. Wherever the question has arisen, the courts have
banned strikes for the collection of fines imposed upon employers
and strikes in violation of trade agreements or in disregard of
individual contracts. Similarly, strikes undertaken to prevent

---

[1] Falls Yarn Mills v. United Textile Workers, 3 *Law and Labor* 125
(Superior Ct. R. I. 1921); Longshore Printing Co. v. Howell, 26 Ore. 527,
38 Pac. 547 (1894); National Fireproofing Co. v. Mason Builders Assoc., 169
Fed. 259 (1909); Minasian v. Osborne, 210 Mass. 250, 96 N. E. 1036 (1911);
Maisel v. Sigman, 205 N. Y. S. 807 (1924).

For cases in which other kinds of strikes not discussed in the text have
been held lawful, see Oakes, *op. cit.*, Secs. 264, 268, 269, 271, 272, 274, and
291.

[2] Roraback v. Motion Picture Operators, 140 Minn. 481, 168 N. W. 766,
169 N. W. 529 (1918); Hughes v. K. C. Motion Picture Operators, 282 Mo.
304, 221 S. W. 95 (1920); Parker Paint and Wall Paper Co. v. Local Union,
87 W. Va. 631, 105 S. E. 911 (W. Va. 1921).

[3] Strikes to compel employers to continue to manufacture were ruled
unlawful in Wilensky v. Hillman, 185 N. Y. S. 257 (1920); Cohen v. Schlesinger, 193 N. Y. S. 928 (1921); Greenberg v. Berlin, 4 *Law and Labor* 309
(1922).   *Contra:* Rutan Co. v. Hatters, 97 N. J. Eq. 77, 128 Atl. 622 (1923).

Strikes to compel employers to employ more men at given operations
were held lawful in Scott-Stafford Opera House Co. v. Musicians, 118 Minn.
410, 136 N. W. 1092 (1912); Empire Theater Co. v. Cloke, 53 Mont. 183, 163
Pac. 107 (1916); and were held unlawful in Haverhill Strand Theater v.
Gillen, 229 Mass. 413, 118 N. E. 671 (1919); Edelman v. Retail, etc., Clerks'
Union, 198 N. Y. S. 17 (1922); Yablonowitz v. Korn, 205 App. Div. 440,
199 N. Y. S. 769 (1923).

Strikes to compel employers to apportion work in slack seasons instead
of discharging workmen were condemned in Jaeckel v. Kaufman, 187 N. Y. S.
889 (1920); Benito Rovira Co. v. Yompolsky, 187 N. Y. S. 894 (1921).

employers from entering into individual contracts with their employees, even when these contracts forbade the employees to join the union, have been held illegal in most jurisdictions where this question has arisen.[1]

It has frequently been suggested that strikes in essential government industries are unlawful. No court, however, has ever held any particular strike of government employees to be unlawful, not considering two cases in which strikes of postal employees were made the bases for criminal indictments for violations of the federal statutes prohibiting interference with the mails.[2]

There is general agreement that strikes which have for their purpose interference with the mails or with interstate commerce are unlawful, but this purpose is seldom if ever the sole object of any strikers. Strikes of persons engaged in interstate commerce which are undertaken for such lawful purposes as an increase in wages or a reduction in hours of labor are not rendered unlawful because they incidentally interfere with interstate commerce or the mails. In only a few cases have strikes of railroad employees been held unlawful.[3] The almost universal

---

[1] Strikes to collect fines have been held illegal in Carew v. Rutherford 106 Mass. 1 (1870); People v. Barondess, 133 N. Y. 649, 31 N. E. 240 (1892); Burke v. Fay, 128 Mo. App. 690, 107 S. W. 408 (1908); People v. Walczak, 315 Ill. 49, 145 N. E. 660 (1924).

A strike to enforce a doubtful private claim was condemned by the U. S. Supreme Court in Dorchy v. Kansas, 272 U. S. 306, 47 Sup. Ct. 86 (1926).

Strikes in violation of trade agreements held unlawful: Reynolds v. Davis, 198 Mass. 294, 84 N. E. 457 (1908); Gilchrist Co. v. Metal Polishers, 113 Atl. 320 (N. J. Chancery 1919); Best Service, etc., Co. v. Dickson, 201 N. Y. S. 173 (1923); Meltzer v. Kaminer, 227 N. Y. S. 459 (1927). A strike in violation of individual contracts was held unlawful in Cook v. Wilson, 178 N. Y. S. 463 (1919).

Strikes against efforts of employers to sign their employees to individual non-union contracts were held illegal in Floresheimer v. Schlesinger, 187 N. Y. S. 891 (1921); McMichael v. Atlanta Envelope Co., 151 Ga. 776, 108 S. E. 226 (1921); Moore Drop Forging Co. v. McCarthy, 243 Mass. 554, 137 N. E. 919 (1923). *Contra:* LaFrance, etc., Co. v. International Brotherhood, 108 Ohio 61, 140 N. E. 899 (1923).

[2] These cases are discussed in Chap. IV, p. 76.

[3] One of these cases dates back to 1877, King v. Ohio & M. Ry. Co., 7 Biss. 513, Fed. Cases 7800. Another was an unreported decision by U. S. Judge Ricks in 1893, published in the *Washington Star*, Apr. 1, 1893. Two other decisions to this effect were rendered in connection with the railroad

opinion is that the lawfulness of railroad strikes is governed by the same principle as that of other strikes, regardless of the effect of these strikes on interstate commerce.

While the legislature may undoubtedly place restrictions upon the right to strike in essential occupations affected peculiarly by the public interest, and probably also upon strikes in war time, in the absence of legislation the courts usually will not interfere with strikes on these grounds.[1]

STRIKES FOR THE CLOSED SHOP

Far more frequently than the strikes discussed in the preceding section, two other principal kinds of strikes, closed-shop strikes and sympathetic strikes, have been challenged in the courts. The question of closed-shop strikes has come before the courts in different ways, but most frequently over the demand of unions for the discharge of workmen (and sometimes of foremen) not belonging to the union, or belonging to a rival union, although sometimes the question before the courts has been that of a strike for the reinstatement of union members discharged by an employer or for recognition of the union. Recognition is not necessarily the same thing as the closed shop but has been so regarded in nearly all cases which have come before the courts.

Closed-shop cases have come up more frequently in the courts of Massachusetts than in any other state, and it is here that such strikes have most frequently been condemned.[2] The attitude

---

shop crafts strike of 1922: U. S. v. Railway Employees Dept., 290 Fed. 978; Michaelson v. Chicago, etc., Ry. Co., 291 Fed. 940.

[1] In Rosenwasser v. Pepper, 172 N. Y. S. 310 (1918), it was held that all strikes are unlawful in war time. In Gottlieb v. Matchkin, 191 N. Y. S. 777 (1921), a strike of milk-wagon drivers was condemned on the ground that it interfered with an essential public service. Both cases are extreme and should not be taken as representing generally accepted law.

That restrictions may be placed upon strikes in industries peculiarly affected with a public interest is generally acknowledged. See Wilson v New, 243 U. S. 332, 37 Sup. Ct. 298 (1917) and People v. United Mine Workers, 70 Col. 269, 201 Pac. 54 (1921).

[2] The following Massachusetts cases involve this question in some form or other: Plant v. Woods, 176 Mass. 492, 57 N. E. 1011 (1900); Berry v. Donovan, 188 Mass. 353, 74 N. E. 603 (1905); Pickett v. Walsh, 192 Mass. 572, 78 N. E. 753 (1906); Aberthaw Construction Co. v. Cameron, 194 Mass. 208, 80 N. E. 478 (1907); Reynolds v. Davis, 198 Mass. 294, 84 N. E. 457 (1908); Folsom v. Lewis, 208 Mass. 336, 94 N. E. 316 (1911); Deminicio

of the Massachusetts courts is not that all closed-shop agreements are illegal or that every strike for the discharge of workmen is necessarily unlawful. Agreements for the closed shop voluntarily entered into and not monopolistic in character have been held to be lawful. So have strikes to procure the discharge of workmen against whom the strikers have a legitimate grievance. The Massachusetts courts, however, hold that it is their function to pass upon the question whether the strikers have just cause for their demand that other workmen be discharged, and they have refused to regard the motive of strengthening the union as a just cause for such a demand. Strikes for the discharge of members of rival unions have been sustained by the Massachusetts Supreme Court in several cases, but in not a single case has this court ever found a strike for the discharge of non-unionists to have been justified. Such strikes have been condemned in more than a dozen cases, as have strikes to procure the reinstatement of union members, or to discharge objectionable foremen. This court has even condemned strikes to gain the preferential shop, which differs from the closed shop in that, while non-union members are not barred, preference is given to the union members. It has likewise ruled unlawful strikes over the recognition of the union, and a similar conclusion has been reached with regard to strikes in which the demand for a closed shop was but one of several demands made by the strikers. Underlying all these conclusions is the conviction that, while labor unions are lawful organizations, all efforts to strengthen their position are illegal if they involve loss to non-union members or to employers.

---

v. Craig, 207 Mass. 593, 94 N. E. 317 (1911); Hanson v. Innis, 211 Mass. 301, 97 N. E. 756 (1912); Hotel and Railroad News Co. v. Leventhal, 243 Mass. 317, 137 N. E. 534 (1912); Fairbanks v. McDonald, 219 Mass. 291, 106 N. E. 1000 (1914); Burnham v. Dowd, 217 Mass. 351, 104 N. E. 841 (1914); Cornellier v. Haverhill Shoe Manufacturers Assoc., 221 Mass. 554, 109 N. E. 643 (1915); Snow Iron Works v. Chadwick, 227 Mass. 382, 116 N. E. 801 (1917); Bausch Machine Co. v. Hill, 231 Mass. 30, 120 N. E. 188 (1918); Smith v. Bowen, 232 Mass. 106, 121 N. E. 814 (1919); Shinsky v. O'Neil, 232 Mass. 99, 121 N. E. 790 (1919); Folsom Engraving Co. v. O'Neil, 235 Mass. 269, 126 N. E. 479 (1920); Plant v. Gould, 2 *Law and Labor* 276 (1920); Mechanics Foundry Co. v. Lynch, 236 Mass. 504, 128 N. E. 877 (1920); Jackson v. Brown, 3 *Law and Labor* 53 (1921); United Shoe Machinery Corp. v. Fitzgerald, 237 Mass. 537, 130 N. E. 86 (1921); Stearns Lumber Co. v. Howlett, 260 Mass. 45, 157 N. E. 82 (1927).

Many cases raising this issue of unionization have come up in New York, but the position taken by the New York courts is much more liberal than that of the Massachusetts courts.[1] It is difficult to reconcile the New York cases except on the assumption that the viewpoint of the New York Court of Appeals has gradually become more favorable to labor. In 1897, this court held that workmen who were discharged pursuant to closed-shop agreements might recover damages from the union. In 1902, the same court held that a strike for the closed shop is lawful and, in 1905, it held enforcible a trade agreement which provided for the exclusive employment of union members. None of these three cases has ever been overruled, and they are still regarded as the leading cases in New York upon the issue of unionization. From these cases and those which have followed, the conclusion seems warranted that strikes to gain union recognition and the closed shop are lawful even though they involve the discharge of non-unionists, unless the effect of the demand of the unions is to create a monopoly for them in a particular community. That the motion of strengthening the union is a legitimate one, justifying the infliction of loss upon employers and non-unionists, has been squarely asserted by the New York Court of Appeals in at least one recent case. The New York and Massachusetts courts have reached opposite conclusions upon this issue, which has long been one of the most debated in the entire law of labor combinations.

---

[1] Decisions of the New York Court of Appeals involving this question are the following: Curran v. Galen, 152 N. Y. 33, 46 N. E. 297 (1902); National Protective Assoc. v. Cumming, 170 N. Y. 315, 63 N. E. 369 (1902); Jacobs v. Cohen, 183 N. Y. 207, 76 N. E. 5 (1905); Kissam v. Printing Co., 199 N. Y. 76, 92 N. E. 214 (1910); McCord v. Thompson-Starrett Co., 198 N. Y. 587, 92 N. E. 1090 (1910) affirming 129 App. Div. 130, 113 N. Y. S. 385 (1909); Exchange Bakery and Restaurant Inc. v. Riffkin, 245 N. Y. 260, 157 N. E. 30 (1927).

Other New York cases of the last two decades, some of which take a position different from that presented in the text, are: Schwarcz v. Ladies' Garment Workers, 68 Misc. 528, 124 N. Y. S. 968 (1910); Newton Co. v. Erickson, 126 N. Y. S. 949, 129 N. Y. S. 1111 (1911); Cusumano v. Schlesinger, 152 N. Y. S. 1081 (1915); Grassi Contracting Co. v. Bennett, 160 N. Y. S. 279 (1916); Coon Co., Inc. v. Meinhart, 112 Misc. 650, 183 N. Y. S. 713 (1920); Michaels v. Hillman, 183 N. Y. S. 195 (1920); Yates Hotel Co. v. Myers, 195 N. Y. S. 558 (1922); Herzog v. Cline, 131 Misc. 816, 227 N. Y. S. 462 (1927). See also Aeolian Co. v. Fischer (1928–1929), 27 F. (2nd) 560, 29 F. (2nd) 679, 35 F. (2nd) 34, construing the New York law.

In other states, there have been fewer cases involving this question. In fact, a majority of the state supreme courts have never passed on the legality of strikes for union recognition or the closed shop. Where this question has come up, the courts have been almost evenly divided between the Massachusetts and New York positions. Strikes for the discharge of non-unionists have been held illegal by the Supreme Courts of Connecticut, New Hampshire, New Jersey, Pennsylvania, and Vermont, and also in an old Maryland case; while in Delaware, a strike for union recognition has been condemned. Strikes for the discharge of non-unionists or of members of rival unions have been sustained by the highest courts in Arkansas, California, Indiana, and Oklahoma, and by the Supreme Court of the District of Columbia (an inferior court). In 1905, the Illinois Supreme Court severely condemned the closed shop in a case where this was only an incidental question. In 1912, in a case in which the issue of the legality of a strike for the discharge of non-unionists was definitely presented, the court divided three to three upon this issue, with a seventh judge holding for labor but refusing to endorse the closed shop. In Texas, no decision has been rendered by the Supreme Court, and the decisions of the intermediate appellate courts are irreconcilable. In the federal courts, there have been few cases involving this issue, and in not a single case has the U. S. Supreme Court passed upon the question of unionization.[1]

SYMPATHETIC STRIKES

Sympathetic strikes have provoked almost as frequent court disagreements as closed-shop strikes, but with a larger percentage of the decisions unfavorable to labor. By the term "sympathetic strike," most people understand a strike by the workmen of one employer or craft in aid of the employees of another. Such strikes occur most frequently in the building trades, due to the

---

[1] Cases in point are:

Connecticut: Wyeman v. Deady, 79 Conn. 414, 65 Atl. 129 (1906); Connors v. Connolly, 86 Conn. 641, 86 Atl. 600 (1913). Slightly contrary: Cohn, etc., Co. v. Bricklayers, 92 Conn. 161, 101 Atl. 659 (1917).

New Hampshire: White Mountain Freezer Co. v. Murphy, 78 N. H. 398, 101 Atl. 659 (1917).

New Jersey: State v. Donaldson, 32 N. J. L. 151 (1867); Blanchard v. Newark Joint District Council, 78 N. J. L. 389, 71 Atl. 1131 (1908); Ruddy v. United Assoc., 79 N. J. L. 467, 75 Atl. 742, (1910); Baldwin Lumber

fact that in this industry labor is organized along craft lines. When one craft, say the electrical workers, has a difficulty with the subcontractor by whom it is employed, it is a common occurrence for all of the other crafts employed on the same building to go on strike with the electrical workers, so as to compel the general contractor and building owner to bring the subcontractor employing the electrical workers to terms. In an industry organized along industrial lines, such as coal mining, much the same situation often arises, but when all the miners go on strike because, perchance, the hoisting engineers are involved in a dispute over wages, no one regards this as a sympathetic strike, because the hoisting engineers and the miners all belong to the same union. In the building trades, however, where each particular craft has its own union, when the same circumstance

Co. v. Local 560, 91 N. J. Eq. 240, 109 Atl. 147 (1920); Bijur Motor Appliance Co. v. International Assoc. of Machinists, 92 N. J. Eq. 644, 111 Atl. 802 (1920); Lehigh Structural Steel Co. v. Atlantic, etc., Works, 92 N. J. Eq. 131, 111 Atl. 376 (1920); Gevas v. Greek, etc., Club, 99 N. J. Eq. 770, 134 Atl. 309 (1926). Contrary: Mayer v. Journeymen Stone Cutters, 47 N. J. Eq. 519, 20 Atl. 492, (1890); Jersey City Printing Co. v. Cassidy, 63 N. J. Eq. 759, 53 Atl. 230 (1902).

Pennsylvania: Erdman v. Mitchell, 207 Pa. 79, 56 Atl. 327 (1903); Bausbach v. Rieff, 244 Pa. 559, 91 Atl. 224 (1914).

Vermont: State v. Dyer, 67 Vt. 690, 32 Atl. 814 (1895).

Maryland: Lucke v. Clothing Cutters, 77 Md. 396, 26 Atl. 505 (1893).

Delaware: Sarros v. Nouris, 138 Atl. 607 (1927).

Arkansas: Harmon v. United Mine Workers, 166 Ark. 255, 266 S. W. 84 (1924).

California: Overland Publishing Co. v. Union Lithograph Co., 57 Cal. App. 366, 207 Pac. 412 (1922); Greenwood v. Building Trades Council, 71 Cal. App. 159, 233 Pac. 823 (1925).

Indiana: Shaughnessey v. Jordan, 184 Ind. 499, 111 N. E. 622 (1916).

Oklahoma: Roddy v. United Mine Workers, 41 Okla. 621, 139 Pac. 126 (1914).

District of Columbia: Bender v. Local Union, 34 Wash. Law Rep. 574 (1906).

Illinois: O'Brien v. People, 216 Ill. 354, 75 N. E. 108 (1905); Kemp v. Division 241, 255 Ill. 213, 99 N. E. 389 (1912).

Texas: Cooks, etc., Union v. Papageorge, 230 S. W. 1086 (1921); Sheehan v. Levy, 238 S. W. 900 (1922). But a strike for a preferential union shop has been held lawful in Underwood v. Texas & Pac. R. R. Co., 178 S. W. 38 (1915).

Federal: National Fireproofing Co. v. Mason Builders' Assoc., 169 Fed. 259 (1909); Tunstall v. Stearns Coal Co., 192 Fed. 808 (1911); Niles-Bement-Pond Co. v. Iron Molders, 246 Fed. 851 (1917).

occurs, it is called a sympathetic strike, and such strikes have in a considerable number of cases been held unlawful.[1]

Sympathetic strikes also occur at times in other industries.   In a few scattered instances, there have been general strikes affecting either all industries in a given community or, more commonly, workmen in related industries.   Such sympathetic strikes have nearly always been condemned as illegal.[2]

But more frequently than any other type of sympathetic strike, the strike against non-union materials has come up.   Such strikes are often referred to as boycotts, but they are boycotts carried out, not through the refusal to patronize, but through the refusal to work, that is, by strikes or threats of strikes.   Such strikes are waged to effect the unionization of the factories supplying the materials against which the strikes are called.   Typical are the strikes which the carpenters in New York conducted for nearly a decade beginning in 1910 against "non-union wood trim," that is, wood trim supplied by non-union factories.   The purpose of the strikes called in New York was to prevent the contractors and building owners in that city from using these non-union materials, with the ultimate end in view of compelling the material manufacturers to deal with the union.

Upon the legality of such strikes against non-union materials, the courts are divided.   The Supreme Courts of California, North Carolina, and New York have ruled them to be legal, and there is at least an intimation to the same effect in a decision of

[1] Beattie v. Callahan, 67 App. Div. 14, 73 N. Y. S. 513, 81 N. Y. S. 413 (1901–1903); Gray v. Building Trades Council, 91 Minn. 171, 97 N. W. 663 (1903); Pickett v. Walsh, 192 Mass. 572, 78 N. E. 753 (1906); Aberthaw Construction Co. v. Cameron, 194 Mass. 208, 80 N. E. 478 (1907); Reynolds v. Davis, 198 Mass. 294, 84 N. E. 457 (1908); New England, etc., Co. v. McGivern, 218 Mass. 198, 105 N. E. 885 (1914); Grant Construction Co. v. St. Paul Building Trades Council, 136 Minn. 167, 161 N. W. 520, 1055 (1917); Leheigh Structural Steel Co. v. Atlantic, etc., Works, 92 N. J. Eq. 131, 111 Atl. 376 (1920); Blandford v. Duthie, 147 Md. 388, 128 Atl. 138 (1925); Bricklayers', Masons' and Plasterers' International Union v. Seymour, Ruff & Sons, Inc., 52 Atl. 232 (Md., 1931).

[2] Booth v. Brown, 62 Fed. 794 (1894); Thomas v. Cincinnati, etc., R. R. Co., 62 Fed. 803 (1894); Burgess v. Stewart, 112 Misc. 347, 184 N. Y. S. 199 (1920), 114 Misc. 673, 187 N. Y. S. 873 (1921); Buyer v. Guillan, 271 Fed. 65 (1921); International Brotherhood of Electrical Workers v. Western Union, 6 F. (2nd) 444 (1925); Bellows Corp. v. Electrical Workers, 10 *Law and Labor* 5 (Ohio Com. Pl. 1927).

the Arkansas Supreme Court. On the other hand, the U. S. Supreme Court in two decisions has held strikes against non-union materials to constitute illegal boycotts, and this is likewise the view of the Supreme Courts of Florida, Massachusetts, New Jersey, and Pennsylvania, and of inferior federal and Ohio courts.[1]

A special form of strike against non-union materials is the strike against "struck materials." Such strikes occur when an employer involved in a strike transfers his orders to another employer and has this other employer fulfill his contracts. In such cases, if the plant of the second employer is organized, his workmen will usually refuse to work upon the "strike orders," since the filling of these orders operates to defeat the men on strike in the other plant. Few such strikes have come before the courts, and in these cases the courts have disagreed. The

---

[1] Strikes against non-union materials, lawful:

New York: Bossert v. Dhuy, 221 N. Y. 342, 117 N. E. 582 (1917); Newton Co. v. Erickson, 126 N. Y. S. 949 (1911) affirmed in 129 N. Y. S. 1111 (1911) and in 221 N. Y. 632, 117 N. E. 1059 (1917); Aeolian Co. v. Fischer, 27 F. (2nd) 560 (1928).

California: Parkinson v. Building Trades Council, 154 Cal. 581, 98 Pac. 1027 (1908).

North Carolina: State v. Van Pelt, 136 N. C. 633, 49 S. E. 177 (1904).

Arkansas: Meier v. Speer, 96 Ark. 618, 132 S. W. 988 (1910) (not directly in point).

Strikes against non-union materials, unlawful:

Ohio: Parker v. Bricklayers, 10 Ohio Dec. 458 (1889); Moores v. Bricklayers, 10 Ohio Dec. 645 (1890).

Pennsylvania: Patterson v. Building Trades Council, 11 Pa. Dist. 500 (1902); Purvis v. Carpenters, 214 Pa. 348, 63 Atl. 585 (1906).

Florida: Jetton-Dekle v. Mather, 53 Fla. 969, 43 So. 590 (1907).

Massachusetts: Burnham v. Dowd, 217 Mass. 351, 104 N. E. 841 (1914); Stearns Lumber Co. v. Howlett, 260 Mass. 45, 157 N. E. 82 (1927), 163 N. E. 193 (1928).

New Jersey: Booth v. Burgess, 72 N. J. Eq. 181, 65 Atl. 231 (1906).

United States: Duplex Printing Press Co. v. Deering, 254 U. S. 443, 41 Sup. Ct. 172 (1921); Bedford Cut Stone Co. v. Stone Cutters, 274 U. S. 37, 47 Sup. Ct. 522 (1927).

Federal: Huttig v. Fuelle, 143 Fed. 363 (1906); Shine v. Fox Brothers Manufacturing Co., 156 Fed. 357 (1908); Irving v. Joint District Council, 180 Fed. 896 (1910); Irving v. Neal, 209 Fed. 471 (1913); Paine Lumber Co. v. Neal, 212 Fed. 259, 214 Fed. 82 (1913); Decorative Stone Co. v. Building Trades Council 13 F. (2nd) 123 (1926).

Supreme Court of Washington has held such strikes to be unlawful, as have appellate courts in Illinois and New York. The opposite conclusion was reached by a U. S. Circuit Court of Appeals and by courts in other New York cases.[1]

COURT ACTION AGAINST ILLEGAL STRIKES

The problem of preventing illegal strikes is one which has given the courts considerable difficulty. Until quite recently, the generally accepted belief was that workmen could not be prevented from striking. In the Ann Arbor case, in 1893,[2] William H. Taft, then a United States circuit judge, did hold that locomotive engineers employed by the Pennsylvania Railroad could by process of injunction be compelled to handle cars from the "struck" Ann Arbor road, but in the same decision he expressly stated that the courts could not by injunction prevent the Pennsylvania engineers from quitting their employment altogether, and further, that since the engineers could not be prevented from quitting work, the union officers could not be enjoined from advising them to quit or assisting them if they should quit. In the Arthur v. Oakes case[3] in the next year, Justice Harlan of the U. S. Supreme Court held that, while workmen might not be enjoined from striking, they might be enjoined from conspiring to quit work with the intent of interfering with the operation of the railroad by which they were employed. Later, it was attempted to prevent or cripple illegal strikes by prohibiting union officers from issuing strike orders, from advising union members to go on strike, or from paying the strikers any strike benefits. Adopting the position taken by Justice Taft, however, such prohibitions were in several cases held invalid by appellate courts on the theory that they amounted

---

[1] Strikes against "strike orders" were condemned in Piano and Organ Workers v. Piano, etc., Co., 124 Ill. App. 353 (1906); Schlang v. Ladies Waist Makers, 124 N. Y. S. 289 (1910); Pacific Typesetting Co. v. Typographical Union, 125 Wash. 273, 216 Pac. 358 (1923). Such cases were sustained in Searle Manufacturing Co. v. Terry, 106 N. Y. S. 438 (1905); Iron Molders' Union v. Allis Chalmers Co., 166 Fed. 45 (1908).

[2] 54 Fed. 730.

[3] 63 Fed. 310.

to an indirect method of compelling workmen to continue in employment, which, it was assumed, could not be done directly.[1]

Within the last ten years, nevertheless, a considerable number of injunctions have been issued not only forbidding union officers from advising or ordering strikes and enjoining the payment of strike benefits but directly forbidding strikes. In some cases injunctions have directed union officers to call off strikes already in progress, and in a few instances definite provisions have been included to make certain that the union officers did observe the court's directions. In comparatively few cases has the validity of such orders been discussed,[2] but their issuance has become a familiar practice.

It remains true, however, that it still does not follow that, because a strike is illegal, it can be prevented. Most decisions holding strikes illegal have been rendered in cases where no attempt was made to prevent the strike. Likewise, it seems that just as many strikes for the closed shop and strikes against non-union materials occur in states in which such strikes have been held unlawful as in states where such strikes have been held lawful, or where there are no supreme court decisions in point. What the future may bring forth in this respect, however, is uncertain, since there has been a distinct tendency in the last decade toward the more extensive and effective use of the injunction to prevent or break up illegal strikes.

PERSUASION AND INTIMIDATION

In the great majority of cases growing out of strikes, the issue is not the legality of the strike itself but rather the conduct of the strikers. Here, there is general agreement on fundamental principles. Persuasion of employees, prospective employees, and customers is lawful; threats, coercion, and intimidation are unlawful.

---

[1] Wabash R. R. Co. v. Hannahan, 121 Fed. 563 (1903); Barnes v. Berry, 157 Fed. 883 (1908); Del., etc., R. R. Co. v. Switchmen, 158 Fed. 541 (1908); Kemp v. Division 241, 255 Ill. 213, 99 N. E. 389 (1912).

[2] Such injunctions were upheld in Burgess v. Ga., etc., R. R. Co., 148 Ga. 415, 96 S. E. 864 (1918) and in Western Union v. International Brotherhood, 2 F. (2nd) 993 (1924). For an opposite view, see Lundoff v. Smith, 24 Ohio App. 294 (1927).

Technically, intimidation is not limited to physical violence or threats of violence. "Any words or acts which are calculated and intended to cause any ordinary person to fear an injury to his person, business, or property are equivalent to threats."[1] Though no word is spoken, the conduct of strikers may be intimidating; their number alone may be sufficient to create fear. Regardless of how the fear is produced, the simple fact of its existence among employees and prospective employees condemns the strikers. Nor is it necessary to prove that any particular person was intimidated. "It is only necessary to prove that the threats and acts are such as would be calculated to cause the ordinary man to fear or to affect his mind in such a way that he could not voluntarily act or assent."[2]

While intimidation is always unlawful, persuasion is not always lawful. Persuasion is lawful only if the purpose of the strike is lawful. Likewise the persuasion must not be directed to bring about a breach of contract. Where the "loyal" employees work under contracts binding them to serve for a definite period of time, acts and words designed to persuade them to join in a strike are illegal. This doctrine has been applied even where the loyal employees are free to quit at any time, the argument being that they would have continued but for the interference by outsiders.[3] A still further extension has occurred in the "yellow-dog contract cases," which are discussed in Chap. X. These cases involve contracts which obligate the loyal employees not to join a labor union or not to join in any strike. In numerous instances in recent years, these contracts have furnished the basis for injunctions prohibiting persuasion designed to induce employees to join in strikes, and for orders prohibiting union officers and organizers from ordering or inducing them to strike.

---

[1] State v. Stockford, 77 Conn. 227, 58 Atl. 769 (1904).

[2] State v. McGee, 81 Conn. 696, 69 Atl. 1059 (1909).

For a more complete discussion as to what constitutes intimidation, see Oakes, *op. cit.*, Sec. 320, and the footnotes thereto.

[3] Walker v. Cronin, 107 Mass. 555 (1871); O'Neil v. Behanna, 182 Pa. 236, 37 Atl. 843 (1897); Frank v. Herold, 62 N. J. Eq. 443, 52 Atl. 152 (1901); George Jonas Glass Co. v. Glass Bottle Blowers, 77 N. J. Eq. 219, 79 Atl. 262 (1911); Southern R. R. Co. v. Machinists, 111 Fed. 49 (1901); Davis Machine Co. v. Robinson, 41 Misc. 329, 84 N. Y. S. 837 (1903).

With the exceptions noted, persuasion is lawful and may be resorted to by strikers to gain recruits and further support. Payment of strike benefits is also for the most part lawful, although there are numerous cases in which such payment has been prohibited, where the courts deemed the strike itself to be unlawful. Likewise, it is lawful to offer transportation back home to prospective employees brought in by the employer to take the place of men who have gone on strike, provided the strike itself be lawful. There are cases on record which hold that the payment of moneys for this purpose represents bribery, but the weight of the courts' decisions sustains this familiar practice in strikes.[1]

Similarly, the distribution of handbills and the display of banners and placards stating the case of the strikers are generally lawful. Such methods of publicity, however, may be prohibited by local ordinance and become unlawful if the information conveyed is false, libelous, or intimidating.

PICKETING

Picketing is the principal method used by strikers to persuade the loyal and "new" employees to join them. It is also frequently employed to induce labor sympathizers and the general public to withhold patronage from employers or merchants with whom labor has a dispute.

Picketing is conducted in a great variety of ways. Most commonly it is carried on by representatives of the strikers stationed outside of the plant or place of business, who address the employees, prospective employees, or customers, as they enter, in an effort to convert them to the strikers' cause. Sometimes the pickets say nothing but present their case by means of banners or placards. Usually picketing is conducted in a systematic and orderly manner, with a limited number of pickets operating on regular beats and schedules.

At other times, so-called "mass picketing" prevails, which means that all of the strikers and others sympathizing with them gather in a body in front of the struck premises. In some instances, such mass picketing is regulated and orderly, but very often it is accompanied by hooting and jeering, and at times by

---

[1] OAKES, *op. cit.*, Secs. 322, 323, and cases cited.

physical violence. Even picketing in limited numbers may be thus conducted, or it may be peaceful in every sense of the word.

There have been more court decisions upon the legality of picketing than upon any other question in the law of labor combinations. In these decisions, there is considerable difference in the statement of the law, but these differences are more apparent than real. The apparent contradictions are largely due to two factors: (1) the use of the term "picketing" in different senses and (2) a difference in the time when the decisions were rendered, a marked change in the law as to picketing having been brought about by two decisions of the U. S. Supreme Court in 1921.

The crucial question in the law of picketing is whether peaceful picketing is lawful. Picketing which is not peaceful is recognized by all courts to be unlawful. Unlawful picketing comprises that characterized by abusive language and threats of violence, veiled or open, as well as by physical violence. It is recognized in all cases that mere numbers may be intimidating so that an "unreasonable" number of pickets is unlawful, even when they conduct themselves in an orderly manner. Some courts go so far as to hold that speaking to employees against their will amounts to intimidation and is unlawful.[1]

Upon the question whether truly peaceful picketing is lawful, the courts were, prior to 1921, seriously divided. One view was forcibly expressed by a federal court: "There is and can be no such thing as peaceful picketing, any more than there can be chaste vulgarity or peaceful mobbing or lawful lynching. When men want to persuade, they do not organize a picket line."[2] This opinion was held prior to 1921 by the Supreme Courts of California, Illinois, Massachusetts, Michigan, New Jersey, Pennsylvania, and Washington, and in many federal cases.[3] The exact

---

[1] Frank v. Herold, 63 N. J. Eq. 443, 52 Atl. 152 (1901); Jersey Printing Co. v. Cassidy, 63 N. J. Eq. 759, 53 Atl. 230 (1902); Goldfield Consolidated Mines Co. v. Miners' Union, 159 Fed. 500 (1908).

[2] Atchison, etc., Co. v. Gee, 139 Fed. 582 (1905).

[3] Pierce v. Stablemen's Union, 156 Cal. 70, 103 Pac. 324 (1909); *ex parte* Williams, 158 Cal. 550, 111 Pac. 1035 (1910), but as to California, see, also, Southern California Iron and Steel Co. v. Amalgamated Assoc., 186 Cal. 604, 200 Pac. 7 (1921), which may be construed as modifying the earlier decisions cited; Franklin Union v. People, 220 Ill. 355, 77 N. E. 176

opposite of this opinion, to the effect that peaceful picketing is not a fiction and that when it is conducted in an orderly manner and without intimidation, it is lawful was the view of the highest courts of Arkansas, Arizona, Indiana, Maryland, Minnesota, Missouri, Montana, New Hampshire, New York, Ohio, Oklahoma, Oregon, and Wisconsin, and also had the support of many federal courts.[1]

The U. S. Supreme Court passed upon the legality of picketing in the cases of American Steel Foundries Company v. Tri-city Trades Council[2] and Truax v. Corrigan,[3] which were decided within a few weeks of each other in 1921. In the first of these cases, the Supreme Court rendered a unanimous decision, written by Chief Justice Taft, in which it held that all "picketing" is unlawful, but that it was lawful for former employees on strike and their fellows in a labor union to have a single representative at each entrance to the plant of the employer to announce the strike and peaceably persuade the employees and

---

(1906); Boston Store v. Retail Clerks, 216 Ill. App. 428 (1920); Vegelahn v. Guntner, 167 Mass. 92, 44 N. E. 1077 (1896); *In re* Langell, 178 Mich. 305, 144 N. W. 841 (1914); Glass Co. v. Glass Blowers, 77 N. J. Eq. 219, 79 Atl. 262 (1911); Keuffel & Esser v. Machinists, 93 N. J. Eq. 429, 116 Atl. 9 (1922); O'Neil v. Behanna, 182 Pa. 236, 37 Atl. 843 (1897); St. Germain v. Bakery Workers, 97 Wash. 282, 166 Pac. 665 (1917); Otis Steel Co. v. Molders, 110 Fed. 698 (1901); Kolley v. Robinson, 187 Fed. 415 (1911); Vonnegut Machinery Co. v. Toledo Machine and Tool Co., 263 Fed. 192 (1920).

[1] Local Union 313 v. Stathakis, 135 Ark. 86, 205 S. W. 450 (1918); Truax v. Bisbee Local, 19 Ariz. 379, 171 Pac. 121 (1918); Shaughnessy v. Jordan, 184 Ind. 499, 111 N. E. 622 (1916); but see, also, Davis v. State, 199 Ind. 739, 161 N. E. 375 (1928); My Maryland Lodge v. Adt, 100 Md. 238, 59 Atl. 721 (1905); Steffes v. Motion Picture Operators, 136 Minn. 200, 161 N. W. 524 (1917); Hughes v. Motion Picture Operators, 282 Mo. 304, 221 S. W. 95 (1920); Empire Theatre Co. v. Cloke, 53 Mont. 183, 163 Pac. 107 (1917); Butterick Publishing Co. v. Typographical Union, 50 Misc. 1, 100 N. Y. S. 292 (1906); White Mountain Freezer Co. v. Murphy, 78 N. H. 398, 101 N. E. 357 (1917); La France Electrical Construction and Supply Co. v. Electrical Workers, 108 Ohio 61, 140 N. E. 899 (1923); *ex parte* Sweitzer, 13 Okla. Crim. 154, 162 Pac. 1134 (1917); Greenfield v. Central Labor Union, 104 Ore. 236, 192 Pac. 783 (1920); Monday Co. v. Automobile Workers, 171 Wis. 532, 177 N. W. 867 (1920); Allis Chalmers Co. v. Iron Molders, 166 Fed. 45 (1908).

[2] 251 U. S. 184, 42 Sup. Ct. 72.

[3] 257 U. S. 312, 42 Sup. Ct. 124.

would-be employees to join them in it.   In the Truax v. Corrigan
case, the court divided five to four upon the constitutionality of
the Arizona statute (as interpreted by the Supreme Court of that
state) which attempted to legalize mass picketing, the majority
of the court holding this statute to be unconstitutional.

The American Steel Foundries Company case is unquestionably the leading case upon the law of picketing and has influenced
practically all subsequent decisions involving picketing.   In this
case, the term "picketing" unfortunately is employed in a sense
different from its common usage.   The court decreed that all
picketing is unlawful; yet it expressly allowed one picket at each
factory entrance.   Despite the unusual application of the term
"picketing," this case did a great deal to clear up the law upon
picketing.   While the state Supreme Courts are not compelled to
follow the decision of the U. S. Supreme Court, they have in
practically all cases since 1921 cited the American Steel Foundries
Company decision and have accepted it as stating the correct rule
of law.[1]

The accepted doctrine since 1921 is that picketing is not
necessarily unlawful.   The stationing of strikers in front of
factory entrances to persuade employees and prospective employees to join them in the strike may or may not be lawful, depending
upon the circumstances and facts in each case.   Such picketing is
unlawful if it actually tends to intimidate the employees, prospective employees, or customers.   Mass picketing is under all
circumstances unlawful, as is picketing characterized by misrepre-
sentations and untruthful statements.   On the other hand,
picketing which is limited to lawful persuasion, where the conduct
of the pickets is not such as to occasion fear, is usually lawful.   All
picketing may become unlawful when the strikers resort to
violence.   Likewise there are a considerable number of cases to

---

[1] The Washington Supreme Court has held that, because Washington
has a statute prohibiting picketing, even peaceful picketing is unlawful,
but it has also held that patrols marching up and down on the sidewalks
with banners stating the strikers' side of the case and never coming nearer
than one hundred feet from the factory entrance are not engaged in picketing: Adams v. Local 400, 124 Wash. 564, 215 Pac. 19 (1923); Danz v.
American Federation of Musicians, 133 Wash. 186, 233 Pac. 630 (1925);
Sterling Chain Theaters, Inc., v. Central Labor Council, 283 Pac. 1081
(1930).

the effect that all picketing is unlawful if the strike itself is unlawful. Upon the question whether picketing in the absence of a strike is lawful, there is still a divergence of opinion. Some courts hold that picketing is illegal in the absence of a strike or after a strike has ended, while other courts take the position that "picketing without a strike" is no more illegal than a strike without picketing.[1] Prior to the U. S. Supreme Court decisions in 1921, injunctions issued in picketing cases which did not forbid all picketing, usually in vague terms forbade picketing for purposes of coercion or intimidation. Practically never would the courts make any attempt in such orders to state definitely what sort of picketing *would* be regarded as lawful. Since the American Steel Foundries decision, however, the tendency has been toward minutely detailed and very strict regulations in injunctions relating to the manner in which picketing may be conducted. In the majority of injunctions issued since 1921, precisely the same number of pickets have been permitted as in the American Steel Foundries Company case, namely, one at each factory gate. This has become almost a fetich, but the correct interpretation of this decision is that the number of pickets and the manner in which they may conduct themselves must vary with the circumstances in each case. In accordance with this conception, some courts have allowed more than one picket at a gate, and it has become quite common to prescribe other regulations besides those relating to the mere number of pickets. While picketing

---

[1] Picketing in absence of strikes held to be unlawful: Dail-Overland Co. v. Willys-Overland Co. 263 Fed. 171 (1919); Heitkemper v. Central Labor Union, 99 Ore. 1, 192 Pac. 765 (1920); Stuyvesant Lunch and Bakery Corp. v. Reiner, 181 N. Y. S. 212, 182 N. Y. S. 953 (1920); Yates Hotel Co. v. Meyers, 195 N. Y. S. 558 (1922); Yablonowitz v. Korn, 205 App. Div. 140, 199 N. Y. S. 769 (1923); Waitress' Union v. Benish Restaurant Co., 6 F. (2nd) 568 (1925); Gevas v. Greek Western Workers Club, 99 N. J. Eq. 770, 134 Atl. 309 (1926); Crouch v. Central Labor Council, 293 Pac. 729 (1930); People v. Jenkins, 246 N. Y. S. 444 (1931).

Picketing in absence of strikes held to be lawful: Stoner v. Robert, 43 Wash. L. Rep. 437 (1915); Clark Lunch Co. v. Cleveland Waiters, 22 Ohio App. 265, 154 N. E. 363 (1926); People v. Phillips, 245 N. Y. 401, 157 N. E. 508 (1927); Exchange Bakery and Restaurant v. Riffkin, 245 N. Y. 260, 157 N. E. 130 (1927). On this question, see The Privilege of Picketing an Establishment Where No Strike Is in Progress, in 27 *Columbia Law Rev.* 190–197 (1927).

is still often prohibited, in the majority of recent injunctions it has been permitted but confined within carefully restricted limits.

BOYCOTTS

The boycott is another means used by strikers to bring employers to their terms.   Boycotts sometimes arise without strikes, but most boycotts grow out of strikes and are often continued after strikes are lost.   Boycotts, in fact, are about the only method that organized laborers have for continuing their struggle with an employer who has defeated them in a strike.

In considering the law of boycotts, the first thing to be noted is that the term itself has no standard meaning.   One writer has said that the boycott is "a chameleon that is impossible of definition," and another that it is a term "of vague signification of which no accurate and exhaustive definition has ever been given."[1]

In its common industrial usage, this term is applied to two quite different phenomena.   One of these is what might be called the "consumers' boycott," a collective refusal to purchase boycotted commodities.   The other is the "workers' boycott," which is the refusal to work upon or with boycotted materials. This latter kind of boycott is carried out through strikes or threats of strikes.   Since this has been discussed in the section dealing with sympathetic strikes, only the commodity boycott will be dealt with in this section.

Explanations of the term "boycott" in court cases often are such as to render boycotts illegal by definition.   In an early and oft-quoted case, a boycott was defined as "a combination of many to cause a loss to one person by coercing others against their will to withdraw from him their beneficial business intercourse, through threats that unless those others do so, the many will cause similar loss to them."[2]   When boycotting is thus defined,

---

[1] The first quotation is from Kestner, "Der Organizationszwang," 344; the second, from Oakes, "Organized Labor and Industrial Conflicts," 602.   See also the exhaustive footnote in Oakes, *op. cit.* (Note 4, pp. 603–606), presenting the various definitions of the term "boycott" that have been given in court decisions and in law books.

[2] Toledo, etc., Co. v. Pennsylvania Co., 54 Fed. 730 (1893).

there can be no question that the boycott is illegal, but clearly this definition does not accurately describe all of the activities which in general industrial usage are regarded as boycotts.

The confusion which results from the use of the term "boycott" with varying signification has been increased by the attempts made in many decisions to distinguish between "primary" and "secondary" boycotts. Wherever this distinction has been drawn, the primary boycott has been accounted lawful and the secondary boycott unlawful. There is no agreement, however, as to what constitutes a primary boycott. Oakes, whose treatment of the law of boycotts is the most exhaustive, defines a primary boycott as consisting "simply of cessation by concerted action of dealings with another; while in the case of the secondary boycott, an attempt is made to procure parties outside of the combination to cease dealing as well."[1] It is obvious that under such a definition, there are but few primary boycotts in labor controversies. When workmen go on strike against an employer, they do not buy his products, but the withdrawal of their patronage alone is not likely to have any effect upon the outcome of the strike. Of necessity, if the boycott is to amount to anything, an attempt must be made "to procure parties outside of the combination to cease dealing as well," which under Oakes' definition would constitute a secondary boycott. The U. S. Supreme Court has defined the term "primary boycott" in a somewhat broader way, so as to include not only the refusal of the workmen directly involved in the dispute to patronize the former employer but also efforts on their part by peaceful means to persuade other persons to refrain from purchasing his goods.[2] In the case where this definition occurs, however, the court found that a strike against non-union materials constitutes a secondary boycott. The New York Court of Appeals, coinciding with the U. S. Supreme Court in holding that primary boycotts are lawful and secondary boycotts are unlawful, reached the opposite conclusion and held a strike against non-union materials to be a primary boycott.[3]

---

[1] OAKES, *op. cit.*, p. 606.

[2] Duplex Printing Press Co. v. Deering, 254 U. S. 469, 41 Sup. Ct. 172 (1921).

[3] Bossert v. Dhuy, 221 N. Y. 342, 117 N. E. 582 (1917).

In the most famous of the boycott cases (the Danbury hatters case),[1] the U. S. Supreme Court said that the courts are nearly unanimous in condemning boycotting. This statement, however, turns upon the definition of the term. It implies a use of this term under which boycotting is unlawful by definition. When it is applied, not only to measures involving the coercion of third parties, but also to the voluntary withdrawal of patronage and the persuasion of others to join in the boycott, it is apparent that the courts are by no means unanimous in condemning all boycotts. The actual situation has been well summarized by Oakes: "Notwithstanding the very considerable number of decisions on the subject, the law as to boycotts is in a confused and more or less chaotic condition."[2]

It is generally not unlawful for a combination of working people to withhold their patronage from a dealer or manufacturer against whom they have a grievance.[3] Usually also it is not unlawful for them to ask and persuade others to join them in withholding patronage. In all cases, however, the purpose of the persons conducting the boycott must be one which the courts regard as justifiable, and the means employed to make the boycott effective must be free from physical violence, coercion, or intimidation. In the conduct of a boycott, there must be no interference with ingress and egress to the boycotted premises. When pickets are stationed in front of the boycotted establishment, they must not interfere with the prospective customers, and their very presence may be unlawful if it tends to attract crowds.

In addition to verbal appeals, persuasion of others to withhold their patronage from an employer with whom labor has a dispute may take the form of the distribution or display of cards, handbills, placards, and banners. Statements made about the employer and his goods must not be false or libelous; must not convey a threat or an implied threat; nor arouse in the persons to whom they are addressed the fear of physical or economic harm if they do not comply with the request.

---

[1] Loewe v. Lawlor, 208 U. S. 274, 28 Sup. Ct. 301 (1908).

[2] OAKES, *op. cit.*, p. 601.

[3] For an exhaustive discussion of the law of boycotts, with citations to all reported cases which have arisen, see Oakes, *op. cit.*, pp. 598–740.

Dealers and manufacturers who are boycotted are termed "unfair" by labor, and lists of persons to be boycotted are known as "unfair" lists. This term "unfair" has led to contradictory decisions. In some cases, the position has been taken that this term implies a threat and that all reference to a dealer or manufacturer as unfair is illegal. In other cases, it has been held that there is nothing unlawful in referring to an employer as "unfair," and further, that injunctions prohibiting the printing and circulation of boycott notices and the spreading of information about the boycott constitute an invasion of the constitutional rights of free speech and free press. The U. S. Supreme Court, however, has held that these constitutional guarantees are of no avail when spoken or written words are employed in furtherance of an unlawful boycott.[1]

The most moot question connected with boycotts is that of the lawfulness of pressure brought to bear upon third parties to induce them to cease dealing with a boycotted employer. This is a very common situation in boycotts growing out of labor controversies. Most manufacturers do not sell their goods directly to consumers but sell through dealers. If labor is to use its patronage to help workmen on strike against such employers, they must refuse to buy from the dealers handling the goods of such manufacturers or threaten to do so if these dealers

---

[1] Among cases holding illegal all reference to dealers or manufacturers as unfair are: Seattle Brewing and Malting Co. v. Hansen, 144 Fed. 1011 (1905); Henrici v. Alexander, 198 Ill. App. 568 (1916); Martin v. Francke, 227 Mass. 272, 116 N. E. 404 (1917); and Campbell v. Motion Picture Operators, 151 Minn. 220, 186 N. W. 781 (1922). The opposite position has been taken in the following cases, among others: People v. Radt, 15 N. Y. Crim. 174, 71 N. Y. S. 846 (1900); State v. Van Pelt, 136 N. C. 633, 49 S. E. 177 (1904); Steffes v. Motion Picture Operators, 136 Minn. 200, 161 N. W. 524 (1917); Clark Lunch Co. v. Cleveland Waiters, 22 Ohio App. 265, 154 N. E. 363 (1926).

Courts have taken the view that all prohibitions of the circulation of boycott notices and of statements urging boycotts represent an invasion of the rights of free speech and free press in: Riggs v. Cincinnati Waiters, 5 Ohio N. P. 386 (1898); Marx, etc., Clothing Co. v. Watson, 168 Mo. 133, 67 S. W. 391 (1901); Lindsay v. Montana Federation of Labor, 37 Mont. 264, 96 Pac. 127 (1908); The leading case to the contrary is the decision of the U. S. Supreme Court in Gompers v. Buck's Stove and Range Co., 221 U. S. 418, 31 Sup. Ct. 492 (1911).

do not give up handling these goods. This is the typical secondary boycott and is the crux of the entire law of boycotts.

All boycotts against dealers, and threats implied or expressed of such strikes, have been regarded as unlawful in the majority of the jurisdictions in which this question has come before the courts, although in Arizona, California, and Montana the courts of final jurisdiction have held that such boycotts if conducted peaceably are lawful. Though its Supreme Court has not spoken, this seems also to be the law in Oklahoma, and there are numerous New York decisions to the same effect, while in Missouri it has been held that the printing and distribution of boycott circulars may not be enjoined.[1]

The boycott was held unlawful as early as 1886 and, from that date on, there were numerous decisions condemning boycotts conducted by organized labor. Not until 1908, however, did these court decisions have much practical effect. In that year the U. S. Supreme Court decided the Danbury hatters case and held that treble damages might be recovered under the Sherman Antitrust Act to compensate a manufacturer for

---

[1] *Arizona:* Truax v. Bisbee Local, 19 Ariz. 379, 171 Pac. 121 (1918); Truax v. Corrigan, 20 Ariz. 7, 176 Pac. 570 (1918).

California: Parkinson Co. v. Building Trades Council, 154 Cal. 581, 98 Pac. 1027 (1908); Pierce v. Stablemen's Union, 156 Cal. 70, 103 Pac. 324 (1909).

Montana: Lindsay v. Montana Federation of Labor, 37 Mont. 264, 96 Pac. 127 (1908); Empire Theatre Co. v. Cloke, 53 Mont. 183, 163 Pac. 107 (1917).

Oklahoma: Oklahoma Electric Planing Mill v. Chickasha Trades Council, (1909), cited in Laidler, "Boycotts and the Labor Struggle," p. 414.

New York: Sinsheimer v. Garment Workers, 77 Hun. 215, 28 N. Y. S. 321 (1894); People v. Radt, 15 N. Y. Cr. 174, 71 N. Y. S. 846 (1900); Cohen v. Garment Workers, 35 Misc. 748, 72 N. Y. S. 341 (1901); Foster v. Retail Clerks, 39 Misc. 48, 78 N. Y. S. 860 (1902); Butterick Publishing Co. v. Typographical Union, 50 Misc. 1, 100 N. Y. S. 292 (1906). *Contra:* Matthews v. Shankland, 25 Misc. 604, 56 N. Y. S. 123 (1898); Sun Printing and Publishing Assoc. v. Delaney, 48 App. Div. 623, 62 N. Y. S. 750 (1900); Mills v. U. S. Printing Co., 99 App. Div. 605, 91 N. Y. S. 185 (1904); Auburn Draying Co. v. Wardell, 89 Misc. 501, 152 N. Y. S. 475 (1915); 178 App. Div. 270, 165 N. Y. S. 469 (1917); 227 N. Y. 1, 124 N. E. 97 (1919).

Missouri: Marx, etc., Clothing Co. v. Watson, 168 Mo. 133, 67 S. W. 391 (1902); Lohse Patent Door Co. v. Fuelle, 215 Mo. 421, 114 S. W. 997 (1908); Root v. Anderson, 207 S. W. 255, Mo. App. (1918); Hughes v. Motion Picture Operators, 282 Mo. 304, 221 S. W. 95 (1920).

losses sustained through an interstate boycott. This was followed in 1911 by the Buck's Stove and Range Company case,[1] in which the American Federation of labor was enjoined from publishing the name of a St. Louis manufacturer on its unfair list. When this injunction was disregarded, Gompers, Mitchell, and Morrison, the three most prominent labor leaders in the country, were cited for contempt and sentenced to a year in jail. This sentence was subsequently set aside, but the net effect of the prosecution was that all boycotts were regarded popularly as unlawful. The American Federation of Labor discontinued its unfair list and, while boycotts were not altogether abandoned by organized labor, they were conducted less boldly, and probably also less effectively. Since then, there have been fewer boycott cases, by no means all of which have gone against labor. Boycotting is still a method used by labor to get its way, and most boycotts are not attacked in the courts, but adverse court decisions have doubtless had an effect, and consumers' boycotts are not now of very much importance in labor struggles.

CRUCIAL ISSUES

In this chapter, only the "high spots" have been touched concerning restrictions which court decisions impose upon employees in their contests with employers. These restrictions are many and varied and for years have been increasing. What labor may do to gain its ends differs from state to state, and it is impossible to say what the entire law is in many jurisdictions.

This is due in part to the fact that the law of labor combinations is comparatively new and is still in the developmental stage. In most states, only a few of the troublesome questions in this field have come before the supreme court. Another source of the existing complexity lies in the use of the common terms of labor controversies in technical and varied senses. Such terms as "strike," "boycott," and "picketing" have often been used in court decisions with various meanings. Many differences in the conclusions reached by different courts upon

---

[1] This view is also very ably presented in the minority opinion of Justice Brandeis of the U. S. Supreme Court in Duplex Printing Press Co. v. Deering, 254 U. S. 469 at 479, 41 Sup. Ct. 172 at 181 (1921).

the legality of the methods employed by labor to gain its ends
really resolve themselves into nothing more than the use of
these terms in varying senses.

Aside from these there are some real disagreements among the
courts in this field of the law. Everywhere labor unions,
other than syndicalist organizations, are recognized to be
lawful. It is also generally admitted that strikes and picketing,
and at times even boycotting, are lawful when conducted for
legitimate ends and in a peaceful manner. Differences of
opinion arise over the question: What ends are legitimate
and what conduct is peaceful? The crucial issues are unionization and the extent to which workmen not parties to the original
dispute may become participants therein. The Massachusetts
courts hold that the strengthening of the union is too remote an
object to justify such injury to employers and non-union men
as is necessarily involved in strikes and boycotts. They also
refuse to recognize that workmen other than those originally
and immediately involved in a dispute have sufficient interest
in its outcome to justify intervention on their part. In Ney
York, on the other hand, the Court of Appeals has held unionization to be sufficient justification for strikes and boycotts. This
court has also recognized that there is a community of interest
among members of the same union wherever they happen to be,
as well as among workmen in related crafts. The position
of the Massachusetts courts upon these crucial questions is also
that of the Connecticut, New Jersey, and Pennsylvania courts
and, on most points, of the Illinois and Michigan courts. On
the other hand, the Ohio decisions parallel those of New York;
while the California and Oklahoma courts have taken a position
even more favorable to labor, holding that strikes and boycotts
are always lawful.

In most other jurisdictions, these crucial questions either have
not arisen or have not been squarely met. Even in the states
named, the law of labor combinations is undergoing constant
change and development. In New York, for example, it is
quite impossible to reconcile all of the decisions except by taking
into account the time when they were rendered. Almost everywhere, the law of labor disputes has still not been crystallized
and will probably be modified as public opinion changes in its
attitude toward labor unions and union activities.

The restrictions upon union activities in this country are very real. While labor unions are recognized as lawful, many of the methods they employ in advancement of their purposes are in many jurisdictions unlawful and, almost everywhere, subject to doubt and legal attack. With the exception of the New York and Ohio courts, moreover, the tendency seems to be toward increasing restrictions.

Bibliographical Note

The original sources for a study of the law of labor combinations are the reported court decisions, many of which are cited in footnotes to this chapter. A considerable number of the leading decisions are reprinted in Francis B. Sayre, "A Selection of Cases and Other Authorities on Labor Law," Harvard University Press, Cambridge (1922), and in A. R. Ellingwood and Whitney Coombs, "The Government and Labor," McGraw Hill Book Company, Inc., New York (1926). The most exhaustive treatise on the law of labor combination is E. S. Oakes, "Organized Labor and Industrial Conflicts," Lawyers' Cooperative Publishing Co., Rochester (1927). Older treatises are W. A. Martin, "A Treatise on the Law of Labor Unions," Bryne, Washington (1910); and F. H. Cooke, "The Law of Combinations, Monopolies and Labor Unions," Callaghan, Chicago (1919). A shorter discussion, of exceptional merit, is the chapter by Prof. Wm. G. Hale on Injunctions against Interference with Trade or Employment; Combinations, Strikes, Boycotts, etc., in J. N. Pomeroy's "Equitable Remedies" (supplement to Pomeroy's "Equity Jurisprudence," Bancroft-Whitney Co., San Francisco, 1919 ed.), Vol. V, Chap. XVIII, pp. 4564–4629. Another very good brief account is Chap. I in Felix Frankfurter and Nathan Greene, "The Labor Injunction," The Macmillan Company, New York (1930).

Good accounts of the substantive restrictions imposed by court decision upon labor in its contests with employers, written by and for laymen, are John R. Commons and John B. Andrews, "Principles of Labor Legislation," pp. 98–122, Harper & Brothers, New York, 1927 ed.; and Solomon Blum, "Labor Economics," Chaps. V and VI, pp. 87–145, Henry Holt & Company, New York (1925). Older accounts are L. D. Clark, "The Law of the Employment of Labor," Chap. XII, pp. 257–300, The Macmillan Company, New York (1911); and G. G. Groat, Attitude of American Courts in Labor Cases, Part II, pp. 57–260, "Columbia University Studies in History, Economics, and Public Law," XLII, No. 108, Longmans, Green and Co., New York (1911).

CHAPTER III

LEGAL THEORIES

Court decisions in labor cases vary greatly in length. Some decisions are brief and consist of little more than a citation of precedents supporting the conclusions reached. Many other decisions are very long. This is a field of law which is so highly controversial that many judges feel the necessity of going back to first principles and developing their conclusions at length, by logical steps and processes, from these first principles.

The first principles or points of departure are not the same in all cases, but there is a recurrence of a relatively small number of what might be called "fundamental theories." None of these is accepted by all courts, but, collectively and separately, they have played such a large role in the law of labor disputes that a comprehension of these theories is essential to an understanding of the present law and the criticisms to which it has given rise.

CONSPIRACY DOCTRINE

The most important of these theories, at least historically, is what has often been called the "conspiracy doctrine." Under this doctrine, all combinations of workingmen were in the earliest English cases held to be unlawful. In this country, such an extreme view appears in only a few early unreported cases,[1] but, until the 1880's practically all legal actions growing out of labor disputes were criminal prosecutions for conspiracy. Since then, injunctions have been the most common form of action in labor cases, but even in injunction cases, the conspiracy doctrine has played and still plays a large role. In the complaints in these cases, the workmen against whom the action is brought are almost invariably charged with having formed a conspiracy,

---

[1] WITTE, E. E., Early American Labor Cases. 35 *Yale Law Jour.* 825–837 (1926).

and everything that has been done by the defendants is represented as having been done in furtherance of the alleged conspiracy. Similarly, the injunctions issued frequently include clauses prohibiting the defendants from "conspiring" to injure the plaintiff or his employees. In decisions of the courts, the words "conspire" and "conspiracy" occur less frequently, but the conclusion reached often depends upon whether, in the opinion of the court, the defendants formed a *lawful combination* or an *unlawful conspiracy*.

The conspiracy doctrine is a very old one and is not confined to labor cases.[1] It rests upon the proposition that the many acting in combination have a power for evil far greater than that of any one individual. "A combination of men is a very serious matter. No man can stand up against a combination: he may successfully defend himself against a single adversary, but when his foes are combined and numerous he must fall."[2]

Because of the great power of combinations, the law inquires into the purposes of those who combine. If the purpose is one which the law condemns, the very combining is illegal. The crime of conspiracy is complete when a group of men agree to do something unlawful, before they have done anything more to carry out their purpose. In most other fields of law, no cognizance is taken of the plans of men until they have done something to put them into execution, but, in the law of conspiracy, the unexecuted intent to do wrong is of itself criminal. Again, much that individuals may lawfully do becomes illegal when done by many in combination.[3] Further, once a combination to effect some unlawful purpose has been formed, every act done in pursuance thereof is illegal, although such act is of itself innocent. All who combine to accomplish an illegal purpose, moreover, are responsible for the acts of any of their number which are done to carry out the common object.

---

[1] The best discussion of the conspiracy doctrine and its history is J. W. Bryan, The Development of the English Law of Conspiracy, published in the "Johns Hopkins University Studies in History and Political Science," Vol. 27, pp. 133–161 (1909).

[2] People v. Wilzig, 4 N. Y. Crim. 403 (1886).

[3] For a good statement of this proposition and the reasons upon which it rests, see the decision of Justice Harlan of the U. S. Supreme Court in Arthur v. Oakes, 63 Fed. 310 (1894).

The essence of conspiracy is agreement, coupled with intention to effect a forbidden purpose. The character of the goal or the means of reaching the goal differentiates a lawful combination from an unlawful conspiracy. Only those combinations which aim to do something unlawful are classed as conspiracies. A conspiracy is "a combination of two or more persons, by concerted action, to accomplish some unlawful, oppressive, or immoral action, or to accomplish some purpose, not of itself unlawful, oppressive, or immoral, by unlawful, oppressive, or immoral means."[1] Even when the conspirators aim "to accomplish some purpose, not of itself unlawful, oppressive, or immoral, by unlawful, oppressive, or immoral means," however, the crime is complete when their concerted plan has been formed, although they have as yet done nothing to carry out their intent.

THE MALICE DOCTRINE

The present is an age of organization. Combinations of all kinds are so common that the mere fact of combination no longer seems adequate to serve as the starting point for decisions condemning many of the activities of labor in controversies with employers. Many courts now take the position that the fact that workingmen acted in concert makes no difference in determining whether their acts are legal or illegal.[2]

In a considerable number of cases in which this view is expressed, however, the courts nevertheless find the legality of the acts of workingmen to turn upon their motives, precisely as do the courts which stress the element of combination. As an illustration, the Minnesota Supreme Court holds that "any right which one man may exercise singly, two or more may lawfully agree to do jointly," but also that "one man singly, or any number of men jointly, having no legitimate interests to protect, may not lawfully ruin the business of another by maliciously inducing his patrons not to deal with him."[3]

---

[1] Commonwealth v. Hunt, 4 Metcalf (Mass.) 111 (1842).

[2] COOKE, FREDERICK H., "The Law of Combinations, Monopolies, and Labor Unions," pp. 23–39, Callaghan & Co., Chicago (1908), and cases cited in footnotes; also, Opera House Co. v. Minneapolis Musicians, 118 Minn. 410, 136 N. W. 1092 (1912); and Shaughnessy v. Jordan, 184 Ind. 499, 111 N. E. 622 (1916).

[3] Opera House Co. v. Minneapolis Musicians, 118 Minn. 410, 136 N. W. 1092 (1912).

The underlying idea here is that a determination of the lawfulness of acts constituting interference with the rights of others depends upon whether these acts were inspired by motives of self-interest or of malice. If the purpose of the persons acting in concert is to advance their own economic interests, their combination is lawful. If, on the other hand, their purpose is to injure their employer or non-union workmen, their combination is unlawful.

In its application to labor disputes, this doctrine at once leads to difficulties. The motives of workmen in going on strike are mixed. They aim both to do injury to the employer and to advance their own interests: to effect the second by means of the first. This has led the courts in many labor cases to draw a distinction between "motive" and "intent." Motive is defined as the ultimate object of those who combine; intent, as the immediate purpose of their combination. Motive, many courts say, has nothing to do with the legality of combinations; only the intent of those combining has legal significance.

Here again, however, there are difficulties. The distinction between motive (the ultimate object) and intent (the immediate purpose) is far from being clean-cut. All strikes are actuated by an immediate purpose to injure the employer. This is the immediate purpose even in a strike for higher wages, and such a strike ought logically to be held unlawful. The courts, however, do not go that far, and, while in closed-shop cases they do say that the combination is unlawful because the intent is to injure the employer or the non-unionist, they never apply the same reasoning to strikes for higher wages. Manifestly, the courts are not deciding these cases solely on the basis of the immediate purpose of the strike, but rather upon what they think of the merits of the entire dispute.

COMBINATION OF THE CONSPIRACY AND MALICE DOCTRINES

In labor cases, there is always present both the element of combination and the element of intentional injury to others. The courts, hence, really do not have to decide whether the element of combination or the element of a malicious motive changes the character of the acts done. It is only the total result which the courts must necessarily consider. In most recent cases, therefore, there has been no discussion of the legal effects of combination or of a bad motive, but only the assumption that the legality of acts done in combination depends upon the purpose of those combining.

It is possible to reach this conclusion although the view is taken that neither the fact of combination nor the fact of a bad motive, each standing alone, is of any legal significance. This was precisely the position taken by the House of Lords, the highest British court, prior to the enactment of the British Trades Disputes Act. In Mogul Steamship Co. v. McGregor,[1] the House of Lords held that an act which is legal when done by one person is not rendered illegal solely because it is done by several persons pursuant to an agreement among them. In Allen v. Flood,[2] it held that it is of no importance whether persons performing acts of interference with the business of others are actuated by malicious or by proper motives, and that the civil law looks only at the results of men's acts and not at their objects. In Quinn v. Leathem,[3] however, the House of Lords held that, when there is a combination, the legality of the acts done by such combination depends upon whether or not they were actuated by malicious motives.

Few American courts have taken precisely the same position as that taken by the House of Lords in these three great English cases. Most of the American courts, however, have reached the same general conclusion: that the presence or absence of malice is the determining factor in the legality or illegality of acts done by combinations of workmen in labor disputes. Many American courts hold that combination makes no difference in the legality of an act.[4] Other courts hold that the motive underlying the acts of workmen involved in labor cases is immaterial.[5] There are but few jurisdictions, however, in which both the combination and the motive are held to be immaterial.

THE "JUST-CAUSE" THEORY

Most of the courts in this country at the present time say comparatively little in their decisions about either the element

---

[1] A. C. 25 (1892).

[2] A. C. 1 (1898).

[3] A. C. 495 (1901).

[4] See Note 6, *ante.*

[5] Cooke, Frederick H., "The Law of Combinations, Monopolies, and Labor Unions," pp. 17–22, Callaghan & Co., Chicago (1908), and cases cited in footnotes.

of combination or that of motive. Court decisions are now based, to a prevailing extent, on what is often called the "just-cause" theory, first expounded by Justice Holmes, then of the Massachusetts Supreme Court.[1] This theory starts with the proposition that everybody is entitled to free and unobstructed access to the commodity market and to the labor market. He who intentionally interferes with this right is *prima facie* guilty of a wrongful act. This presumption, however, can be rebutted by showing that there was a just cause for the interference. Interference is justified when it results from the exercise of equal or superior rights. A business man who draws customers from his competitor is guilty of a *prima facie* wrong; but if he competes fairly, he has a just cause for interfering with the expectancies of his competitor, because competition is a right superior to the competitor's claim upon the patronage of his old customers. The injury done to the competitor is *damnum absque injuria;* that is, although the plaintiff suffered loss, he cannot recover because the defendent acted within his rights.

In cases arising in connection with labor disputes, there is always interference with the expectancies of the employer, and frequently also with those of non-union workmen. In all cases, thus, under the just-cause theory, there is a presumption of illegality which can be rebutted only by a showing satisfactory to the court that interference was justified.

This theory has been presented as if it has no connection with either the conspiracy doctrine or the view that the test of legality is the presence or absence of malice. This claim, however, will not bear examination. The crucial question under the just-cause theory is, as has been noted, whether labor acts in pursuance of rights equal or superior to those of capital. Competition and self-interest are such rights; but when does labor compete with capital, and when is it pursuing merely its own interests? The two cases in which the just-cause theory was first logically developed were the Massachusetts cases of Vegelahn v. Guntner[2] and Plant v. Woods.[3] In these cases, both the majority and the

---

[1] Privilege, Malice, and Intent, in 8 *Harvard Law Rev.* 114 (1894); reprinted in Oliver Wendell Holmes, "Collected Legal Papers," 117–152, Harcourt, Brace & Howe, New York (1920).

[2] 167 Mass. 92, 44 N. E. 1077 (1896).

[3] 176 Mass. 492, 57 N. E. 1011 (1900).

minority ably expounded the just-cause theory, but their conclusions upon the legality of the workmen's conduct were exactly
opposite.   As these cases illustrate, there is nothing inevitable in
the application of the just-cause theory in concrete situations.
Justice Holmes, who might be called the "father" of this theory,
has almost always held for labor; the Massachusetts Supreme
Court, which first accepted this theory and has carried it furthest,
has generally held against labor.   Verily, as Justice Holmes
wrote in the article in which he first presented this theory:

> The ground for decision really comes down to a proposition of policy
> of rather a delicate nature concerning the merit of the particular benefit
> to themselves intended by the defendants and suggests a doubt whether
> judges with different economic sympathies might not decide such a case
> differently when brought face to face with the same issue.[1]

How the just-cause theory is actually applied will appear from
the following sentence from a recent Massachusetts decision:

> It is settled that an act lawful in an individual may be the subject of a
> civil conspiracy when done in concert, provided it is done with the
> direct intention to injure another, or when, although done to the
> benefit of the conspirators, its natural and necessary consequence is
> the prejudice of the public or the oppression of individuals.[2]

As this sentence illustrates, the just-cause theory is really a
combination of the conspiracy and malice doctrines, expressed in
slightly different language but reaching the same conclusions as
these older theories.

The essential agreement between the just-cause theory and the
conspiracy doctrine has been obscured by the distinction drawn
between "malice in fact" and "malice in law."   "Malice in fact"
is personal ill will and spite; "malice in law" is the intentional
infliction of injury without justification.   The courts which accept
the just-cause theory say that malice in fact is of no legal significance.   This sounds like a repudiation of the basal proposition in
the conspiracy doctrine, that the legality of acts which are done
in combination depends upon the motives of those who combine.
However,

> . . . those who say with Justice Wells that man is liable for the harm
> he does if he does it maliciously, meaning by malice, without legal

---

[1] Cited in Note 13 *ante.*

[2] A. T. Stearns Lumber Co. v. Howlet, 260 Mass. 45, 157 N. E. 82 (1927).

excuse, naturally turn to the defendants' motives as at least one of the elements on which the existence of a "legal excuse" depends.[1]

The term "malice in law" is more inclusive than the term "malice in fact"; and the advocates of the just-cause theory can correctly claim that motive is but one of many factors determining the legality of the acts of labor unions and strikers in labor disputes. The courts' conception, however, of what these unions and strikers are trying to do—what the object is at which they are aiming—unquestionably is one of the principal factors in determining the legality of their acts.

THE TEST OF ILLEGAL MEANS

Many recent cases, particularly in the federal courts, turn not upon motive or intent, but upon the means used to gain the ends sought by the combination. "There is a pronounced tendency in recent cases throughout the country to say little about the illegal motives of the workingmen and to find the illegality of their conduct in the unlawful means they employ."[2]

The courts applying this test are in agreement in the terms they use to describe lawful and unlawful means. Violence, force, threats, coercion, and intimidation are unlawful, while combination and persuasion are lawful. Beyond these terms, there is little agreement. Violence is a definite concept, but force and threats are descriptive terms which admit of widely different interpretations. A "threat" may be a warning of violence; it may also be a warning of intention to do a legally permissible act. "The unlawfulness of threats depends upon what you threaten."[3] Coercion and intimidation are still less exact. In a Connecticut case, these terms were defined to include "any words or acts which are calculated or intended to cause an ordinary person to fear injury to his person, business, or property."[4] As this definition indicates, these terms can be applied to almost everything that is done by working people in strikes, or they may be limited to physical violence and threats of physical violence.

---

[1] LEWIS, DEAN WILLIAM DRAPER, 5 *Columbia Law Rev.* 107, 118 (Feb. 1905). See also J. B. Ames in 18 *Harvard Law Rev.* 411–422 (1905).

[2] COMMONS, JOHN R., and JOHN B. ANDREWS, "Principles of Labor Legislation," Harper & Brothers, New York, p. 110 (1927).

[3] Justice Holmes in Vegelahn v. Guntner, 167 Mass. 92, 44 N. E. 1077 (1896).

[4] State v. Stockford, 77 Conn. 227; 58 Atl. 769 (1904).

With such vague concepts to guide them, the courts which have applied the test of illegal means naturally have often reached different conclusions. This test was the one most usually applied in picketing cases, but it was not until the U. S. Supreme Court, in the American Steel Foundries Company case,[1] suggested the rule of one picket at each factory entrance that a definite standard for judging the legality of picketing was developed. What constitutes coercion or intimidation is in the last analysis almost as subjective as what constitutes motive or intent, and the final results have been much the same, whether the motives or the means have been taken as the test of the legality of collective actions.

RESTRAINT OF TRADE

Another theory which has been historically of much significance in the law of labor disputes is the "restraint of trade" doctrine. This theory makes the test of the legality of workmen's and employers' conduct in labor controversies the injury occasioned to the public at large, that is, whether or not such conduct restrains trade. In the early American labor cases, this doctrine was closely interwoven with the conspiracy doctrine and figured very prominently in the court decisions. Nowadays, it occurs principally in cases arising under the federal antitrust acts, which are discussed at length in Chap. IV.

At this point, it need only be noted that not all conduct which restrains trade is unlawful. This was finally decided, as regards the general scope of the federal antitrust acts, in the Standard Oil and American Tobacco Company cases in 1911,[2] when it was held that the Sherman Antitrust Act forbids not all restraints of trade, but only *unreasonable* restraints of trade. In labor cases, no other view has ever been entertained. Every strike and every boycott to some extent restrains trade. No court has ever held, however, that all strikes and boycotts are unlawful on this ground. No strike exclusively for higher wages, no matter how extensive, has ever been enjoined solely on the ground that it violated the federal antitrust acts; but strikes causing great public inconvenience have been condemned on this score. In

---

[1] 257 U. S. 184; 42 Sup. Ct. 72 (1921).

[2] Standard Oil Co. v. U. S., 221 U. S. 1, 31 Sup. Ct. 502 (1911); American Tobacco Co. v. U. S., 221 U. S. 106, 31 Sup. Ct. 632 (1911).

other words, while the legal test is restraint of trade, the actual decision seems to turn rather upon the court's conception of the legitimacy of the workmen's demands and their methods than upon this legal formula.[1]

CRITICISMS AND DISSENTS

None of these fundamental theories, which recur again and again in labor cases, has found universal acceptance. On the contrary, all of them have been challenged, not only by interested parties, but by many of the most eminent legal writers and jurists of the country.

The conspiracy theory has in recent decades become steadily less significant. Comparatively few courts of final jurisdiction have repudiated this theory, and it has been advanced at one time or another by many of the strongest courts of the country, but it is now seldom brought into labor cases and when used is usually combined with some other theory.[2]

The reason for the decreasing emphasis upon the element of combination is that this theory is manifestly unfounded in many situations which arise in disputes between employers and employees. It is true that a combination often has much greater power for harm than any individual can exert. There can, for instance, be no question that picketing by large numbers of strikers and strike sympathizers is an entirely different matter from picketing by one man or only a few men. On the other hand, it is certainly

---

[1] Besides the theories discussed in this chapter, there are a number of others which have played a considerable part in the development of the law of labor disputes. One of these is the doctrine that property in the hands of receivers is under the special protection of the courts. Out of this doctrine grew the first use of injunctions in labor disputes [see Walter Nelles, A Strike and Its Legal Consequences: an Examination of the Receivership Precedent for the Labor Injunction, 40 *Yale Law Jour.* 507, 534–554 (1931); and E. E. Witte, Early American Labor Cases, 35 *Yale Law Jour.* 825–837 (1926)]. In the last three decades, however, it has been of comparatively minor importance, due to the fact that comparatively few large railroad and industrial properties have been in receivers' hands. Another theory of considerable importance in labor cases is the old legal doctrine that action will lie against outsiders who persuade one of the parties to a contract to breach the same. This doctrine is the foundation of the "yellow-dog" contract cases which have caused labor great alarm in recent years, and which are discussed in Chap. X.

[2] OAKES, E. S., "Organized Labor and Industrial Conflicts," p. 291.

not always true that a combination has greater power than a single person. In labor controversies, the usual situation is that on the one side there is a labor union or a group of unorganized workmen and, on the other, a corporation. The corporation in law counts as a single person; the labor union or group of unorganized workmen, as a combination of many persons. In this age of billion-dollar corporations, it is absurd to ascribe to a combination of a few hundred or a thousand workmen much greater power than is possessed by such a corporation.

The idea that there is something peculiarly dangerous about labor combinations and that they must be kept under the closest scrutiny of the courts has been vigorously attacked in many court decisions. "It ignores the fact that in every line of trade and business, combination is the tendency of the age."[1] In similar vein, another judge has said that this doctrine, which "compels every man to be a stranger in action to every other man" is "abhorrent to free men."[2]

The concept which makes the legality of the acts of workmen in labor disputes turn upon whether or not they are actuated by malice has also been much criticized and has been used far less in recent cases than earlier. These criticisms have turned for the most part upon the difficulty of determining whether or not workmen are inspired by malicious or proper motives. The motives which influence any particular workman who takes part in a labor dispute are very likely to be mixed. There is an element of ill will toward the employer or the non-unionist, and also a desire for improved conditions of labor. When the entire group of workmen are considered, their motives obviously are still more mixed. Nor are courts well equipped to get at the true motives of the participants in labor controversies. Judges have little or no special training for getting at underlying causes in such controversies, nor have they facilities for comprehensive

---

[1] Dissenting opinion of Judge Minturn in Geo. Jonas Glass Co. v. Glass Blowers, 77 N. J. Eq. 219, 79 Atl. 262 (1911).

[2] Dissenting opinion of U. S. Circuit Judge Caldwell in Hopkins v. Oxley Stove Co., 83 Fed. 912 (1897). Justice Holmes, expressing the same thought a little differently, said in his dissenting opinion in Vegelahn v. Guntner, 167 Mass. 92, 44 N. E. 1077 (1896): "Combination on the one side is patent and powerful. Combination on the other side is a necessary and desirable counterpart if the battle is to be carried on in a fair and equal way."

research or independent investigation. In the trial of a case, formal procedure and rigid rules as to the admissibility of evidence prevail. To make the legality of the acts of participants turn upon their motives, hence, puts to the courts a problem which they cannot solve fairly and satisfactorily. As long ago as 1887, Dean Wigmore warned: "There is no more persistent and unfounded notion than that the motive—I do not say intention—can become the turning point of civil liability—no notion more fitted to reverse legal relations and to make chaos out of definite principles."[1] In similar vein, Alton B. Parker, as chief judge of the Court of Appeals of New York, said: "It seems to me illogical and little short of absurd to say that the everyday acts of the business world, apparently within the domain of competition, may be either lawful or unlawful according to the motive of the actor."[2]

Most present-day cases start neither with the element of combination nor with the element of motive, but with the proposition that interference with the rights and expectancies of others must be justified to be lawful. This is the just-cause theory discussed above, which undoubtedly now has more support than any other theory in the law of labor combinations. As noted above, however, this theory is little more than a restatement of the older conspiracy and malice doctrines and involves elements of both of these older theories.

The doctrine of "just cause of excuse" inevitably operates so as to leave to judges and juries the decision of questions not so much of law, as of ethics and economics.[3]

Neither this nor any formula will save courts the painful choice of judgment, whether, in a given conflict, privilege has been overstepped. The broad questions of law—what are the permissible purposes for damage, and the intricate issues of fact to which they must be applied—together constitute the area of discretion within which diversity of opinion finds ample scope.[4]

---

[1] WIGMORE, JOHN H., Boycott and Kindred Practices as Ground for Damages, 21 *Amer. Law Rev.* 509 (1887).

[2] National Protective Assoc. v. Cummings, 170 N. Y. 315, 63 N. E. 369 (1902).

[3] GELDART, PROFESSOR W. M., The Present Law of Trade Disputes and Trade Unions, *Polit. Quarterly* 19–61 at 24 (May, 1914).

[4] FRANKFURTER, FELIX, and NATHAN GREENE, The Use of the Injunction in American Labor Controversies, in *Law Quarterly Rev.* 174 at p. 182 (April, 1928).

The application of the just-cause theory compels a determination as to what are superior, and what inferior, rights. This in turn involves the passing of judgment upon the social value of the rights claimed by the contesting parties and introduces the same elements of uncertainty and possibility for bias which characterize the conspiracy and malice doctrines.

The test of illegal means, which, next to the just-cause theory, is probably the one most often applied in present-day labor cases, is subject to similar difficulties. Such terms as "force," "threats," "coercion," and "intimidation" are incapable of precise definition. Often they represent merely the giving of a bad name to a course of conduct that is not approved or is regarded as antisocial. "Names," however, "are not things. It is the thing done or threatened to be done that determines the quality of the act, and this quality is not changed by applying to the act an opprobrious name or epithet."[1]

The restraint of trade theory is equally inconclusive, introducing, if possible, even more subjective elements. It is a doctrine under which some strikes which cause complete stoppage of all business in a very large area are allowed to go on unchallenged, while other strikes causing far less disturbance are held to be illegal. Restraint of trade which results from disputes that the courts deem justified is regarded as merely incidental, while disputes which the courts do not approve are held to be unlawful because they restrain trade.

These several theories figuring in labor cases were not concocted to injure labor, nor to hold labor in subjection, as labor leaders and labor sympathizers have often claimed. Every one is a very old concept and, moreover, is now applied in other fields of law. It is nevertheless true that these theories, separately and collectively, are far from convincing and entirely satisfying. All of them are essentially subjective. In the last analysis, the conclusions arrived at through the application of these theories reflect the opinion of the court upon the merits of the controversy. If the judge is sympathetic with the demands of the workmen, he is very likely to decide in their favor, and *vice versa*. As Prof. W. W. Cook has stated, the real procedure of the courts is not so much to apply the principles to the instant case as to decide

---

[1] Judge Caldwell in Hopkins v. Oxley Stove Co., 83 Fed. 912 (1897).

the case first and then to find the principles to bolster the decision.[1]

The fundamental theories upon which the law of labor combinations is premised are more of a hindrance than a help in arriving at rules of law to govern labor disputes which are both fair and workable. It is not so much that these theories are unsound as that they are vague and uncertain. There is little, if anything, to be gained by going back to these "first principles," and certainly none of them is of such convincing weight as to justify ignoring the concrete facts in labor controversies.[2]

ABSOLUTE-RIGHTS THEORY

The theories discussed thus far in this chapter have often been met by what might be regarded as a countertheory of labor. Opposed to the claims of bad motives, illegal means, and unjustified interference, organized labor and its attorneys are very apt to cite the constitutional guarantees of free speech, free press, the right of public assemblage, and the other privileges guaranteed in the bill of rights of the state and federal constitutions. These rights are conceived as absolute prerogatives which under no circumstances may be denied or abridged. This "absolute-rights theory" has little, if any, support in court decisions or in articles in legal periodicals but recurs time and again in labor literature.

This concept is no more a solution of the problems which arise in the law of labor disputes than are the theories that are employed in decisions adverse to labor. The constitutional

---

[1] Scientific Methods and the Law, *Johns Hopkins Alumni Mag.* 15, Nos. 3, 5 (1927).

[2] Another line of attack upon the generally accepted theories in the law of labor combinations is suggested by the searching criticisms of the late Prof. W. N. Hohfeld of the University of California and Prof. W. W. Cook of Johns Hopkins University of the loose and varying manner in which the courts use such fundamental terms as "rights," "liberty," "privilege," etc. In nearly all labor cases, the courts speak of the "right" of employers to expectancies arising from their relations to customers and employees, while in fact these relations are no "rights" or "privileges." If this distinction were observed, the "just-cause" theory, in particular, would fall, as it is based upon the "right" of the employer to uninterrupted relations with the commodity and labor markets. See W. N. Hohfeld, Fundamental Legal Conceptions, 23 *Yale Law Jour.* 16–59 (particularly pp. 36–37).

guarantees are not a complete guide for conduct to be permitted and condemned in labor disputes.   A conclusive answer to the absolute-rights theory is that given by one of labor's staunchest friends, Justice Holmes of the U. S. Supreme Court:

No conduct has such absolute privilege as to justify all possible schemes of which it may be a part.   The most innocent and constitutionally protected of acts and omissions may be a step in a criminal plot, and, if it is a step in a plot, neither its innocence nor the Constitution is sufficient to prevent the punishment of the plot by law.[1]

Legal theories and principles will not solve the labor problem. What is needed is an examination of the facts and a study of how the law is actually working out, rather than *a priori* reasoning, nice deductions, and reversion to old doctrines and phrases.

Bibliographical Note

The original sources for a study of the legal theories underlying the law of labor combinations are the reported decisions in labor cases.   Some of the more important of these decisions are reprinted in Francis B. Sayre, "A Selection of Cases and Other Authorities on Labor Law," Harvard University Press, Cambridge (1922).

Secondary accounts of outstanding merit which present and support the accepted theories include the following: E. S. Oakes, "Organized Labor and Industrial Conflicts," Chap. 21, pp. 289–374, Lawyer's Cooperative Publishing Co., Rochester (1927); William G. Hale, Injunction against Interference with Trade or Employment; Combinations, Strikes, Boycotts, etc., in J. N. Pomeroy's "Equitable Remedies" (supplement to Pomeroy's "Equity Jurisprudence," 1919 ed. Bancroft-Whitney Co., San Francisco), Vol. V, Chap. XVIII, pp. 4564–4629; W. A. Martin, "A Treatise on the Law of Labor Unions," Chaps. II and III, John Bryne & Co., Washington (1910); Ames, How Far an Act May Be a Tort Because of the Wrongful Motive of the Actor, in 18 *Harvard Law Rev.* 411–422 (1905).

Good criticisms of the accepted theories include: John R. Commons and John B. Andrews, "Principles of Labor Legislation," pp. 106–110, 125–129, Harper & Brothers, New York (1927); J. Wallace Bryan, "Proper Bounds for the Use of Injunctions in Labor Disputes," 36 *Ann. Amer. Acad. Polit. Soc. Sci.* 288–301 (1910); William D. Lewis, Should the Motive of the Defendant Affect the Question of his Liability, 5 *Columbia Law Rev.* 107–123 (1905); Felix Frankfurter and Nathan Greene, "The Labor Injunction," pp. 24–26, The Macmillan Company, New York (1930); Frederick H. Cooke, "The Law of Combinations, Monopolies and Labor Unions," Callaghan & Co., Chicago (1919).

---

[1] Aikens v. Wisconsin, 195 U. S. 194, 25 Sup. Ct. 3 (1904).

CHAPTER IV

STATUTES

The law governing labor disputes appears mainly in court decisions and is grounded principally upon theories derived from the common law, rather than upon statutory enactments. There is, nevertheless, a considerable and increasing body of statutes peculiar to the problems presented by labor disputes.

THE SHERMAN ANTITRUST ACT

Of these, the most important are the federal antitrust laws. In many accounts, these laws are treated as the principal restrictions upon labor combinations. This undoubtedly exaggerates their importance, but that labor unions have been increasingly restricted by them cannot be gainsaid.

The first and most important of the federal antitrust acts was the Sherman Act of 1890, a general law which makes no specific mention of labor combinations or labor disputes. In general terms, it prohibits all combinations in restraint of interstate or foreign commerce and all attempts to monopolize such commerce.

Whether the Sherman Act was intended to apply to labor unions has long been a subject of controversy. The U. S. Supreme Court in the Danbury hatters case[1] stated that an examination of the debates in Congress at the time this act was passed clearly established that it was the intent of Congress to include labor combinations within its scope. On the other hand, the most exhaustive study which has been made of this subject reached the opposite conclusion.[2] The belief that the Sherman Act was intended to apply to labor combinations is supported

---

[1] Loewe v. Lawlor, 208 U. S. 274, 28 Sup. Ct. 301 (1908).

[2] BERMAN, PROF. EDWARD, "Labor and the Sherman Act," Harper & Brothers, New York (1930). The opposite view is presented in James A. Emery, Labor Organizations and the Sherman Law, 20 *Jour. Polit. Econ.* 599–612 (1912); W. W. Thornton, "A Treatise on the Sherman Antitrust Act," pp. 1–31, The W. H. Anderson Co., Cincinnati (1913); and Alpheus T. Mason, "Organized Labor and the Law," Chaps. VII and VIII, Duke Univ., Durham, N. C. (1925).

chiefly by the fact that an amendment offered by Senator Sherman which would have expressly exempted labor unions and which was at one stage adopted by the Senate was omitted in the final draft. The omission of this amendment from the final draft is regarded as conclusive proof that Congress intended this act to apply to labor. In opposition to this, it is argued that the final draft was so altered in other respects that no one in Congress thought that the act in its amended form could possibly be construed to apply to labor unions and that the Sherman amendment was omitted solely because it seemed superfluous. It appears from an examination of the *Congressional Record* that every member in both houses who discussed the question of the application of this act to labor, with the exception of Senator Edmonds and Congressman Stewart, took the position that the antitrust law should not be applied to labor unions. This included many of the ablest members of Congress: among others, Senators Hoar, George, and Teller.

That the great majority of the members of the Congress which passed the Sherman Act were in favor of the policy represented by the Sherman amendment is clear from the Congressional debates. Whether Congress intended merely that labor organizations *per se* should not be rendered unlawful, or that no action whatsoever should under any circumstances be brought under the antitrust laws against labor organizations, is debatable. Upon this point the congressional debates throw no light; probably no member of Congress thought of the distinction. The Sherman amendment read that nothing in the act should be "construed to apply to any arrangements, agreements, or combinations by laborers, made with a view of lessening the hours of their labor or of increasing their wages." This clearly means nothing further than that labor unions *per se* shall not be considered unlawful and does not grant labor complete exemption from the antitrust laws. Had this amendment been included in the final draft of the Sherman Act, it would have made little or no difference in the application of this law to labor unions. In only one case was a labor union held to constitute an unlawful combination in violation of the Sherman Act, and that decision was reversed upon appeal.[1] In all other cases the question involved has been not

---

[1] Hitchman Coal and Coke Co. v. Mitchell, 202 Fed. 512 (1912); reversed in 214 Fed. 685 (1914).

that of the legality of the union, but of acts done in its behalf. Had the Sherman amendment become law, it would have made no difference in the outcome of any of these cases.

Labor-union activities were attacked under the Sherman Act within three years of its passage, and in 1893 and 1894 there were altogether seven cases in which this statute was invoked against labor.[1] All but one of these cases grew out of railroad strikes, and all of them involved direct interference with the transportation of interstate commerce. The legal question raised in these cases was: Does such interference constitute an illegal restraint of trade under the Sherman Act? In these cases, it was definitely established that interference with the transportation of interstate commerce by acts of violence and intimidation does constitute such an illegal restraint of trade. In one case, a district judge expressed the opinion that the Sherman Act rendered every railroad strike unlawful,[2] but this was a mere dictum and has never been accepted as good law. In the American Railway Union (Pullman) strike of 1894, several district judges held that this sympathetic strike was a violation of the Sherman Act, and the injunction out of which grew the famous Debs case was premised upon this law. The U. S. Supreme Court, however, justified the issuance of this injunction upon other grounds and refused to pass upon the question whether the Sherman Antitrust Act had any application to a nation-wide sympathetic strike on the railroads.[3]

After the Debs case, little was heard of the Sherman Antitrust Act in connection with labor disputes until the decision of the U. S. Supreme Court in the Danbury hatters case in 1908. In fact, this act was pleaded in but one case and in that case the decision of the U. S. Circuit Court of Appeals was reassuring, being to

---

[1] Blindell v. Hagen, 54 Fed. 40, 56 Fed. 696; U. S. v. Workingmen's Amalgamated Council, 54 Fed. 994, 57 Fed. 85; Waterhouse v. Comer, 55 Fed. 149; U. S. v. Debs, 64 Fed. 724; U. S. v. Agler, 62 Fed. 824, U. S. v. Elliott, 62 Fed. 801, 64 Fed. 27; *in re* Charge to Grand Jury, 62 Fed. 828; *in re* Grand Jury, 62 Fed. 834; U. S. v. Debs, 63 Fed. 436; *in re* Grand Jury, 62 Fed. 840; U. S. v. Cassidy, 67 Fed. 898; U. S. v. Debs, Dist. Ind., summarized in "The Federal Antitrust Law with Amendments," p. 87, published by the U. S. Department of Justice, Nov. 30, 1928.

[2] Waterhouse v. Comer, 55 Fed. 149 (1893).

[3] *In re* Debs, 158 U. S. 564, 15 Sup. Ct. 900 (1895).

the effect that the Sherman Act does not prohibit an "agreement not to work except under certain conditions, even if the cost of interstate traffic would be thereby enhanced."[1]

In the Danbury hatters case, labor received a rude jolt. This case involved a suit for $240,000 damages against some 250 members of the hatters' union under the seventh section of the Sherman Act, which allows triple damages to persons injured by conduct in violation of this act. The D. E. Loewe Company of Danbury, Conn., had refused to unionize its plant, whereupon its employees went on strike and the union instituted a nation-wide boycott against its goods. In claiming damages, this company alleged that the defendants had conspired to prevent it from engaging in interstate commerce, and that the strike and the boycott were the means used to carry out this conspiracy. To this complaint, the defendants entered a demurrer in which they contended that the Sherman Act was not applicable to the situation. This demurrer was overruled by the U. S. Supreme Court and the case sent back for trial, after which it remained in the courts for seven years more, finally resulting in recovery by the plaintiff of practically the entire amount sued for.[2]

The decision of the Supreme Court in this case alarmed organized labor more than any other decision that has ever been rendered in this country. It was reported in the labor press and elsewhere as holding that labor unions are trusts and that "the labor of a human being is a commodity." As a matter of fact, neither of these propositions was so much as hinted at by the court. The decision was not based on the claim that the defendants had conspired to monopolize the labor supply of the hatters of the country, but that they had aimed to stop the interstate trade in Loewe hats. By many lawyers, this decision was interpreted as holding only that secondary boycotts are unlawful under the Sherman Act. This, in turn, is too narrow an interpretation. The strike and the boycott figured identically in this case: namely, as means employed to carry out the unlawful conspiracy to prevent the Loewe Company from engaging in

---

[1] Wabash R. R. Co., v. Hannahan, 121 Fed. 563 (1903).

[2] Loewe v. Lawlor, 208 U. S. 274, 28 Sup. Ct. 301 (1908), 235 U. S. 522, 35 Sup. Ct. 170 (1915). For a further discussion of this case, see Chap. VII.

interstate commerce.   What the Supreme Court actually decided
was that the Sherman Antitrust Act applies not only where there
is physical interference with the transportation of interstate
commerce, but also where there is interference with the right of
persons freely to engage in interstate commerce.   The gist of
the decision occurs in the following sentence:

If the purpose of the combination were, as alleged, to prevent any
interstate transportation at all, the fact that the means operated at
one end before the physical transportation commenced and at the other
end, after the physical transportation ended, was immaterial.

The Supreme Court held that a combination whose purpose
is to prevent an employer or business man from freely engaging
in interstate commerce is unlawful under the Sherman Act,
whether or not the means used to carry out this purpose are of
themselves lawful.   It did not define what constitutes a combination to interfere with interstate commerce.   The court concluded
that a nation-wide and effective boycott is unlawful under the
Sherman Antitrust Act, but some of its language could be
interpreted as holding that a strike affecting the supply of goods
shipped in interstate commerce may also be unlawful under
the Sherman Act; and labor leaders feared that perhaps the
unions themselves might be held unlawful.

In the six years between the first decision of the Supreme
Court in the Danbury hatters case and the enactment of the
Clayton Act in 1914, between fifteen and twenty cases arose in
inferior federal courts in which the Sherman Act was invoked
in connection with labor disputes.   Most of these cases were
unreported and many of them never brought to trial, but all
of them were commented upon with alarm in the labor papers.

Among these cases were several which proceeded considerably
further than the Danbury hatters decision.   In one case, twenty-
two members of the New Orleans Dock and Cotton Council were
found guilty upon criminal charges of having conspired to violate
the Sherman Act by adopting a resolution directing the coal-
wheelers' union to refuse to coal the vessels of an "unfair"
steamship company.   These men were fined small sums, and
upon appeal, these convictions were sustained by the circuit
court of appeals.   Judge Foster in his charge to the jury took
the extreme position that all strikes which in fact tie up inter-

state commerce are unlawful under the Sherman Act.[1] In another case, five negro longshoremen at Jacksonville, Fla., pleaded guilty to charges of conspiring to violate the Sherman Act and were sentenced to short terms in prison, although neither this case nor the New Orleans case involved any acts of intimidation or violence.[2] Even more alarming to labor was the decision of Judge Dayton in the Hitchman Coal and Coke Co. case[3] to the effect that the United Mine Workers of America were an unlawful combination within the meaning of the Sherman Act.   Though this conclusion was later overruled by the circuit court of appeals, it increased the fear felt in labor circles that the very existence of labor unions was menaced by the Sherman Act.

CLAYTON ACT, SECTION 6

As early as 1900, the American Federation of Labor was instrumental in having bills introduced in Congress proposing amendments to exempt labor unions from the Sherman Act.   When the U. S. Supreme Court decided the Danbury hatters case in 1908, efforts to secure such legislation were redoubled.   This became organized labor's foremost objective, leading the unions to take a very active part in the presidential and congressional elections of 1908, 1910, and 1912.   In all of these elections, the American Federation of Labor conducted campaigns to defeat members of Congress who did not support its proposals for injunction legislation and amendment of the Sherman Act, and in the two presidential campaigns it endorsed the Democratic candidates, who ran upon platforms which, at least vaguely, promised the relief sought by labor.

In March, 1913, Woodrow Wilson became President and the Democratic party, for the first time in twenty years, controlled both houses of Congress.   The President and most of the Democratic members of Congress had been actively supported in the preceding campaign by organized labor, which now demanded and expected legislation exempting it from the Sherman Act.

---

[1] U. S. v. Ray *et al.*, E. D. La., Indictment in 1908.   Trial in 1911, in which defendants were found guilty and fined an aggregate of $110.   Judgment affirmed by the Circuit Court of Appeals ("The Federal Antitrust Laws with Amendments," p. 102).

[2] U. S. v. Haines *et al.*, S. D. Fla., 1911 ("The Federal Antitrust Laws with Amendments," p. 115).

[3] 202 Fed. 512 (1912), reversed in 214 Fed. 685 (1914).

The hopes which labor entertained of getting what it called "relief from the antitrust laws" were, at least in its opinion at the time, fulfilled by the inclusion of Sec. 6 in the supplementary antitrust law known as the Clayton Act, enacted in the first regular session of this Democratic Congress:

That the labor of a human being is not a commodity or article of commerce. Nothing contained in the antitrust laws shall be construed to forbid the existence and operation of labor, agricultural, or horticultural organizations, instituted for the purpose of mutual help, and not having capital stock or conducted for profit, or to forbid or restrain individual members of such organizations from lawfully carrying out the legitimate objects thereof; nor shall such organizations, or the members thereof, be held or construed to be illegal combinations or conspiracies in restraint of trade, under the antitrust laws.

Exactly what Congress intended to accomplish by this section is as debatable as is the question whether Congress intended to make the Sherman Act applicable to labor. There is some justification for opinions like the following:

With a legislative history like that which surrounds the Clayton Act, talk about the legislative intent as a means of construing legislation is simply repeating an empty formula. The Supreme Court had to find meaning where Congress had done its best to conceal it.[1]

An examination of the debates in Congress, as well as personal contacts which the present author had at the time with members of the Judiciary Committee of the House, in which this bill originated, justify the conviction that most of the members of Congress believed Sec. 6 of the Clayton Act simply precluded suits for the dissolution of labor unions under the antitrust laws and actions directed against their normal and lawful activities. This was President Wilson's interpretation as given in a newspaper interview at the time.[2]

The exemption of labor from the antitrust laws in Sec. 6 of the Clayton Act was not in the form originally suggested by the representatives of organized labor. As originally introduced in the House of Representatives, this section did not include the first sentence of the final draft or the last clause of the second sentence. In this form, the section merely provided that

---

[1] FRANKFURTER, FELIX, and NATHAN GREENE, 38 *Yale Law Jour.* 888 (1929).

[2] Interview carried in nearly all of the daily newspapers of June 2, 1914.

the antitrust laws should not be construed to forbid the existence and operation of labor unions, or to forbid the members of such unions from "lawfully carrying out the legitimate objects thereof." President Gompers, finding this unacceptable, addressed a letter to each member of Congress, protesting that the proposed exemption was wholly unsatisfactory and asking for the substitution of a clause to the effect that "nothing contained in the antitrust laws should be construed to apply to labor organizations."[1] Immediately before the bill came up for action in the House, a compromise resulted in the addition, to the original draft of this section, of what is now the last clause in the second sentence: that labor unions and their members shall not "be held or construed to be illegal combinations or conspiracies in restraint of trade."[2] This change caused labor enthusiastically to support the Clayton Bill. In the Senate, the first sentence of Sec. 6 as it now stands was added and acclaimed by labor as expressing exactly what it wished to secure, although it would seem the change was not at labor's instigation. There is nothing in the congressional debates to indicate that any member understood that this section had been altered in meaning, but these changes resulted in an about face on labor's part.

Organized labor felt very sure of its complete exemption from the antitrust laws through Sec. 6 of the Clayton Act. Samuel Gompers referred editorially to this provision as "the Industrial Magna Charta upon which the working people will rear their construction of industrial freedom."[3]

Labor retained this enthusiasm for the Clayton Act for about five years, and for some time longer it insisted that the courts were misconstruing the act. No one thinks now that the Clayton

---

[1] This letter was signed by the president and secretary of the American Federation of Labor, the legislative representatives of the four railroad brotherhoods and an officer of the Farmers' Union and the Farmers' National Congress. The same position was later taken in a resolution adopted by the executive committee of the American Federation of Labor, which was published in the *A. F. of L. Weekly News Letter* of May 23, 1914, and in 21 *Amer. Federationist* 584–585, July, 1914.

[2] Upon how this compromise was arrived at, see the speech of Chairman Henry of the Rules Committee on June 1, 1914 (*Cong. Rec.*, 63rd Congress, 2nd Sess., Vol. 51, p. 9540). For a somewhat different version, see *Philadelphia Inquirer*, May 27, 1914.

[3] 21 *Amer. Federationist* 971, November, 1914.

Act was labor's "Magna Charta." What Sec. 6 of the Clayton Act really accomplished, or rather did *not* accomplish, has been set forth authoritatively by the U. S. Supreme Court:

There is nothing in this section to exempt such an organization or its members from accountability where it or they depart from its normal and legitimate objects and engage in an actual combination or conspiracy in restraint of trade. And by no fair or permissible construction can it be taken as authorizing any activity otherwise unlawful, or enabling a normally lawful organization to become a cloak for an illegal combination in restraint of trade as defined by the antitrust laws.[1]

Section 6 of the Clayton Act means this: that labor organizations are not rendered illegal by the federal antitrust laws; it does not exempt all activities by, or on behalf of, labor unions from the antitrust laws. When a labor combination seeks by lawful means to increase wages, reduce hours of labor, or otherwise improve conditions of work, incidental restraint of trade does not render these activities unlawful. When the court finds, however, that the combination aims primarily at restraint of trade, then all activities to this end are unlawful, whether or not they are undertaken by or on behalf of a labor organization. Thus, labor gained from the Clayton Act only a statement that the antitrust laws did not forbid all strikes affecting the interstate transportation of goods, as was suggested in a few cases in inferior courts prior to the passage of the Clayton Act.

In one respect, the Clayton Act made the position of organized labor under the antitrust laws distinctly worse than before because of a provision allowing private parties to obtain injunctions under the antitrust laws against persons guilty of conduct in violation of these laws. Whereas prior to the act, the federal government alone could secure injunctions against unlawful restraint of trade, Sec. 16 provided that any private party injured through any unlawful restraint of interstate or foreign commerce might maintain an injunction suit against persons guilty of such conduct.

PRESENT APPLICATION OF THE FEDERAL ANTITRUST LAWS

In the fifteen years' history of the Clayton Act, there have been a great many more cases against labor under the federal antitrust

---

[1] Duplex Printing Press Co. v. Deering, 254 U. S. 443 at 469, 41 Sup. Ct. 172 at 177 (1921).

laws than during the previous twenty-four years. As many of them are unreported, their exact number is not known, but in this period have occurred at least twenty-three criminal prosecutions, six damage suits, and about forty suits for injunctions. Twenty-eight of these criminal prosecutions and injunctions were instituted by the federal Department of Justice, or by United States district attorneys.[1] In more than half of the criminal cases convictions have resulted, with long prison sentences in several instances. Considerably more than half of the injunctions sued for have been allowed, and there have been settlements for large damages in two actions.[2]

Most of the criminal prosecutions have involved conduct which was clearly criminal aside from the antitrust laws—graft and extortion or acts of violence and sabotage.[3] A few others have involved exclusive agreements between unions and employers' associations, in which the employers have obligated themselves to hire union men only, and the unions to work only for employers belonging to employers' associations.[4] Still others

---

[1] All actions instituted by the government under the antitrust laws are summarized in the publication of the Department of Justice, "The Federal Antitrust Laws with Amendments," Nov. 30, 1928.

[2] The cases referred to are the Coronado Coal and Coke Co. case (cited in Note 2, p. 72), in which there was at one time a judgment of $600,000 against the defendants, but which was finally settled out of court by payment of $27,500, and the suit brought by the Southern Illinois Coal Co. against the United Mine Workers of America, District 12, for damages sustained through the Herrin, Ill., "massacre" of 1922, which was settled by the unions' buying the plaintiff's property, at what was reported to be an exorbitant price. Another important damage suit under the federal antitrust laws was the Pennsylvania Mining Co. case, 300 Fed. 965 (1924), 266 U. S. 630 (1924), 28 F. (2nd) 851 (1928), in which, after fourteen years of litigation, the plaintiff took a nonsuit. Still another is the case of Decorative Stone Co. v. Building Trades Council, in which a jury in the District Court of the Southern District of New York in March, 1931, awarded $43,000 damages and costs against three union councils which boycotted the plaintiff's non-union store.

[3] Among cases of this kind are the following reported cases: U. S. v. Norris, 255 Fed. 423 (1918); U. S. v. Hency, 286 Fed. 165 (1923); U. S. v. Williams, 295 Fed. 302 (1923); Vandell v. U. S., 6 F. (2nd) 188 (1925). Very similar are: U. S. v. Rinteleen, 233 Fed. 793 (1918) and Lamar v. U. S., 260 Fed. 561 (1919), which involved the activities of German spies during the World War in promoting strikes in munition plants.

[4] Boyle v. U. S., 259 Fed. 803 (1919); Belfi v. U. S., 259 Fed. 822 (1922).

have involved boycotts which apparently were closely associated with racketeering activities.[1]

Other cases are more far-reaching. In one criminal prosecution, five pickets were found guilty of having violated the antitrust laws by interfering with the shipment of a single steel billet across a state boundary, and four of them received sentences of eight months in jail.[2] In another, eight union agents who induced a train crew to abandon a passenger train in the middle of its run were fined a total of ten thousand dollars and the U. S. Supreme Court denied a writ of certiorari to review the case.[3]

Even more alarming to organized labor were several injunctions premised upon the antitrust laws. In 1922, at the instance of the Department of Justice, a consent decree was entered in New York City against the bricklayers' union which not only prohibited this union from attempting to limit production and to prevent employers from using non-union materials but, furthermore, directed the union to print this decree in every issue of its rules.[4] More extreme still were twelve injunctions issued by the federal courts in West Virginia during the years 1920–1922, out of which arose the reported case International Organization, U. M. W. of A., v. Red Jacket Consolidated Coal and Coke Co.[5] These injunctions forbade all attempts to organize the coal miners, in addition prohibiting the sending of money from union fields into West Virginia and the raising of funds by means of the "check-off" system.[6] The circuit court of appeals modified these injunctions, but even in their changed form they forbade all attempts to dissuade employees who had signed individual non-union contracts from joining the union. The U. S. Supreme Court denied a writ of certiorari to review this decision,[7] thus indirectly giving it endorsement. In another case, during the

---

[1] A case in point is U. S. v. Brims, 272 U. S. 549, 47 Sup. Ct. 169 (1926).

[2] O'Brien v. U. S., 209 Fed. 185 (1923).

[3] Clements v. U. S., 297 Fed. 206 (1924); 266 U. S. 605, 45 Sup. Ct. 92 (1924).

[4] U. S. v. Bricklayers' Union, 4 *Law and Labor*, 95. The bricklayers' convention in 1926 voted to try to get this injunction modified and claimed that the union was "bulldozed" into accepting the consent decree.

[5] 18 F. (2nd) 839 (1927).

[6] Borderland Coal Corp. v. International Organization, 275 Fed. 871 (1921), modified in 278 Fed. 57 (1921).

[7] 275 U. S. 536, 48 Sup. Ct. 31 (1927).

great coal strike of 1927–1928, a federal district court at Pittsburgh ruled that this strike violated the antitrust laws.[1]

Most important, however, have been the decisions of the U. S. Supreme Court, especially the Duplex Printing Press Co. case, the two Coronado Coal and Coke Co. decisions, the Herkert & Meisel Trunk Co. case, and the Bedford Cut Stone Co. case.[2] The first of these settled that interstate boycotts of non-union materials could still be enjoined under the antitrust laws.[3]   The first Coronado Coal and Coke Co. decision established that a local coal miners' strike and acts of violence connected therewith are not an interference with interstate commerce, and the Herkert & Meisel Trunk Co. case applied the same doctrine to a strike in a manufacturing plant.   In the second Coronado Coal and Coke Co. decision, however, the court modified its former position, holding that the coal strike and the accompanying acts of violence did constitute an illegal interference with interstate commerce, punishable under the antitrust laws.   This was followed by the Bedford Cut Stone Co. case, in which a rule of the Journeymen Stone Cutters' Union providing that no member should work upon stone cut by non-members was held a violation of the Sherman Act, although no effort was made to persuade persons other than members of this union to take any action against the "unfair" stone.[4]

---

[1] Pittsburgh Terminal Coal Corp. v. United Mine Workers, 22 F. (2nd) 559 (1927).

[2] Duplex Printing Press Co. v. Deering, 254 U. S. 443, 41 Sup. Ct. 172 (1921); United Mine Workers v. Coronado Coal and Coke Co., 259 U. S. 344, 42 Sup. Ct. 570 (1922); 268 U. S. 295, 45 Sup. Ct. 551 (1925); Herkert & Meisel Trunk Co. v. Leather Workers, 265 U. S. 457, 44 Sup. Ct. 623 (1924); Bedford Cut Stone Co. v. Journeymen Stone Cutters' Assoc., 274 U. S. 37, 47 Sup. Ct. 522 (1927).

[3] In the earlier case Paine Lumber Co. v. Neal, 244 U. S. 459, 37 Sup. Ct. 718 (1917), an injunction against a boycott of non-union materials was refused, but solely upon the ground that the action arose prior to the Clayton Act, which first authorized private parties to maintain suits for injunctions under the antitrust laws.

[4] Besides the decisions mentioned in this paragraph two other cases growing out of labor disputes and involving the federal antitrust laws have come before the U. S. Supreme Court.   In National Assoc. of Window Glass Manufacturers v. U. S., 263 U. S. 403, 44 Sup. Ct. 551 (1925), a restrictive trade agreement was held not to violate the antitrust laws; while in Anderson v. Ship Owners, 271 U. S. 652, 47 Sup. Ct. 125 (1926), an alleged combination in effect to blacklist workmen was held to come under their ban.

The last decision mentioned is notable for the emphatic language in the dissenting opinion of Justice Brandeis: "If on the undisputed facts of this case, refusal to work can be enjoined, Congress created by the Sherman Act an instrument for imposing restraints upon labor which reminds of involuntary servitude." This sentence has been quoted repeatedly in labor periodicals and represents labor's appraisal of the antitrust laws.[1] That these laws are a growing menace to organized labor is unquestionable. No one can be entirely certain how far the federal antitrust acts go in restricting the activities of labor unions in industrial disputes.[2] That they go very far indeed is apparent. Acts of violence of any kind affecting the transportation of goods in interstate or foreign commerce are punishable criminally under these laws; labor union members may be enjoined and triple damages recovered for any resulting loss. It is established that these laws apply to all boycotts affecting goods shipped interstate, whether these be commodity boycotts or strikes against the use of non-union materials.[3] Further, it is clear that these laws render unlawful *some* strikes affecting the production of goods shipped in interstate commerce, but exactly when strikes become illegal is not clear. It would seem that even a nation-wide strike which is conducted for a purpose that the courts deem lawful is not rendered illegal because it ties up interstate commerce.[4] On the other hand, a much more limited strike for purposes that the courts do not approve seems to fall under the ban of the Sherman and Clayton Acts. This, as one

---

[1] For a longer statement of the views labor now holds of the antitrust laws, see Mathew Woll, Organized Labor Demands a Repeal of the Sherman Act, in 147 *Ann. Amer. Acad. Polit. Social Sci.* 185–188 (1930).

[2] Wheeler P. Bloodgood, 147 *Ann. Amer. Acad. Polit. Social Sci.* 111, 112 (1930), holds that "every strike, no matter how peaceful, if it interferes with commodities in interstate commerce, is unlawful." This seems to the author an extreme view, unsupported by the weight of the court decisions, but Mr. Bloodgood is an eminent lawyer and has given this subject special study as the chairman of the Committee on the Study of Antitrust Legislation of the National Civic Federation.

[3] Upon this point see Aeolian Co. v. Fischer, 27 F. (2nd) 560, 29 F. (2nd) 679, 35 F. (2nd) 34, 40 F. (2nd) 189 (1928–1930).

[4] TAFT, W. H., "The Antitrust Act and the Supreme Court," p. 97, Harper & Brothers, New York, (1914).

recent writer puts it, "comes near to being judicial hocus pocus,"[1] but these statements represent the best appraisal that can at this time be made upon the application of the federal antitrust laws to strikes affecting interstate commerce.

The federal antitrust laws, however, are not the sole, or even the principal, restriction upon labor's actions in controversies with employers. Of the total number of cases which have grown out of labor disputes, only a small percentage were cases under the antitrust laws. The author's list of more than six hundred injunctions issued against labor unions by the federal courts contains but forty involving the federal antitrust laws. Moreover, far-reaching as are the decisions in cases arising under these laws, the conduct condemned therein generally has been previously held illegal under the common law. Boycotts were held unlawful even before the Sherman Act was passed, and there have been numerous cases in which strikes against non-union materials have been condemned by state courts without invoking the antitrust statutes. Despite these considerations, however, it is undeniable that the federal antitrust laws constitute a vague and undefined danger to organized labor, which is ever becoming more menacing.

OTHER FEDERAL STATUTES

Besides the antitrust laws, three other sets of federal statutes are of some importance in the law of labor combinations. Foremost are the interstate commerce acts, often pleaded in injunction cases and less often in criminal prosecutions growing out of labor disputes. These figured prominently in the great railway strikes of 1893–1894, and in the railroad shop crafts' strike of 1922, but nearly always have been pleaded in conjunction with the antitrust laws.

In several federal decisions, as was noted in Chap. II, language is found which suggests that all strikes on railroads and all strikes which interfere with any other instrumentalities of interstate commerce are in violation of the interstate commerce acts. The real import of these cases, however, is suggested by the language of one of the most sweeping injunctions ever premised upon these

---

[1] TERBORGH, G. W., The Application of the Sherman Law to Trade Union Activities, 37 *Jour. Polit. Econ.* 203, 224 (1929).

acts, allowed by Judge Wilkerson to the Western Union Telegraph Company in a dispute with the electrical workers' union.[1] In this injunction, the defendants were enjoined from "calling a strike or threatening to call a strike, or from striking or threatening to strike"; but the injunction also contained a proviso to the effect that "nothing herein shall be construed to prohibit any employee from voluntarily ceasing work unless said act is in furtherance of the conspiracy charged." As this proviso indicates, the interstate commerce acts do not forbid strikes which hinder interstate commerce, but only those in pursuance of *conspiracies* to interfere with interstate commerce. The application of these acts to labor disputes rests upon substantially the same basis as does the application of the antitrust laws. When strikes affecting interstate commerce are conducted for purposes which the courts deem improper, then the interstate commerce acts may be invoked against them; but if the purpose is otherwise lawful, these acts have no application.[2]

Cited somewhat less frequently, but scarcely less important in labor cases, have been the federal statutes relating to interference with the mails. These statutes have led to many injunctions in railroad strikes, prohibiting interference with the mails and, more frequently, to counts in indictments growing out of such strikes. Seldom, however, have injunctions or criminal prosecutions been premised solely upon these statutes, and still less frequently has any conduct been punished under these statutes which was not also punishable under some other law. Convictions upon indictments charging interference with the mails premised upon conduct growing out of labor disputes have

---

[1] Western Union Telegraph Co. v. International Brotherhood, 2 F. (2nd) 993 (1924), 6 F. (2nd) 444 (1925).

[2] The most important cases arising under the federal interstate commerce acts were probably those of the early nineties which involved the legality of the rule of the Brotherhood of Locomotive Engineers, prohibiting the movement of cars from railroad lines on which there was a strike. The most important of these cases was the decision of Judge Taft (then a U. S. Circuit judge) in the so-called Arthur case in 1893, 54 Fed. 730, which had the effect of compelling the locomotive engineers to abandon this rule. The doctrine upon which this case proceeded was that while the interstate commerce acts did not prevent railroad men from quitting work, they did prohibit them from refusing to perform their full duties as employees of common carriers while continuing in employment.

been rare. The railroad strikes of 1877 and 1893–1894 were followed by a considerable number of such indictments, but only one of them resulted in a conviction.[1] Since then, the mail statutes have figured in railroad strikes principally in the clause often included in injunctions which prohibits the defendants "from in any manner interfering with, hindering, or stopping any trains carrying the mail." In only one recent case, which arose during the railroad shop crafts' strike of 1922, has there been a prosecution and conviction of strikers under the mail statutes.[2]

Besides these cases growing out of railroad strikes, the mail statutes have on two occasions been invoked in strikes of postal employees. The first of these, occurring in New York City in 1914, resulted in the conviction of eleven chauffeurs and their sentence to jail for interference with the mails through acts of violence. The second was a prosecution in 1916 of twenty-four postal employees at Fairmont, W. Va., premised upon their "resigning in a body" when a new postmaster discharged thirty of their number. In this case, the defendants pleaded *nolle contendere* and were thereupon fined from five to five hundred dollars.[3] These two postal cases suggest that the statutes prohibiting interference with the mails may possibly be construed to forbid all strikes of postal employees. In the New York case, however, the presiding judge, in his charge to the jury, expressly stated that while it was not unlawful for these men to strike, the

---

[1] Clune v. U. S., 159 U. S. 590, 16 Sup. Ct. 125 (1895). For other criminal prosecutions premised upon the mail statutes in connection with these strikes, see U. S. v. Clark, Fed. Cases 14,805 (1877); U. S. v. Stevens, Fed. Cases 16,392 (1877); U. S. v. Thomas, 55 Fed. 380 (1893); U. S. v. Cassidy, 67 Fed. 698 (1895). For unreported cases, see *Chicago Tribune*, July 31, 1877; *New York Sun*, Aug. 2, 19, 1877; *Indianapolis Jour.*, July 13, 20, 1894; *Chicago Tribune*, June 30, 1894; *Chicago Times*, July 3, 5, 10, 24, 1894; 29 *Amer. Law Rev.* 512–522 (1895).

[2] Clements v. U. S. 297 Fed. 206 (1924). A writ of certiorari was denied in this case by the U. S. Supreme Court in 266 U. S. 605, 45 Sup. Ct. 92.

[3] The New York case referred to was U. S. v. Hochberg in the southern district of New York, which is not reported, but a full account of which appeared in the *New York Call* in various issues from November, 1913, to February, 1914. The Fairmont, W. Va., case is discussed in *U. S. Postal Clerk*, Nov. 17, 1915, and in a speech by Congressman John I. Nolan in the House of Representatives on Feb. 24, 1916 (*Cong. Rec.*, 64th Cong., 1st Sess., Vol. 53, pp. 3098–3100).

acts of violence which they committed during the strike brought them within the scope of the mail statutes. The Fairmont prosecution seems to have rested squarely upon the concept that a strike of postal employees is *per se* unlawful; but since the defendants entered the plea of *nolle contendere*, there was no real discussion of principles.

The third of the federal statutes which has figured to some extent in labor cases is the "conspiracy statute," Sec. 5440 of the *Revised Statutes*. This penalizes conspiracies to commit offenses against the United States and has been cited in practically all criminal indictments growing out of labor disputes which have been brought in the federal courts. In all but one case, however, the gist of the offense charged has been a violation of either the federal antitrust laws, the interstate commerce acts, the mail statutes, or a combination of these.[1]

STATE LEGISLATION RESTRICTING LABOR COMBINATIONS

The volume of state legislation relating to labor combinations and labor disputes is very much greater than that of the federal legislation, but the state laws are far less important. Every state has a law declaring "conspiracy" to be a criminal offense. These are all broadly worded, yet they are no more inclusive than the definitions of what constitutes a conspiracy in court decisions.

Most states also have antitrust laws, with prohibitions against restraints of trade and attempts at monopoly in intrastate commerce similar to those contained in the federal antitrust laws with reference to interstate commerce. Many of these laws exempt farmer and labor organizations; none has any clause aimed specifically at labor combinations. Although in a few cases these laws have been invoked against labor unions, the total number of prosecutions under the state antitrust laws is small as compared to the number of such cases under the federal antitrust laws.[2]

---

[1] The exception is Pettibone v. U. S., 148 U. S. 197, 13 Sup. Ct. 542 (1893). The offense charged in that case was a conspiracy to obstruct the administration of justice and was premised upon the violation of an injunction issued by a federal court.

[2] For injunction and criminal actions premised upon the state antitrust laws, see: Irving v. Neal, 209 Fed. 471 (1913); Standard Engraving Co. v. Volz, 200 App. Div. 758, 193 N. Y. S. 831 (1922); State v. Employers of Labor, 102 Neb. 768, 169 N. W. 717, 170 N. W. 185 (1918); Webb v. Cooks,

Besides the general conspiracy statutes and the antitrust laws, nearly all the states have laws which prohibit coercion, intimidation, and threats, whether these acts are committed singly or collectively.   These laws are couched for the most part in general language, but many of them owe their enactment to labor difficulties, especially to the railroad strike of 1877 and the strikes and riots of 1886.   Typical is the law of Connecticut, which penalizes

. . . every person who shall threaten or use any means calculated or intended to intimidate any person to compel such person against his will to do or abstain from doing any act which such person has a legal right to do, or injure or threaten his property, with intent to intimidate him.[1]

In addition to these laws, which are to be found in all, or nearly all, states, there are several states which have laws more specifically directed against certain activities of labor combinations. Illinois and Wisconsin have conspiracy laws which include prohibitions of boycotting; Colorado also prohibits boycotting and picketing; Alabama has an antipicketing law, as have also Nebraska and Hawaii; while Utah has a law prohibiting picketing in connection with boycotts.[2]   Several states have laws prohibiting unlawful interference with the operations of railroads and mines, similar to the general antiintimidation statutes, but forbidding as well acts of sabotage and attempts to retard the movement of trains.[3]   All of these several laws, aimed specifically at

---

etc., Union, 204 S. W. 465 (Tex. Civil App. 1918); Campbell v. Motion Picture Operators, 51 Minn. 220, 186 N. W. 781 (1922); Overland Publishing Co. v. Crocker Co., 193 Cal. 222, 222 Pac. 812 (1924); State ex rel. Miller v. Electrical Business Assoc., 13 Law and Labor 74 (Ohio Com. Pl. 1931). Unsuccessful actions include Shaughnessy v. Jordan, 184 Ind. 449, 111 N. E. 622 (1916); Seubert v. Reiff, 164 N. Y. S. 522 (1917); Grant Construction Co. v. Building Trades Council, 136 Minn. 167, 161 N. W. 1055 (1917); People v. Epstean, 102 Misc. 476, 170 N. Y. S. 68 (1918).

[1] Conn. Gen. Stat. sec. 6358 (1918).

[2] In addition to these laws, Texas includes a prohibition of boycotting in its antitrust law, and Illinois and New Jersey have special statutes against calling strikes for purposes of graft. Washington passed an antipicketing law in 1915, but this was turned down by the people in a referendum vote in 1916. On the other hand, the Nebraska antipicketing law was approved by the people upon a referendum vote.

[3] Special laws relating to interference with railroads are to be found in: Connecticut, Delaware, Illinois, Kansas, Kentucky, Maine, New Jersey, Pennsylvania, Texas, Wisconsin; statutes prohibiting interference with

acts of labor combinations, are broader than the common law and at the time of their enactment were bitterly opposed by organized labor. They have, however, been seldom invoked in labor disputes.

As a final type of legislation restricting labor combinations, there are the antisyndicalism laws to be found on the statute books of twenty-two states and territories.[1] Most of these were enacted during the years 1917–1921 and were aimed at the Industrial Workers of the World and the communist organizations. They prohibit the commission of acts of sabotage and the advocacy of the overthrow of government by violence and, many of them, membership in organizations which practice or preach such doctrines. These statutes have been sustained by the U. S. Supreme Court and every state court in which they have been tested.[2] These laws very probably have had something to do with the decline in the last ten years of the Industrial Workers of the World and of labor organizations controlled by communists and have certainly compelled change in the tactics of these organizations. They have never been used, however, against the regular trade unions and have not been regarded by these unions as being particularly objectionable.

---

mines in South Dakota and West Virginia. A similar law was the Texas "open-port" law of 1920 (*General and Special Laws of Texas, 4th called Sess.*, c. 5 [1920]), which aroused violent opposition from labor and was held unconstitutional in Ratcliff v. State, 289 S. W. 1073 (1926).

[1] Antisyndicalism laws exist in Alabama, Alaska, Arizona, California, Hawaii, Idaho, Illinois, Indiana, Iowa, Kansas, Michigan, Minnesota, Montana, Nebraska, Nevada, Ohio, Oklahoma, Oregon, South Dakota, Utah, Washington, and Wyoming. Very similar are the New York criminal anarchy statute and the Pennsylvania and New Jersey sedition laws, enacted many years ago.

[2] Whitney v. California, 274 U. S. 357, 47 Sup. Ct. 641 (1927); Fiske v. Kansas, 274 U. S. 380, 47 Sup. Ct. 665 (1927); State v. Moilen, 140 Minn. 112, 167 N. W. 345 (1918); State v. Steelik, 187 Cal. 361, 203 Pac. 78 (1921); State v. Hennessy, 114 Wash. 351, 195 Pac. 211 (1921); People v. Lloyd, 304 Ill. 23, 136 N. E. 505 (1922); State v. Dingman, 37 Ida. 253, 219 Pac. 760 (1923); State v. Laundy, 103 Ore. 443, 204 Pac. 958, 206 Pac. 290 (1922); People v. Ruthenberg, 229 Mich. 315, 201 N. W. 358 (1924); Berg v. State, 29 Okla. Crim. 112, 233 Pac. 497 (1925). The Pennsylvania sedition law was held constitutional in Commonwealth v. Widovich, 295 Pa. 311, 145 Atl. 295 (1929).

STATE LEGISLATION FAVORABLE TO LABOR COMBINATIONS

There are more laws intended to safeguard labor combinations than to restrict their activities, but these laws are of little significance. Seven states have laws which expressly legalize combinations to increase wages, or to reduce hours of labor.[1] These merely restate what the courts in this country practically from the beginning have held to be the common law. While originally heralded with great enthusiasm, they have been without practical effect. Considerably broader are the laws of Maryland, California, and Oklahoma, which were modeled after the British Conspiracy and Protection of Property Act. These laws provide that acts done in labor disputes by two or more persons in concert shall not be deemed criminal or unlawful unless these acts are criminal if done by one person without agreement. While the English act after which these laws were patterned profoundly changed the law of labor combinations in England, its American counterparts have been cited very seldom and seem to have exerted little influence on the trend of judicial decisions in these three states.[2]

Ten states[3] have expressly exempted labor unions from their antitrust laws; but, as noted, even in states where there is no such exemption, the antitrust laws are seldom used against labor.

Besides these laws, the purpose of which is to legalize labor unions, there are other statutes in practically all states which recognize unions to be lawful organizations and give them statutory protection.[4] Of this character are the laws permitting labor unions to incorporate. These were enacted during the eighties, in response to a demand from the Knights of Labor.

---

[1] Colorado, Minnesota, Nevada, New York, North Dakota, Pennsylvania, and Texas. West Virginia also has a provision in its statutes declaring labor unions to be lawful, but this occurs in a law which penalizes interference with the operation of mines.

[2] In Oklahoma, this statute has been held to legalize picketing: *ex parte* Schweitzer, 13 Okla. Crim. 154, 62 Pac. 1134 (1917).

[3] California, Iowa, Louisiana, Michigan, Nebraska, New Hampshire, New Mexico, Oklahoma, Virginia, and Wisconsin. Montana had a similar provision, but this was held unconstitutional in State v. Cudahy Packing Co., 33 Mont. 179, 82 Pac. 833.

[4] For citations to these laws, see the footnote in the decision of the U. S. Supreme Court in United Mine Workers v. Coronado Coal and Coke Co., 259 U. S. 344, at 386–389, 42 Sup. Ct. 570 at 574–575.

At that time, incorporation was thought of as a method of gaining legal recognition and of getting away from the common law doctrine of conspiracy. Once these laws were enacted, labor lost all interest in them, and but few unions have incorporated. Of much greater practical value are the laws in force in most states protecting union labels from infringement, and the laws of a somewhat smaller number of states prohibiting forgery of union cards, the unauthorized wearing of union buttons, or any false representation of union membership. Less numerous are special laws to protect union funds from embezzlement, and to prohibit bribery of union members.

Of more recent origin are the antiinjunction laws enacted in about a dozen states.[1] In addition to these, laws in five states expressly legalize peaceful persuasion[2] and Massachusetts has a law permitting unions to fine their members for failure to observe strike orders or union rules.[3] Finally, there are some laws exempting labor unions from taxation.

This completes the enumeration of laws favorable to labor combinations. Altogether, these laws have not fundamentally altered the legal status of labor organizations, although the union-label laws and a few others have been of some value.[4]

Bibliographical Note

The original sources for a study of the statutes affecting labor combinations and labor disputes are the compiled statutes and session laws of the several states and the U. S. Statutes-at-Large. Most of these laws are reprinted in *Bull.* 370 of the U. S. Bureau of Labor Statistics, Labor Laws of the United States with Decisions Relating Thereto. This comes down to January, 1925, and includes citations to decisions construing these statutes. Supplementing this bulletin, the U. S. Bureau of Labor Statistics annually issues a bulletin upon the new labor legislation of the preceding year, and the December number of the *American Labor Legislation Review* contains a summary of all new labor legislation of the year.

---

[1] These laws are discussed in Chap. XII, pp. 270–273.

[2] Such laws exist in Massachusetts, New Hampshire, New Jersey, Texas, and Wisconsin.

[3] *Mass. Gen Laws*, c. 180, s. 19 (1921). This statute was rendered necessary by Willicutt v. Bricklayers', etc., Union, 200 Mass. 110, 85 N. E. 897 (1908) and nullifies this decision.

[4] Legislation placing restrictions upon the conduct of employers in labor disputes, of which there is a considerable volume, although also of but slight practical importance, is discussed in Chap. X

There is no recent secondary account covering all statutes in this field. Lindley D. Clark, "The Law of the Employment of Labor," pp. 213–240, The Macmillan Company, New York (1911), is a general account of this kind but is now twenty years old.

The federal antitrust acts in their relation to labor unions have been discussed quite frequently. Alpheus T. Mason, "Organized Labor and the Law with Especial Reference to the Sherman and Clayton Acts," Duke University Press, Durham, N. C. (1926), devotes more than one hundred pages to this subject. A longer study is "Labor and the Sherman Act," by Edward Berman of the University of Illinois, Harper & Brothers, New York (1930); another, J. F. Christ, "The Federal Courts and Organized Labor," four parts of which have been published serially in 3 and 4 *Jour. of Business of the University of Chicago* (1930–1931). A shorter account is G. W. Terborgh, The Application of the Sherman Law to Trade Union Activities, 37 *Jour. Polit. Econ.* 203–224 (1929); and another brief account, Felix Frankfurter and Nathan Greene, "The Labor Injunction," 7–9, 137–146, The Macmillan Company, New York (1930). For source material, the publication of the United States Department of Justice, "The Federal Antitrust Laws with Amendments," issued in November, 1928, is invaluable. Berman, "Labor and the Sherman Act," has an Appendix giving all essential facts in each labor case which has arisen under the antitrust laws; and the articles by Christ, *op. cit.*, give tables listing all reported cases and their outcome.

CHAPTER V

INJUNCTIONS: PROCEDURE

The preceding chapters have dealt with the substantive law, the rights of the contending parties in labor disputes as laid down in statutes and court decisions. This and the succeeding three chapters deal with the procedural law, the enforcement of the rights of the contending parties through injunctions, damage suits, and criminal actions. Of these, injunctions are by far the most important, although criminal prosecutions are far more numerous.

Injunctions are an old and familiar remedy in wide use in many fields of the law.[1] They are ordinarily negative in character, prohibiting the commission of specified acts under pain of punishment for contempt. Their purpose is preventive; and in theory at least, they are designed primarily for the protection of property. In recent years, their use has been growing apace, injunctions now being resorted to in many kinds of controversies in which they were unheard of earlier.[2]

Among these is their use in industrial disputes, which began in England in 1868, although few labor injunctions have since been issued in that country. In the United States the first injunctions were issued in the early 1880's, but not until the Debs case[3] in 1894 did they attract much notice, since which time they

---

[1] The best presentation for the layman of the history, purposes, and the principles governing the issuance of injunctions generally is F. W. Maitland, "Lectures on Equity," The Macmillan Company, New York (1909).

[2] The extension of the use of injunctions has in most fields aroused no opposition. Besides the labor injunctions, objection has been confined principally to the "padlock injunctions" under the National Prohibition Act and to injunctions to restrict publications of matter deemed libelous or seditious.

[3] U. S. v. Debs, 64 Fed. 724 (1894); *in re* Debs, 158 U. S. 664, 15 Sup. Ct. 900 (1895).

have at all times been the best known and most debated of the legal remedies employed in labor controversies.[1]

NUMBER OF INJUNCTIONS

The exact number of injunctions in labor disputes is unascertainable. This results from the fact that most injunctions are issued by inferior courts, whose decisions are not noted in any series of official or unofficial reports.

Some idea of the number of injunctions can be gathered from the fact that the author has definite references to 508 cases in federal courts and 1,364 cases in state courts in which injunctions were issued prior to May 1, 1931, on the application of employers. In addition, there were 32 federal cases and 191 state cases in which injunctions were sought without being allowed.

On the author's list are injunctions in every state except South Carolina, but with the great industrial states predominating, particularly New York, Massachusetts, and Illinois. The unreported cases exceed the reported cases in the ratio of five to one. Of the grand total of 1,845 injunctions, 28 were issued in the 1880's, 122 in the 1890's, 328 from 1900 to 1909, 446 from 1910 to 1919, and 921 between Jan. 1, 1920, and May 1, 1930. Very probably this list includes a larger percentage of all injunctions in the last two decades than in earlier periods, and for the last ten years is swelled by the large number of injunctions issued in the railroad shop crafts strike of 1922. Yet the author believes the impression of a steadily increasing number of injunctions, created by the figures cited, to be substantially correct. In the last six or eight years there has probably been a decrease in absolute numbers, but this is believed to have been smaller than the reduction in the number of strikes.[2]

---

[1] For the history of injunctions in labor disputes, consult Felix Frankfurter and Nathan Greene, "The Labor Injunction," 17–24, The Macmillan Company, New York (1930); Walter Nelles, A Strike and Its Legal Consequences, in 40 *Yale Law Jour.* 507–554 (1931); and E. E. Witte, Early American Labor Cases, in 35 *Yale Law Jour.* 825, 832–836 (1926).

[2] From 1898 to 1916, 265 injunctions were issued in Massachusetts, as listed in *Bulls.* 70, 78, and 117 of the Massachusetts Bureau of Labor Statistics. In the railroad shop crafts strike of 1922, nearly 300 injunctions were issued (G. W. Pepper, Injunctions in Labor Disputes in 49 *Amer. Bar Assoc. Rep.* 174, 177 [1924]). A list of 389 injunctions issued in recent years was filed by the American Federation of Labor

COMPLAINTS AND ANSWERS

Injunctions are most commonly sought while strikes are in progress; far less frequently, to prevent strikes or to break up boycotts. Usually, they are preceded by picketing and quite often by clashes between the strikers and the loyal or new employees (usually called "strike breakers").

In situations of serious violence, however, employers far more commonly resort to criminal prosecutions than to injunctions and seek the protection of the militia rather than that of the courts. Why this is so appears clearly from the explanation given by Walter Drew, counsel for the National Erectors' Association, to a Senate committee in 1912, telling why no injunctions were sought against the structural iron workers in their long series of dynamite outrages which culminated in the McNamara case in 1911:

It may have occurred to the Senators to inquire why we did not begin injunction suits, but an injunction suit against dynamite would have been far less effective than criminal action, if we had the evidence to prove it. We could not very well enjoin anyone from using dynamite until we had the evidence, and the moment we had the evidence, criminal action was the proper course.[1]

Injunctions usually are sought by a single employer or a group of employers.[2] In a few cases, the United States Government acting under the antitrust laws has been the complainant; somewhat more frequently, a non-union workman or a stock- or bondholder of the corporation involved in the labor trouble or

---

with the Senate Committee on the Judiciary in 1928 (Hearings on "Limiting Scope of Injunctions in Labor Disputes," 70th Cong., 1st Sess., pp. 39, 503). From 1894 to 1929, there were 250 applications for injunctions in labor cases in New York City, in nearly all of which injunctive orders were allowed (P. F. Brissenden and C. O. Swayzee, The Use of the Labor Injunction in the New York Needle Trades, 44 *Polit. Sci. Quart.*, 548 [1929]).

[1] 62nd Cong., 2nd Sess., Senate Committee on the Judiciary: "Limiting Federal Injunctions," Hearings before subcommittee on H. R. 23635, p. 216 (1912).

[2] Any number of employers involved in the same difficulty may join as complainants: Inter. Organization, United Mine Workers v. Red Jacket Consolidated Coal and Coke Co., 18 F. (2nd) 839 (1922), in which 316 corporations were joined as complainants. Injunctions, however, cannot be extended to any employers who do not appear as complainants: Gasaway v. Borderland Coal Corp., 278 Fed. 56 (1921).

some outsider with whom it has contractual relations.   In the latter group of cases, the real complainant is practically always the employer, whose motive in not appearing openly as such is to make it possible to bring the suit in a federal court.[1]

Everywhere suits for injunctions are started by the filing of a bill of complaint (bill in equity) in a trial court having jurisdiction.[2]   Often more than one court or judge has jurisdiction, and in such situations the complainants naturally select the one whom they believe most likely to grant them an injunction, so that in many industrial communities a few judges get the great bulk of all labor injunction cases—the "injunction judges" whom organized labor hates so cordially.

The complaints in these cases are thoroughly standardized, varying only in details.   All of them begin with a recital of the

---

[1] To give federal courts jurisdiction, the case must either be brought under some federal statute or there must be diversity of citizenship between the complainants and the defendants.   The facts in most cases preclude bringing the suit under any federal statute, so that normally diversity of citizenship must be established.   This is a simple matter where the complainant is a foreign corporation; but if it is a domestic corporation it can get into the federal courts only if the defendants are non-residents, or if a non-resident stockholder, bondholder, or third party with whom the corporation has contractual relations brings the suit and names the corporation as one of the defendants.   Earlier such suits were quite common, but more recently the principle has been applied that there must be no collusion between the nominal complainants and the corporation.   Most recent attempts to get into the federal courts in this manner have failed, among others the following: Niles-Bement-Pond Co. v. Iron Molders, 258 Fed. 408 (1918), 254 U. S. 77, 41 Sup. Ct. 31 (1920); Davis v. Henry, 266 Fed. 261 (1920); Gable v. Vonnegut Machinery Co., 274 Fed. 66 (1921); Washington Cleaning, etc., Co. v. Cleaners, etc., Union, 34 F. (2nd) 897 (1929); Detroit Tile and Mosaic Co. v. Mason Contractors Assoc., 38 F. (2nd) 284 (1930).   Sometimes, however, stock- or bondholders' suits are still successful in getting labor injunction cases into the federal courts which otherwise would have had to be brought in the state courts, a recent example being U. S. Trust Co. v. Amalgamated Assoc. of Street and Electric Railroad Employees, W. D. La., July, 1929.

[2] The complaints in many reported cases are summarized in the decisions, and copies of the complaints in current cases can usually be obtained by writing to the attorneys for the complainants.   For reprints of some recent complaints see the Senate Hearings on "Limiting Scope of Injunctions in Labor Disputes," pp. 516–524 (1928), and the Senate Hearings on "Conditions in the Coal Mines of Pennsylvania, West Virginia, and Ohio," pp. 1863–1873 (1928).

property holdings and the nature and scope of the business of the complainants, followed by a description of the defendants. Next, it is alleged that the defendants have conspired to injure the plaintiffs. Then follows a recital of the strike and of all clashes between strikers and strike breakers, which are represented as having been undertaken in furtherance of the unlawful conspiracy. If actual violence has occurred, this is set forth at length. Otherwise, "coercion," "threats," "intimidation," and so forth, are alleged in general terms. These allegations are followed by the claim that the defendants will continue their unlawful course unless restrained and that the injury to the complainants will be irreparable. Concluding the complaint is the prayer for relief, which usually states the precise terms of the injunction sought. This is followed by the verification, an affidavit of some officer of the employing corporation, to the effect that the allegations set forth are true to the affiants' best knowledge and belief.

To the complaint, the defendants usually file an answer contradicting everything set forth in the complaint except the statements relating to the business and property of the complainants. They deny that they have conspired to injure the complainants and frequently make the counterclaim that the complainants have conspired to destroy the union. Likewise, there is a contradiction of all unlawful acts, including a version of the specific difficulties between the strikers and the strike breakers which places all the blame upon the strike breakers. Concluding the answer is a request for the dismissal of the suit and sometimes for a counterinjunction.

Both sides customarily file supporting affidavits with their complaint or answer, which relate principally to the specific unlawful acts alleged in the complaint and are usually directly contradictory.[1] On the employer's side, these affidavits are usually made by officers and employees or by detectives and guards hired by them for service during the strike. In the strikers' behalf, the affidavits are made by the men specifically charged with unlawful acts and by strike sympathizers who claim to have witnessed these occurrences.

---

[1] For illustrations of contradictory affidavits in labor cases, see Felix Frankfurter and Nathan Greene, "The Labor Injunction," pp. 69-72, The Macmillan Company, New York (1930).

That the complainants and the defendants should present their respective sides in the most favorable light possible is only to be expected. In many cases, the courts have criticized the complaints as amounting to a mass of glittering generalities presenting rather the conclusions of the pleader than a statement of the facts,[1] and this characterization of the complaints applies equally to the answers. The affidavits, although more specific, are no less unreliable. It is human nature for partisans to see the occurrences in dispute through colored glasses. Particularly questionable are the affidavits of private detectives, of whom Mr. Justice McReynolds of the U. S. Supreme Court said in a recent non-labor case: "All know that men who accept such employment commonly lack fine scruples, often wilfully misrepresenting innocent conduct, and manufacturing charges."[2]   To quote the opinion of another judge:[3]

Affidavits are an untrustworthy guide for judicial action. That is the case in all legal proceedings, but is peculiarly true of litigation growing out of a strike, where feelings on both sides are necessarily wrought up, and the desire for victory is likely to obscure nice moral questions and poison the minds of men by prejudice.

TEMPORARY RESTRAINING ORDERS

In the complaints, it is customary to ask for a temporary restraining order prohibiting the defendants from doing any of

---

[1] Davitt v. American Bakers Union, 124 Cal. 99, 56 Pac. 775 (1889); Builders Painting and Decorating Co. v. Advisory Board, 116 Ill. App. 264 (1904); Badger Brass Manufacturing Co. v. Daly, 137 Wis. 601, 119 N. W. 328 (1909); Hogle Co. v. Mulvaney, Sup. Ct. Queens Co. N. Y., May 9, 1912 (Judge Blackmar); Grant Construction Co. v. St. Paul Building Trades Council, Dist. Ct. Ramsay Co., Minn., June 27, 1916 (Judge Dickson). See also Frankfurter and Green, *op. cit.*, pp. 60–64.

[2] Sinclair v. U. S., 279 U. S. 749, 49 Sup. Ct. 471 (1929). For labor cases in which judges have severely condemned private detectives and questioned their reliability, see Consolidated Steel and Wire Co. v. Murray, 80 Fed. 811, 815 (1897), and Great Nor. Ry. Co. v. Brosseau, 286 Fed. 414, 416 (1923).

[3] United States District Judge Amidon in Great Nor. Ry. Co. v. Brosseau, 286 Fed. 414 (1923). For other criticisms to much the same effect see Garrigan v. U. S., 163 Fed. 16, 19 (1908); Berg Auto Truck and Specialty Co. v. Wiener, 121 Misc. 796, 200 N. Y. S. 745 (1920); Piermont v. Schlesinger, 196 App. Div. 658, 188 N. Y. S. 35 (1921); Great Nor. Ry. Co. v. Local, Great Falls Lodge of Inter. Assoc. of Machinists, 283 Fed. 557 (1922); Aeolian Co. v. Fischer 29 F. (2nd) 679 (1928).

the acts complained of until the case can be heard. The issuance of such orders is entirely discretionary with the court but in non-labor cases is very much a matter of course, their professed purpose being to preserve the *status quo* until the merits of the dispute can be determined.

While there has been little objection to the issuance of temporary restraining orders in non-labor cases, no feature of the use of injunctions in labor disputes has aroused more adverse criticism. The fundamental reason for this is that labor disputes are dynamic occurrences, and there is no possibility of merely preserving the *status quo*. Strikes are usually won or lost within a few days, so that, for practical purposes, the temporary restraining order is the most important of all injunctive writs in labor cases. This was clearly, although moderately, stated by the late President and Chief Justice Taft:

The temporary restraining order is served upon all strikers; they are not lawyers; their fears are aroused by the process with which they are not acquainted, and, although their purpose may have been entirely lawful, their common determination to carry through the strike is weakened by an order which they have never had an opportunity to question, and which is calculated to discourage proceeding in their original purpose.[1]

Due to such criticisms, temporary restraining orders are decreasing in labor disputes. Twenty years ago, temporary restraining orders seem to have been issued as a matter of course in all jurisdictions except Massachusetts. Now three states—Minnesota, New York, and Wisconsin—prohibit the issuance of restraining orders or injunctions in labor cases without opportunity for a hearing;[2] and elsewhere, without legislation, an

---

[1] Quoted in *Congressional Record*, 60th Cong., 1st Sess., Appendix 576.

[2] Of these, the Wisconsin law (Wis. Stats., s. 133. 07 [2]), enacted in 1925, is the broadest, prohibiting the issuance of any injunctive order in a labor case on less than forty-eight hours' notice to the adverse party to show cause why an injunction should not be allowed. The New York law (Laws 1930, c. 378) prohibits the issuance of injunctions in any field without notice to the adverse party but leaves it discretionary with the judge to determine the time and manner of notice. The Minnesota law (Laws 1929, c. 260) also prohibits the issuance of injunctions without notice but expressly authorizes *ex parte* temporary restraining orders where necessary to prevent violence. A 1931 Pennsylvania act (Laws 1931, Act 310) provides that *ex parte* temporary restraining orders shall in no case remain in effect longer than five days.

increasing number of judges are taking the same position.   Yet, even in recent years, *ex parte* temporary restraining orders have been issued in nearly one-half of all labor injunction cases.[1] A common practice is for the complainants' attorneys to draft the temporary restraining order and then to take it to the judge for his signature, often at his home or wherever they can find him. And while judges sometimes make changes in the draft submitted, the more usual practice is to sign the order as prepared by the complainants' attorneys.

Under the circumstances, it is not surprising that the court frequently finds after a hearing that the temporary restraining order issued *ex parte* was either entirely unjustified or too broad in its terms.   In Appendix B are listed 120 cases in which temporary restraining orders were either dissolved or materially modified after a hearing.[2]   But the dissolution or modification of such unwarranted restraining orders does not correct the harm done, as the strike is usually either won or lost by that time.   In forty-one cases on which the author has definite information regarding the time elapsing between the date of the allowance of an *ex parte* temporary restraining order and its dissolution or modification after a hearing, the intervening period was less than a month in only sixteen cases; and in the most extreme case it was nearly a year.[3]

---

[1] In 118 reported federal cases from 1901 to 1928, *ex parte* temporary restraining orders were granted in 70 cases, but in the last 25 of these cases, there were restraining orders in only 4 instances (Frankfurter and Greene, *op. cit.*, p. 64 and Appendix I).   In 45 cases in which injunctions were allowed in the clothing trades in New York City from 1910 to 1927, *ex parte* restraining orders were issued in 26 cases.   Of these *ex parte* temporary restraining orders 2 never came to any hearing, 9 were vacated after a hearing, 2 others after the trial, and 1 on appeal   (P. F. Brissenden and C.O. Swayzee, The Use of Injunctions in the New York Needle Trades, 44 *Polit. Sci. Quart.* 548, 563 (1929), 45 *Polit. Sci. Quart.* 87, 88 (1930). In Massachusetts, on the other hand, in 234 applications for injunctions from 1898 to 1916, *ex parte* temporary restraining orders were granted in only 29 cases (author's computation from data in *Mass. Labor Bull.* 70, 78, and 117).

[2] See Appendix B, p. 335.

[3] Detroit Tile and Mosaic Co. v. Mason Contractors Assoc., 38 F. (2nd) 284, in which a temporary restraining order was issued in March, 1929, and dissolved Feb. 21, 1930.

Nor does the requirement of a bond to indemnify the defendants, if it shall subsequently be found that no injunction order should have been granted, adequately protect them. Under general equity practice and the statutes of all states, such bonds must be furnished by the complainants before any sort of injunction can be issued, but it is a claim of labor attorneys that this requirement is often overlooked in the issuance of temporary restraining orders, or that the bond is set at a ridiculously low figure. Be that as it may, it is practically impossible to indemnify the defendants in labor cases for the losses they sustain. Court costs and attorneys' fees are definite amounts but the effect of the injunction upon the strike cannot be measured in terms of dollars and cents. It has been held, moreover, that no recovery on the bond can be had until after the denial of a permanent injunction,[1] and but a small percentage of all labor cases ever reach this stage. Hence, it is not surprising that recovery on the bond in labor cases is almost unknown.[2]

PRELIMINARY HEARINGS AND TEMPORARY INJUNCTIONS

At the time the complaint is filed or shortly thereafter, whether a temporary restraining order is allowed or not, the court sets a date for a preliminary hearing, which is always to be within ten days after the filing of the complaint.[3] This does not mean, however, that the case is heard and decided within this period. Postponements frequently are granted, in the discretion of the court, either on its own initiative or at the request of one of the parties. Again, after the trial, the court may take the matter under advisement and delay making a decision. During all these delays, any temporary restraining order remains in effect. The

---

[1] Slingerland v. Albany Typographical Union, 115 App. Div. 15, 100 N. Y. S. 569 (1906).

[2] The three cases known to the author in which there was any recovery upon the bond are: R. R. Donnelley & Sons Co. v. Chicago Typographical Union, Sup. Ct., Cook Co., Ill., in which $2,000 was paid to the union in 1925 for court costs and attorneys' fees (*Toledo Union Leader*, June 19, 1925); Local Union 368 v. Barker Painting Co., 56 *Wash. Law Rept.* 151 (1928); and Herkert & Meisel Trunk Co. v. Leather Workers' Union, in which after the dissolution of the injunction in 265 U. S. 457, the union recovered $7,500 costs and attorneys' fees (*A. F. of L. News Service*, June 13, 1927).

[3] Prior to Equity Rule 73, promulgated by the U. S. Supreme Court in 1912, a longer period was common in the federal courts, and occasionally in the state courts. Now the ten-day rule prevails in all jurisdictions.

time actually consumed at this stage varies greatly.[1]   In many cases it is less than ten days; in others, many months.   The average appears to be around thirty days, but in Sullivan v. U. S.[2] more than two years elapsed and there are other cases which were nearly as long drawn out.

The preliminary hearings in injunction cases are generally conducted without oral examination of the witnesses in court, being confined to the complaint, answer, and affidavits, with arguments by opposing counsel.[3]   No jury is impanelled, the judge determining all questions of fact as well as law.   This throws upon him the burden of determining where the truth lies amid the contradictions of the affidavits presented by the contending parties, without opportunity to see or question any of the witnesses.[4]

After the preliminary hearing and consideration of the claims and counterclaims of the respective parties, the judge renders a

---

[1] Out of 152 cases on which the author has the exact dates, the time between the filing of the complaint and the decision of the court upon the motion for a temporary injunction was less than ten days in 25 instances, between 11 and 30 days in 60 cases, and more than 30 days in 61 cases. These figures correspond very closely to those given by Brissenden and Swayzee regarding the injunctions issued in the New York needle trades, in 44 *Polit. Sci. Quart.* 557 (1929) and 45 *Polit. Sci. Quart.* 89 (1930).

[2] 4 F. (2nd) 100.   In this case an *ex parte* temporary restraining order was issued July 12, 1922, and the temporary injunction July 21, 1924.

[3] This does not apply to Massachusetts, where the usual practice is to refer injunction cases to masters who take oral testimony.   Federal Equity Rule 46 requires the testimony of witnesses in injunction cases to be taken in open court, not by depositions, unless there are good reasons for waiving this requirement.   While this rule has been in effect since Jan. 1, 1913, however, the case-by-case analysis of the procedure in the reported labor injunction cases, presented in Frankfurter and Greene's "The Labor Injunction" (Appendix C), indicates that the great majority of the preliminary hearings in the federal courts even in recent years have been conducted without appearance of the witnesses in court.

[4] It is generally agreed that the proof for a temporary injunction does not have to be so clear and conclusive as for a permanent injunction, some cases going so far as to hold that all that is necessary to warrant the issuance of a temporary injunction is a showing that there is some danger of irreparable injury to the property of the complainants: Goldfield Consolidated Mines Co. v. Goldfield Miners' Union, 159 Fed. 500, (1908); Hall Lace Co. v. Javes, 76 N. J. Eq. 92, 79 Atl. 439 (1909); Irving v. Joint District Council, 180 Fed. 896 (1910); Skolny v. Hillman, 114 Misc. 571, 187 N. Y. S. 706 (1921).

decision allowing or refusing a temporary (interlocutory) injunction. This may be merely a continuance or modification of the temporary restraining order, or an entirely new writ.

TRIALS AND PERMANENT INJUNCTIONS

In theory, temporary injunctions are intended to control the actions of the parties only until a full trial; in fact, they are usually the final orders issued in labor injunction cases. Of eighty-eight reported federal cases between 1901 and 1928 in which temporary injunctions were allowed, only thirty-two went to a final hearing, and of the total of thirty-five temporary injunctions issued in New York City in the five years 1923–1927 not a single one was followed by a permanent injunction.[1] Many permanent injunctions, moreover, are issued without a contest, for the same reason that far more cases never reach this stage, that the strikes occasioning the appeal to the courts are settled before a trial can take place.

When there is a contest, there is a full trial, with oral examinations of all witnesses in court and opportunity for cross-examination. These trials generally do not come until months after the beginning of the suit, but in this respect again there are great variations. Cases have occurred where a permanent injunction was issued within one month after the filing of the complaint; years have intervened in others.[2]

After the trial, the court determines whether a permanent (final) injunction shall be issued. In form and content, this

---

[1] FRANKFURTER and GREENE, *op. cit.*, p. 79. Of forty-five temporary injunctions allowed in disputes arising in the clothing industry in New York City from 1910 to 1927, only seven went to trial, and only five permanent injunctions were issued, one of which was dissolved on appeal (Brissenden and Swayzee, 44 *Polit. Sci. Quart.* 548, 566 [1929] and 45 *Polit. Sci. Quart.*, 87, 90 [1930]).

[2] Of fifty-three cases for which the author has the exact dates, permanent injunctions were allowed within less than a month in three instances, within a period of more than a month but less than a year in twenty-five cases, and not until after a year in twenty-five cases. The cases of the longest delays are: Stearns Lumber Co. v. Howlett, 260 Mass. 45, 157 N. E. 82, 163 N. E. 193, begun June 20, 1916, final injunction July, 1927; West Virginia-Pittsburgh Coal Co. v. White, U. S. Dist. Ct., N. D. W. Va., temporary restraining order September, 1913, permanent injunction, 1923; and California Federation of Labor v. Loewe, 139 Fed. 71, temporary injunction July 1, 1905, permanent injunction July 25, 1911.

usually does not differ much from the temporary injunction but represents a final adjudication of the rights of the parties, subject only to the right of appeal to a higher court.[1]

APPEALS

Either party may appeal to a higher court from the allowance or refusal of a temporary or permanent injunction,[2] though not from a temporary restraining order.[3] Such appeals in labor cases have nowhere any special preference and usually consume a very long time.   Particularly is this true in states where there is an intermediate appellate court, from which further appeal can be taken to the supreme court, as is the situation in the federal judicial system and in about a dozen of the most populous states.

---

[1] A permanent injunction has no application to a new dispute between the same parties: Tosh v. Western Kentucky Coal Co., 252 Fed. 44 (1918); but it governs the rights of the contending parties with reference to the original controversy for all future time.   This means that ordinarily the injunction expires, for all practical purposes, with the strike, but injunctions prohibiting boycotts or union organization, where the employees have been signed to individual non-union contracts, are enforceable for many years. Contempt proceedings were started and certain defendants fined in April, 1922, for violating the injunction in the famous case Hitchman Coal and Coke Co. v. Mitchell, 245 U. S. 225, in which the temporary restraining order was issued in 1907 and the permanent injunction in 1912 (Senate Hearings on "Conditions in the Coal Fields of Pennsylvania, West Virginia, and Ohio," 2122–2133 [1928]).

[2] This is the general rule but is not true of all jurisdictions.   For examples, see U. S. Heater Co. v. Molders Union, 129 Mich. 354, 88 N. W. 889 (1902); Grimes v. Durnin, 80 N. H. 145, 114 Atl. 273 (1921).

Besides being subject to review by appeal, injunctions may be attacked collaterally in appeals from convictions for contempt.   In such proceedings, however, only the court's power to issue the injunction may be challenged, not the correctness of the order: Gompers v. Bucks' Stove and Range Co., 221 U. S. 418, 450, 31 Sup. Ct. 492, 501 (1911); McLaughlin v. U. S., 251 U. S. 541, 40 Sup. Ct. 178 (1920); Lyon & Healy v. Piano Co., etc., Workers Union, 289 Ill. 176, 124 N. E. 443 (1919); Hoeffken v. Belleville Trades and Labor Assembly, 229 Ill. App. 28, 32 (1923); Irving v. Howlett, 229 Mass. 560, 118 N. E. 901 (1918).

[3] The defendants may move for the dissolution or modification of a temporary restraining order at any time after it is issued.   This, in most jurisdictions, has the effect of bringing the case on for a preliminary hearing within a few days, after which hearing and the trial court's decision, either party may appeal to a higher court.

Between these courts and the several stages of injunction proceedings, some labor injunction cases have dragged out for years: the two longest, the Stearns Lumber Company case in Massachusetts and the Hitchman Coal and Coke Company case in the federal courts, respectively, for twelve and ten years.[1] Less than six months is very good time for the disposition of appeals, and more than a year not at all uncommon.[2] Pending disposition of the appeal, injunctive orders appealed from remain in full force and effect.[3]

Upon appeal, the record alone is reviewed, without further testimony. As a general rule, every phase of the proceedings may be gone into by the higher court, but it can set aside or modify the decision of the trial court only if it was clearly wrong.[4] Nevertheless, higher courts upon appeal have in numerous instances reversed or modified the decisions of the trial courts. In Appendix C are listed sixty-three cases in which temporary or permanent injunctions were dissolved or modified by appellate courts upon appeals taken by the defendants, and thirty-six in which the complainants were successful. This probably does not represent a larger percentage of successful appeals than occur in other legal actions, but, because strikes generally are of such short duration that the appellate court's decision comes too late, errors by trial courts are more serious. In labor cases the law

---

[1] Stearns Lumber Co. v. Howlett, 260 Mass. 45, 157 N. E. 82, 163 N. E. 193: started in 1916; final decision in 1928. Hitchman Coal and Coke Co. v. Mitchell, 245 U. S. 229: begun in 1907; finally concluded in 1917.

[2] From Frankfurter and Greene's study of reported federal cases ("The Labor Injunction," Appendix II), it appears that the largest number of appeals from temporary injunctions were disposed of in from six to twelve months, but in more than one-third of these cases the appeals took more than a year; while in appeals from permanent injunctions the great majority were not decided until after two years. In sixty-nine cases in federal and state courts upon which the author has definite dates regarding appeals, only thiry-one were disposed of within one year after the filing of the complaint.

[3] Theoretically, a writ of *supersedeas* may be allowed suspending the injunction pending appeal, but this practice has been almost unknown in labor cases.

[4] Gasaway v. Borderland Coal Corp., 276 Fed. 56 (1921); Kinloch Telephone Co. v. Local Union, 275 Fed. 241 (1921); Shaughnessy v. Jordan, 184 Ind. 499, 111 N. E. 622 (1916); Jordahl v. Hayda, 1 Cal. App. 696, 82 Pac. 1079 (1905); Decorative Stone Co. v. Building Trades Council, 13 F. (2nd) 123 (1927); Aeolian Co. v. Fischer, 29 F. (2nd) 679 (1929).

which, for practical purposes, counts most is the "law of the trial judge, not that of the Supreme Court."[1]

SCOPE AND CONTENT OF INJUNCTIONS

Temporary restraining orders, temporary injunctions, and permanent injunctions are much alike in scope and content. All of them run against named parties, who are usually the strike leaders and those of the strikers who have been guilty of violence or intimidation. Besides these individual defendants, injunctions frequently are directed against labor unions as entities. This is expressly sanctioned by statutes or Supreme Court decisions in some jurisdictions,[2] and elsewhere the rule prevails that objection may be made only when the case is first heard.[3]

Besides the named defendants, injunctions invariably apply by their terms to their attorneys and agents and to "all persons acting in aid of or in connection with them or each of them." Many injunctions go further and, to quote a clause from an injunction approved by the U. S. Supreme Court, embrace "all persons whomsoever."[4] Whether such blanket clauses are included or not, it is settled law that injunctions apply to all persons who, with actual knowledge of their issuance, aid or assist the named parties in violations. Such actual knowledge is not presumed but may be inferred, although direct, positive proof is lacking.[5] To be in a position to establish such actual knowl-

---

[1] COOK, WALTER WHEELER, The Injunction in the Railway Strike, 32 *Yale Law Jour.* 166–171 (1922).

[2] See the discussion on How Trade Unions May Be Sued, in Chap. VII, pp. 141–144.

[3] For a complete discussion of the principles controlling the issuance of injunctions against unincorporated associations, see E. S. Oakes, "Organized Labor and Industrial Conflicts," pp. 110–128 (1927).

[4] American Steel Foundries v. Tri-cities Central Trades' Council, 257 U. S. 184, 42 Sup. Ct. 72 (1921). For variations of this phrase having the same effect, see Felix Frankfurter and Nathan Greene, *op. cit.*, pp. 88, 89, and cases cited.

[5] Leading cases upon the application of injunctions to persons not named therein are: *in re* Lennon, 166 U. S. 548, 17 Sup. Ct. 658 (1897); Bessette v. Conkey Co., 194 U. S. 324, 24 Sup. Ct. 665 (1904); Forrest v. U. S., 277 Fed. 873 (1922) (certiorari denied, 258 U. S. 629, 42 Sup. Ct. 462); Minerich v. U. S., 29 F. (2nd) 565 (1928); Berger v. Superior Court, 175 Cal. 719, 167 Pac. 143 (1917); State *ex rel* Continental Coal Co. v. Bittner, 102 W. Va. 677, 136 S. E. 202 (1927). See also Oakes, *op. cit.*, Secs. 643 to 645, and cases cited.

edge in the event of violations and to make injunctions as widely effective as possible, it is customary for the complainants to have the marshal or sheriff serve copies not only upon the named defendants, but upon all other persons who appear on the picket line and as many strikers as can be conveniently located. Copies also are posted at all factory entrances, on poles and buildings in the vicinity, and sometimes are published in newspapers in all of the languages represented amongst the strikers.[1]

Coming now to the restraining clauses in injunctions, we find these varying with the situation, the jurisdiction, and the judge. Most prohibitions, however, occur again and again throughout the country. Nearly all injunctions forbid the defendants from resorting to "force," "threats," "coercion," and "intimidation." Picketing is either altogether prohibited or more commonly regulated in minute detail. Less frequent, though not at all unusual, are clauses against boycotting, trespass on company property, persistent following of the complainants' employees, calling them "scabs," offering them transportation back home; and in cases of unlawful strikes, threatening, calling, or advising such strikes, or paying any strike benefits.

Some injunctions have gone further, directly forbidding workmen to go on strike,[2] or to persuade the complainant's employees

---

[1] Such posting and publication are sometimes directed by the court itself. For recent examples, see Clarkson Coal Mining Co. v. United Mine Workers of America, 9 *Law and Labor* 290 (Fed. 1927), and N. Y. Trust Co. v. Amalgamated Assoc., 11 *Law and Labor* 176 (Fed. 1929).

Whether posting and newspaper publication alone are sufficient to establish actual knowledge of the issuance of an injunction on part of the strikers and strike sympathizers not named therein is an unsettled question of law: Garrigan v. U. S., 163 Fed. 16 (1908) (certiorari denied in 214 U. S. 514); *ex parte* Richards, 117 Fed. 658 (1902); Borden's Farm Products Co. v. Sterbinsky, 117 Misc. 585, 192 N. Y. S. 757 (1922).

[2] Among these are the following recent injunctions: Bausch Machine Tool Co. v. Hill, 231 Mass. 30, 120 N. E. 188 (1918); Bedford Cut Stone Co. v. Journeymen Stone Cutters, 9 *Law and Labor* 297 (Fed. 1927); Alco-Zander Co. v. Amalgamated Clothing Workers, 35 F. (2nd) 209 (1929). Union officers were enjoined from calling or counseling strikes, among others, in American Can Co. v. Inter. Assoc. of Machinists, 2 *Law and Labor*, 256 (N. J. 1920); U. S. v. Railway Employees' Dept, 283 Fed. 479 (1922); Keating v. Allison, Common Pleas, Philadelphia Co., Pa. (Judge McDevitt), Sept. 27, 1926; General Woodcraft Co. v. Teamsters, Chancery Ct., N. J. (Vice Chancellor Church), Apr. 16, 1927. Cairo Dress Co. v. Sigman, Sup.

to leave or other workmen to refuse employment.[1]   Others have forbidden the holding of any union meetings and all attempts at union organization.   A few injunctions have enjoined unions from using their funds to help their members fight eviction from company houses, and one such writ directed the marshal to dispossess the strikers' families.[2]   The same order enjoined aliens from serving on the picket line, although it provided that the injunction should be published in four languages, as most of the strikers were foreigners.   Another injunction in the same strike forbade the strikers to assemble on church property near the complainants' mines for the purpose of singing "Onward, Christian Soldiers" and similar church hymns which the court considered intimidating.[3]

Still other extreme injunctions might be cited, but these are not typical.   As a general rule, the specific clauses in injunctions do not go beyond forbidding conduct which is either prohibited by the criminal law or has been held unlawful by the highest court of the jurisdiction.   While the trial judges do make the law on

---

Ct. New York Co., N. Y., Oct. 4, 1926 (Text in 45 *Polit. Sci. Quart.* 104 [1930]).

Union officers were directed to call off strikes already in progress in U. S. v. Hayes, U. S. Dist. Ct., Dist. Ind., Nov. 19, 1919 (reprinted in Sayre, "Cases in Labor Law," p. 757); Londoff-Bicknell Co. v. Building Trades Council, Com. Pleas., Cuyahoga Co., Ohio, Sept. 10, 1925; Selden-Breck Co. v. Blair, 7 *Law and Labor* 255 (Fed. 1925); Selden-Breck Construction Co. v. Local Union 253, 7 *Law and Labor* 302 (Fed. 1925); Londoff-Bicknell Co. v. Smith, 8 *Law and Labor* 298, (Ohio Com. Pleas, 1926); Clearfield Bituminous Coal Corp. v. Phillips, Com. Pleas, Indiana Co., Pa., Nov. 8, 1927.

[1] Such prohibitions have most frequently occurred where the complainants' employees were bound by individual non-union agreements (yellow-dog contracts) but have sometimes been used in other situations.   Among recent injunctions prohibiting all persuasion are Graceline Dress Co. v. Joint Board International Ladies Garment Workers Union, Sup. Ct., Cook Co., Ill., March 4, 1924; West Virginia-Pittsburgh Coal Co. v. United Mine Workers, U. S. Dist. Ct., N. D. W. Va., May 19, 1925; Red Jacket Consolidated Coal and Coke Co. v. Lewis, U. S. Dist. Ct., S. D. W. Va., Oct. 9, 1925; Leonard v. Bittner, Cir. Ct., Marion Co., W. Va., Sept. 26, 1925.

[2] Clarkson Coal Mining Co. v. United Mine Workers of America, 23 F. (2nd) 208 (1927).

[3] Jefferson and Indiana Coal Co. v. Aikens, Com. Pleas Ct., Indiana Co., Pa., reprinted in Senate Hearings on "Limiting Scope of Injunctions in Labor Disputes," p. 599 (1928).

points on which the Supreme Court has not spoken, there have been few orders for which there was no support in decisions elsewhere. In the main, it is the unfavorable state of the substantive law and the vagueness of the theories upon which it rests which account for the drastic restraints imposed by injunctions, rather than the unfairness or prejudices of the trial judges.

Following the specific restraining clauses, most injunctions include catch-all "blanket" clauses. Typical are the following from a 1929 federal injunction: "interfering in any way with the complainants, their agents, or employees in the legitimate conduct, management, or operation of their business," and "from combining or conspiring together or with any persons, firms, or corporations to injure or interfere with the business of the complainants or any of them, or to interfere with the production and shipment of clothing of the complainants or any of them."[1] Blanket clauses probably add little to the injunctions in legal effect,[2] but they are likely to discourage the strikers. At all events, they violate the cardinal principle "that the language of an injunction should be so clear and explicit that an unlearned man can understand its meaning without the necessity of employing counsel."[3]

METHODS OF ENFORCEMENT

Violation of an injunction constitutes an indirect contempt of court. This is an offense which the court which issued the order has inherent power to punish, although to some extent the proceedings and penalties may be regulated by statute.[4]

Contempts are classified as civil and criminal, between which there is theoretically a great distinction. In actual practice, however, this distinction, as the Massachusetts Supreme Court

---

[1] Alco-Zander Co. v. Amalgamated Clothing Workers, U. S. Dist. Ct., E. D. Pa., Sept. 9, 1929.

[2] Contempt proceedings have only very seldom been premised upon the blanket clauses. An exception is Schwartz v. U. S., 217 Fed. 866 (1914).

[3] Laurie v. Laurie, 9 Paige 234 (N. Y. 1841). See also, Great Nor. Ry. Co. v. Brosseau, 286 Fed. 414, 415 (1923); and Zechariah Chafee, "The Inquiring Mind," pp. 190–197, Harcourt, Brace & Company, New York (1928).

[4] Michaelson v. U. S., 266 U. S. 42 at 66, 45 Sup. Ct. 18 at 20 (1923) and cases cited.

has stated,[1] "rests in shadow." Almost everywhere, any violation of an injunction can be treated as either a civil or a criminal contempt, as the complainants and the court prefer, and regardless of the choice the procedure is much the same.[2]

Contempt proceedings are generally initiated by the complainants in the original action, either by a petition asking for the punishment of persons alleged to have been guilty of violations of the court's injunction or, in the federal courts, by the filing of affidavits charging such violations. Whereupon the court issues an order for the arrest of the alleged contemnors, citing them to appear on a date specified and show cause why they should not be punished for contempt.[3]

On this date, the court conducts a hearing to determine the guilt or innocence of the accused. The trial is usually conducted by the judge who issued the injunction, although another judge

---

[1] Root v. McDonald, 260 Mass. 344, 358 (1927).

[2] The U. S. Supreme Court drew a very clear distinction between civil and criminal contempts in Gompers v. Bucks' Stove and Range Co., 221 U. S. 418, 31 Sup. Ct. 492 (911). In compliance with this decision, criminal contempt cases in the federal courts are nominally initiated by the court, entitled in the name of the United States, and prosecuted by the United States district attorneys. In actual practice, however, the complainants initiate these contempt proceedings and their attorneys conduct the prosecution (Frankfurter and Greene, op. cit., pp. 128–129).

In some other respects it does make a difference whether contempt proceedings are treated as criminal or civil. In civil contempt cases, all fines imposed are payable to the complainants and either side may take an appeal to a higher court, while in criminal contempts fines go into the public treasury and only the defendants can appeal. Further, in the federal courts, the right of jury trial is limited to criminal contempts where the offense charged also constitutes a crime. While there are these differences, it seems to be true everywhere that the complainants actually determine whether they wish to proceed for criminal or civil contempt, and the courts often allow a mixed procedure: State ex rel Rodd v. Verage, 177 Wis. 295, 187 N. W. 830 (1922); Michaelson v. U. S., 291 Fed. 940 (1922); Reeder v. Morton-Gregson Co., 296 Fed. 785 (1924). For a more complete discussion of the distinction between civil and criminal contempts and its shadowy character, see Oakes "Organized Labor and Industrial Conflicts," Secs. 647–649 (1927), and cases cited.

[3] In West Virginia, arrests may be made for contempt without a show-cause order: ex parte Kirby, 100 W. Va. 30, 130 S. E. 86 (1925). See also Castner v. Pocahontas Collieries Co., 117 Fed. 184 (1902).

may be called in.[1] Except in a few jurisdictions, the trial is conducted without a jury. In the federal courts, the defendants may now demand trial by jury in criminal contempt cases in which the acts upon which the charge of contempt is premised also constitute a crime, and the same provision applies in Utah. Oklahoma and Wisconsin allow jury trial in all cases of indirect contempt, Pennsylvania in all cases of indirect criminal contempt, while New Jersey leaves submission of the case to a jury discretionary with the court.[2] In other respects, contempt cases are conducted as ordinary criminal trials, except that the prosecution is ordinarily conducted by the attorneys for the complainants and not by the public prosecutors.[3]

For conviction, proof of guilt beyond a reasonable doubt is required, but the modification of the injunction subsequent to the offense but prior to the trial is no defense.[4] From decisions of the trial judge in contempt cases, appeals may be taken to the appropriate higher court.[5] The extent to which such appeals

---

[1] For a suggestion by the U. S. Supreme Court that, at least in cases in which the contempt charge is premised upon a criticism of the court, another judge ought as a matter of propriety to be called in, see Craig v. Hecht, 263 U. S. 255, 279 (1923).

[2] 38 U. S. Stats.-at-Large 730, ss. 21–35; Utah Laws 1917, c. 68, s. 5; Okla. Const. art. II, s. 25, and Rev. Laws 1909, s. 2278; Wis. Stats. 1929, s. 113.07 (4); Pa. Laws 1931, Act 311; N. J. Laws 1925, c. 169. The jury trial provision of the federal law was held constitutional in Michaelson v. U. S., 266 U. S. 42, 45 Sup. Ct. 18 (1924). The Oklahoma law was held constitutional in McKee v. DeGraffenreid, 33 Okla. 136, 124 Pac. 303 (1912). The other jury trial laws have not been passed on by the supreme courts.

[3] In the federal courts and in New York, the public prosecutors nominally conduct all prosecutions for criminal contempts, but even in these jurisdictions the complainants' attorneys sit in the prosecution, and usually control the same: Frankfurter and Greene, *op. cit.*, pp. 128–129.

In a few instances, contempt proceedings have been disposed of entirely upon affidavits, without examination of the witnesses in court: Union v. People, 220 Ill. 355, 77 N. E. 176 (1906); Garrigan v. U. S., 141 Fed. 679 (1905) (reversed in 163 Fed. 16).

[4] In civil contempt cases only a preponderance of evidence is necessary for a conviction. For a complete discussion of this subject, see Oakes, *op. cit.*, p. 1005, and cases cited.

While the defendants can neither plead the subsequent modification of the injunction nor the fact that its provisions were too broad as an excuse for their violations, they have a good defense if it can be shown that the court altogether exceeded its jurisdiction in issuing the order.

[5] In criminal contempt cases, only the defendants can secure a review, and in some jurisdictions only after they have actually been sentenced, not if the

open up the case varies in different jurisdictions, some states virtually confining the review to questions of law and others allowing the appellate court to go into all questions of law and fact without, however, taking any new testimony.[1]

It has been widely assumed that contempt cases are disposed of most expeditiously. On this point, the scanty information available indicates that while many contempt cases are handled very promptly, long periods of time are consumed in others.[2]

---

sentence is suspended: Pocketbook Workers' Union v. Orlove, 148 Atl. 826 (Md. 1930).

[1] Except where changed by statute, convictions for criminal contempt can be reviewed only by writ of error, certiorari, or habeas corpus. Upon writ of error, the court's finding of guilty can be challenged only if there is no credible evidence supporting the conviction. Certiorari, in most jurisdictions, is available only if the court exceeded its powers in issuing the injunction. Habeas corpus can be employed only to challenge the injunction itself, not the facts upon which the conviction for contempt was had or the regularity of the proceedings. Wherever these three processes only are available for the review of criminal contempts, the higher court virtually can pass only on questions of law. Many states, however, have enacted statutes providing for a review of criminal contempts by appeal, which has the effect of allowing the higher court to pass upon all aspects of the case. In civil contempt cases, review is always by appeal.

Leading cases upon the right of higher courts to review convictions for contempt and what constitutes ground for reversal are: Bessette v. Conkey Co., 194 U. S. 324, 24 Sup. Ct. 665 (1904); *in re* Reese, 107 Fed. 942 (1901); Garrigan v. U. S., 163 Fed. 16 (1908); Phillips Sheet and Tin Plate Co. v. Amalgamated Assoc., 208 Fed. 335 (1913); Schwartz v. U. S., 217 Fed. 866 (1914); Oates v. U. S., 233 Fed. 200 (1916); Binkley v. U. S., 282 Fed. 244 (1922); Gravely v. U. S., 288 Fed. 837 (1923); Michaelson v. U. S., 291 Fed. 940 (1923); U. S. v. Bittner, 11 F. (2nd) 93 (1925); Hake v. People, 230 Ill. 174, 82 N. E. 561 (1907); Eastern Consolidated Steel Co. v. Bricklayers, 200 App. Div. 714, 193 N. Y. S. 368 (1922); International Pocketbook Workers' Union v. Orlove, 148 Atl. 826 (Md., 1930).

[2] In the author's report to the United States Commission on Industrial Relations, in 1915, on Injunctions in Labor Disputes, Appendix C, pp. 32–39, he listed seventeen cases in which contempt proceedings were disposed of within fourteen days after they were begun, nine cases in which the time consumed was fifteen days to two months, and ten cases in which more than two months elapsed.

The case involving the longest delay in the disposition of a contempt proceeding by a trial court was the contempt action begun under the injunction Typothetae v. Typographical Union 6, in the Supreme Court in New York Co., N. Y., Apr. 26, 1906. In this case, hearings were conducted by a referee and sentences were not imposed until Mar. 2, 1908 (G. A. Stevens,

It is probable that, on the average, contempt cases consume less time than ordinary criminal trials except those for minor offenses in the police courts. When contempt cases are referred to masters or referees, when appeals are taken to higher courts, and sometimes for no apparent reason whatsoever, they drag out for months and years and are not decided until long after the strike is ended.

It has been further assumed that the percentage of convictions in contempt cases is much greater than in ordinary criminal trials and that sentences are distinctly more severe. Upon this point also, there is really no basis for comparison. It is probable that the percentage of convictions is higher, and there have been many cases in which the sentences imposed were very severe.[1] On the other hand, it is a frequent practice in the first contempt case arising under an injunction to dismiss the defendants with a warning.[2]

"*History of Typographical Union No. 6*," pp. 379–389, J. B. Lyon Co., State Printers, Albany [1913] and *Machinists' Journal*, 352, April, 1908). In six other cases the contempt proceedings were not concluded in the trial court until five to twelve months after the action was started, including the well-known reported cases, U. S. v. Debs, 64 Fed. 724 (1894); Gompers v. Bucks' Stove and Range Co., 221 U. S. 418 (1911); and U. S. v. Garrigan, 163 Fed. 16 (1908).

In contempt cases in which appeals were taken the author knows of two which were finally disposed of within six months after the defendants were cited for contempt, fourteen in which the intervening time was six to twenty-four months, and fourteen others in which this time was more than two years. In the Lennon case, 64 Fed. 320, 166 U. S. 548, four years intervened between the arrest of Lennon on Mar. 18, 1893, and the final affirmation of the conviction for contempt on Apr. 19, 1897.

[1] For specific examples of the penalties imposed in contempt cases, see Frankfurter & Greene, *op. cit.*, pp. 58–59, and Oakes, *op. cit.*, Sec. 665. The author discussed this subject very fully in his report to the U. S. Commission on Industrial Relations of Injunctions in Labor Disputes, Appendix, B, pp. 178–187, and Appendix C., pp. 44–50, in which are listed the penalties imposed in scores of contempt cases, both state and federal.

[2] This has even occurred where the defendants were guilty of assaults and similar crimes. Thus, eighteen strikers were, on July 18, 1924, found guilty in the Circuit Court of Monongalia Co., W. Va., of having violated the injunction (Brady-Warner Coal Corp. v. United Mine Workers) through an attack on the company's property with rifles and dynamite but were dismissed without any penalty upon the promise not to repeat the offense

Whatever may be the advantages of contempt proceedings as compared with criminal prosecutions in such matters as the time consumed, the likelihood of conviction, and the severity of the sentence, it is certain that the number of such cases is much smaller. Only thirty-seven contempt cases, involving 108 individuals, are noted in all of the federal reports from 1901 to 1928; and in forty-eight injunctions in the needle trades strikes in New York City from 1894 to 1928, there were only three motions for contempt, two of which were denied.[1]　Hundreds of arrests are often made on criminal charges after the issuance of injunctions, without a single contempt proceeding.[2]

CRITICISM OF INJUNCTION PROCEDURE

The use of injunctions in labor disputes has been under fire from its inception, not only from organized labor but from judges, legal writers, and prominent public men.　These criticisms may for convenience be grouped into three main classes: (1) those holding that injunctions should not be used in labor disputes at all, (2) those concerned with the content of injunctions, and (3) those which relate to procedure.　The second of these lies outside the scope of this chapter, as it comes back to the substantive law of labor disputes, discussed in prior chapters.[3]　The first and third, however, require attention at this point.

(testimony of Samuel D. Brady of the complainant corporation in the Senate Hearings on "Conditions in the Coal Fields in Pennsylvania, West Virginia, and Ohio," pp. 2080–2084 [1928]).　A similar instance is given in the testimony of James E. McCloskey, Jr., an employers' attorney, in the House Hearings on "Injunction Bills," pp. 444–446 (1904).

[1] FRANKFURTER and GREENE, *op. cit.*, p. 130; BRISSENDEN and SWAYZEE, The Use of the Injunction in the New York Needle Trades, 45 *Polit. Sci. Quart.* 101 (1930).

[2] In the first fifteen weeks of the ladies garment workers' strike in New York City in 1926, there was an average of eight hundred arrests of pickets on criminal charges each week.　At the outset of this strike, an injunction prohibiting mass picketing was issued, but there was not a single prosecution for contempt: 8 *Law and Labor* 302.　Under the injunction, Allen A Co. v. Steele, U. S. Dist. Ct. E. D. Wis. (1928–1929), there were over fifty arrests for contempt—wellnigh the largest number ever brought under a labor injunction, but even in this strike there were over eight hundred arrests on criminal charges after the issuance of the injunction.

[3] See particularly the section on the Crucial Issues, pp. 43–45.

The contention that injunctions should not be issued at all[1] has been advanced principally by labor advocates and rests upon the belief that injunctions are used in industrial disputes as in no other kind of controversies. This in turn is based upon the claim that it is only by giving a revolutionary and strained definition to property that injunctions can be justified in labor disputes. The time-honored function of injunctions is to prevent irreparable injury to property, which term was formerly applied only to tangible things. In labor cases there often is no claim of danger to the plant and materials; the charge is that the defendants' conduct interferes with profits which the complainants expected to realize. It is these expected profits which injunctions in labor disputes are primarily designed to protect, and the courts have justified their issuance by extending the concept of property to include the right of free access to the commodity and labor markets, often called the right "to do (or continue) business," from which profits normally arise. This the labor people claim to be a perversion, insisting that the right to do or continue business is a personal, not a property, right and not entitled to equitable protection.

This attack upon injunctions has little support among legal scholars,[2] although they admit that it is only within the last century that expectancies have come to be regarded as property and that injunctions have been invoked for their protection. But they insist that this change corresponds with the facts of present-day economic life and, further, that it involves no dis-

---

[1] For a good presentation of this argument see John P. Frey, "The Labor Injunction," Equity Publishing Co., Cincinnati (1922); also the argument of T. C. Spelling before a subcommittee of the Senate Judiciary Committee published as *Sen. Doc.* 944, 62nd Cong., 2nd Sess. (1912).

[2] The person who apparently had most to do with the development of the criticism that the use of injunctions in labor disputes involves an unwarranted extension of the definition of property was T. C. Spelling, an eminent writer upon the law of equity and long one of the most influential advisors of the American Federation of Labor. Spelling in his most recent book (T. C. Spelling and J. H. Lewis, "A Treatise on the Law Governing Injunctions," pp. 224–229, Thomas Law Book Co., St. Louis [1926]), while insisting that his earlier position is historically correct, acknowledges that there are now so many decisions to the contrary that there is no longer anything to be gained by attacking injunctions in labor disputes on this score.

crimination against labor, since the same concept of property is now applied in all fields of the law[1]: a claim which is undoubtedly correct.

Similarly, there is slight foundation for any claim of discrimination in the procedure followed in labor cases. The procedure in injunction cases arising in connection with labor disputes, described in this chapter, is substantially the same procedure as is followed in other injunction cases. It seems to the author that, in labor cases, the courts have given insufficient consideration to the familiar equity principles that the complainants must come into court with clean hands and that an injunction should be issued only when the loss which would result if no such order is granted is greater than the injury which the defendants would sustain if it were allowed.[2] But even as to these principles, there is no court which has ever held that they are inapplicable to labor cases.

Aside from the question of discrimination, there are strong grounds for complaint regarding procedure. The more important of these can be summarized as follows:

1. That injunctions are issued without affording the defendants a fair opportunity to present their side of the case. This complaint is directed against *ex parte* temporary restraining orders

---

[1] According to the modern view, property consists of rights, duties, and relationships. Things are not property, but merely the objects of property, and there is property which has no connection with anything physical. Market opportunities, thus, are conceived of as being property just as much as are the rights to physical things.

[2] For a good presentation of this criticism, see Frankfurter and Greene, *op. cit.*, pp. 200–202.

Labor cases in which the clean-hands doctrine was applied to deny injunctions sought by employers are: Schwartz v. Hillman, 115 Misc. 61, 189 N. Y. S. 21 (1921); Yarbloom v. Freedman, 3 *Law and Labor* 278 (N. Y. Sup. Ct. 1921); Post-McCord v. Morin, 6 *Law and Labor* 220 (N. Y. Sup. Ct. 1921); Segenfeld v. Friedman, 117 Misc. 731, 193 N. Y. S. 128 (1922); and Adler & Sons Co. v. Maglio, 228 N. W. 123 (Wis. 1929). This doctrine was applied against labor in Cornellier v. Haverhill Shoe Manufacturers Assoc., 221 Mass. 554, 109 N. E. 643 (1915) and was pleaded but held inapplicable in Carpenters' Union v. Citizens' Committee, 333 Ill. 225, 164 N. E. 393 (1928).

The balance of convenience doctrine has never been comprehensively discussed in any labor case, but a suggestive statement of the injury done to strikers through the issuance of injunctions occurs in Wood Mowing and Reaping Co. v. Toohey, 114 Misc. 185, 186 N. Y. S. 95 (1921).

and the conduct of preliminary hearings without oral examination of the witnesses. The net result of these practices is that usually there is no full hearing until the trial preceding the issuance of a permanent injunction, which stage is seldom reached before the strike is ended.

2. That injunctions are often issued upon insufficient proof— a result of the foregoing practices. *Ex parte* temporary restraining orders can be based only upon the complaints and supporting affidavits, manifestly partisan statements; and while in preliminary hearings the defendants can present counterclaims and affidavits, this is an undependable way of getting at the truth. An additional factor is that some courts take the position that so long as the defendants are merely forbidden what they have no lawful right to do, no harm can result from the issuance of an injunction,[1] a view manifestly untenable, since an injunction stigmatizes the defendants before the public as law breakers and subjects them to costs and penalties.

3. That injunctions are a species of judicial legislation, which, besides representing an unwarranted extension of judicial powers, has the vice of extreme vagueness. Clauses are often included which make injunctions applicable to "all persons whomsoever" who have notice of their issuance, by which means injunctions are virtually given the effect of statutes governing the conduct of everybody in entire industrial communities. And while there has been distinct improvement with respect to making injunctions more specific, it is still common to conclude with blanket prohibitions of all interference with the complainants' property and employees, which workmen may well understand as preventing

---

[1] This view was expressed, among others, in the following cases: Davis v. Zimmerman, 91 Hun. 489, 36 N. Y. S. 303 (1895); Foster v. Retail Clerks, 39 Misc. 48, 78 N. Y. S. 860 (1902); Herzog v. Fitzgerald, 74 App. Div. 110, 77 N. Y. S. 366 (1902); Golf Bag Co. v. Suttner, 124 Fed. 467 (1903); Davis Machine Co. v. Robinson, 41 Misc. 329, 84 N. Y. S. 837 (1903); Martin v. McFall, 65 N. J. Eq. 91, 55 Atl. 465 (1903); My Maryland Lodge v. Adt, 100 Md. 238, 59 Atl. 721 (1905); Piano and Organ Workers, v. Piano and Organ Supply Co., 124 Ill. App. 353 (1906); New York Central Iron Works v. Brennan, 105 N. Y. S. 865 (1907); Iron Molders' Union v. Niles-Bement-Pond Co., 258 Fed. 408 (1910); Wyckoff Amusement Co. v. Kaplan, 183 App. Div. 205, 170 N. Y. S. 548 (1918); United Traction Co. v. Droogan, 115 Misc. 672, 189 N. Y. S. 39 (1921). To much the same effect are Jersey City Printing Co. v. Cassidy, 63 N. J. Eq. 759, 53 Atl. 230 (1902), and Hall Lace Co. v. Javes, 76 N. J. Eq. 92, 79 Atl. 439 (1909).

any sort of activity in support of the strike and of whose meaning not even a lawyer can be certain.

4. That there are no adequate provisions for prompt appeals, so that in labor injunction cases the law actually enforced is the law of the trial court, not that of the supreme court. In this respect, there is no discrimination against labor, but the situation presented is such that, when labor injunction cases must take the same course as other cases, there is for practical purposes little value in appeals.

5. That injunctions deny persons accused of crime a fair trial. Trial of contempts before the judge who issued the injunction and without a jury is not confined to labor cases, but it is in connection with labor cases that the greatest popular demand has come for a change in this respect.

These several major complaints regarding the procedure in injunction cases will be further discussed in the concluding chapter of this book. Here, attention is directed only to the fact that all these complaints rest not upon the claim that a procedure is followed in labor cases different from that in other injunction suits, but rather upon the argument that a different procedure ought to be applied because the situation presented in industrial disputes differs radically from that of ordinary legal controversies. Rules and practices which are objectionable in other suits work badly and unjustly in labor cases. It is not that labor is discriminated against, but that industrial disputes present special problems requiring special treatment.

Bibliographical Note

Many articles have been written in legal and other periodicals on the use of injunctions in labor disputes, but there have been but few studies of the actual procedure in such cases. By all odds, the best of these is the recent book by Felix Frankfurter and Nathan Greene, "The Labor Injunction," The Macmillan Company, New York (1930). A similar study of more limited scope is P. F. Brissenden and C. O. Swayzee's The Use of the Labor Injunction in the New York Needle Trades, in *Polit. Sci. Quart.* Vol. 44, 548–568 (1929) and Vol. 45, 87–111 (1930). The author has dealt with this subject in an article Injunctions in Labour Disputes in the United States, 21 *Inter. Labour Rev.* 317–347 (1930), and in 1915 made a report to the U. S. Commission on Industrial Relations on Injunctions in Labor Disputes, with a detailed appendix on The Actual Practice in Injunction Cases Arising in Connection with Labor Disputes, which has never been published but is on file in the libraries of Harvard Law School and the Wisconsin Historical Society.

Recent general accounts of the use of injunctions in labor disputes, representing little original research but informing and popular, are the article by Wayne Gard, The Injunction Process in Labor Disputes, *Current History*, 829–831, March, 1931, the *Bulletin* of the Department of Research and Education of the Federal Council of the Churches of Christ in America on The Use of Injunctions in Labor Disputes, Information Service of the Council, Vol. IX, No. 10 (1930), and the report bearing the same title, issued by Editorial Research Reports, Washington, February, 1928. An earlier study of the same general character is that of the Illinois Legislative Reference Bureau on Injunctions in Labor Cases, *Ill. Constitutional Convention Bull.* 14 (1919).

The legal doctrines underlying labor injunctions are discussed in all text books on the law of equity and in numerous articles in law magazines. Extended discussions are to be found in E. S. Oakes, "The Law of Organized Labor and Industrial Conflicts," 865–948, 973–1011, Lawyers' Cooperative Publishing Co., Rochester (1927), and in T. C. Spelling and J. H. Lewis, "A Treatise on the Law Governing Injunctions," 224–282, Thomas Law Book Co., St. Louis (1926).

Among numerous short critical articles on this subject, the symposium on The Scope and Limits of the Injunction, 36 *Ann. Amer. Acad. Polit. Social Sci.* 87–144 (1910) and the paper by J. Wallace Bryan, Proper Bounds for the Use of Injunctions in Labor Disputes, in the same volume of this magazine, pp. 288–310 (1910), although old, still must be highly rated. More recent articles of this character include a chapter in Rev. John A. Ryan, "Declining Liberty and Other Papers," pp. 203–212, The Macmillan Company, New York (1927); an essay in Zechariah Chafee, "The Inquiring Mind," pp. 183–216, Harcourt, Brace & Company, New York (1928); Francis B. Sayre, The Labor Injunction, in 85 *Forum and Century* 56–61 (1931); the symposium on Injunctions in Labor Disputes by several different authors, *Proc. Acad. Polit. Sci.* 37–89, New York (1928); and the pamphlet of the Committee on Labor Injunctions, "Labor Injunctions: What are they?" (1931).

Labor's point of view is presented very ably in the book by John P. Frey, "The Labor Injunction," Equity Publishing Co., Cincinnati (1922); in William Green, "Labor and Injunctions," American Federation of Labor, Washington (1927); and Maurice Sugar, "Working Class Justice," Detroit Federation of Labor (1916); also, in the numerous editorials and other articles on injunctions in labor disputes by Samuel Gompers and Andrew Furuseth in the *Amer. Federationist*. The employers' point of view is briefly outlined in the article, The Injunction in Labor Disputes, in 6 *Law and Labor* 115–117 (1924).

Comprehensive bibliographies are the "Select List of References on Boycotts and Injunctions in Labor Disputes," published in 1911 by the Library of Congress, and Laura A. Thompson's Injunctions in Labor Disputes: Select List of Recent References, in 27 *Monthly Labor Rev.* (3) 201–220, September, 1928.

Material for original studies of the practice in labor injunction cases is exceedingly abundant, much of it readily obtainable. The reported decisions present not only the law applicable but often give also such facts as the time elapsing at various stages, the pleadings of the parties, the injunctional orders, etc. Generally, the facts regarding the actual procedure to be gathered from the reported decisions, however, are incomplete and need to be supplemented by examinations of the original court records, newspaper accounts, interviews, correspondence, and so forth; and these are the only available sources for the much larger number of unreported cases. The court records are the only completely accurate source, but these are themselves often incomplete and difficult of access. Newspaper and partisan accounts are not reliable but furnish valuable clues and, if used intelligently, convey an approximately accurate picture of the actual practice in labor injunction cases.

Many injunctions in labor disputes as well as some of the pleadings have been reprinted, and copies in any current case can usually be obtained free by writing to the attorneys or the judge. Important collections of labor injunctions, with some of the complaints and decisions, include the following congressional documents: A Compilation of Documents Relating to Injunctions in Conspiracy Cases, *Sen. Doc.* 504, (57th Cong., 1st Sess., 1908); and "Injunction Data Filed by Samuel Gompers," Government Printing Office, (1908); three bulletins of the Massachusetts Bureau of Labor Statistics, *Bulls.* 70, 78, and 117, on Labor Injunctions in Massachusetts, issued, respectively, in 1909, 1910, and 1916; Francis B. Sayre, "A Selection of Cases and Other Authorities on Labor Law," pp. 717–799, Harvard University Press, Cambridge, Mass. (1922); A. R. Ellingwood and W. Coombs, "The Government and Labor," pp. 209–263, McGraw-Hill Book Company, Inc., New York, (1926); and E. S. Oakes, "Organized Labor and Industrial Conflicts," pp. 1124–1147, Cooperative Law Publishing Co., Rochester (1927).

Other important sources of information on the actual practice in injunction cases are the hearings before Congressional committees on antiinjunction bills and in investigations of labor difficulties. These reprint numerous labor injunctions and decisions and give the stories of the contending parties upon the procedure followed in many of these cases. Such hearings have been conducted in nearly every Congress since 1895 and a complete list of them is given in the two bibliographies cited above. The most recent and, for present-day use, the most valuable of these Congressional hearings is that conducted in the 70th Congress, 1st Session (1928) by a subcommittee of the Committee on the Judiciary on "Limiting the Scope of Injunctions in Labor Disputes."

CHAPTER VI

INJUNCTIONS: RESULTS

We come now to another aspect of the use of injunctions in labor disputes—their social consequences, a problem hitherto almost wholly neglected. How do injunctions actually work out? How valuable are they to employers? How greatly do they handicap labor? Above all, do they operate for the protection of the public and the improvement of the relations between employers and employees, or the reverse?

INJUNCTIONS AND ACTS OF VIOLENCE

Injunctions are customarily associated with the preservation of law and order in labor difficulties. There is a widespread belief that, but for injunctions, violence and bloodshed would be much more frequent than they now are and that "the alternative [to the injunction] is the soldier and the bayonet."[1] This is a natural association. Many injunctions are sought after much violence has occurred in labor disputes,[2] and, even when this is not so, acts of intimidation and violence are generally alleged in the bills of complaint by the artful use of descriptive terms such as "force," "coercion," "threats," and so forth. Practically all injunctions include clauses prohibiting such conduct, and some of them, prohibitions of specific criminal or near-criminal acts, such as assaulting the complainants' employees, calling them "scabs," and persistently following them.

While these features suggest a close connection between injunctions and acts of violence, it does not follow that they have any real value in preserving law and order. Injunctions do not make acts of violence or intimidation any more unlawful than they

---

[1] A good statement of this view occurs in a speech of Senator William E. Borah, Aug. 19, 1914, reported in the *Cong. Rec.*, 63rd Cong., 2nd Sess., Vol. 51, Part 14, p. 13978.

[2] A recent injunction which appears to have been preceded by much violence is Wil-Low Cafeteria v. Kramberg, 134 Misc. 841, 237 N. Y. S. 76 (1929).

are without such orders. "The most drastic, severe, and permanent of all injunctions against violence is the penal law."[1] The only difference that an injunction makes is that thereafter acts of violence may be punished as contempts of court. In actual practice this is not an additional, but an alternative, penalty. In theory, persons committing acts of violence after the issuance of injunctions may be proceeded against on both counts. The author knows of only eight cases, however, where this actually occurred;[2] and while these are probably not the only instances, they were certainly exceptional.

Contempt proceedings are usually initiated by the complainants, who must bear the burden and expense of prosecution.[3] Getting such prosecutions under way is quite cumbersome. Before anyone can be arrested for contempt, a motion, petition, or affidavit must be filed and the court must issue an order directing the contemnor to show cause why he should not be punished—a much slower and less direct procedure than arrest and prosecution for crime. When a police officer witnesses a fight or other breach of the peace, an order from any court for the arrest of the participants is not necessary; but although such conduct may have been specifically prohibited by an injunction, the persons caught "red-handed" cannot be arrested for contempt until the facts have been presented to the court and it has issued a show-cause order.

The supposed advantages of contempt proceedings over criminal prosecutions are the more rapid disposition of such cases, the greater certainty of conviction, and the imposition of severer sentences. As indicated in the preceding chapter, there are some doubts regarding these claimed advantages, but in any event they scarcely offset the difficulties of initiating contempt proceedings.

---

[1] Segenfeld v. Friedman, 117 Misc. 731, 193 N. Y. S. 128 (1922).

[2] These include two reported cases: Anderson v. Indianapolis Drop Forging Co., 34 Ind. App. 100, 72 N. E. 277 (1904); U. S. v. Colo., 216 Fed. 654 (1914). (The defendants convicted of contempt in the latter case were in November, 1914, indicted for conspiracy and in January, 1915, pleaded guilty to this charge, *Chicago Tribune*, Nov. 20–26, 1914; Jan. 20, 1915.)

[3] An illustration of the expense of contempt proceedings to employers is the expenditure of $45,000 for counsel fees by the employers' association in the 240 contempt cases brought during the strike in the Chicago dress and waist industry in 1924, which resulted in but thirteen convictions.

When crimes are committed after their prohibition in injunctions, the offenders are much more apt to be prosecuted for crime than for contempt. On many injunctions there are no contempt proceedings at all; seldom are there very many; while in practically every important strike there are scores of arrests on criminal charges.

While strongly suggesting that injunctions have far less value as measures for law enforcement than is commonly supposed, the facts cited fall short of establishing the complete uselessness of injunctions for this purpose. Contempt proceedings are more disconcerting to the strikers than the usual run of criminal prosecutions on petty charges. Besides this, the possibility that charges of contempt may be brought if the police officers fail in the enforcement of the criminal law gives the complainants an additional weapon. Many employers' attorneys frankly acknowledge that they seldom advise contempt proceedings; yet they insist that injunctions have a distinct value in setting a standard for peace officers and the police courts, and in giving them backbone to enforce the criminal law. How much there is to this, it is difficult to say, but at the best the value of injunctions in keeping violence in check is indirect and uncertain.

The same story can be gathered from a study of the results of particular injunctions. Beyond question there have been cases in which much violence preceded injunctions, while very little occurred thereafter. There also have been cases in which injunctions did not check violence but apparently gave it impetus.

Such a result followed the injunction which preceded the famous damage suit Coronado Coal Co. v. United Mine Workers.[1] This case arose in the Hartford Valley in west Arkansas in the spring of 1914 and involved nine affiliated domestic mining corporations. These terminated their trade agreement with the United Mine Workers, made a contract with a private detective agency for "strike service," and barricaded their mines in preparation for war. They also incorporated a holding company in the

---

[1] At this stage, the case was known as Mammoth Vein Coal Mining Co. v. Hunter (U. S. v. Colorado, 216 Fed. 654, and U. S. v. Stewart, 236 Fed. 838 [1914] involved contempt proceedings under this injunction). The facts presented in this and the succeeding paragraph on the actual working out of this injunction are based mainly on a field investigation made by Special Agent L. A. Brown of the U. S. Commission on Industrial Relations.

state of West Virginia (which was referred to by Chief Justice Taft in his decision as a "hugger mugger corporation"), apparently to enable them to apply to the federal courts for an injunction. These preparations completed, the complainants secured their injunction, which included an unusual clause directing the United States marshal to swear in sufficient deputies for protection of the mines. The marshal telegraphed to the Department of Justice at Washington for authority to employ fifty additional deputies to carry out the order of the court. This authority was refused by John W. Davis, Acting Attorney-general, on the ground that this part of the court's order was unlawful; whereupon it was withdrawn.

The complainants, nevertheless, reopened one of their mines with strike breakers and guards furnished by the detective agency. The strikers and their sympathizers, already greatly incensed by the breach of the trade agreement and the issuance of the injunction, very soon clashed with the strike breakers and the strike guards; fights and shooting followed. Contempt proceedings against some of the strike leaders broke the camel's back. A great mob of union sympathizers, embracing practically everybody in the community, attacked the mine at which operations had been begun and drove off the strike breakers and guards, killing a number of them and setting fire to the mines. The mining companies then passed into the hands of a receiver, federal troops were sent to the district, some of the strike leaders were convicted of contempt and later also for conspiracy, and finally the famous damage suit was started, which dragged on for eleven years and in the end yielded the plaintiffs only a part of their court costs and attorneys' fees. This last part of the story will be told more fully in the next chapter; here we are interested only in how the injunction worked out. This was stated tersely in a letter which the principal stockholder wrote to the Attorney-general of the United States after the destruction of the mines:

I still insist that it is the duty of the government in such cases to appoint deputy marshals in sufficient numbers to make the court's order of some value. If such is not the law, then the order of the federal court is not worth the paper upon which it is written. Such an order, if it cannot be enforced, before the property is destroyed, is of no value whatever.

Numerous other cases might be cited in which violence followed the issuance of injunctions, but two recent illustrations must suffice.[1] One of these was the injunction issued by the U. S. District Court of the Western District of Missouri on Jan. 4, 1919, in the street-railway strike then in progress in Kansas City. *Law and Labor*,[2] reporting upon the situation in this strike, records that, despite the injunction, "the ex-employees have been dynamiting cars nearly every night and sometimes as many as four explosions have occurred in one night." A similar situation developed under the injunction (Clarkson Coal Mining Co. v. United Mine Workers) issued by the U. S. District Court of the Southern District of Ohio in 1927. This injunction was described by the judge, in a newspaper interview, as "the big stick in the form of regulations" and as having "a lot of teeth."[3] It failed, nevertheless, to forestall fifty serious acts of violence, and there were only seven contempt proceedings all told.[4]

The effectiveness of injunctions in preventing violence is of necessity a matter of opinion. Even when much violence occurs after the issuance of an injunction, it is still uncertain whether worse things would not have occurred without the court's intervention. Employers, judges, and complainants' attorneys as a rule claim that injunctions have great value in checking violence, but its widespread prevalence in American labor disputes, despite the many injunctions, makes this most doubtful.

---

[1] The author cited a considerable number of such cases in his report to the U. S. Commission on Industrial Relations on Injunctions in Labor Disputes, Appendix C, pp. 55–60. See also the author's Value of Injunctions in Labor Disputes, 32 *Jour. Polit. Econ.* 335, 339 (1924). For an illustration to the opposite effect, of an injunction which apparently did have value in curbing violence, see the *Bulletin* of the National Association of Manufacturers on The New Orleans Street-railway Strike of 1929–1930, p. 19 (1930). For an excellent discussion of the results of the injunctions in numerous concrete cases, see the unpublished Ph. D. thesis at the University of Chicago by Howard B. Meyers, "The Policing of Labor Disputes in Chicago," pp. 1111–1126 (1929).

[2] February, 1919.

[3] *Baltimore Sun*, Feb. 28, 1924.

[4] A list of these several acts of violence is included in the testimony of Ezra Van Horn, vice president of the complainant company, in the "Hearings on Conditions in the Coal Fields of Pennsylvania, West Virginia, and Ohio," conducted by a subcommittee of the Committee on Interstate Commerce of the U. S. Senate, 70th Cong., 1st Sess. pp. 2249–2250 (1928).

Injunctions usually add nothing to the police protection afforded the complainants' property and employees; efficient policing is at least as important as are summary court proceedings and drastic sentences in law enforcement. Logically, if the courts assume the duty of protecting the complainants' property against acts of violence, they cannot confine themselves to the issuance of injunctions but must take control of, and be responsible for, the policing of strikes. In about a dozen cases, courts have taken this step, including in their injunctions a direction to the marshal to protect the complainants' property and to swear in special deputies for this purpose.[1] This practice has twice come before the courts and has twice been passed upon by attorney-generals of the United States with opposing conclusions.[2] In the case most squarely in point, a federal district judge directed the marshal to commission as deputies strike guards employed and paid by the complainants.[3] John W. Davis, in 1914, took the position that the Department of Justice, not the courts, has the determination of the employment of additional deputies and that guarding the complainants' property is not a function of the marshal's office. Attorney-general William Mitchell, on the other hand, in 1929 held that it is within the sound discretion of the court to issue such an order, and that the marshal and the department of justice are in duty bound to observe the court's directions so long as the number of deputies to be sworn in is reasonable.[4] To date, the practice of directing marshals to

---

[1] The earliest example of such an order probably was the direction to the marshal given by Judge Woods of the Northern District of Illinois during the Pullman strike of 1894, to deputize nine hundred of the employees of the railroad companies to enforce the injunction under which arose the famous Debs case (*Chicago Times*, July 3, 1894). Recent cases in which similar directions were given to the marshals include Clarkson Coal Mining Co. v. United Mine Workers, U. S. Dist. Ct., S. D. E. Div., Ohio, 9 *Law and Labor* 290 (1927); and N. Y. Trust Co. v. Amalgamated Assoc., U. S. Dist. Ct., E. D. La., 11 *Law and Labor* 176 (1929). In American Bemberg Corp. v. Miller, Mar. 18, 1929, the Chancery Court at Elizabethton, Tenn., issued a similar direction to the sheriff of the county.

[2] Consolidated Coal and Coke Co. v. Beale, 282 Fed. 934 (1922).

[3] Dail-Overland Co. v. Willys-Overland, 263 Fed. 171 (1919).

[4] The opinion of John W. Davis was given in connection with the coal strike, discussed earlier in this section, out of which developed the Coronado Coal Co. case; that of Attorney-general Mitchell, in connection with the injunction in the New Orleans street-car strike in which the injunction

undertake the protection of the complainants' property is still exceptional, but it is a logical, if not inevitable, extension of injunctions in labor disputes. This development is contrary to the American theory of the separation of governmental powers[1] but is likely to come into widespread use in the not distant future.

EFFECTIVENESS OF RESTRAINING CLAUSES

How effective are injunctions aside from the prevention of violence? This is a question which cannot be answered by any single statement.

First, injunctions aimed at the strike itself: As noted in the preceding chapter, such injunctions have been most frequently issued in connection with strikes against non-union materials. While most of the earlier injunctions of this character seem to have been ineffective,[2] at least some of the more recent of such injunctions have been entirely successful. The decision of the U. S. Supreme Court in 1927 allowing an injunction to the Bedford Cut Stone Co. against the rule of the stonecutters' union prohibiting its members engaged in construction work from setting stone quarried by non-union men not only compelled the abandonment of this rule throughout the country but led the electrical workers' unions in New York City to give up their practice of refusing to install non-union electrical equipment.[3] After years of struggle featured by many injunctions, non-union wood trim is now freely used in both Chicago and New York, where until recently the use of such materials was certain to lead to a strike.[4]

New York Trust Co. v. Amalgamated Assoc. was issued by Judge Borah of the U. S. District Court, E. D. La. This opinion was expressed in response to a protest filed against this order with the Attorney-general by William Green, president of the American Federation of Labor. (Copies of the entire correspondence in this matter have been furnished to the author by the American Federation of Labor.)

[1] In this connection, Montesquieu's observation, that where "the power to judge . . . [is] joined to the executive power the judge might behave with all the violence of an oppressor," is timely.

[2] See WITTE, E. E., Value of Injunctions in Labor Disputes, 32 *Jour. Polit. Econ.* 335, 340–341 (1924).

[3] 9 *Law and Labor* 269 (1927).

[4] There is some question whether this result is to be ascribed to the injunctions. This is claimed by employers, but union officials say that

Injunctions against other kinds of strikes have been infrequent, but the best known of these illustrates the difficulties of preventing strikes through injunctions. This was the injunction procured by Attorney-general Palmer late in October, 1919, which prohibited the officers of the United Mine Workers from calling a nation-wide coal strike.[1] When this injunction was issued the strike order had already gone out and before any further legal action could be taken the union coal miners of the country had quit work. Hereupon, the court issued a second order, directing the union officers to call off the strike. This they did, but the strike continued. Not until more than a week later, when President Wilson had arranged an agreement between the operators and the union providing for arbitration, did the miners resume work.

Coming, secondly, to injunctions directed against methods used to make the strike effective, let us first consider restrictions upon picketing. Here again the story is one of injunctions gradually becoming more effective, but still not always accomplishing their purpose. As long as the usual picketing clause was a prohibition of "unlawful" picketing or of picketing for the purpose of intimidating the complainants' employees, they had little effect. Since it has become the custom, following the decision of the U. S. Supreme Court in the American Steel Foundries case in 1921, to prescribe minutely how the picketing must be conducted, enforcement is greatly facilitated and the injunctions against picketing are distinctly more effective. Yet they do not always work out as expected. An illustration is the injunction issued at Kenosha, Wis., in 1928 against striking full-fashioned hosiery workers.[2] At the preliminary hearing in this case, the judge offered to modify the temporary restraining order so as to permit one picket at the factory

---

these boycotts of non-union wood trim were abandoned because there were so few union manufacturers that they could not possibly supply all of the materials needed, so that the practical alternative presented to the union carpenters was either that they must work on non-union materials or let non-union men do the work.

[1] This case, entitled U. S. v. Hayes, is not reported, but the injunction is reprinted in Sayre, "Cases on Labor Law," p. 757. The facts given regarding the way this injunction worked out are taken from the daily press reports while the strike was in progress.

[2] Allen A Co. v. Steele, U. S. Dist. Ct., E. D. Wis. (March 1928).

entrance, but this offer was scorned by the defendants. They preferred complete prohibition which would assure them the support of all other workmen in the city. Thereafter all of the picketing was done by these sympathizers, and as proof that they acted in concert with the defendants could not be furnished they could not be prosecuted for contempt. In this case, an injunction absolutely prohibiting picketing operated to make possible the continuance of mass picketing.

Injunctions against boycotting have still more often proved boomerangs, as illustrated by the Bucks' Stove and Range Co. case.[1] An injunction issued in 1907 prohibited the American Federation of Labor from continuing to publish the name of the Bucks' Stove and Range Co. in its unfair list. At that time, this list, published inconspicuously each month in the *American Federationist*, had on it the names of over eighty firms. It is a safe guess that not 1 per cent of the trade unionists of the country knew that the Bucks' Stove and Range Co. was one of these eighty firms. After this injunction was issued and, particularly, after contempt proceedings were started against the three most prominent labor leaders of the country, under which they were, for a time, under sentence to one year in jail, all union members knew that Bucks' stoves and ranges were "unfair" and avoided purchasing them. The unfair list in the *American Federationist* was discontinued, but the sales of the Bucks' Stove and Range Co. fell off. Within three years this company, under new management, made its peace with organized labor.[2]

The American Federation of Labor has never resumed its unfair list, and boycotts have been resorted to less frequently and conducted less openly than prior to the Bucks' Stove and Range Co. injunction. This cannot be ascribed, however, wholly to this injunction, as the decision of the U. S. Supreme Court in the Danbury hatters case occurred almost simultaneously. The latter case, holding that treble damages could be recovered under

---

[1] Bucks' Stove and Range Co. v. American Federation of Labor, 35 Wash. Law Rep. (1907); A. F. of L. v. Bucks' Stove and Range Co., 33 App. D. C. 83 (1909); Gompers v. Bucks' Stove and Range Co., 33 App. D. C. 516 (1909), 221 U. S. 418, 31 Sup. Ct. 492 (1911); Gompers v. U. S., 233 U. S. 604, 34 Sup. Ct. 693 (1914).

[2] LAIDLER, H. W., "Boycotts and the Labor Struggle," pp. 147–148, John Lane Co., New York (1913).

the Sherman Antitrust Act for losses sustained through interstate boycotts, occasioned much greater alarm in labor circles than the former.[1] Moreover, many labor boycotts are still conducted, especially against local institutions like restaurants and theaters, which can be most effectively boycotted; and injunctions have proven valueless against such boycotts. By giving them wider publicity, they, in fact, increase their effectiveness.

Some of the less universal clauses in injunctions appear to be more effective. This is particularly true of injunctions directed against union organization. The combination of the individual non-union agreement ("yellow-dog" contract) with injunctions to enforce these agreements is perhaps the most serious menace now confronting organized labor. There is good reason for believing, as the union claims, that the individual non-union agreements and the injunctions to enforce them kept the United Mine Workers out of most of the coal fields of West Virginia at the time when this was the strongest of American unions; and the inability to organize West Virginia has played a large part in the near collapse of this union within the last few years. The individual non-union agreement is practically meaningless without the injunction, but with the injunction it can be turned into a powerful weapon to all but annihilate unionism. Similarly, injunctions to prohibit the payment of strike benefits and to prevent the use of union funds to aid strikers when arrested or when threatened with eviction from company houses are most difficult to evade and seriously hamper the conduct of strikers.

Injunctions have grown steadily more sweeping and their phraseology better adapted to secure compliance. Undoubtedly, they are more effective now than formerly, although not nearly so valuable as many employers think. Many times they prove disappointing and it is only when they tie labor hand and foot that they have any value at all.

INJUNCTIONS AND THE OUTCOME OF STRIKES

The net purpose and effect of injunctions, organized labor claims, is to defeat strikes, and numerous specific strikes are cited to prove this point.[2] Many of these seem to bear out this claim;

---

[1] WOLMAN, LEO, "The Boycott in American Trade Unions," pp. 129–135, The Johns Hopkins Press, Baltimore (1916).

[2] A good statement of this view is the article by Lilienthal, Labor and the Courts, 34 *New Republic* 314–316 (1923).

but it is difficult, if not impossible, to isolate the influence of injunctions from other factors which may have had a part in causing labor's defeat.

The difficulties of determining how much injunctions have to do with the failure of strikes are illustrated by the Pullman (American Railway Union) strike of 1894, often cited as an outstanding example of the harmful effects of injunctions. Eugene Debs, the leader of this strike, stated that it was the injunction which defeated the strikers. Yet the injunction taken out by Attorney-general Olney was not issued until a week after the federal troops had been sent to Chicago; and for nearly two weeks thereafter there was not a single citation for contempt, while there were hundreds of arrests for violation of state and federal laws. Debs himself was arrested for "conspiracy" a week before he was cited for contempt. By that time, railroad operations were almost normal and the backbone of the strike had been broken. Not until six months later, when the strike had long terminated, was Debs convicted and sentenced to jail. He may have been right in claiming that the defeat of the strike was due to the injunction, but the record suggests that the troops and the criminal prosecutions had quite as much to do with this result.

That injunctions do handicap labor is undeniable. For one thing, they prejudice public opinion, and public opinion is an important factor in the outcome of many strikes. The issuance of an injunction gives the public the impression that the strikers have been lawless—a difficult prejudice to overcome. Again, injunctions tend to undermine the morale of the strikers. When such an order is issued, the rank and file may well feel that everything is lost, and even the leaders may become panicky. Injunctions tend to dissipate the energies of the leaders and divert their primary attention from the strike to the battle in the courts. It is the leaders who are designated by name in the complaints and in the injunctions, and they are the ones who are more commonly proceeded against for contempt. Injunctions cost labor unions large amounts in attorneys' fees and court costs. Injunctions cost the ladies garment workers' union $41,000 in the Chicago dressmakers' strike of 1924, and the International Molders Union spent $26,000 in counsel fees in injunction cases in the five-year period 1912–1917, in which there were comparatively few injunctions.[1]   And this financial cost is small compared with the loss in time and energy of the leaders, coming, as it usually does, at the most crucial period of the strike.   Strikes are usually won or lost within the first few days, and it is at this time that injunctions are most devastating.

Union leaders who have had a great deal of experience with injunctions often boast about the number of such orders that have been served upon them.   This is largely idle braggadocio; but it is a fact that such men are far less frightened by injunctions than the ordinary workingmen and leaders who have had no experience with such writs.   Injunctions do not hamper strong and well-organized unions nearly so much as weak or new organizations.   Injunctions have been least effective in the building trades, where labor is most strongly organized, and have proved most serious when, combined with individual non-union agreements, they are directed against union organizations—an obstacle which, thus far, organized labor has found practically insurmountable.

While injunctions are not the sole and, probably, not even the principal cause of the relatively weak position of labor unions in the United States, they have been a factor in producing this situation.   And injunctions are a greater menace to organized labor today than ever before.

LABOR'S REACTIONS

There is no question as to what labor thinks about injunctions. In the belief that they are unfair and prejudiced, labor is an absolute unit.   The most conservative of labor leaders are as bitter in their denunciation of injunctions as are the left-wing elements in the labor movement.   This feeling, to a great extent, is shared throughout the ranks of organized workingmen and, to some degree, unorganized workingmen.   All that any public speaker has to do to get an enthusiastic response from a workingmen's audience is to denounce the use of injunctions in labor disputes; and a politician can make no better play for the labor vote than to pledge support to antiinjunction legislation.

---

[1] MEYERS, HOWARD B., "The Policing of Labor Disputes in Chicago," University of Chicago thesis, p. 987 (1929); report of President Valentine to the 1927 convention of the International Molders' Union, published as an Appendix to Vol. 53 of the *International Molders' Journal*, p. 17 (1917).

The attitude of labor toward injunctions is, in part, one of defiance. This is expressed in one of *The Trade Union Epigrams*, an official publication of the American Federation of Labor: "In the case of an injunction in labor disputes, contempt of court is respect for law." Samuel Gompers, the guiding genius of the American labor movement for more than forty years preceding his death in 1925, always urged that trade unionists be willing to go to jail for contempt rather than obey injunctions which clearly violate their constitutional rights. This sentiment has ever met with a hearty response. Conviction for contempt is to a trade unionist proof positive of whole-hearted devotion to the interests of labor. The labor leader who is sent to jail for the violation of an injunction is almost sure of his position ever after. Even the Socialists, who hated him so bitterly, voted for the reelection of Gompers as president of the Federation after he was sentenced to a year in jail for violating the injunction in the Bucks' Stove and Range Co. case.

Besides being defiant of injunctions, labor is resentful towards the courts. In the language of an editorial in *The American Federationist*, labor believes that the courts have "become the allies of employers in a partisan struggle." George Perkins, long president of the cigar makers and a conservative of conservatives, once said:

It is not a new experience to have the United States Supreme Court decision added to the attacks of the Farleys, the Currys, and the organized bands of strike breakers. What cut-throat financiers and grasping employers cannot do themselves, they confidently expect the courts to do for them.[1]

This expresses forcibly but accurately the sentiments which labor entertains toward the courts; many other quotations to like effect might be given.

In recent years labor itself, and particularly radical labor, has made some use of injunctions in contests with employers.[2] This does not mean that labor unions have become reconciled to the use of injunctions in labor disputes. They are as much opposed to injunctions as ever; if possible, more so. There is a growing disposition to give employers a boomerang blow, but

---

[1] 15 *Amer. Federationist* 164 (1908).
[2] See Chap. X, pp. 231–234.

this is tinged with quite as much bitterness over injunctions as ever.

Labor's feeling against injunctions has found expression in literally hundreds of editorials in the *American Federationist* and other trade-union publications and in thousands of speeches of labor leaders. There has not been an annual convention of the American Federation of Labor since injunctions first attracted public notice in the early nineties which has not taken a strong stand against the abuse of injunctions in labor disputes and demanded legislative relief.

A further reaction of labor appears in its political activity. The story of the long battle which organized labor has waged to gain relief through legislation from "the abuse of injunctions" and the extent to which in this struggle it has been drawn into politics will be told in Chap. XII. Here, only the fact need be noted that relief from injunctions has been labor's foremost legislative demand and the principal attraction drawing it into politics.[1] Although there is no independent labor party in the United States, our labor unions—national, state, and local—are today just as active in politics as organized labor in Europe, with injunctions occupying the center of interest; often to the exclusion of all other issues.

The efforts made by organized labor to elect legislators who will support antiinjunction legislation have, naturally, been countered by efforts of employers' organizations to prevent this. Nationally, the National Association of Manufacturers has been most active in this respect. In the Mulhall *exposé* of 1913 and the Congressional investigation which followed, this organization was revealed as being engaged in lobbying of the most pernicious kind.[2]

Such coarse methods appear no longer to be employed by this or any other employers' association, but the National Association of Manufacturers, the League of Industrial Rights, the U. S. Chamber of Commerce, and other organizations representing the point of view of employers are still actively interested in preventing antiinjunction and similar legislation. These employ-

---

[1] WALLING, W. E., "American Labor and Democracy," p. 20, Harper & Brothers, New York (1926).

[2] House Lobby Committee Hearings, 63rd Cong., 1st Sess. (1913).

ers' organizations usually do not endorse candidates for Congress or the state legislature as does labor, but without doing so they have perhaps more effective control of the influence and votes of their group than does labor.

INJUNCTIONS AND THE SELECTION OF JUDGES

Both the labor organizations and the employers' associations are interested not only in the election of friendly legislators but equally in the selection of judges. For many years, organized labor in many industrial communities has fought the reelection of "injunction judges," and has endorsed judicial candidates whom it considers friendly.[1] These campaigns, on the whole, have met with indifferent success and have grown less frequent.[2] Nevertheless, one or more still occur somewhere every year, and by no means all of them end in failure. After the judicial elections in New York City in November, 1929, the New York State Federation of Labor claimed credit for the defeat for reelection of Supreme Court Justice Callaghan; and a similar, though futile, campaign was conducted against the reelection of Judge Dennis E. Sullivan in Chicago.[3] In 1927, a successful fight was waged by labor against the reelection of Judge Crow in the third judicial district of Illinois, and in the same year Supreme Court Justice H. J. Lynch of the ninth judicial district of New York was reelected with the endorsement of the New York State Federation of Labor, although not on the slate of the bar association.[4] Many similar reports might be cited,[5] but these

---

[1] The American Federation of Labor in its 1918 convention adopted a resolution urging all affiliated unions to exert themselves "in changing the personnel of the judiciary so as to secure judges who can understand economic problems." (*Proc.* 280.)

[2] The first known instance of an attempt to defeat a judge considered hostile to labor occurred in 1899 when the Detroit Trades and Labor Council inaugurated a campaign against the reelection of Judge Claudius B. Stone of the Michigan Supreme Court (*Amer. Federationist* 44, April, 1899). For an extended account of labor's activities in judicial elections prior to 1915, see the author's report to the U. S. Commission on Industrial Relations on Injunctions in Labor Disputes, Appendix F, pp. 24–32.

[3] *Bull. N. Y. State Fed. Labor*, November, 1929; *Labor*, Oct. 26, 1929.

[4] *A. F. of L. Weekly News Service*, Apr. 23, 1927; *Labor*, June 25, 1927, and Oct. 29, 1927.

[5] A case illustrating labor's tactics is the successful campaign engineered by the Cleveland Federation of Labor in 1918 against the renomination

will serve the purpose of illustrating labor's interest in judicial elections and the claims it makes of at least partial success in its policy of rewarding friends and punishing enemies in judicial offices.

Illustrative of the situation which prevails in many industrial communities are the advertisements of judicial candidates with which the labor papers are filled before every judicial election. Some of these bids for labor votes are most startling.   In behalf of a candidate the following advertisement was run in a Minneapolis labor paper in 1914:

John R. Coan is a candidate for municipal judge. As a lawyer of ability he has fought many battles for labor. His sympathies are with the men who toil. With Coan acting as judge and jury in our municipal court there would be one law for the employer and the same law for the employee. If Coan happened to make a mistake it would probably be in our favor. Remember John R. Coan election day and you will have done your part in securing justice for yourself and organized labor.[1]

In similar vein, Nicholas Klein, a candidate for a vacancy on the Ohio Supreme Court in 1924, appealed for labor support on the plea:

Short as my term will be, I intend to devote every moment of it to the task of bringing to the people of our state an understanding of the outrage that adheres to the use of injunctions in labor disputes.   I shall take the opportunity of making a state-wide attack on the whole system of government by injunction and my words will not soon be forgotten by the judges.[2]

---

of Judge Robert D. Morgan of the Court of Common Pleas. This judge had incurred the enmity of labor by the issuance in the preceding year of an injunction against the iron molders' union. On the eve of the primary, 60,000 dodgers attacking Judge Morgan were distributed in the labor wards, and these, according to the labor press, accounted for Judge Morgan's defeat (54 *Int. Molders Jour.* 707 [1918]). Illustrative of the situation which exists in Cleveland is also the item in the *Cleveland Citizen*, Oct. 18, 1924, to the effect that Judge Gilbert appeared at a meeting of the Cleveland Federation of Labor and pleaded for endorsement for reelection, on the ground that in eighteen years on the bench his record has been uniformly friendly to labor. This endorsement was given and Judge Gilbert was reelected.

[1] *Minneapolis Labor Rev.*, Oct. 9, 1914.
[2] *Toledo Union-Leader*, Oct. 24, 1924.

At times, the election of judges in industrial centers has developed into a regular "show-down" fight between labor and capital, centering upon the attitude of the candidates on injunctions in labor disputes. This was the situation in the judicial elections in Chicago in 1921 and 1923.[1] In both years, the Chicago Federation of Labor launched campaigns to defeat Superior Judges Sullivan and Holdom on their injunction records, the second of which was participated in by Samuel Gompers himself. These were countered by the organization of The Minute Men of the Constitution, headed by General Charles G. Dawes and backed by the employing interests of the city, whose purpose was to prevent labor from gaining control of the judiciary. Victory in both contests rested with employers, but today labor is to be reckoned with in all judicial elections in Chicago, as in many other cities.

Nothing that has been said should be construed as either approving or condemning the election of judges with reference to their attitude on the use of injunctions in labor disputes. The point intended to be made is that this has become an important question in many judicial elections, and that both the labor unions and the employers' associations often concern themselves with electing "fair" judges.

Since federal judges are appointed, somewhat different tactics have been found necessary to influence the federal judiciary. But labor and the employers' associations have interested themselves no less actively in the selection of federal judges. The most noteworthy instance of such activities was the successful fight which organized labor made in 1930 against the confirmation of Judge John T. Parker as a justice of the Supreme Court of the United States, the first time in more than a quarter century

---

[1] Accounts of these campaigns are given in the *Chicago Tribune*, Dec. 16, 1921; *New Majority*, Nov. 3, 1923; *Labor*, Nov. 17, 1923.

An even more striking, although less important, illustration of a judicial election contested along these lines was the campaign for the county judgeship of Letcher County, Ky., in 1920. This county, at that time, had a strong membership in the United Mine Workers and Judge Combs had incurred the enmity of this union. Fess Whitaker, a member of the union, who had been sentenced by Judge Combs to six months in jail for contempt of court, was brought out as a candidate against him and while serving in jail was elected as his successor. (*Survey*, Dec. 18, 1920.)

that any appointment to the Supreme Court has failed to get the approval of the Senate. While other factors entered into this result, the principal cause for the rejection of Judge Parker was his concurrence in a decision sustaining an injunction premised upon a yellow-dog contract.[1] Similar, although unsuccessful and less well-known, efforts have been made by organized labor to defeat confirmation of other appointments to federal judgeship, and it has repeatedly urged the President to appoint named individuals to the Supreme Court, or, in general terms, "persons whose leanings and sympathies are toward the newer concepts of social justice."[2] Employers' associations have not so openly interested themselves in the selection of federal judges, but when President Wilson appointed Louis D. Brandeis to the Supreme Court, they fought his confirmation, precisely as labor fought Judge Parker's.

The labor record of federal judges, likewise, has figured prominently in attempts at impeachment. At least four federal judges who have resigned while investigations to determine whether they should be impeached were under consideration or impeachments pending were "injunction judges," bitterly opposed by labor: namely, Judge Hanford of the District Court of the District of Washington in 1912, Judge Wright of the Supreme Court of the District of Columbia in 1914, Judge

---

[1] The unexpected votes of some conservative senators cast against Judge Parker were probably influenced more by his decisions against equal rights for negroes than his labor record, but these were offset by the southern Democrats, who rallied to his support on the same issue. The long debate over confirmation was confined almost exclusively to the yellow-dog contract decision, and this was clearly the main reason for the rejection of Judge Parker.

[2] In May, 1929, President Green and other members of the Executive Council of the American Federation of Labor, as reported by the International Labor News Service, called on President Hoover and "asked the President for fair judges on the federal bench, calling his attention to abuses by federal judges, notably in issuing injunctions," and "more emphasis was put on this subject than on any other in the conference." (*Toledo Union-Leader*, May 31, 1929.)

During the Wilson administration, the national conventions of many labor unions endorsed Frank P. Walsh for the Supreme Court and lauded the appointment of Louis D. Brandeis. In the Harding administration, labor opposed confirmation of the appointments of William H. Taft and Pierce Butler.

Dayton of the Northern District of West Virginia, also in 1914, and Judge English of the Southern District of Illinois in 1925.[1] In each of these cases, there were charges other than those connected with injunctions in labor disputes, but organized labor had much to do with starting the proceedings against these judges, particularly in the cases of Judges Wright and Dayton. In this connection, it is worthy of note that John P. Frey, one of the ablest of present-day labor leaders, in his book "The Labor Injunction"[2] urges that impeachment is one of the most effective weapons that labor has to secure relief from the abuse of injunctions.

EFFECTS UPON THE COURTS

What have been the reactions of the judges to the bitter criticisms to which they have been subjected and to the efforts which unions and employers' associations have made to secure "friendly" judges? Naturally, these reactions have differed with the individual judge. Some have thereby been made blind partisans, incapable thereafter of impartiality.[3] Others have been made afraid of injunction cases, long delaying their findings and sometimes holding for labor even when decisions

---

[1] A similar attempt at the impeachment of an "injunction judge" occurred in the Colorado legislature in 1911. This involved Judge Whitford, who had imposed most drastic sentences upon certain strike leaders for violations of the injunction Northern Coal and Coke Co. v. United Mine Workers. Charges looking toward impeachment growing out of this case were brought by a labor member of the House of Representatives but collapsed when Judge Whitford freed the convicted unionists before the expiration of their sentences.

[2] Pp. 84–85.

[3] Numerous illustrations of such partisanship are given in John A. Fitch, "The Causes of Industrial Unrest," 324–340, Harper & Brothers (1924). Other illustrations were given by the author in his report on Injunctions in Labor Disputes, Appendix F, pp. 32–38. A recent example is the following statement in Schwartz & Jaffee v. Hillman, 189 N. Y. S. 21, 25 (1925):

"Courts cannot find the balancing point (in the conflict between employers and workers) by boxing the compass of judicial opinion from extreme radicalism to ultraconservatism. They must stand at all times as the representatives of capital, or captains of industry, devoted to the principle of individual initiative, protecting property and persons from violence and destruction, strongly opposed to all schemes for the nationalization of industry, and yet save labor from oppression and be conciliatory towards the removal of the workers' just grievances."

of the highest court of the jurisdiction clearly indicated the opposite conclusion.[1] Clarence Darrow once said, "In labor cases it depends altogether upon the point of view of the judge. If the judges are your friends, you will get favorable decisions."[2] To much the same effect *Law and Labor*, on the other side, has said editorially: "Whatever may be the written words of the law, we realize today as we have never before that public opinion dictates the trend of the law. The courts cannot escape pressure from this opinion."[3]

While these statements from both opposing camps are true to some extent, it is the author's belief that the majority of the judges decide labor cases fairly and impartially. The average judge does not have much of an understanding of industrial problems. He probably never had a labor injunction case before his elevation to the bench. His contacts generally have been more with the employer class than with the working class. He does know enough about labor cases, however, to realize that this is a most controversial subject, that his "labor record" will be closely scanned when he comes up for reelection. These considerations alone are sufficient to make most judges anxious to follow strictly the decisions of the supreme courts. That trial courts are in this class of cases often reversed is due rather to the newness and vagueness of this entire field of the law than to a deliberate disregard of the rights of either side. It is not corruption,[4] nor usually even prejudice, which accounts

---

[1] Strong statements, from employer sources, upon the timidity of judges in labor cases (and favoritism to labor) occur in the "Recommendations to the Industrial Relations Commission of the American Anti-boycott Association," p. 14 (1914), and in testimony of Dudley Taylor in 4 *Final Report and Testimony of the U. S. Commission on Industrial Relations* 3239 (*Sen. Doc.* 415, 64th Cong., 1st Sess.).

[2] Quoted in *Inter. Socialist Rev.* 151, September, 1910.

[3] 3 *Law and Labor* 237 (1921).

[4] Charges of improper interests, verging on corruption, have been made against a few, but only a few "injunction judges." The most serious were those made by the Committee of the Judiciary in *House Rep.* 1490, 63rd Cong., 3rd Sess., concerning Judges Jackson and Dayton, who successively presided over the U. S. District Court of the Northern District of West Virginia and who issued more extreme injunctions in labor cases than any other two judges in the history of the country. According to this report, after Judge Jackson resigned in 1905, he was placed on the pay roll of the Baltimore and Ohio R. R. Co. without ever rendering any services. Of

for so many injunctions against labor, but the present condition of the substantive law and the unfairness of the usual equity procedure when followed in labor cases.

The most important aspect of the reaction of labor injunctions upon the courts is their weakened prestige. The issuance of injunctions in labor disputes has done more to destroy the confidence of the workingmen in the courts than any other development of recent decades. Workingmen regard the interference of courts in labor disputes as an act of partisanship. They believe that injunctions are used against labor as against no other group or class. They think that through injunctions they are denied their constitutional rights, to the end that labor unions may be destroyed and strikers defeated in their demands for higher wages and better working conditions. Jane Addams once expressed this state of affairs as follows:

There is a growing distrust of the integrity of the courts, the belief that the present judge has been a corporation attorney, that his sympathies and his experience and his whole view of life is on the corporation side.[1]

The belief that the courts favor the rich and powerful has always prevailed to some extent, among the poor and the weak.[2] On the whole, this feeling has been less prevalent in the United States than in any other country. Of all branches of government, the courts have the strongest popular support, but there is abundant evidence that they are losing their reputation for impartiality—among, at least, the organized workingmen. As President Roosevelt stated in a special message to Congress on Apr. 27, 1908:

Judge Dayton the committee said that he was interested as a stockholder in coal-mining companies, and that his manner and language toward union coal miners in cases before him "was that of hatred and bitterness" and that he "was very impatient of hearing what the defendants had to say, his manner was heated and impassioned, he was laboring under much emotional excitement, and his conduct generally was that of one that had prejudged the cases before him."

[1] 13 *Amer. Jour. Sociology* 70, 72 (1908).

[2] Shakespeare expressed this complaint in King Lear (Act IV, Sc. 6):
　　"Through tattered clothes great vices do appear;
　　Robes and furred gowns hide all. Plate sin with gold,
　　And the strong lance of justice hurtless breaks;
　　Arm it in rags, a pigmy's straw does pierce it."

They are blind who fail to realize the extreme bitterness caused among large bodies of worthy citizens by the use that has been repeatedly made of the power of injunctions in labor disputes.[1]

Spokesmen of militant employers' associations have charged that this dissatisfaction has been artificially created by the labor leaders, pursuant to a deliberate attempt "to bring contumely down upon the leaders of the judiciary and disrespect for the courts, in order that their own special and mismanaged purposes may be furthered."[2] This may seem an adequate explanation to some but does not make the distrust of the courts any the less serious.   Whether labor leaders have just grievances against labor injunctions, as the author believes, or whether they are merely raising a smoke screen to hide their own misdeeds is not nearly so significant as the fact that their views are shared by the great mass of the organized workingmen, and to a very considerable extent also by the unorganized.   Walpole's dictum, "You cannot indict a nation," is applicable; the working people are such an important element in our society that what they think of the courts vitally affects their usefulness and the safety of the entire social structure.   Distrust of the courts by workingmen is a fact, and injunctions in labor disputes are an important factor in keeping alive and stimulating this feeling.

Bibliographical Note

There have been few comprehensive discussions of the social consequences of the use of injunctions in labor disputes.   The notable address of former Senator George W. Pepper on Injunctions in Labor Disputes, made in 1924 at a joint meeting of the American Bar Association and the Pennsylvania Bar Association, which is published in 49 *Amer. Bar Assoc. Rept.* 174 and also separately, dealt mainly with this aspect of the injunction question. The present author discussed this subject in his report in 1915 to the U. S. Commission on Industrial Relations on Injunctions in Labor Disputes and in Appendices C to F thereto, devoted, respectively, to Injunctions and Acts of Violence, Injunctions and the Outcome of Strikes, Injunctions and Trade Union Boycotts, and Injunctions and the Courts.   (This report and the appendices were never published, but typewritten copies are to be found in the libraries of the Wisconsin Historical Society and the Harvard Law School.)   More recently, he has dealt with this subject in four articles:

---

[1] *Congressional Record*, 60th Cong., 1st Sess., Vol. 42, Part 6, p. 5327.

[2] HICKEY, MICHAEL J., Legislation Affecting the Right to Operate the Open Shop, *Open Shop Bull.* 25, published by the National Association of Manufacturers, Dec. 10, 1929.

Results of Injunctions in Labor Disputes, 12 *Amer. Labor Legis. Rev.* 197–201 (1922); Value of Injunctions in Labor Disputes, in 32 *Jour. Polit. Econ.* 335–356 (1924); The Labor Injunction—a Red Flag, 18 *Amer. Labor Legis. Rev.* 315–317 (1928); and Social Consequences of the Use of Injunctions in Labor Disputes, 24 *Ill. Law Rev.* 772–785 (1930). An excellent detailed account of the effects of particular injunctions (issued in the city of Chicago) is the unpublished Ph. D. thesis of Howard B. Meyers, "The Policing of Labor Disputes in Chicago," Chicago (1929).

Other discussions of certain phases of the results of injunctions include David E. Lilienthal, Labor and the Courts, 34 *New Republic* 314–316 (1913); A. De Silver, The Injunction—a Weapon of Industrial Power, 114 *Nation* 89–91 (1922); T. Yeoman Williams, Injunctions in Labor Disputes, 13 *Proc. Acad. Polit. Sci.* 78–83 (1928), and the discussion of this paper by Morris Hillquit in the same magazine, pp. 84–87; the article What Does the Average Workman Believe about Injunctions? 6 *Law and Labor* 175–176 (1924); Felix Frankfurter and Nathan Greene, "The Labor Injunction," Appendix VIII (1930); J. H. Hollander, "Economic Liberalism," 121–132, Abingdon Press, New York (1925); and Duane McCracken, "Case Studies of the Effects of Injunctions Growing out of Industrial Disputes in North Carolina, Elizabethton, Tennessee, and Danville, Virginia," University of North Carolina Press, Chapel Hill (1931). A good presentation of labor's criticisms and reactions to injunctions is Frey, "The Labor Injunction" (1923).

Information for a study of the results of injunctions is scattered and difficult to obtain. Some data can be gleaned from accounts regarding particular injunctions in newspapers, the labor and employer press, and sometimes from the court proceedings and reported decisions. The many Congressional hearings on injunctions in labor disputes (listed in the bibliographical note to Chap. V) contain much pertinent information. Correspondence and interviews with employers, labor leaders, and their attorneys can be made to yield much data not otherwise obtainable; and still better are field studies, including an examination of all available published material and talks with the interested parties on the ground. Practically all statements obtained from these sources, however, need to be checked, particularly if made to influence public opinion for or against injunctions.

CHAPTER VII

DAMAGE SUITS

Damage suits are an older remedy in labor controversies than injunctions, but far less important. Yet twenty years ago it seemed that damage suits would prove a more serious menace to labor unions than even injunctions. Nothing has since occurred to lessen this danger, but the actual results have not been so very alarming.

DANBURY HATTERS CASE

The great alarm over damage suits arose from the decision of the U. S. Supreme Court in Loewe v. Lawlor[1] in 1908. This decision occurred in a suit begun in 1903 by a hat manufacturer of Danbury, Conn., against 197 members of the hatters' union and was premised upon an alleged conspiracy to prevent the manufacturer from selling his products in interstate commerce, pursuant to which the union called a strike in his factory at Danbury and instituted a nation-wide boycott against his hats. Treble damages were asked for under the Sherman Antitrust Act, the amount sued for being $240,000. To the complaint, the defendants filed a demurrer based upon the theory that their acts did not constitute a violation of the Sherman Act, inasmuch as there was no interference with the physical transportation of the hats between states. This demurrer was overruled by the Supreme Court, and this decision led not only labor leaders but most of the leading students of labor problems in this country to predict that it would compel the labor unions to adopt a secret form of organization, if indeed they could survive.

Thereafter came the trial of the cause upon its merits, which culminated in a jury award in 1912 of the full amount of the damages sued for, plus costs. Then the case was again carried

---

[1] 208 U. S. 274, 28 Sup. Ct. 301. For other decisions in this case, see 148 Fed. 924 (1907); 187 Fed. 552 (1911); 223 U. S. 721 (1912); 209 Fed. 72 (1913); 235 U. S. 522, 35 Sup. Ct. 170 (1915).

to the U. S. Supreme Court, which in 1915 sustained the award of damages. This was the final litigation, but it was not until two years later that a settlement was made with the Loewe Co. In the meantime, the hatters' union and the American Federation of Labor sought by voluntary contributions to raise the funds to pay the judgment. A "hatters' day" was staged throughout the country, all union members being asked to contribute their wages for the day to the hatters. Through these appeals the major portion of the amount was collected, and in the summer of 1917 the case was settled for a total of something over $234,000, of which amount the American Federation of Labor furnished $216,000.[1]

The most significant feature of this case is that it was an action against individual members of the hatters' union, who were sued not as representatives of the union but by reason of their individual membership. Only 2 of the 197 defendants were prominent in the union; nearly all the others had no active part in the boycott. Many of them had not attended a union meeting for years and testified that they did not even know of the existence of the boycott. They were sued solely because they were union members and had property not exempt from execution. At the outset, their savings accounts and homes were placed under attachment. In the final wind-up, they lost their savings accounts, and their homes were returned to them after they had been under attachment for fourteen years, during which no repairs were made on any of them. The theory upon which these defendants were held responsible will be discussed in later sections of this chapter. At this point, it suffices to note that this suit was an action against individual union members who were held responsible for acts of union officers in which they did not directly participate.

This case has often been regarded as a parallel to the Taff-Vale case in England,[2] in which the House of Lords ruled that a labor union might be sued for damages caused by its officers and agents. This decision led to the enactment of the British Trades' Disputes

---

[1] The judgment with interest amounted to a total of $310,000 but the Loewe Co. was in receivers' hands and, moreover, it was doubtful whether the property attached was worth more than the $234,000 for which the suit was settled.

[2] Taff-Vale Railway Co. v. Amalgamated Soc., (1901) A. C. 426.

Act in 1906, which provides that no damage action may be brought against a trade union or its members for any act committed in behalf of the union. The American counterpart of this British case was a suit not against the union as an entity but against individual members and, while it aroused a similar outcry, has never resulted in any legislation. Unlike the Taff-Vale case, the Danbury hatters case is still the law.

THE CORONADO CASE

Involving even larger sums, and for many years promising to become a second Danbury hatters case was the Coronado case,[1] before the federal courts from 1914 to 1927. The happenings preliminary to this damage suit have been recited in the preceding chapter.[2] Eight affiliated mining companies of western Arkansas breached a trade agreement and became involved in a strike, in connection with which they procured an injunction from the federal courts and attempted to operate their properties with strike breakers and armed guards. District 21 of the United Mine Workers met these tactics by supplying the strikers with firearms and ammunition, whereupon the plaintiffs instituted contempt proceedings against the strike leaders. This led to an attack on the mines by the strikers and their sympathizers, the killing of some of the employees, the driving off of the rest, and the setting fire to the properties. Subsequently, the mining companies went bankrupt, and the receiver brought suit for treble damages under the Sherman Antitrust Act against the national organization of the United Mine Workers, District 21, and certain individual union members who were directly involved in the troubles described. The total amount sued for was $2,200,000.

The defendants entered a demurrer, claiming that no case was made out under the Sherman Act, since mining is not interstate commerce. This demurrer was sustained by the District Court,

---

[1] Reported decisions in this case are the following: Dowd v. United Mine Workers, 235 Fed. 1 (1916), 242 U. S. 653 (1917); Coronado Coal Co. v. United Mine Workers, 258 Fed. 829 (1919); United Mine Workers v. Coronado Coal Co., 259 U. S. 344, 42 Sup. Ct. 570 (1922); Finley v. United Mine Workers, 300 Fed. 972 (1924); United Mine Workers v. Coronado Coal Co., 268 U. S. 295, 45 Sup. Ct. 551 (1925).

[2] See pp. 113–114.

but reversed upon appeal by the Circuit Court of Appeals. Then the case came on for trial, and a jury in 1918 awarded $600,000 damages to the plaintiffs, which, with attorneys' fees, costs, and interest, brought the entire amount of the judgment to $745,600. This award was sustained by the Circuit Court of Appeals but, in 1922, was reversed by the U. S. Supreme Court, with directions sending the case back for new trial.

This decision, though heralded by the United Mine Workers as a great victory, was denounced by Samuel Gompers in unmeasured terms.[1] The explanation is that there were in this decision features both favorable and unfavorable from labor's point of view. The court held that, upon the evidence presented, no case was made out under the Sherman Act, and that the evidence fell short of connecting the national organization of the United Mine Workers with any of the unlawful acts in western Arkansas. The court, however, also held that unincorporated labor unions may be sued as entities, and further, that the responsibility of District 21 was clearly established.

After the Supreme Court's decision, came a new trial in the District Court, at which time the plaintiffs presented additional testimony to prove that the defendants' acts amounted to a substantial interference with interstate commerce. The trial judge did not believe this evidence to be sufficiently strong and directed a verdict for the defendants. From this direction, an appeal was taken which culminated in what is usually called the "second Coronado decision" of the Supreme Court; reversing a part of its former decision on the ground that the evidence now presented did make out a case under the Sherman Act.

Again the case went back for a new trial, which this time resulted in a disagreement. For a fourth time, a jury was impaneled, but before another trial could be held, a settlement was reached in October, 1927. Under this settlement, District 21 paid to the plaintiffs $27,500,[2] each side paying its own costs.

---

[1] In the *A. F. of L. Weekly News Letter*, June 10, 1922, Gompers is quoted as saying: "This decision means that big business has won its objective in its long campaign for trade-union incorporation . . . These laws are no longer necessary. The Supreme Court of the United States has arranged matters to suit the convenience of big business, which can hereafter turn its strike breaking over to the judiciary."

[2] *Baltimore Sun*, Oct. 14, 1927, and other newspapers of this date.

These are believed to have amounted to over $100,000, so that, as a final result of the long litigation, the coal companies received considerably less than the amount they expended in the suit. In the course of the litigation, however, the U. S. Supreme Court had held that, under the provisions of the federal antitrust acts and also on principle, unincorporated labor unions may be sued as entities and that treble damages may be recovered in certain circumstances under the antitrust laws for acts of interference with mining or manufacturing.

OTHER DAMAGE SUITS

The Danbury hatters case and the Coronado Co. case are by no means the only damage suits against labor unions. The author has a list of 314 cases in which damages were sought against unions or their members for acts committed by, or on behalf of, the union. About two-thirds of these were actions in tort; the rest, suits in equity, in which the plaintiff asked for an accounting for damages already sustained as well as for an injunction to prevent future injury. Not all were suits by employers; many were brought by non-unionists or expelled union members. A few were suits by third parties who in some manner were injured through strikes or other union activities.

The more than three hundred damage suits against labor unions or their members were premised upon a great variety of acts claimed to have been illegal. Most of them grew out of strikes or threats of strikes. Damages to property through acts of violence, losses of business profits through illegal strikes, and the destruction of goodwill and established relations have all figured in damage suits by employers; and a considerable number have been premised upon boycotts. Non-unionists and former union members have generally sued for damages resulting from loss of employment caused by the action of the union, but at times for insurance rights and other privileges of union membership; and there have been a few cases where damages were claimed for personal injuries, such as assaults and libelous statements. The amounts sued for have ranged from a few hundred dollars to several millions.[1]   Most of these damage suits were brought

---

[1] The largest suit ever brought against a labor union appears to have been the action started in 1924 by members of the National Erectors Association and the Iron League in New York City against the structural iron workers'

in the state courts and were based upon the general principles of the law of torts and agency. Only five out of the entire number were brought under the Sherman Antitrust Act, but among these were the Danbury hatters case and the Coronado case. The advantage which the Sherman Act affords to plaintiffs is that it allows treble damages; the disadvantage, that interference with interstate commerce, as well as an actionable wrong against the plaintiffs, must be established.[1]

One of the earliest of labor cases was a damage suit, the Thompsonville Carpet Weavers case in 1834, which is included in the early American labor cases reported in Commons and Gilmore's "Documentary History of American Labor." There were at least thirty-three damage suits against unions or their members before 1900, including eleven in which the plaintiffs recovered damages. Since then, there have been damage suits every year, but with no tendency toward an increase in numbers. If there has been any concentration it was in the five or six years following the first decision of the U. S. Supreme Court in the Danbury hatters case in 1908; and there have been fewer successful suits in the last ten years than in the preceding decade.

A large proportion of these damage suits were never brought to trial. It would seem that damage suits are often started as a bluff or to tie up the union funds during strikes and then quietly dropped when the difficulty is over. And only very rarely is the demand for damages pressed when this is made in a suit for an injunction. There have been, however, at least sixty-six cases in which damages were recovered from labor unions or their members.[2] In addition, there are fifteen cases in which the plaintiffs were held to have a cause of action upon their pleadings, but whose final outcome is unknown to the author.

---

union, in which total damages of $5,000,000 were asked. The union met this suit by a counterclaim for $10,000,000 (*Toledo Union Leader*, July 4, 18, 1924).

[1] Under the federal antitrust laws, damages cannot be recovered in the same action in which an injunction is sought. While these acts give injured parties the right to sue for an injunction and also the right to claim treble damages, these remedies may be obtained only by separate proceedings, one in equity, the other at law. Decorative Stone Co. v. Building Trades Council, 23 F. (2nd) 426 (1928) (certiorari denied, 277 U. S. 594, 48 Sup. Ct. 530 [1928]).

[2] See Appendix D for a complete list of these cases.

Only a few of the numerous damage suits against labor unions can be discussed here in any detail. One of the most lengthy of these was the suit of the Pennsylvania Mining Co. v. United Mine Workers, District 21,[1] which closely paralleled the Coronado case. Like that case, it arose in Arkansas in 1915, was premised upon a strike in which there was much violence, and was brought under the Sherman Antitrust Act. In the first trial, an award of $300,000 damages, plus costs and attorneys' fees, was allowed. Thereafter it came twice before the Circuit Court of Appeals and once before the U. S. Supreme Court, once also being retried. In the end (May, 1929), the plaintiffs took a non-suit and paid all of the costs.

Another case involving the United Mine Workers was Southern Illinois Coal Co. v. United Mine Workers, District 12.[2] While this suit never came to trial, it appears to have cost labor a larger sum than the Danbury hatters case. This action grew out of the Herrin, Ill., massacre of 1922, in which a mob of union sympathizers killed twenty-two employees of the plaintiff company and destroyed its mines. When the company sued District 21 for treble damages under the Sherman Act, it purchased the property of the plaintiffs for a price reported in excess of $700,000, although the mines were worth only between $200,000 and $300,000, doubtless because it feared that the plaintiffs might recover the even greater amount sued for.

A more recent successful damage suit was that of Alden Brothers v. Dunn,[3] in which the plaintiffs were milk distributors and the defendants a union of milk-wagon drivers of Boston. In this case, the trial court awarded more than $63,000 damages for losses sustained through an alleged illegal strike. The Massachusetts Supreme Court affirmed this decision in 1928, with a slight reduction in the judgment. As the union had no substantial funds, the plaintiffs began action to attach the wages

---

[1] Reported decisions in this case are to be found in 300 Fed. 965 (1924), 266 U. S. 630 (1924), 28 F. (2nd) 851 (1928). For additional information upon this case, see Law and Labor, May, 1920, and November, 1924. The final outcome was reported in an Associated Press dispatch of May 29, 1929.

[2] 6 Law and Labor 295; Milwaukee Jour., July 3, 1923.

[3] 264 Mass. 355, 162 N. E. 773 (1928). The account of the final outcome given is from Freedom in Employment (published by the Milwaukee Employers' Council), December, 1928.

of all of its members. This led to a settlement for $35,000, of which $5,000 was paid in cash and the balance raised through an assessment upon the members of the union.[1]

Aside from these, there have been only a few cases involving the recovery of any large amounts.[2] In a 1923 Alabama case,[3] a union member wrongfully expelled from a local of the Brotherhood of Locomotive Engineers was allowed $12,500 as damages for his expulsion. An unreported and undefended case in New York City resulted, in 1926, in the allowance of $25,000 to a non-unionist who sued the furriers' union for keeping him out of employment.[4] In a 1922 Connecticut decision,[5] a manufacturer of non-union hats was awarded $5,139 as damages for losses sustained through a boycott. A suit for damages along with an injunction in a St. Louis federal case in 1920 culminated in a stipulation under which the defendants paid $8,250 to the plaintiffs.[6] In no other case were the damages recovered in excess of $5,000, and in only ten other cases did the amounts recovered exceed $1,000.

HOW UNIONS MAY BE SUED

While the total number of successful damage suits is much larger than is generally known, the fears expressed after the Supreme Court's decision in the Danbury hatters case have not

---

[1] Other cases in which judgments rendered against unions were recovered from the individual members are: Patterson v. Building Trades Council, 11 Pa. Dist. 500 (1902); Patch Manufacturing Co. v. Capeless, 79 Vt. 1, 63 Atl. 938 (1906); and Hanson v. Innis, 211 Mass. 301, 97 N. E. 756 (1912). In the last-mentioned case this fact does not appear in the reported decision, but Frederick W. Mansfield, Boston, attorney for the defendants, advised the author that after judgment was rendered the plaintiff attached the houses of some of the individual union members, whereupon the union paid in full.

[2] Besides the cases mentioned in this paragraph, $50,000 damages were awarded by a jury in a Colorado case in 1923, but this award was set aside upon appeal and the case remanded for a new trial in Order of Railway Conductors v. Jones, 78 Colo. 80, 239 Pac. 882 (1925).

[3] Grand International Brotherhood of Locomotive Engineers v. Green, 210 Ala. 496, 98 S., 569 (1923).

[4] Joe Cohen v. Furriers' Union, *N. Y. Times*, Sept. 2, 1926.

[5] R. & W. Hat Shop, Inc., v. Sculley, 98 Conn. 1, 118 Atl. 55.

[6] Langenberg Hat Co. v. United Cloth Hat and Cap Makers, 262 Fed. 127 (1920). Facts about settlement from 11 *Monthly Labor Rev.* 195 (1920).

materialized. Damage suits have not destroyed labor unions nor driven them into secrecy, nor have they proved by any means as serious as have injunctions. The reasons why the dire predictions have not come true are mainly two: (1) procedural difficulties in suing labor unions and (2) inability under the established principles of agency law to connect unions or their members with alleged unlawful acts.

At common law, unincorporated associations can neither sue nor be sued,[1] and nearly all labor unions are unincorporated. In the absence of statutes or decisions modifying the common-law rule, unions are not legal entities and have no existence apart from their members. It is the members and not the union that must be sued for acts done by, or in, its behalf. The union funds belong to the members or are held in trust for their benefit and probably can be levied against only when all of the members are shown to have been responsible for the unlawful acts complained of. Since most unions have a large membership, it is practically impossible to join all of them in a single suit, where each must be served individually and his responsibility for the alleged unlawful acts established upon a personal basis. Under the common-law rule, hence, union funds are for practical purposes exempt from execution.

This rule has been modified by statutes or decisions in fourteen states to allow suits against unincorporated associations in their common name. These fourteen states are Alabama, California, Connecticut, Louisiana, Maryland, Michigan, Missouri, Montana, Nevada, New Jersey, South Carolina, Texas, Vermont, and Virginia.[2] In five other states, statutes permit

---

[1] St. Paul Typothetae v. Bookbinders, 94 Minn. 351, 102 N. W. 725 (1905); Pickett v. Walsh, 192 Mass. 572, 78 N. E. 753 (1906); Tucker v. Eatough, 186 N. C. 505, 120 S. E. 57 (1923); District 21 v. Bourland, 169 Ark. 796, 277 S. W. 546 (1925).

[2] The following states expressly authorize suits against unincorporated associations in their usual name: Alabama, Code 1928, ss. 5723–5728; Connecticut, G. S. 1918, s. 5611; Maryland, Annot. Code 1924, art. 23, s. 104; Michigan, Howell's Stats., s. 13558; Missouri, Rev. Stats. 1919, s. 1186; New Jersey, 3 Comp. Stats. p. 4064; South Carolina, Civ. Code 1922, s. 5070; Texas, Vernon's Stats. 1914, art. 6149 (in San Antonio Fire Fighters v. Bell, 223 S. W. 506 [1902], this statute was held to authorize suits against unions only when property interests are at stake); Vermont, Gen. Laws 1917, s. 1743; Virginia, Code 1924, s. 6058. California (Deering's Code of

unions to be sued by starting the action against the union officers or selected members as representatives of the entire membership: New York, Ohio, Rhode Island, Washington, and Wisconsin.[1] In all other states, there are either no statutes or Supreme Court decisions upon the manner of suing unincorporated associations or, more frequently, it is settled law that unions cannot be sued through either of the two methods. Even where such decisions have been rendered, if objection is not made before the case is tried, the defendants cannot later raise the point that unincorporated unions cannot be sued in their common name.[2] But if timely objection is made, any such suit must be dismissed in the courts of more than half of all states.

In the federal courts, the contrary rule has prevailed, since the U. S. Supreme Court in the first Coronado case[3] in 1922 held that unincorporated unions can be sued in their common name. This decision was based squarely upon grounds of public policy, the court holding that, although no law expressly authorizes such suits and the common-law rule is to the contrary, the recognition of unions as entities in many statutes according them privileges requires that they should also be treated as

Civil Procedure 1923, s. 388) and Montana (Rev. Codes 1921, s. 9089) have narrower statutes authorizing only suits against unincorporated associations engaged in business, but in both states the courts of final jurisdiction have held that these statutes authorize suits against unincorporated labor unions: Vance v. McGinley, 39 Mont. 46, 101 Pac. 247 (1909); Armstrong v. Superior Ct., 173 Cal. 341, 159 Pac. 1176 (1916). Similar statutes in Minnesota and Nebraska were held not applicable to labor unions: St. Paul Typothetae Co. v. Book Binders, 94 Minn. 351, 102 N. W. 725 (1905); Cleland v. Anderson, 66 Neb. 252, 92 N. W. 306, 96 N. W. 212, 98 N. W. 1075 (1902). Nevada has a statute authorizing unincorporated associations to be sued through representative members (Rev. Laws 1912, s. 5001), but in Branson v. I. W. W., 30 Nev. 270, 95 Pac. 354 (1908), this statute was held to authorize suits against such associations in their common name. Louisiana (Marr's Rev. Code of Practice 1927, p. 114) authorizes suits against voluntary associations in their common name "on any obligation incurred for the benefit of the association."

[1] New York, General Associations Law, ss. 12–13; Ohio, Throckmorton's Code 1929, s. 11257; Rhode Island, Gen. Laws 1923, s. 5190; Washington, Remington's Code and Stats. 1915, s. 190; Wisconsin, Stats. 1929, s. 260.12.

[2] United Mine Workers v. Cromer, 159 Ky. 605, 167 S. W. 891 (1914); Barnes v. Typographical Union, 232 Ill. 402, 83 N. E. 932 (1908).

[3] United Mine Workers v. Coronado Coal Co., 259 U. S. 344, 42 Sup. Ct. 570 (1922).

entities when claims are made against them. The prestige of the U. S. Supreme Court is such that the state courts might reasonably be expected to follow this conclusion. No such tendency, however, has been discernible to date. No state Supreme Court which had not previously held unincorporated unions to be suable has since followed the lead of the U. S. Supreme Court. Likewise, efforts made by the League of Industrial Rights and other employers' associations since the World War to secure the enactment of statutes allowing unions to be sued in their common name have resulted in the enactment of but one additional statute of this kind.[1]

CONDITIONS OF LIABILITY

Having cleared the procedural hurdle (which in many states is insurmountable), the plaintiff employer or non-unionist still has the burden of establishing the responsibility of the defendants for the alleged unlawful acts. Where the unions cannot be sued as entities, this involves proving that all individual members were responsible for these acts. Even where unions can be sued in their common name or through representative members, it is doubtful whether it is not necessary to prove the responsibility of all members before the union funds can be touched. This is the position of the New York Court of Appeals,[2] which regards the statute of that state allowing unions to be sued through their officers as merely a method of getting the union into court, but as not altering the rule that the union is responsible only if each individual member is responsible. And even the U. S. Supreme Court in the Coronado case did not expressly hold unions to be entities distinct from their members, although this is perhaps implied.

The responsibility of unions as entities (where they are so regarded) and of their members for unlawful acts allegedly committed in their behalf must be determined in accordance with the general principles of agency law. A relationship of principal and agent must be established between the union and its members

---

[1] Alabama enacted such a law in 1921. The Massachusetts legislature passed the same measure in 1922, but this was carried to a referendum and defeated by a narrow majority.

[2] Schouten v. Alpine, 215 N. Y. 225, 109 N. E. 244 (1915); People *ex rel.* Solomon v. Brotherhood of Painters, 218 N. Y. 115, 112 N. E. 752, (1916).

on the one hand, and those who personally committed the unlawful acts on the other. Such a relationship can be established either on the grounds of antecedent authorization or subsequent ratification. Unions and their members are liable for unlawful acts committed in behalf of the union when they have directly or indirectly authorized these acts in advance of their commission. Again, they are liable, although these acts were not authorized in advance, if they subsequently ratified them by expressing approval thereof or by accepting without protest the benefits resulting therefrom.

These general principles are not peculiar to labor law; they appeal to everyone's sense of justice. In their application to concrete situations in labor cases, however, serious questions of public policy arise, as illustrated by the two most famous of damage suits, the Danbury hatters and the Coronado cases. In the former, although many members had not attended a union meeting for years and testified under oath that they knew nothing about the boycott, the Supreme Court found both antecedent authorization and subsequent approval of the unlawful boycott by the individual members sued in that the constitution of the union directed the officers to make every possible effort "to unionize the trade," which the court regarded as a euphemistic way of saying that they might institute boycotts against non-union manufacturers. It found subsequent approval in the continued union membership of the defendants after the boycott had been repeatedly discussed at union meetings and in the union journal. The denial of the defendants that they had actual knowledge of these acts was held immaterial, on the theory that under the circumstances they must or ought to have known about them. In the Coronado Coal Co. case, on the other hand, the Supreme Court found neither antecedent authorization nor subsequent ratification of the acts of violence on part of the international organization of the United Mine Workers but did find antecedent authorization by District 21. The evidence in this case was to the effect that the strike in which the acts of violence sued upon were committed was mentioned in the *United Mine Workers' Journal* and was discussed in speeches by the national president of the union, in a manner which might be interpreted as inciting, or at least sanctioning, violence. Since, however, under the national constitution this was a purely local strike, for which no sanction by the national officers was necessary, the court held that the national union had not authorized the unlawful acts. Because it did nothing to indicate approval of these acts (except the vague references in the speeches of the national president), it was held not to have subsequently ratified it. District 21, which conducted and financed the strike, whose officers furnished the firearms used in the attack upon the mines, and which paid the attorneys who defended the men guilty of the acts of violence, on the other hand, was held to be responsible for the damages resulting from these acts.[1]

The Danbury hatters and the Coronado Coal Co. cases are the leading decisions upon the conditions under which unions and their members may be held liable for unlawful acts alleged to have been committed in their behalf, but the same problem has arisen in a considerable number of more obscure cases. As yet, however, the precise limits of responsibility have been defined only vaguely.

With regard to the liability of unions as organizations, the most important question is: When is a union which undertakes a strike liable for acts of violence occurring thereafter? One view is that the union is liable for all of the violence, even when proof is lacking that it was committed by union members. A little milder is the position that the union is responsible for all acts of its pickets. The most liberal opinion holds unions responsible only when they deliberately, as organizations or through their officers, inaugurate campaigns of violence, or if, subsequent to their commission, they ratify the unlawful acts of individual members and sympathizers, through furnishing attorneys to fight their cases in court, paying their fines, or failing to discipline or expel such members.[2]

---

[1] In 32 *Yale Law Jour.*, 59–65 (1922), the Supreme Court's decision is criticized on the assumption that the court holds District 21 liable solely because it sanctioned the strike. There is language in the decision which suggests that this fact alone was sufficient to establish liability, but the court no doubt had in mind all of the facts of the situation, which included not merely the calling of the strike but the furnishing of the firearms and almost direct incitation to violence by certain district officers.

[2] In the following cases (some of which involved injunctions, others actions in tort) unions were held responsible for unlawful acts committed during strikes because they inaugurated and controlled the picketing although there was no proof that these acts were committed by pickets: Union Pacific v.

With reference to the liability of the individual members of unions, the crucial question is whether continued membership is of itself sufficient proof that they sanctioned the unlawful acts committed in behalf of the union. Upon this point, as upon practically every other phase of the general question of the liability of unions and their members, there are conflicting court decisions. Cases have arisen in which liability by reason of membership alone was asserted on the conspiracy theory, under which all parties to the conspiracy are chargeable with the unlawful acts done by any of their number in pursuance of the unlawful object. There are other cases in which the same conclusion was reached upon the assumption that violence is a natural by-product of all strikes. A larger number of decisions have held that something more than mere union membership is necessary to establish liability. There must be proof that the members had knowledge of the unlawful acts and in spite of them continued payment of union dues.[1] But even this doctrine leaves union

---

Ruef, 120 Fed. 102 (1902); Jones v. Maher, 62 Misc. 388, 116 N. Y. S. 180 (1909) (affirmed in 125 N. Y. S. 1126); Clarkson v. Laiblan, 202 Mo. App. 682, 216 S. W. 1029 (1919); Herkert & Meisel Trunk Co. v. United Leather Workers, 268 Fed. 662 (1920); U. S. v. Railway Employers' Dept., 283 Fed. 479 (1922). *Contra:* Cumberland Glass Manufacturing Co. v. Glass Blowers, 59 N. J. Eq. 49, 46 Atl. 208 (1899).

On the following cases the union was held liable because it failed to discipline members guilty of unlawful acts: Southern Ry. Co. v. Machinists, 111 Fed. 49 (1901); Franklin Union v. People, 220 Ill. 355, 77 N. E. 176 (1906); Alaska S. S. Co. v. International Longshoremen's Assoc., 236 Fed. 964 (1916); Kroger Grocery and Baking Co. v. Retail Clerks, 250 Fed. 890 (1918); Nederlandsch, etc., v. Stevedores, 265 Fed. 397 (1920); United Traction Co. v. Droogan, 115 Misc. 672, 189 N. Y. S. 39 (1921); Great Northern Ry. Co. v. Local Great Falls Lodge, 283 Fed. 557 (1922). In Hillenbrand v. Building Trades Council, 14 Ohio Dec. 628 (1904), the union was held liable because it paid the fines of members guilty of acts of violence.

[1] All members were held responsible for unlawful acts committed in behalf of the union on the theory that all were engaged in a common conspiracy in U. S. v. Debs, 64 Fed. 724, 762 (1894); Dayton Manufacturing Co. v. Metal Polishers, 11 Ohio Sys. and C. P. Dec. 643 (1901); Gulf Bag Co. v. Suttner, 124 Fed. 467 (1903); and in Patch Manufacturing Co. v. Protection Lodge, 77 Vt. 294, 60 Atl. 74 (1905). Mere membership in the union was held sufficient to establish liability for unlawful acts in behalf of the union: O'Neil v. Behama, 182 Pa. 236, 37 Atl. 843 (1897); Illinois Central R. R. Co. v. International Association of Machinists, 190 Fed. 910, 911 (1911);

members in a most hazardous situation. Under it, a man with property may be held responsible for the unlawful acts of others, simply because he continued his union membership after it became known to him, or after he should have known, that unlawful acts were being committed in behalf of the union. To such a union member, the choice may be one between giving up his insurance in the union, to which he may have contributed for years, and losing his job, or taking a chance upon being mulcted in damages for the unlawful acts committed in behalf of the union; but, however serious the practical consequences may be to him, many cases assert that to avoid liability he must give up membership as soon as his union engages in any unlawful acts.

THE FUTURE OF THE DAMAGE SUIT

The present status of the law regarding the liability of labor unions and their members is satisfactory to no one. There are distinct possibilities that under the doctrines announced in many cases, including the decisions of the U. S. Supreme Court in the two leading cases, unions may be destroyed in the future. As the law stands, both the union and its members may be held responsible, without limit, for unlawful acts committed in behalf of the union. There is no limited liability for union members as for stockholders in corporations.

The existing situation is no more satisfactory to employers. The possibilities expressed in the preceding paragraph have existed now for twenty years; yet employers have been able to collect substantial damages from unions or their members in comparatively few cases. Employers have spent far more in attorneys' fees and court costs in trying to collect damages from unions and their members than they have realized in damages. Despite the Coronado decision, it is still impossible to sue unincor-

---

Nalty v. Local Union 65, 5 *Law and Labor* 307 (Fed. 1923). To much the same effect is Church Shoe Co. v. Turner, 218 Mo. App. 516, 279 S. W. 232 (1926). Among the larger number of cases holding the opposite are Schneider v. Local Union 60, 116 La. 270, 40 So. 700 (1905); Lawlor v. Loewe, 187 Fed. 522 (1911); Hill v. Eagle Glass Manufacturing Co., 219 Fed. 719 (1915); Michaels v. Hillman, 112 Misc. 395, 183 N. Y. S. 195 (1920); Diamond Block Coal Co. v. United Mine Workers, 188 Ky. 477, 222 S. W. 1079 (1920).

porated labor unions in many jurisdictions. Likewise, despite the conspiracy doctrine and the loose application of principles of agency law in labor cases, it is most difficult to hold either the union or its members for unlawful acts. For these reasons, the League of Industrial Rights has advocated the enactment of legislation allowing unincorporated unions to be sued in their common name but has made little headway with this proposal. The prospect that employers will find damage suits the most powerful of all weapons against labor unions seems as remote as ever.

To the legal profession, the view that it ought to be possible to sue labor unions precisely as corporations may be sued has always had a strong appeal. Louis D. Brandeis, one of labor's most sincere friends, some thirty years ago, before he became a Supreme Court Justice, advocated the incorporation of unions.[1] More recently, Professor Berman and others have urged that the Coronado decision is really a boon to the labor unions, as it will allay all talk about the irresponsibility of unions and give them a convincing argument against the allowance of injunctions in labor disputes.

Organized labor has not taken kindly to these suggestions. In the 1880's, labor championed incorporation laws, apparently in the belief that incorporation would give unions legal recognition and remove all doubts regarding the legality of their normal activities. Laws permitting the incorporation of unions were passed in most of the states, but, after they had been placed upon the statute books, labor changed front and few of the unions incorporated. From regarding incorporation as a relief from its dangerous legal position, the unions have passed to thinking of incorporation as a measure for completely shackling them. They fear not only suits by employers, but still more, suits by members in matters of discipline and expulsion and concerning pension and other benefits. Nor have the unions taken kindly to the present-day suggestions that the union be regarded as a unit apart from its members. They see in the Coronado decision what amounts to compulsory incorporation, without a statute to that effect. And for all that has happened to date, labor's position cannot be described as contrary to its own interests,

---

[1] For a statement of the position of Justice Brandeis, see his article Incorporation of Labor Unions in 15 *Greenbag* 11–14 (1903).

though the time may come when labor unions will prefer to be treated as entities readily suable.

Bibliographical Note

There is no satisfactory account of damage suits against labor unions and their members, particularly of their actual results. The legal questions of the suability of unions and of liability for unlawful acts committed in their behalf are most adequately dealt with in Oakes, "Organized Labor and Industrial Conflicts," pp. 49–51, 97–128 (1927). Sayre, "A Selection of Cases and Other Authorities on Labor Law," pp. 517–553 (1922), reprints most of the leading decisions in this field. Commons and Andrews, "Principles of Labor Legislation," pp. 129–133 (1927 ed.), summarizes the principles of liability and briefly discusses their social consequences.

Worth while articles on the legal aspects of the damage suit include: T. Megaarden, The Danbury Hatters' Case, Its Possible Effect on Labor Unions, 49 *Amer. Law Rev.* 417–428 (1915); The Coronado Coal Company Case, 32 *Yale Law Jour.* 59–65 (1922); Felix Frankfurter, The Coronado Case, 31 *New Republic* 328–330 (1922); K. B. McGill and F. Roswell, The Suability of Labor Unions, 1 *North Carolina Law Rev.* 81–94 (1922); Francis B. Sayre, The Coronado Decision, 48 *Survey* 385–386 (1922); G. C. Fay, The Coronado Coal Case and Its Consequences, 8 *Iowa Law Bull.* 162–176 (1923); W. A. Sturges, Unincorporated Associations as Parties to Actions, 33 *Yale Law Jour.* 383–405 (1924); Civil Liability of Members of Unincorporated Labor Unions, in 42 *Harvard Law Rev.*, 550–555 (1929); Zechariah Chafee, Jr., The Internal Affairs of Associations Not for Profit, 43 *Harvard Law Rev.* 993–1029 (1930).

The position of employers on the suability of unions and their liability for unlawful acts committed in their behalf is best presented in the statement "Proposed Legislation on Public Policy and Industrial Warfare," submitted in 1919 by the League of Industrial Rights to the (President's) Industrial Conference. Taking much the same position, but representing a research study rather than the mere statement of a program, is F. R. Black's Should Trade Unions and Employers' Associations Be Made Legally Responsible? published by the National Industrial Conference Board as *Special Report* 10 in 1920.

Labor's views are perhaps best shown in the symposiums on the Danbury hatters case in 15 *Amer. Federationist* 161–179, 354–364 (1908) and in the editorial by Samuel Gompers, Is Shylock Satisfied? in 22 *Amer. Federationist* 105–108 (1915).

On the question of the compulsory incorporation of unions there are two symposiums, now more than twenty-five years old, but still the best presentations of both sides of this question. One of these is a debate before the Boston Economic League participated in by Louis D. Brandeis and Samuel Gompers, which is reported in the Boston newspapers of Dec. 5, 1902 (the address of Brandeis on this occasion is reprinted in 15 *Greenbag* 11–14 [1903]). The other was published in the first issue of the *National Civic Federation Review* in 1903. Another valuable discussion is Part

III of the *Report* of the Massachusetts Bureau of Statistics for 1906, pp. 125–144, which besides presenting opinions upon the question of the incorporation of labor unions gives a digest of the laws then in force on this subject in all states and in foreign countries. Articles dealing with the legal aspect of this question are Eug ne Wambaugh, Should Trade Unions Be Incorporated? in 15 *Greenbag* 260–265 (1903), and C. G. Walter, Incorporation of Labor Unions, in 68 *Albany Law Jour.* 68–70 (1906). A good statement of labor's position occurs in an interview with P. M. Draper on Why Labor Unions Do Not Favor Incorporation Idea, published in *Labor*, Dec. 21, 1929.

An eighteen-page "List of References on the Legal Responsibility of Trade Unions" was issued in November, 1924, by the Library of Congress.

CHAPTER VIII

CRIMINAL PROSECUTIONS

Injunctions have received so much attention that many well-informed people do not realize that other legal remedies figure in labor disputes. Yet criminal prosecutions are far more numerous, bring more workmen before the courts, result in a much larger number of fines and sentences of imprisonment, and are almost as potent a cause of discontent.

NUMBER OF ARRESTS

The number of arrests and prosecutions on criminal charges is astonishing. No one has ever attempted to ascertain the number of persons arrested in any really great American strike, but an examination of contemporary newspapers will convince anyone that it runs into the thousands. For some smaller strikes, the totals are definitely known. In the ladies garment workers' strike in New York City in 1926, which involved about 40,000 people, there were 7,500 arrests in the first fifteen weeks. The New York furriers' strike in the same year led to 884 arrests and 477 convictions. The New Bedford textile workers' strike in 1928 was featured by more than 2,000 arrests on criminal charges. The strike against the Allen A Hosiery Company at Kenosha, Wis., in 1928 and 1929, which involved only a few hundred employees, many of them women, resulted in 800 arrests. In the short strike in New York City in 1929 fomented by the Needle Trades Workers Union, a left-wing organization, there were 65 arrests on Feb. 7, 63 on Feb. 8, and 250 on Feb. 11; and in the textile workers' strike at Elizabethton, Tenn., later in the same year, there were 300 arrests on a single day.[1] Similar totals might be cited for many other strikes.[2]

---

[1] The figures given in this paragraph on the arrests on the ladies garment workers' strike in New York City in 1926 are taken from 8 *Law and Labor* 302; those for the furriers' strike from the *New York Times*, Apr. 27, 1927 (8 *Law and Labor* 184 gives the number of arrests in this strike as one thousand); the New Bedford strikes figures from the *Report* of the American Civil Liberties Union, The Fight for Civil Liberty (1928–29); those for the New York needle trades' strike from the *New York Times*, Feb. 8, 9, 12, 1929; and for the Elizabethton strike, from the *New York Times*, May 15, 1929.

[2] In the ladies garment workers' strike in Chicago in February, 1917, there were 1,400 arrests among the 2,500 strikers (24 *Amer. Federationist*

PROSECUTION CHARGES

The charges upon which the arrests are made are many and various. Few of them have occurred under statutes relating particularly to labor disputes. Of all the laws discussed in Chap. IV, only the federal antitrust and mail statutes, the Colorado antipicketing law, and the several state antisyndicalism laws have been invoked in recent labor troubles, the last mentioned only against the Industrial Workers of the World and the Communist organizations, never against the railroad brotherhoods or the unions affiliated with the American Federation of Labor.[1]

A great many arrests and prosecutions have occurred under the general felony statutes, for such offenses as treason, sedition, conspiracy, murder, dynamiting, kidnaping, extortion, criminal libel, rioting, inciting to riot, assault, malicious mischief, and unlawful assembly. Treason is a crime almost unknown to this country and is thought of as occurring only in times of war, but there have been arrests and trials for treason growing out of labor disturbances in recent years in both West Virginia and North Carolina, and earlier in Pennsylvania and Ohio.[2] Pro-

---

373 [1917]). In the men's clothing industry strike in Chicago in 1919, there were 1,150 arrests in four weeks (*A. F. of L. Weekly News Letter*, June 21, 1919). In a series of small strikes in St. Louis in the last five months of 1913, there were 2,400 arrests (*Report* of Special Agent R. S. Brennan to the U. S. Commission on Industrial Relations). In the Paterson silk workers' strike in the same year, there were 2,238 arrests and 300 convictions (*Final Report U. S. Commission on Industrial Relations* p. 67 1915]).

[1] There were over five hundred prosecutions under the California antisyndicalism law between the date of its taking effect, Apr. 30, 1919, and Aug. 1, 1924 (Study by Dean George W. Kirchwey, reported in 57 *Survey* 494 [1927]); and while probably no other state approached these totals, there were numerous prosecutions in the years following the war in all twenty-three states and territories which have antisyndicalism laws. From 1924 to 1929, these laws were little used, but within the last year, there has been a revival of prosecutions of communists under antisyndicalism laws in many states: Back to Red Hysteria, 63 *New Republic* 168–169 (1930); Seiler, Cantaloupes and Communists, 131 *Nation* 243–244 (1930).

The antipicketing statute of Colorado was made the basis for many arrests in the Colorado coal miners' strike of 1913 and again in the I. W. W. strike in the southern Colorado coal fields in October, 1927.

[2] No less than fifty-four men were indicted for treason in connection with the march from union coal fields in West Virginia to the non-union fields in Logan County in 1921, but only a few of these were ever brought to trial.

secutions for conspiracy, the principal legal actions in connection with labor disputes until the injunction came into general use about 1890, now occur chiefly in connection with the federal antitrust and mail statutes.[1] Charges of "rioting" and "inciting to riot" are exceedingly frequent in labor troubles, as are indictments for assault or murder.[2]

In the leading case, that against William Blizzard, president of a subdistrict of United Mine Workers, District 17, which engineered this march, the jury acquitted, but in a subsequent case, one William Allen was convicted ("The United Mine Workers in West Virginia," brief of the bituminous operators' special committee submitted to the U. S. Coal Commission Aug., 1923; and *Chicago Tribune*, Apr. 24, 1922). Alfred Hoffman, organizer for the United Textile Workers of America, and four others were tried for treason at Marion, N. C., in November, 1929, but were acquitted on direction of the court after the prosecution had presented its evidence (Associated Press dispatch Nov. 22, 1929). Numerous indictments for treason were returned against participants in the Homestead, Pa., strike in 1892 (23 *Pittsburgh Legal Jour.* n. s. 106). One Joseph Kobylak, a local coal miners' union secretary, was arrested for treason at Dillonville, Ohio, in 1914, and held for months in jail, but he was never brought to trial; and a few months thereafter the same charge was brought against Joseph J. Ettor, I. W. W. leader, at St. Clairville, Ohio, with the same outcome (Testimony of Joseph Kobylak in *Final Report and Testimony, U. S. Commission on Industrial Relations* 10, 513–534, and *Report* of Special Agent Patrick Gill to the United States Commission on Industrial Relations, on the Kobylak case). Charges of sedition were brought against four officials of the Amalgamated Textile Workers' Union at Paterson, N. J., in 1919, but were dismissed by Supreme Court Justice Minturn (42 *Survey* 751 [1919]).

[1] For a discussion of the criminal prosecutions under the antitrust and mail statutes, nearly all of which charged a conspiracy to violate these laws, see pp. 70–71, 75–77. Other reported cases involving criminal prosecutions for conspiracy include: Pettibone v. U. S., 148 U. S. 197, 13 Sup. Ct. 542 (1893); State v. Dyer, 32 Atl. 814, 67 Vt. 690 (1895); People v. Davis, 30 *Ch. Leg. News* 212, Feb. 19, 1898; State v. Kidd, Municipal Ct., Oshkosh, Wis. (1898) (*U. S. Labor Bull.* 23, 575–579); People v. Radt, 71 N. Y. S. 846 (1900); State v. Stockford, 77 Sup. Ct. 227, 58 Atl. 769 (1904); People v. McFarlin, 89 N. Y. S. 527 (1904); People v. Yannicola, 117 N. Y. S. 381 (1909); People v. Davis, 159 App. Div. 464, 30 N. Y. Crim. 270 (1914); People v. Curran, 286 Ill. 302, 121 N. E. 637 (1919); People v. Seefeldt, 141 N. E. 829, 310 Ill. 441 (1920); People v. Raymond, 296 Ill. 599, 130 N. E. 329 (1921); Taylor v. U. S., 2 F. (2nd) 444 (1925); People v. Makvirta, 231 N. Y. S. 279 (1928).

[2] Reported cases growing out of prosecutions for felonies alleged to have been committed in labor disputes, in addition to the Haywood, McNamara, Mooney, and other famous cases discussed later in this chapter, and those

The majority of arrests in labor disputes, however, have been made not for grave felonies but for petty misdemeanors. Some of these have been premised upon state statutes; a larger number, upon local ordinances. Favorite charges under state statutes are disorderly conduct, obstructing traffic, disturbing the peace, trespass, and intimidation. Prosecutions under local ordinances are directed at picketing,[1] loitering, the holding of gatherings without permits, the unauthorized distribution of handbills, and a long list of other activities, some of them almost ludicrous.[2]

---

involving charges of conspiracy listed in the preceding note, include the following:

Murder or Conspiracy to Murder: People v. Schmidt, 33 Cal. App. 426, 165 Pac. 555 (1917); Richardson v. People, 69 Col. 155, 170 Pac. 189 (1918); Venable v. State, 156 Ark. 564, 246 S. W. 860 (1922); State v. Stafford, 89 W. Va., 301, 109 S. E. 326 (1921).

Rioting: People v. Brown, 193 App. Div. 203, 38 N. Y. Crim. 518 (1920); Bolin v. State, 139 N. E. 659, 193 Ind. 302 (1923).

Kidnaping: Hackbarth v. State, 229 N. W. 83 (Wis. 1930).

Extortion and Conspiracy to Extort: People v. Mader, 313 Ill. 277, 145 N. E. 137 (1924); People v. Walsh, 322 Ill. 195, 153 N. E. 357 (1924); People v. Barondess, 16 N. Y. S. 433, 133 N. Y. 649 (1892); People v. Walczak, 315 Ill. 49, 145 N. E. 660 (1924); State v. Kramer, 31 Del. 454, 115 Atl. 8 (1921).

Malicious Mischief: State v. Schliefer, 102 Conn. 708, 130 Atl. 184 (1925).

Unlawful Assembly: State v. Butterworth, 104 N. J. Law, 579, 142 Atl. 57 (1928); McGehee v. State, 23 Tex. Ct. of App. 330 (1887).

[1] Under an antipicketing ordinance adopted by Los Angeles in 1910, there were 472 arrests in the metal workers' strike in that year (Letter of Prof. Ira Cross of the University of California to the U. S. Commission on Industrial Relations, Jan. 18, 1915). Other antipicketing ordinances were adopted in San Francisco (1916), Oakland (1916), Portland (1916), El Paso (1917), Noblesville, Ind. (1917), Anniston, Ala. (1917), San Diego (1919), Indianapolis (1919). A somewhat similar ordinance against loitering was enacted by Boston in 1916. The antipicketing ordinance of Los Angeles was sustained as constitutional in *in re* Williams, 158 Cal. 550, 111 Pac. 1035 (1910), and that of El Paso in *ex parte* Stout, 198 S. W. 967 (Tex. Civ. App. 1917), while the Portland ordinance was held unconstitutional in Hall v. Johnson, 87 Ore. 21, 169 Pac. 515 (1917).

[2] An Indianapolis ordinance which prohibited signs placed over or across streets without a permit was made the basis for police-court prosecutions of pickets in 1916 who carried placards on their backs calling attention to a labor-union boycott (*Indianapolis News*, Jan. 19, 1916). Andrew McAndrew, president of the International Tobacco Workers' Union, which gives some small insurance benefits to its members, was in 1919 arrested at Winston-Salem, N. C., on the charge of selling insurance without a license

PETTY CRIMINAL PROSECUTIONS

The misdemeanors mentioned, for which the greatest number of arrests are made in strikes, are not indictable offenses and are punishable by fines only, but they have given rise to many complaints by labor impugning the fairness of the police, the prosecutors, and the judges. The police (including sheriffs and their deputies) are charged with arbitrary and unwarranted arrests and brutal treatment of strikers and strike sympathizers. Against the public prosecutors and the police magistrates, charges are made that they demand excessive bail, prosecute and convict upon insufficient evidence, and impose excessive penalties.

Employers, too, have their complaints. They claim that local authorities often deliberately blink at acts of disorder and intimidation by strikers and strike sympathizers or deal with them so leniently that they are encouraged to commit more serious crimes. Far from being dealt with unfairly, persons guilty of misdemeanors during strikes, they insist, have been pampered by public officials fearful of the labor vote.

Numerous illustrations can be cited in support of every charge made by labor, and on the other hand there is no doubt that peace officers and police magistrates have in some strikes favored the strikers. This country is so large and the criminal prosecutions in connection with labor disputes so little studied that no generalizations can be made.

Illustrative of the wrongs of which strikers have often been victims is the steel strike of 1919. The Senate Committee on Education and Labor, after an extensive investigation of this strike, reported:

Apparently there have been cases of unoffending men and women arrested without reason by the officers, put in jail, and in some cases fined by magistrates without warrant or justification . . . As to the complaint of the action of the courts, we are inclined to believe that there is some ground for complaint and that the action of the magisterial courts in the taking of bonds and the forfeiting of bonds, in the arrest of people merely as suspicious characters and in sending them to jail therefor has not in every instance been justifiable.[1]

because he attempted to organize the tobacco workers (*A. F. of L. Weekly News Letter*, Mar. 29, 1919).

[1] 66th Cong., 1st Sess., *Sen. Rept.* 289, pp. 24–25. Another account of the prosecutions in the steel strike is S. Adele Shaw's Closed Towns: Intimidation as It Is Practiced in the Pittsburgh Steel District—the Contrast in Ohio, 43 *Survey* 58 (1919).

Much the same story can be told of other conflicts. In the Paterson silkworkers' strike in 1913, bonds of $500 to $2,000 were demanded from each of the hundreds of strikers arrested on the charge of unlawful assembly. As this strike was conducted by a weak "outlaw" union, the bonds could not be furnished and many of the strikers were kept in jail for weeks and months, without being brought to trial. Of the 2,238 men arrested, however, some 300 were convicted, all without a jury trial, as New Jersey does not allow jury trial for misdemeanors. Yet in this strike, involving some 25,000 workmen, the total property damage amounted to less than $25.[1]

In the strike of waitresses employed by the Philip Henrici Company, Chicago, in 1914, there were 153 arrests, although Judge McGoorty, who conducted extensive hearings upon this strike, in connection with an application for an injunction, said that "it is admitted that no acts of violence were committed by any of the pickets." Bail amounting to as high as $1,400 was demanded from some of those arrested, and the only one of the entire number brought to trial was acquitted.[2]

Little violence accompanied the Lawrence textile strike in 1912; nevertheless, 224 strikers were arrested and most of them convicted, principally on charges of "rioting." In one day during this strike, a police magistrate sentenced thirty-four strikers to a year in prison after giving but five to ten minutes' consideration to each case, and, when the attorney for the convicted men served notice of an appeal, held each of them under $800 bonds. The Massachusetts Supreme Court, after review-

---

[1] The facts set forth in this paragraph are based upon the *Final Report, U. S. Commission on Industrial Relations*, p. 67, (1915), an unpublished report made by Special Agent R. S. Brennan on this strike to this commission, and an article by Rabbi Mannheimer, Darkest New Jersey, 74 *Independent* 1190–1192 (1913).

In addition to the prosecutions for misdemeanors, a considerable number of prosecutions were instituted against the leaders of the strike for felonies, which resulted in convictions subsequently set aside upon appeal: State v. Scott, 86 N. J. 133, 90 Atl. 235 (1914); State v. Boyd, 87 N. J. L. 328, 560, 94 Atl. 807; 86 N. J. L. 75, 91 Atl. 586; 87 N. J. L. 328, 93 Atl. 599 (1915); Quinlan v. State, 87 N. J. L. 333, 93 Atl. 1,086 (1915).

[2] This strike was investigated by Miss Nelle B. Curry, a special agent for the U. S. Commission on Industrial Relations. The decision of Judge McGoorty of the Superior Court of Cook County in the injunction case on Apr. 6, 1914, throws additional light on the criminal prosecutions.

ing these cases, dismissed several of the defendants and reduced the sentences upon the others to fines of $15 to $20.[1]

Trials of persons arrested on petty charges are few, and convictions fewer. Twenty-four hundred arrests in St. Louis strikes in the autumn of 1913 which were investigated by a special agent of the U. S. Commission on Industrial Relations culminated in less than fifty convictions. On one day during the ladies garment workers' strike in New York City in 1926, according to the *New York Times*, the police made four hundred eighty arrests, out of which number only twenty were fined small amounts.[2] These instances are somewhat extreme, but it is safe to say that less than one-half of the persons arrested during strikes are convicted. This may mean either that they are wrongfully arrested or that the prosecutors and magistrates are unduly lenient, the one alternative inevitably resulting in resentment against government and the other in contempt for government.

Especially antagonizing are long periods in jail awaiting a trial which never takes place. Although the unions customarily furnish bail for all their members and supporters, when large numbers are arrested some of them must stay in jail for a considerable time before the mechanics of getting them released can be completed. Further, bail bonds, attorneys' fees, court costs, and fines place a heavy strain upon the union treasury which many a weak union has been unable to stand. In the New York furriers' strike in 1926, the bonds in the nearly nine hundred arrests totaled $903,000.[3] Instances can be cited of workingmen arrested on petty charges and kept in jail for months because they could not furnish bail, only in the end to be released without

---

[1] An account of the action of the police magistrate referred to is given in 28 *Survey* 509 (1912), in which this appropriate comment is made: "The haste, the heavy bail, and the long sentences all seem to have the earmarks of disciplinary strike measures, rather than judicial decisions upon the merits of the case." For the final outcome of these cases, see Kate H. Claghorn's "The Immigrant's Day in Court," pp. 271–283 (1923).

[2] The statements on the arrests and convictions in the St. Louis strikes in 1913 are based upon the investigation made by Special Agent R. S. Brennan for the U. S. Commission on Industrial Relations; the account of one day's arrests in the ladies' garment workers' strike from the *New York Times*, Sept. 14, 1926.

[3] 8 *Law and Labor* 184.

trial.[1] Not only have the victims of such procedure a just grievance for erroneous imprisonment, but the fact that the charges upon which they were arrested were never cleared up may prevent their finding reemployment.[2]

Meriting comment as another aspect of the many arrests which characterize labor troubles is the fact that very often the same persons are arrested over and over again. These are not always brawlers, but often union organizers whose real offense is their effort at organization. Thus, two organizers who figured in the injunction case U. S. v. Armstrong, at Indianapolis, were within a period of sixty days in the early summer of 1926 arrested no less than fifty-six times on charges of loitering and vagrancy, but not once so much as fined.[3] Again, in many strikes immigrants constitute an unduly large percentage of persons arrested, not because they are peculiarly lawless, but because of their foreign birth.[4]

MAJOR FELONY CASES

Despite the great number of petty criminal prosecutions and the many complaints concerning them, the less numerous major felony cases have been responsible for much wider dissatisfaction among workingmen. Practically every great strike and many lesser ones have had their aftermath of such cases, but it is the less than a dozen big trials which principally account for

---

[1] In the metal workers' strike in Los Angeles in 1910, several of the pickets were kept in jail for fifty-six days because they could not furnish bail and then were released without being brought to trial (*San Francisco Bull.*, Jan. 10, 1911).

[2] This fact was stressed by the district attorney in Boston in 1912, when he made a formal motion to dismiss all charges pending against workingmen who participated in the strike on the elevated lines in that city. In making this motion, he stated that the company had refused to reemploy anyone who had been arrested, although the charges were never brought to trial.

[3] Testimony of former Governor Groesbeck of Michigan in the Senate Hearings on "Limiting Scope of Injunctions," p. 227 (1928). For somewhat similar experiences of a common workman, see the testimony of Joseph Kobylak in *Final Report and Testimony, U. S. Commission on Industrial Relations*, 10, 513–534.

[4] This was noted by the U. S. Senate Committee on Education and Labor in its report on the steel strike of 1919 (66th Cong. 1st Sess., *Sen. Rept.* 289), with the comment: "The foreigners whom the industries bring among us cannot be dragooned into love for America and loyalty to its institutions."

a widespread belief among workmen that the criminal law is all too often made use of to discredit and destroy labor organizations.[1] During the last quarter century, there never has been a time when at least one such case was not before the public, attracting nation-wide attention and arousing both sympathy and resentment.

The first of these in the present century was the Haywood-Moyer-Pettibone case, which involved the principal officers of the Western Federation of Miners[2] and grew out of the killing in 1905 of former Governor Steunenberg of Idaho by a bomb planted at his home by one Harry Orchard. After arrest, this

---

[1] At least one case prior to the turn of the century attracted quite as much attention as any of those discussed in the text. This was the Chicago anarchist case in 1886, which originated in the throwing of a bomb among a squad of policemen who were engaged in the suppression of a riot on the Haymarket Square. For this crime, eight anarchists, some of whom were rather prominent in the labor movement in Chicago, were convicted of murder on the theory that they were responsible for the crime by inciting the workmen to violence. Seven of these men were sentenced to death, but one of them committed suicide and two others had their sentences commuted to life imprisonment. These two and the eighth man, who was sentenced to fifteen years' imprisonment, were in 1893 pardoned by Governor Altgeld. The governor's account "Reasons for Pardoning Fielden, Neebe, and Schwab," is a powerful presentation of the viewpoint that the evidence against the anarchists was wholly inconclusive and that they did not receive a fair trial, while the reply by the presiding judge Joseph E. Gary, "The Chicago Anarchists of 1886: the Crime, the Trial, and the Punishment," is perhaps the best statement to the opposite effect. Organized labor never took up the cause of the anarchists but suffered from being identified with them in popular opinion.

[2] Haywood was the secretary-treasurer and Moyer the president of the Western Federation of Miners. Pettibone had long been prominent in the organization but, at the time of the murder, lived in retirement. Besides these, one Jack Simpkins, member of the executive board of the Western Federation of Miners for Idaho, was charged with actual participation in the bombing but fled and was never apprehended. Steve Adams, named by Orchard as a confederate in all his crimes, and who first signed a confession in corroborating Orchard, which he later repudiated, was tried for murder in both Idaho and Colorado, but in the end cleared of all charges.

The best accounts of this case are the articles by Luke Grant, Idaho Murder Trial, 85 *Outlook* 805–811 (1907) and The Haywood Trial: A Review, 86 *Outlook* 855–862 (1907). Orchard's confession was published in several installments in *McClure's Mag.* in 1907 (Vol. 29, pp. 294–306, 367–379, 507–529, 658–672 and Vol. 30, pp. 113–129) and Darrow's great plea for Haywood, in *Wayland's Monthly* in October of that year.

assassin turned state's evidence and gave an account of bombings and murders committed by him and a confederate under the direction of the three union leaders mentioned, extending over a period of six years and resulting in at least twenty-one deaths. As these union leaders were in Denver when former Governor Steunenberg was killed, it was doubtful whether they could have been legally extradited, but extradition papers were secretly obtained and the three men rushed by special train to Idaho, without opportunity to apply for a writ of habeas corpus. This "kidnaping" feature of the case was appealed to the U. S. Supreme Court, but that court held that no federal right was infringed in the mode of their being brought into Idaho.[1]

Each of the defendants demanded a separate trial, and the first to be tried was Haywood. This trial lasted for months and gave national reputations to Senator Borah, special counsel for the state, and Clarence Darrow, the leading defense attorney. On behalf of the prosecution, evidence presented to corroborate the Orchard confession included proof that the officers of the Western Federation of Miners arranged for his defense before his real name was known or anyone had suggested that labor troubles had anything to do with the murder. The defense on its part charged a counterconspiracy by the mine owners' association to destroy the Western Federation of Miners, and the manufacture of false evidence by detectives against the accused union officers.[2] A jury of farmers and ranchmen acquitted Haywood, and thereafter Pettibone was tried and acquitted, and Moyer released without trial.

The next famous case growing out of labor troubles, the McNamara case, started much like the Haywood affair but had a very different ending.[3] In 1910, a bomb exploded in the *Los*

---

[1] Pettibone v. Nichols, 203 U. S. 192, 27 Sup. Ct. 111 (1906).

[2] Steunenberg, as governor, had ordered out the militia in the Coeur d'Alene miners' strike in 1899. Both Orchard and Simpkins had been involved in this strike and the former imprisoned in the "bull pen." It was the theory of Darrow for the defense that Orchard and Simpkins murdered Steunenberg as a matter of private revenge, while the prosecution claimed that this was but one of the many acts of violence instigated by the officers of the Western Federation of Miners to intimidate all who opposed them.

[3] Upon the McNamara and structural iron workers' cases, the most nearly impartial accounts are the article by John A. Fitch, The Dynamite Case, 29 *Survey* 607–617 (1913), the report by Luke Grant, The National Erectors

Angeles Times building killed ten people. Organized labor was at once suspected because the Los Angeles Times and its publisher, General Harrison Gray Otis, were among its most determined opponents, and some months later J. J. McNamara, secretary-treasurer of the International Structural Iron Workers, was arrested as the instigator of this crime and his brother, J. B. McNamara, and one Ortie McManigal as the persons who planted the bomb. As in the Haywood case, the principal defendant was far from the scene of the crime at the time of its commission and likewise was legally "kidnaped" at his office in Indianapolis and rushed to California without opportunity to apply for a writ of habeas corpus. This "kidnaping," plus the fact that McNamara and his union were in the best of standing with the American Federation of Labor and the knowledge that the case against the accused was being worked up by William J. Burns and his force of private detectives, aroused a great outcry from labor that this was another plot by the "open shoppers" to destroy the labor unions. The American Federation of Labor itself undertook to raise a defense fund, and Clarance Darrow once more was employed as principal defense counsel.[1] When the case came on for trial, after the jury had already been selected, however, the McNamaras pleaded guilty and were sentenced to life imprisonment.

The true reasons for the unexpected plea of guilty by the McNamaras were not known until, some months later, fifty-four members of the structural iron workers' union, including all of its general officers and the officials of many of its largest locals, were indicted by a federal grand jury at Indianapolis for conspiracy to transport dynamite interstate. These indictments, it developed at the trial which followed, were premised upon a confession by Ortie McManigal, in which he recounted that he

---

Association and the International Association of Bridge and Structural Iron Workers, published by the U. S. Commission on Industrial Relations in 1915, and the symposium on the Larger Bearings of the McNamara Case, 27 *Survey* 1407–1436 (1911). *Bulletins* 25 and 30 of the National Association of Manufacturers, entitled, respectively, The Crime of the Century and Its Relation to Politics (1912) and Deeds against Words (1913), and McManigal's Own Story: The National Dynamite Plot (1913) are the principal accounts from sources hostile to labor.

[1] Following McNamara's plea of guilty, Darrow was tried and acquitted of attempted bribery of a juryman.

and J. B. McNamara were employed by the structural iron workers' union, with the full knowledge and active assistance of its officers, to blow up bridges and other structures erected by members of the National Erectors Association, with which the union was engaged in a life-and-death struggle over recognition. According to the confession, this conspiracy, extending over a period of more than six years, led to 102 bombings in various parts of the country. Yet during the entire campaign no one was killed until the *Los Angeles Times* explosion.[1] The MeManigal confession was supplemented by documents seized in a raid on union headquarters at Indianapolis, which established conclusively the existence of a great dynamite conspiracy.[2] After a long trial, thirty-eight of the forty-five union officers actually tried were convicted and all of them sentenced to prison, the longest terms being for seven years. Some of them were granted new trials by the Circuit Court of Appeals, after which their cases were dismissed.[3] Twenty-five served prison sentences, after which some of them were reelected to their old positions.

The next case on a par with the Haywood and McNamara cases in the interest aroused was the Mooney case in San Francisco.[4] The principal defendant, Tom Mooney, was a local

[1] According to McManigal, the *Los Angeles Times* explosion was not a part of the structural iron workers' dynamite campaign but was engineered by the San Francisco building trades unions, which felt its hold upon San Francisco slipping because Gen. Harrison Gray Otis had made Los Angeles a 100 per cent open-shop town. The loaning of J. B. McNamara to the San Francisco unions to do this bombing job was the only connection of the structural iron workers with the crime.

[2] According to Luke Grant, *op. cit.*, pp. 105–106, detectives of the Burns Agency followed McManigal and J. B. McNamara around on their last ten bombing jobs, and H. S. Hockin, a member of the international executive board who was elected secretary-treasurer when J. J. McNamara pleaded guilty in the Los Angeles trial, made regular reports to the Burns Agency upon all contemplated bombings during 1910 and 1911.

[3] The U. S. Circuit Court of Appeals decision is reported in Ryan v. U. S., 216 Fed. 13 (1914). Matthew A. Schmidt and David Caplan, who assisted J. B. McNamara in the *Los Angeles Times* bombing, escaped arrest until 1915, when they were in separate trials in Los Angeles convicted of participation in the murder. The conviction of Schmidt was affirmed in People v. Schmidt, 33 Cal. App. 426, 165 Pac. 555 (1917).

[4] The following reported decisions relate to this case: People v. Billings, 34 Cal. App. 549, 168 Pac. 396 (1917); People v. Mooney, 175 Cal. 666,

union leader of decidedly radical leanings but in good standing as a member of the molders' union. The case grew out of a bomb explosion during a preparedness parade in 1916, which killed ten marchers and bystanders and injured fifty others. Five people were indicted for this crime, and, in the trials which followed, two of them, Mooney and Billings, were convicted and the former sentenced to be executed, upon the evidence of a considerable number of witnesses who claimed to have seen them with the suitcase in which the fatal bomb was planted near the scene of the crime, within a few minutes previous thereto.

This case did not at first arouse much interest in labor circles, despite the fact that the convicted men made the claim that the real motive of the prosecution was that they had incurred the enmity of the public utilities and other antiunion employing interests of San Francisco through their radical labor activities. Before their appeals had been disposed of by the Supreme Court, evidence was unearthed which cast much doubt upon the reliability of the prosecution witnesses. This doubt has become stronger with the lapse of years, practically every witness against the convicted men having by this time either repudiated his testimony or had his integrity seriously impeached. By 1918, Judge Griffin, who conducted the trial, asked the Attorney-general and the Supreme Court of California to grant a new trial and has since been a most active leader in the movement to secure a pardon for the convicted men. Every one of the

166 Pac. 999 (1917); 176 Cal. 105 (1917), 177 Cal. 642, 171 Pac. 690 (1918); 178 Cal. 525, 174 Pac. 325 (1918).

A good presentation of the evidence in behalf of Mooney is the publication of the Tom Mooney Molders Defense Committee, San Francisco, "Pardon Tom Mooney," the latest edition of which was issued in 1929. Other accounts favorable to the defendants are the report of the President's Mediation Commission on the Mooney case, January, 1918, reprinted in 64 *New Republic* 72–74 (1930); *House Doc.* 567 of the 66th Cong., 1st Sess., on Connection of Certain Department of Labor Employees with the Case of Thomas J. Mooney (1919); John A. Fitch, The San Francisco Bomb Cases, 38 *Survey* 305–312 (1917); and Duncan Aikman, Justice: California Brand, 155 *Outlook* 530–533, 557–558 (1930). Literature on the other side is scant. "Review of the Mooney Case," by John M. Olin, published privately at Madison, Wis., in 1919, is perhaps the best. F. R. Welch, "America's Greatest Peril: the Bolsheviki and the Mooney Case," privately published, 109 S. Fourth St., Philadelphia, is an attempt to establish that the agitation for Mooney's pardon originates with the Bolsheviki in Russia.

jurymen has joined in the petition for a pardon, as has the present prosecuting officer of the city and county of San Francisco. Organized labor, which was at first indifferent, if not hostile, has come to look upon the Mooney imprisonment as a labor case, and every convention of the American Federation of Labor since 1922 has adopted resolutions asking for a full pardon. All appeals for a pardon, however, have thus far been of no avail, although the death sentence on Mooney was commuted to life imprisonment in 1918, at the request of President Wilson, after a commission he named to investigate this case, headed by Secretary of Labor William B. Wilson, reported that there were grave doubts regarding the guilt of the convicted men. The most determined efforts to gain a pardon have been made since Governor Young, a reputed liberal, took office in 1927, but these culminated in failure in 1930 after the State Pardon Board and the Supreme Court, upon review of the cases of Mooney and Billings, respectively, made recommendations against pardons.

No other case of the present century has attracted such wide attention in labor circles as these three, but there have been many others in which large defense funds were raised by nation-wide appeals and which were discussed for months in all of the labor papers.[1] Of these, only the wholesale prosecutions grow-

---

[1] The Sacco-Vanzetti case attracted as much attention as the Haywood, McNamara, and Mooney cases but implicated labor only to the extent that the accused were Italian workmen who had attained some local prominence in I. W. W. strikes. The crime for which these men were convicted was the murder of a paymaster and pay-roll guard at South Braintree, Mass.; motive, robbery. These men were executed in 1927, six years after their conviction, during which interval, great interest was aroused in their case among liberals throughout the country as facts were brought to light casting doubt upon their guilt and indicating that the doomed men were convicted because they were foreigners, draft evaders, and radicals. Many labor unions and labor leaders contributed funds to the defense committee and joined in the unsuccessful petitions at first for a new trial, later for a pardon, but the prime movers in the great efforts to save these men were intellectuals, not labor people. For a good account of this case, see Felix Frankfurter: "The Case of Sacco and Vanzetti," Little, Brown & Company, Boston (1927); for opposite conclusions regarding the innocence of the defendants, see the decision of Governor Fuller in refusing a pardon, reprinted in 61 *Amer. Law Rev.* 944–949 (1927).

Less well-known criminal prosecutions growing out of labor troubles which attracted something like nation-wide interest include, besides the cases discussed in the text:

ing out of the Colorado coal miners' strike of 1913–1914, the West Virginia mine troubles of 1919–1922, and the Herrin massacre of 1922 will here be discussed.

1. The Sam Parks case in New York City in 1903, a conviction for graft of the president of the New York Building Trades Council. For an account of this case, see the article by Hayes Robbins, The New York Building Trades Paralysis of 1903, 9 *Amer. Jour. of Sociology* 755–767 (1904).

2. The Ettor Giovanatti case in 1913, in which the leaders in the I. W. W. strike of the textile workers at Lawrence, Mass., were charged with murder on the theory that they incited violence. This trial ended in acquittal after the defendants had been kept in jail without bail for months. A good account of this case is the article by James P. Heaton, The Salem Trial, 29 *Survey* 301–304 (1912–1913).

3. The Wheatland riot case, arising out of riots in August, 1913, among the hop pickers in California, in which four men were killed. Two I. W. W. leaders were convicted of this murder and sentenced to life imprisonment, which sentences were affirmed in People v. Ford, 25 Cal. App. 388, 143 Pac. 1075 (1914).

4. The Carl Persons case, in which the editor of a labor paper at Clinton, Ill., was tried in 1914 for the slaying of a strike breaker but was acquitted on grounds of self-defense (*Chicago Tribune*, Sept. 20, 1914; *Chicago Daily News*, Oct. 5, 1914).

5. The New York cloak makers' murder trial. Seven members of the International Ladies Garment Workers Union, including Morris Sigman, the secretary-treasurer of the international union, were in 1915 arrested for the murder of a non-union cloak maker during the cloak makers' strike in 1910. After being kept in jail for twelve weeks, they were released on $120,000 bonds and upon trial were acquitted (*Inter. Ladies Garment Workers Jour.*, pp. 4–8, June, 1915; *United Mine Workers Jour.*, p. 9, June 15, 1916).

6. In the Calumet copper strike in northern Michigan in 1913, there were seven hundred arrests, the great majority of them on felony charges. After the strike, thirty-seven strike leaders, including President Moyer and Vice President Mahoney of the Western Federation of Miners, were indicted for conspiracy. These men, however, were never brought to trial, and in May, 1915, the indictments were dismissed (*Miners Mag.*, Feb. 14, 1914, and June 3, 1915; *Chicago Tribune*, May 18, 1915).

7. Chicago graft cases. There have been many criminal prosecutions for graft against Chicago labor leaders throughout the last fifteen years. The most important of these, however, occurred in 1915–1916, when fifty-four labor leaders were indicted for extortion and graft, fourteen of whom were convicted. For accounts of these cases, see the Chicago newspapers during this period, particularly in the first part of December, 1915, and in June–July, 1916.

8. The Everett I. W. W. trials. These grew out of a clash between deputy sheriffs and I. W. W. in a "free-speech fight" at Everett, Wash., in the summer of 1916, in which seven men were killed. Seventy-four members of the I. W. W. were indicted for murder; all were released after

The Colorado strike was an unusually bitter contest, during which at least seventy-four persons were killed. Much of this

---

Thomas Tracy was tried and acquitted in 1917. See the articles by Miss Anna L. Strong in 37 *Survey* 475–476; 38 *Survey* 160–162 (1917).

9. The Centralia I. W. W. cases. These grew out of an attack by American Legionaries on the I. W. W. hall at Centralia, Wash., on Armistice Day, 1919, in which a number of persons were killed. Ten members of the I. W. W. were tried for murder in connection with this difficulty in 1920, and seven of them were convicted and sentenced to from twenty-five to forty years in prison. Since then, seven jurors have joined in a petition to the governor for a pardon, stating that the jury verdict was a compromise brought about by fear that the defendants would .otherwise be lynched. The Washington Federation of Labor has also joined in the request for a pardon, although none of the men involved are "regular" unionists, but all but one man (who was released August, 1930) are still in jail. For a brief review of this case, see the editorial The Centralia Case Again, 62 *New Republic* 340 (1930).

10. San Francisco carpenters' strike cases. Several hundred strikers were arrested on various charges in connection with the San Francisco carpenters' strike in 1926. Five men were sentenced to long prison terms, while forty-two were fined or received prison sentences. (Information from Paul Eilel, director of Industrial Relations Department of the Industrial Association of San Francisco.)

11. The North Carolina cases in 1929–1930. There have been several distinctly criminal prosecutions in connection with the textile workers' strike at Gastonia and Marion. At Gastonia, in the "outlaw" strike of the National Textile Workers' Union, seventy-one of the strikers were indicted for the murder of Police Chief Aderholdt and the wounding of several others in a riot in the summer of 1929. Seven of these men, all communists, were convicted of second-degree murder and assault in October, 1929, and given long prison sentences. Thereafter an appeal was taken and the defendants released on bond, whereupon they fled to Russia and escaped having to serve their sentences.

At Marion, the strike was conducted by the United Textile Workers of America, an A. F. of L. organization. Alfred Hoffman, an organizer for this union, and four others were in November, 1929, tried for treason, but the charge was dismissed by direction of the judge. Thereafter, Hoffman and three others were tried and convicted on the charge of rioting, and these sentences were sustained by the North Carolina Supreme Court in State v. Hoffman, 154 S. E. 314 (1930).

Besides newspaper accounts, the following magazine articles may be consulted upon these cases: N. B. Lewis, Tar Heel Justice, 129 *Nation* 272–273 (1929); Nelson, North Carolina Justice, 60 *New Republic* 314–316 (1929); Spofford, Marion, North Carolina, 46 *Christian Century* 1502–1503 (1929); Weimar Jones, Southern Labor and the Law, 131 *Nation* 14–16 (1930); L. S. Gannett, Skipping Bail, 131 *Nation* 437–438 (1930).

violence was attributed by the miners to company guards and militiamen, but the only persons indicted were strikers. Of these, a total of 408 were charged with serious felonies, principally murder, but the great majority were never tried. Only four men were convicted, and all four were released after appeal to the Colorado Supreme Court, because of gross irregularities in their trials: conduct of the prosecution in at least one case by attorneys for the coal operators without any participation by the state; refusal by a trial judge who had been an attorney for the prosecution prior to his elevation to the bench to allow the defendants a change of venue; denial of the right of the defense to cross-examine prospective jurymen as to their prejudices and business connections after they had stated that the juries had been deliberately stacked to secure the conviction of the defendants.[1]

The criminal actions growing out of the West Virginia labor troubles[2] were even more numerous, with a greater number of

---

[1] These statements are based upon the decisions of the Colorado Supreme Court in Zancannelli v. People, 63 Col. 252, 165 Pac. 612 (1917), and Lawson v. People, 63 Col. 270, 165 Pac. 771 (1917). The convictions of the other two convicted men were set aside in People v. Richardson, 69 Col. 155, 170 Pac. 189 (1918), this action being based upon a confession of error by a newly elected attorney-general. Frank Swancara, A Prosecution in a "Strike Case," 18 *Jour. Amer. Inst. Criminal Law and Criminology* 539–551 (1928), severely scored the disposition of these two cases, calling it wholly unwarranted and an instance of the common practice of showing favoritism to labor men when accused of crime. Even in this article, however, the statements made in the Zancannelli and Lawson cases concerning the unfair methods of prosecution are not questioned.

Other sources of information upon the Colorado strike cases include the report of President Wilson's Colorado Coal Strike Commission, which was published as *House Doc.* 859, 64th Cong., 1st Sess. (1914); George P. West, *Report on the Colorado Coal Strike*, made to, and published by, the U. S. Commission on Industrial Relations (1915); the extensive hearings on The Colorado Coal Miners' Strike, published in 7 and 8 *Final Report and Testimony, U. S. Commission on Industrial Relations* 6347–7425 (1915); a booklet of the statistical department of the United Mine Workers, "The Lawson Case" (1915); and articles by Martha Gruening, Methods of Law and Order, 3 *New Republic* 200–202 (1915), and John A. Fitch, Law and Order: the Issue in Colorado, 30 *Survey* 241–258 (1914).

[2] "The United Mine Workers in West Virginia," a brief by the Bituminous Operators' Special Committee filed with the U. S. Coal Commission in August, 1923, gives an account of the violence and criminal actions arising therefrom in the West Virginia troubles, from the operators' point of view.

convictions. More than twenty union members were tried for murder for the killing of several private detectives in a fight at Matewan in 1920, claimed by each side to have been provoked by the other. Three hundred two indictments in Boone County and no less than nine hundred in Logan County were returned as a result of the "marches" promoted by the union, from union coal fields to the Logan and Mingo fields in the southern part of the state in 1921, and 230 union men were indicted for an attack upon the Cliftonville mine in northern West Virginia early in 1922. Among the persons indicted and tried were nearly all of the officers of the district organization of the United Mine Workers, as well as most of the subdistrict officials. There were trials for treason, murder, inciting to murder, assault, and other crimes. The majority of these ended in acquittals, but no less than forty-one union men either pleaded guilty or were convicted for the attack on the Cliftonville mine, and there were also a number of convictions growing out of the mine marches, including one for treason and several for murder. No very prominent union man was convicted, but the plethora of criminal actions undoubtedly had something to do with the complete collapse of the United Mine Workers in that state.

The last stages of the West Virginia difficulties were connected with the nation-wide coal strike of 1922. This strike led to an unusually large number of criminal actions, not only in that state but in Illinois, Ohio, Pennsylvania, and elsewhere. A survey made by the Associated Press in October, 1922, disclosed that no less than 631 members of the United Mine Workers were under indictment for serious crimes, of whom 411 were held for murder.[1]

Next to the West Virginia cases, the largest number of indictments have resulted from the Herrin, Ill., massacre, one of the most shocking crimes ever committed in labor troubles. This massacre involved an attack upon some unarmed non-union

---

The report of the U. S. Coal Commission on Civil Liberties in the Coal Fields, published in *Sen. Doc.* 195, Part I, 68th Cong., 2nd Sess., pp. 168–174 (1925); the *Report* of the special Senate investigating committee on the West Virginia Coal Fields (67th Cong., 2nd Sess., *Sen. Rept.* 457) in 1922, and Winthrop D. Lane's booklet "Civil War in West Virginia," B. W. Huebsch, New York (1921), are other sources of information on this strike.

[1] *Milwaukee Jour.*, Oct. 29, 1922.

(or rival-union) men by a mob of strikers and strike sympathizers, who killed nineteen of them. Two hundred fourteen indictments were returned, of which ninety-eight were for murder or conspiracy to murder. Two trials followed, both resulting in acquittal, after which all of the defendants were released.[1]

These strikes will suffice to illustrate the situation with regard to felony cases in labor troubles. Literally thousands of strikers, including many labor leaders, have been indicted on such charges, but comparatively few have been convicted. To labor, this fact is proof that the prosecutions were unjust, while its opponents see in it evidence only that it is very difficult to bring labor criminals to justice; and there is some basis for both opinions, contradictory as they are.

Instances can be cited of unwarranted arrests and prosecutions and even of convictions obtained by unfair methods or on doubtful evidence. Accused workingmen are sometimes handicapped by lack of funds, although as a general rule, particularly where unions have stepped into the breach, the defense seems to have been represented by quite as able counsel as the prosecution. Prejudice, notably in the case of I. W. W.'s and other radicals, is a greater hindrance. In most communities, comparatively few workingmen are chosen for jury duty.[2] Even when selected for the jury panel, they are likely to be stricken by the prosecution.

On the other side of the picture are situations like that of Herrin. While there exist communities with a strong prejudice

---

[1] The best account of the Herrin massacre, which, however, does not deal with the legal cases arising therefrom, is the *Report of the U. S. Coal Commission on Civil Liberties in the Coal Fields*, published in *Sen. Doc.* 195, Part I, 68th Cong., 2nd Sess., pp. 164–168 (1925). Accounts of the legal cases are to be found in *Literary Digest*, Vol. 76, pp. 11–12, Feb. 3, and pp. 48–54, Feb. 10, 1923, and 36 *New Republic* 114–115 (1923).

[2] A survey made by a committee of the Lawyers' Association of Illinois disclosed that out of 3,440 persons selected for jury service in Chicago from Sept. 15, 1913, to March 1, 1914, only 350 were mechanics or other workmen (*Chicago Examiner*, Sept. 6, 1914; *Chicago Tribune*, Oct. 25, 1914).

Workingmen are likely to be inadequately represented on juries wherever they are selected by special jury commissioners or from assessment lists. These methods of selecting juries are very general and are prescribed by statute in most states.

Special complaints have been made by labor regarding the selection of grand juries. According to these accounts, workingmen almost never are chosen for grand juries, even when they are selected for petit-jury service.

against labor organizations, particularly radical ones, some districts are dominated by organized labor. While workingmen may be inadequately represented on juries and handicapped by lack of resources, public prosecutors often fear the loss of labor votes, and judges, because they know they will be subjected to severe criticism, make every possible concession to the defense.

It is thus well-nigh impossible to generalize about the fairness of the major criminal prosecutions growing out of labor cases. There are places where it seems impossible to convict a labor man, and others where a strike leader cannot get a fair trial.

CRIMES AGAINST STRIKERS

Labor claims not only that strikers do not get a fair deal in the courts, but that crimes committed by guards, militiamen, and police officers go unpunished and often unnoticed. Here again it is impossible to generalize. Illustrations can be presented of unpunished crimes against strikers or union leaders. In the North Carolina textile-mill strikes in 1929, Mrs. Ella May Wiggins, a communist, was seized by a mob and murdered, and it was not until Governor Gardner intervened that anyone was indicted for this crime. Then the accused were acquitted, despite much evidence identifying them as participants. The same thing happened in the trial of seven North Carolinians charged with having been among the mob which in broad daylight kidnaped and flogged Ben Wells and two other communists.[1] These are matched by the Barkowski case in Pennsylvania, also in 1929. This concerned a union miner who was arrested by three coal and iron policemen (company guards) and brutally beaten to death because he would not confess to a crime of which he was probably innocent. The coal company is reported to have paid the widow $13,500 damages, but the coal and iron policemen who committed this crime were found guilty only of involuntary manslaughter and sentenced to one year in prison although one of them had previously served a prison sentence for murder.[2] Many earlier illustrations could be given, but only

---

[1] Upon these North Carolina cases, see Weimar Jones, Southern Labor and the Law, 131 *Nation* 14–16 (1930).

[2] This case aroused a great outcry in Pennsylvania against the coal and iron police and led to the enactment of legislation intended to curb the private police system which has long been maintained in the Pennsylvania

the Bisbee, Ariz., deportation cases of the war time, which were investigated by a commission appointed by President Wilson, will be mentioned.[1] These developed from an I. W. W. strike in the copper fields, to end which a local mob seized 1,186 of the strikers (about 30 per cent of whom were members of American Federation of Labor unions) and transported them by train into the desert, where they were left without food until rescued near the point of starvation by a United States army force. Indictments against 25 members of the mob returned by a federal grand jury were dismissed on the ground that no federal question was involved, and of the 210 men indicted in the state courts, only one was ever tried and he was acquitted.[2]

But crimes committed against strikers do not always go unpunished. Only within the last year, a private detective who tried to bribe a union organizer at Passaic, N. J., was convicted and fined $500.[3] There also have been several cases holding employers liable for crimes committed by company guards against strikers, the most recent of which was that of P. T.

---

mine fields. For accounts of this case, see E. E. Ericson, Good Men and True, 60 *New Republic* 292 (1929); *Nation*, Feb. 12, 1930; *Labor*, July 7, 1930.

[1] Two other cases widely discussed in the labor press which should perhaps be noticed were those against John J. Breen, who during the Lawrence Textile Workers' strike in 1912 planted dynamite to discredit the strikers, for which he was only fined, while William H. Wood, president of the American Woolen Co., charged with conspiracy in connection with this crime, was never brought to trial (19 *Amer. Federationist* 817 [1912]); and the failure of a jury to convict two company guards who killed Mrs. Fannie Sellins, organizer for the United Mine Workers at Brackenbridge, Pa., in 1919 (*A. F. of L. Weekly News Letter*, June 16, 1923).

[2] This outrage is reviewed in the report of the President's Mediation Commission published in the *Official Bull. of the Committee on Public Information*, Nov. 27, 1917; 24 *Amer. Federationist* 742–744 (1917); 42 *Survey* 457 (1919); 43 *Survey* 571 (1920); and 139 *Nation* 225–227 (1921). The federal phase of this case is reported in U. S. v. Wheeler, 254 Fed. 611 (1918).

[3] *A. F. of L. Weekly News Service*, Sept. 2, 1929. A reported case involving a successful prosecution for the kidnaping of a strike leader is State v. Newman, 127 Minn. 445, 149 N. W. 945 (1914). Three guards and a deputy sheriff were convicted of manslaughter during the Calumet copper strike in 1913 and given long terms in prison (*Philadelphia Inquirer*, Feb. 16, 1915; *Chicago Herald*, May 18, 1915). Sam Crews, a Baldwin-Felts operative, was convicted of the murder of a union member at Raleigh, W. Va., in 1920, and sentenced to fifteen years' imprisonment (*United Mine Workers Jour.*, Aug. 1, 1920).

Fagan, president of the United Mine Workers, District 5, who recovered $3,000 damages in May, 1929, from the Pittsburgh Coal Corporation because he was arrested without warrant by its coal and iron policemen.[1]

Such actions seem to be on the increase. In recent years, the American Civil Liberties Union, which is not a labor organization but apparently quite closely connected with some of the radical labor groups, has started actions in scores of cases against guards and police officers alleged to have been guilty of unlawful arrests or other criminal acts against strikers.[2] It is becoming a creed of radical labor that the best way to meet interference with union meetings or violence on part of guards and police officers is to start civil suits against the parties responsible for these actions and, where possible, to take out criminal warrants.[3] There is some evidence that more conservative labor unions as well have come to see the advantage in such a course, and it is certainly doubtful whether crimes committed against strikers are any less likely to be punished than crimes committed by them.

CONCLUDING OBSERVATIONS

Little further need be said regarding arrests and prosecutions on criminal charges growing out of labor troubles. Both sides can point to many facts indicating a most unsatisfactory state

---

[1] This case is discussed in *Labor*, May 11, 1929.

Other cases in which employers have been held liable for unlawful acts committed by company guards include Pennsylvania Mining Co. v. Jarnigan, 222 Fed. 889 (1915); Walters v. Stonewell Cotton Mills, 136 Miss. 361, 101 S. 495 (1924); St. Louis S. W. R. Co. v. Hudson, 282 S. W. 257 (Tex. Civ. App. 1926) reversed by Hudson v. St. Louis S. W. R. Co., 293 S. W. 811 (Tex. Com. of App. 1927). In Ruffner v. Jamieson Coal and Coke Co., 247 Pa. 34, 92 Atl. 1075 (1915), an action failed because it was not shown that the defendant corporation which employed the coal and iron policemen had directed them to commit the unlawful acts complained of. Besides these reported cases, there are a number of unreported cases in which damages were recovered from employing corporations on account of unlawful acts against strikers committed by guards in their employ.

[2] Accounts of these cases are given in the *Annual Reports* of this organization, which carry the title The Fight for Civil Liberty, and can be secured from its headquarters in New York City.

[3] This is the thesis of the booklet "Don't Tread on Me!" by Wood, Coleman, and Hays, Vanguard Press, New York (1928), a program of action for radical labor.

of affairs. The great majority of the serious crimes growing out of labor disputes, whether committed by strikers and strike sympathizers or by company guards, militiamen, or policemen, go unpunished. Yet there have been many occasions on which workingmen have been arrested on most flimsy evidence, and some cases where innocent men have been convicted. Police officers have at times pursued anything but a neutral course, favoring now the one side or the other; and sometimes, although less frequently, trial courts have been similarly prejudiced.

Neither side complains of the content of the criminal law. Labor does not argue that there should not be laws against assault and murder, nor even that the statutes against rioting or disorderly conduct should be repealed. Nor do employers claim that the penalties in the criminal law are not adequate. But both are dissatisfied with the administration of the criminal law. Thus, the arrests and prosecutions in connection with labor troubles are but a phase of the larger problem of the enforcement of law and order, which will be further dealt with in the next chapter.

Bibliographical Note

While numerous articles have been written about particular cases (many of which are cited in the notes in this chapter), the only connected accounts of the criminal prosecutions growing out of labor difficulties are a few pages in Fitch, "Causes of Industrial Unrest," pp. 323–340 (1924), and in Kate H. Claghorn, "The Immigrant's Day in Court," pp. 255–296, Harper & Brothers, New York (1923). Plus these, there is a brief discussion of some phases of this subject in the report of the director of research and investigation included in the *Final Report of the U. S. Commission on Industrial Relations*, pp. 64–69 (1915).

The last account is a summary of data gathered by a number of special agents who made field studies of the legal actions arising out of the great strikes of the years 1913 and 1914. The reports of these agents, like practically all other studies of the staff, were never published but were turned over to the U. S. Bureau of Labor Statistics upon the wind-up of the commission. (Several of these reports are cited in the notes in this and the next chapter.) While difficult to get at, these reports are a most important source of information and a good starting point for further studies.

Besides these reports of special agents of the U. S. Commission on Industrial Relations, the articles upon the famous criminal cases which are listed in the notes to this chapter are valuable to students of the subject. Other sources of information are the labor press, the general newspapers, and the original court records. This is a field in which genuine research is much needed and, while difficult, is likely to prove profitable.

CHAPTER IX

LAW ENFORCEMENT

EXTENT OF VIOLENCE

The year 1926 witnessed fewer strikes and workmen involved in strikes in the United States than any previous year for which there are records. In contrast, England had more strikes and more working days lost through strikes than in any other year, with more than eight times as many men implicated as in the United States.[1] For months, more than a million coal miners were on strike, and for ten days in May there was a general strike which paralyzed all industries of the country.

When it comes to violence in connection with strikes, the picture is radically different. In the British general strike, the—for England—unusual course was pursued of operating essential services by "volunteers" and strike breakers. This led to the smashing of a few bus and street-car windows and to some arrests of strikers for calling the volunteers "black legs." But this was the extent of the disorder. From newspaper accounts, it is doubtful whether there was an assault, and certainly no murder or bombing took place.[2] The prolonged coal strike was equally peaceful.

In this country, three strikes of importance were in progress at the time of the British general strike, those of the Passaic silk workers, the New York furriers, and the San Francisco carpenters.[3] The Passaic strike was then in its fourth month,

---

[1] The U. S. Bureau of Labor Statistics reported 329,592 employees involved in strikes in 1926; the British Labor Department, 2,721,000 workmen directly involved in strikes, not counting millions indirectly affected by the general strike.

[2] These statements are taken from the very full accounts of this strike in the *New York Times*, May 4-14, 1926. No English newspapers were published during the strike.

[3] The facts recited in this paragraph regarding the Passaic strike are from 8 *Law and Labor* 106-112, 121-122 (1926); the *New York Times*, Mar. 16, 1916, and July 26, 1926; and the decision of the Court of Chancery

and seldom has any long-drawn-out American strike involving more than ten thousand men been more peaceful, but even here occurred mass picketing on the one hand and police interference with all union meetings on the other. Clashes between strikers and police culminated in bloodshed and a request to the governor for the militia. In the furriers' strike, which involved a smaller number of men and much less time, much more violence prevailed. There were numerous street fights, several mob invasions of plants employing non-union men, raids on the homes of strike breakers, and shooting affrays; 874 arrests were made, 116 of them on a single day. Some months after the strike, the American Federation of Labor, as the result of an investigation which it conducted, laid before Mayor Walker evidence to the effect that the striking furriers had paid large sums to the police officers in two New York precincts; and while this charge must be put down as not proved, it is certain that both sides felt bitter toward the police. In the San Francisco carpenters' strike, 272 assaults were made on non-union carpenters during the first months of the strike, and one non-union man was killed. The union defended every striker and strike sympathizer arrested, and the Industrial Association of San Francisco furnished bonds and attorneys for every strike breaker and guard involved in any difficulty.

Other strikes of this year were similarly turbulent. In the Indianapolis street-car strike, the president of the local union, who was subsequently shown to have been a spy in the employ of the street-car company, publicly told the strikers that the time had come to "cut loose," after which cars were stoned, dynamite placed on the tracks, and passengers injured. At Clarksburg, W. Va., a clash took place between three hundred strikers and state troopers, the latter using machine guns. The plant of the Manville-Jenckes Co. at Pawtucket, R. I., was set

in Furstman and Huffman v. United Front Committee, reported in 8 *Law and Labor* 125. The account of violence in the furriers' strike is from news stories in the *New York Times*, particularly under dates of Mar. 3 and June 4, 7, 21, 1926, and Jan. 15, Apr. 6, 27, 1927, and the article in 8 *Law and Labor* 184 (1926). The San Francisco carpenters' strike story is from Warren Ryder, San Francisco's Successful Labor Plan, 25 *Current Hist.* 539–543 (1927); San Francisco's Labor War, 143 *Outlook* 363–364 (1926), the *New York Times*, Oct. 3, 31, 1926, and the complaint in the case of Barrett and Hilp v. United Brotherhood of Carpenters, 8 *Law and Labor* 320 (1926).

on fire during a strike. In a butcher workmen's strike in Chicago involving a single retail shop, two men were stabbed. The window cleaners' strike in New York City was featured by five assaults on non-union men in its first day, with shooting in front of the Flatiron Building in the heart of the city. In a strike against the Interborough Rapid Transit Co., strikers and the police engaged in a fight which Samuel Untermeyer, counsel for the union, characterized as an unprovoked attack by the police and which the president of the Interborough attributed to the fact that the strikers mistook the plain-clothes men for spies in the employ of the street-car company. In the strike of the paper-box workers, also in New York, formal charges were made by the union to the police commissioner of the alleged brutality of the police in clubbing pickets.[1]

This by no means exhausts the account of the lawless acts in labor disputes committed in 1926, a year of few strikes and relatively little violence. In proof, only the fact need be cited that the militia was not called out in any labor trouble of this year, which is most unusual. For 1927 and 1928, if not for 1929, the record of violence was distinctly longer, and earlier years were much worse.

Yet it is possible to overstate the violence in labor disputes. In many strikes there is no violence of any kind; in numerous others, nothing more serious than a few fights and opprobrious epithets. On the whole, violence in labor disputes has probably decreased since the turn of the century. Despite this, there are

---

[1] The recital of the violence in the Indianapolis street-car strike, and particularly the connection therewith of Harry Boggs, union president and company spy, is derived from the testimony of former Governor Groesbeck of Michigan, counsel for the strikers, W. H. Latta, counsel for the street-car company, and Albert Ward, U. S. District Attorney for Indiana, in Senate Hearings on "Limiting Scope of Injunctions," pp. 225–282 (1928). The Clarksburg, W. Va., clash is from the *Baltimore Sun*, June 23, 1926; the Pawtucket, R. I., disturbance from the *New York Times*, Aug. 31, 1926; the account of the first day of the New York window cleaners' strike from the *New York Times*, Oct. 25, 1926; the violence in the small Chicago butcher workmen's strike from the *Chicago Herald-Examiner*, Sept. 6, 1926; the fight between the strikers and the police in the Interborough Rapid Transit Co. strike and the two versions of this affair from the *New York Times*, July 23, 1926; and the charges regarding police brutality in the paper-box workers' strike from the *New York Times*, Dec. 11, 1926.

still many strikes marked by loss of life and property. Some strikes have developed into a veritable state of civil war, *e.g.*, the Colorado coal strike in 1913–1914 and the West Virginia mine troubles of 1919–1922.[1] During the latter, thousands of armed union miners marched from central West Virginia to the southern West Virginia coal fields, where they were met by forces of company guards and militiamen. Battles ensued, with casualties on both sides. In 1922, several hundred miners from Pennsylvania crossed the state border and attacked the Cliftonville mine in the northern part of the state; and while these lawless acts were being committed in labor's behalf, company guards and public officials, in equal disregard of law, were deporting union organizers and breaking up union meetings.

Sometimes the casualties have equalled those of minor battles. In the Colorado coal strike, as was noted in the preceding chapter, at least seventy-four persons were killed, including thirteen women and children who lost their lives along with six strikers and one militiaman in the Ludlow massacre,[2] in which militiamen and company guards shot into, and set fire to, a strikers' tent colony. This is perhaps the most serious crime ever committed against strikers, but it is matched by the Herrin massacre,[3] eight years later, in which twenty-one unarmed strike breakers were clubbed to death by a mob of strike sympathizers.

Frequently, it has been necessary to call out the militia to restore a semblance of law and order. No study has ever been made of the number of times this has occurred, but some idea of the situation can be obtained from a few known facts.[4] Of

---

[1] For reference to reports and articles upon the Colorado strike of 1913–1914, see p. 168, Note 1; and for the West Virginia mine troubles, Note 2, pp. 168–169.

[2] A good account of the Ludlow massacre is given in George P. West, *Report on the Colorado Coal Strike*, pp. 124–138, U. S. Commission on Industrial Relations, Washington (1915).

[3] The best account of this massacre, including an explanation of this tragic occurrence, is given in the report of the U. S. Coal Commission on Civil Liberties in the Coal Fields, *Sen. Doc.* 195, Part I, pp. 164–168, 68th Cong., 1st Sess. (1925).

[4] The authorities for the statements in this paragraph are Carroll D. Wright, A Report on Labor Disturbances in Colorado from 1880 to 1904, published as *U. S. Sen. Doc.* 122, 58th Cong., 3rd Sess. (1905); 28 *New Republic* 92, Sept. 21, 1921; and the *Bulletin* of the National Association of Manufacturers, The New Orleans Street-railway Strike of 1929–1930, pp. 19–22 (1930).

thirteen strikes in the Colorado coal fields from 1880 to 1904, the militia was ordered out in ten. Federal troops had to intervene in West Virginia on three distinct occasions in the two years 1920 and 1921. The militia or the federal troops have been called out in twenty-three strikes of the Amalgamated Association of Street and Electric Railway Employees alone.

Nor is lawlessness in controversies between capital and labor confined entirely to strikes. Most of the dynamite outrages in the long war of the structural iron workers' union with the erectors' association were committed while no strikes were in progress; similarly, the kidnappings to prevent union organization, which are discussed later in this chapter, have most frequently been resorted to in the absence of strikes. The racketeer, who has become an important factor in industrial relations in many large cities, flourishes both in times of strike and in anticipation of trouble.

Racketeering, a phase of the problem of the professional criminal, has within the last decades developed an industrial aspect.[1] Finding labor unions a convenient agency for extorting money from employers and others by violence and threats of violence, racketeers have organized unions and seized control of others through the failure of reputable union men to attend meetings. In furtherance of their criminal purposes, they have placed gunmen on the pay rolls of their unions and have used them to terrorize their victims and opponents.

But racketeering has by no means been restricted to labor unions, as some accounts try to make out. Its greatest prevalence seems to be in connection with the liquor traffic, and it has appeared on the employers' side in labor controversies as well as on the employees'. Employers' associations have had gunmen on their pay rolls, among them men simultaneously in the employ of labor unions. As an illustration, the Illinois Crime Survey records that George Martini, a Chicago gunman, was killed in an automobile belonging to the hardware dealers' association, while his wife was being paid a regular monthly allowance by the bar-

---

[1] G. L. Hostetter and Thomas Q. Beasley, "It's a Racket," LesQuin Book Co., Chicago (1929), is an account of labor racketeering from employer sources. John Landesco, Organized Crime in Chicago, *Ill. Crime Survey* pp. 960–975 (1929), is more impartial and altogether the best treatment of this subject.

bers' union, and he himself was a member of a gang whose principal activity was the bombing of barber shops.[1]   The police commissioner of New York in October, 1929, charged that both the union and the employers involved in the gasoline truck drivers' strike had hired gangs of gunmen to assault the strike breakers and the pickets.[2]   Union men, no less than employers, have been victimized by racketeers.[3]   It is a mistake to regard racketeering as a union development or a problem peculiar to labor disputes,[4] but it is a factor which complicates law enforcement in strikes, not only in Chicago, but also in New York, Detroit, Boston, and perhaps other great cities.

SOME PSYCHOLOGICAL FACTORS

The violence chargeable to racketeers is easily explained.   It represents the activities of professional criminals who use unions and employers' associations as disguises and means to foster their schemes of extortion.   It is much more difficult to understand why so much violence occurs, particularly during strikes, for which employers and employees who are honorable men, not criminals, are responsible.

One factor is clearly the general American attitude toward laws and law observance.   We in this country have great faith in laws, as is manifested by our passion for lawmaking; but their enforcement is quite another matter.   More unpunished crimes are committed in the United States than in any other civilized land.   Our homicide rate is double that of the next highest

---

[1] *Ill. Crime Survey*, pp. 973–974 (1929).

[2] *Baltimore Sun*, Oct. 15, 1929.

[3] An illustration is the incident reported from Chicago late in December, 1929, of the shooting of four gangsters by the police in the office of a trade-union secretary, to which they had come to collect ten thousand dollars they had demanded from this union official with the threat that he would be "taken for a ride" unless the money was forthcoming (*A. F. of L. Weekly News Service*, Jan. 4, 1930).

[4] John Landesco, research director of the Illinois Crime Survey in a letter to the author in December, 1928, summarized the conditions existing in Chicago as follows:

"The extent to which merchants are using gangsters to stabilize prices and to exclude competition is increasing.   To my astonishment, not only little business men but the large-scale business is availing itself of these gangsters.   There are sections of Chicago where almost every line of business is 'racketed'; slugging, bombing, and homicide are the means."

country keeping vital statistics and is nine times as great as that of England or Wales.[1] More murders are committed in Memphis, with its population of 250,000, than in all Canada, one-half as many as in all England. This does not mean that the great majority of the people of this country sanction murder or violence, but that we have not developed adequate governmental machinery to cope with professional criminals.

This, clearly, is only one part of the explanation of the widespread violence in labor disputes. The average American may not think it so very wrong to violate traffic laws, trade laws, and many others, but he commits assaults, bombings, or murder only under great provocation. Business competition gives rise to bitter feelings and many sharp practices but seldom leads to physical violence. Labor disputes cause men who are ordinarily law-abiding to commit or sanction serious crimes and are responsible for far more lawless acts than might be regarded as normal for this country. Contrasts with England, again, are helpful. In that country, organized labor is firmly established and recognized. Strikes are seldom life-and-death struggles for the unions involved. Usually, the employers make no attempt to operate their plants with strike breakers. In some American industries, the unions are almost outlaws. Employers are far better organized than in England, and the majority of them believe it to be an American creed not to deal with labor organizations. When strikes occur, the employment of strike breakers is almost universal.

In such an atmosphere of strife, neither side is overscrupulous about law observance. Neither sanctions violence, but each is inclined to minimize or excuse lawlessness in furtherance of its own cause.[2] Employers seldom personally commit lawless acts

---

[1] Evans Clark, U. S. Indicted as the Most Lawless Country, *New York Times*, Nov. 2, 1924.

[2] A good presentation of the view expressed, that both sides are prone to excuse, if not sanction, lawlessness in their behalf, is found in the report of the U. S. Coal Commission on Civil Liberties in the Coal Fields, *Sen. Doc.* 195, Part I, pp. 163–180, 68th Cong., 1st Sess. (1925). This contrasts conditions in West Virginia with conditions at Herrin, Ill., the one an outstanding example of lawlessness against union organizers, and the other of violence against strike breakers.

A similar illustration is afforded by two successive articles in the *Literary Digest* 11–13, Feb. 3, 1923, which carry the titles Labor's Right to Murder

or give instructions for their commission, but they employ detective agencies to break strikes and make no inquiries as to how this is accomplished. They give little or no assistance in running down crimes against union organizers or strikers, just as organized labor has seldom interested itself in bringing anyone to justice for unlawful acts against strike breakers or company guards.

The fundamental difficulty is that each side regards its own interests and rights as paramount to all other considerations. Each believes that its opponent not only is wholly wrong but will not hesitate to resort to unfair methods. In such an atmosphere, both are apt to take the law into their own hands. "Trifles pull triggers," and, without anybody's particularly intending it, loss of life and property results.[1] In this connection, it is to be noted that native-born Americans are just as much disposed toward violence as immigrant workmen. Both West Virginia and Herrin were mining fields in which nearly all of the workmen were native Americans, and there have been few unions in which the foreign born constituted so small a percentage of the total membership as the structural iron workers' union during the years of its dynamiting campaign.

Unfortunately, also, the power of government and the force of public opinion are not exerted effectively in behalf of law and order. The public is shocked by violence in labor troubles but stops in its analysis of the problem with damning organized labor. There is little realization that it usually takes two to make a quarrel, and that employers by unintelligent action may provoke violence unthought of by their workmen. Still less is it appreciated that the occurrence of physical strife is evidence of the inability of government to cope with the situa-

---

and The Right to Murder Labor. The first deals with the Herrin massacre and the acquittal of all the union men charged with murder; the second with the activities of a vigilance committee during a strike on the Missouri and North Arkansas Railroad at Harrison, Ark., which included the lynching of a striker, the deportation from the state of scores of other strikers, the public whipping of strike sympathizers, and the burning of the furniture in the union hall.

[1] A good illustration of the trivial causes which often provoke serious troubles in labor controversies is given in the article by Erwin F. Meyer, Six Killed, Twenty Wounded: a Case Study of Industrial Conflict, 59 *Survey* 644–646 (1928).

tion. To the lack of efficient strike policing and impartial law enforcement is added the use of injunctions to preserve law and order in labor disputes. Not only do injunctions, as noted in a previous chapter, increase the tension; they represent a wrong approach to law enforcement. Courts cannot efficiently police strikes, even though they are more impartial than the executive officials. Law enforcement is essentially an executive, not a judicial, function. By their reliance on injunctions, employers help executive officers to dodge their responsibility. Injunctions, far from being a solution of the problem of law enforcement, are themselves a cause of the general lawless disposition pervading American labor disputes.

INDUSTRIAL ESPIONAGE

Coming to more tangible causes of violence, consideration will first be given to the industrial work of the private detective agencies—a peculiarly American institution. There are a few private detective agencies in England and continental Europe, none of them engaged in industrial work.[1]

In the United States, this is a very large business, although many well-informed people have no suspicion of its existence. Examination of the classified telephone directories of any large city will disclose five to ten, and in some cities twenty or more of these agencies listed under the titles "Detective Agency," "Investigator," or "Industrial Engineer." The largest agencies —the W. J. Burns Agency, the Pinkerton Agency, Sherman Service, Inc., Corporations' Auxiliary, and some others—have offices in most of the large cities. The Sherman Service, Inc., paid $258,000 federal income taxes in one year during the war period.[2] The president of Howard W. Russell, Inc., testified

---

[1] This statement was made to the author by F. W. Leggett, chief factory inspector of the British Ministry of Labor, on his visit to the United States in 1926. A strike-breaking agency for dock labor was once started in London but soon went out of business.

[2] Sidney HOWARD, "The Labor Spy," New Republic Publishing Co., p. 19 (1924).

Jean E. Spielman, "The Stool Pigeon," American Publishing Co., Minneapolis (1923), estimates the combined earnings of the Pinkerton, Burns, and Thiel agencies at $65,000,000 per year and states that they once employed more than 135,000 persons. This is undoubtedly an overstatement but represents what labor people believe to be the facts regarding the extent of the detective-agency business.

in hearings conducted by the Industrial Commission of Wisconsin[1] that in 1920 this small detective agency, with offices only in Milwaukee, had one thousand inside operatives in plants of the middle west and "handled" 217 strikes; and that a strike which does not yield it a revenue of $50,000 to $75,000 is considered a "piker's strike." When the "work-or-fight" order was issued during the war, the detective business was classified as non-essential, but the Sherman Service persuaded so many employers to protest against this classification that the provost marshal modified his order to exempt its operatives from the draft.[2]

The beginnings of the industrial work of private detective agencies date back to about 1890,[3] with its greatest expansion during the World War and in the years immediately following. Since then, there probably has been some decline in this business. This is not certain, but it would seem that the vast amount of adverse publicity received through the publication of Howard's

---

[1] This tendency was taken in 1921 in connection with charges against the Russell Agency of violating the Wisconsin private employment-agency law in a building trades strike at Wausau, Wis. It has not been published but is on file in the offices of the Industrial Commission at Madison.

[2] To the author's personal knowledge, the salesmen of the Sherman Service in 1919 exhibited copies of the letters written to the provost marshal in endorsement of their service by many of the largest corporations of the country, as a talking point for new contracts. See also Howard, op. cit., p. 19.

[3] The earliest known illustration of something akin to industrial espionage was the work of McPartland, an employee of the Pinkerton agency, in securing the evidence which led to the conviction of the Molly McGuires, a band of criminals that infested the anthracite-coal regions, by becoming a miner and joining the labor and other organizations which the "Mollys" had formed to disguise their criminal purposes. This was in the early seventies, but the detective agencies received no attention from the labor press until, in 1892, three hundred guards supplied by the Pinkerton agency participated in the Homestead, Pa., riots, in which scores of strikers were killed and injured. Due to the early prominence of the Pinkerton agency in this industrial work, all labor spies and strike guards were long called "Pinkertons."

For a good brief account of the Molly McGuires and their exposure, see John R. Commons and associates' "History of Labor in the United States," Vol. II, pp. 181–185, The Macmillan Company, New York (1921); and for a longer account, R. W. Rowan, "The Pinkertons," pp. 238–270, Little, Brown & Company, Boston (1931). On the Pinkertons in the Homestead riot, see House Rept. 2447, 52nd Cong., 1st Sess. (1892), and Howard, op. cit., pp. 181–182.

study "The Labor Spy,"[1] the growth of genuine personnel work in industry, the decrease in the number of strikes, and the tendency for employers' associations and large corporations to develop their own spy and guard services must have had this result. Yet the larger agencies have as many branches as ever and still have many small competitors.

The industrial work of private detective agencies includes three principal services. One of these is the industrial espionage carried on through what are technically known as "inside operatives"; another is the furnishing of strike breakers; and the third, the supplying of company and strike guards. All of these are combined in what the detective agencies speak of as "handling" strikes, the contracts made with employers often, in fact if not in exact words, calling for the detective agency to "break the strike."

The inside operatives carry on the work of industrial espionage while working for the client employer under assumed names as ordinary mechanics or workmen, or in some other capacity.[2] They do their daily work and draw pay checks like other workmen, and their fellow employees and immediate superiors— often the superintendents themselves—have no inkling that they are spies. But every day they make a report to the detective agency, and this agency in turn reports to the employer. Practically never do the operatives report directly, the roundabout method of reporting being represented to the employer as necessary to preserve secrecy, but it is no doubt primarily resorted to to enable the home office to make the employer think that he is getting a valuable service.[3]

The purpose of this espionage is to enable the employer to get rid of slackers and pilferers and, above all, agitators and

---

[1] This study was made under the auspices of the Cabot Fund for Industrial Research by Sidney Howard, in collaboration with Robert Dunn. It was first published in the *New Republic* in 1921. A revised and enlarged edition was published in 1924.

[2] In the hearings before the Industrial Commission of Wisconsin in 1921, Howard W. Russell testified that many of his operatives were personnel men, he regarding personnel work as affording the best opportunity for a detective really to ascertain everything about the workmen in the plant.

[3] Original reports from operatives and the revised accounts furnished employers by the home offices are reproduced in Howard, *op. cit.*, pp. 44–86. These indicate that operatives often report the merest drivel, but that the employer is made to think that the information given is most valuable.

trouble makers, by which are usually meant all union members. To this end it is an almost invariable practice of the inside operatives to join the union. The great detective agencies seem to have membership cards in all unions and, at least at times, have union officers on their pay rolls.[1] The spies attend all union meetings and take an active part in all union affairs, including strikes.

To employers, the detective agencies represent these union activities as being undertaken solely for their protection. Through this means, employers are informed of what the union is doing and enabled to get rid of agitators. The detective agencies claim further that the spies often disrupt unions. Accounts of how this is brought about differ, ranging from the pious statement that the spies use their opportunities as union members and officers to present the employer's side to the deluded union men, to an occasional frank acknowledgment that they create strife within the union, arouse racial hatreds, and spread suspicions.[2]

There is reason to believe that this is not the whole explanation of the spies' union activities. Normally, a detective agency is first employed while a strike is brewing, or perhaps while it is in progress.[3] Its contract is very likely to be terminated

---

[1] Howard recounts the exposure as industrial spies in the pay of private detective agencies of the following union officers, who when exposed held the positions indicated: J. C. Cronin, president of the Central Labor Union of Philadelphia; Jack Peters, president of the Central Labor Council of Wheeling; Beattie, president of the Pittsburgh Labor Bank; William H. Downs, secretary-treasurer of the timber workers' union at Wausau; Ray Smith, who organized the strike in the Cudahy Packing Co. at Cudahy, Wis., in 1919. Luke Grant, in his report to the U. S. Commission on Industrial Relations on the National Erectors Association and the Structural Iron Workers Union, charged that J. C. Hockin, a member of the executive board and later secretary-treasurer of this union and the man from whom Ortie McManigal and J. B. McNamara received their orders in their bombings, was, at least during the last year of the dynamite campaign, an employee of the W. J. Burns detective agency. Another such incident is recited in Note 4, *ante.*

[2] Statements from the literature of the Sherman Service, Inc., to this effect are quoted in Howard, *op. cit.*, pp. 32–43.

[3] The great detective agencies keep informed, through clipping services and other methods, of threatened industrial disputes throughout the country and then promptly send their salesmen to the employers involved.

when the trouble is ended.[1] Under the circumstances, it is to be expected that the detective agencies should themselves stir up and endeavor to prolong trouble, and there is abundant evidence that they have done so on many occasions. Spies have organized unions, fomented strikes, and counseled violence in labor troubles.[2] As is to be expected from the nature of the

---

[1] In a booklet issued by the Sherman Service during the World War with the reassuring title "Industry, Society, and the Human Element," the story is told of a plant (perhaps imaginary) which employed this agency in a time of strike, with the result that within a comparatively short time the detectives gained control of the union and disrupted the organization, whereupon the employer foolishly dispensed with the services of the spies only to have trouble again within a few months. This booklet was withdrawn from circulation, probably because the obvious moral of the story, that once an employer ties up with a detective agency he must keep on with it forever, was too revealing of the methods and implications of the detective-agency business.

[2] For proof of these charges, see Howard, *op. cit.*, pp. 178–197.

During the World War, the author had an experience which illustrates the point made, that industrial spies may play as false with employers as with unions. In a Wisconsin city in which the author organized a government employment office, the labor unions made a protest against the man who was appointed superintendent of the office on the ground that he had built his home with non-union labor. To straighten out this difficulty, a meeting was arranged with the central labor council. Shortly before this meeting, two executives of the principal manufacturing plant of the city called on the author, with the startling information that the labor representative on the community labor board controlling this employment office was one of four Sherman Service operatives in this plant. This man had come to the Wisconsin city just six weeks before and had organized the molders' union. He was elected its representative on the trades and labor council and, by this council, elected to the community labor board. This last step was apparently taken without prior knowledge of the client employer corporation. Fearing that this man's spy service might in some manner become public through his acting as labor representative on the community labor board, the employer revealed the operative's identity to the author and offered to ask the detective agency to take him away from the city, as was subsequently done.

At the meeting with the trades and labor council, much discussion developed over the unfair attitude of this manufacturing corporation. The complaint was made that it had been discharging all men who joined unions, particularly molders, and it developed that the real objection to the man who had been appointed superintendent of the office was that he was believed to be aligned with this corporation. At this point, the labor representative on the community labor board arose and delivered a most violent attack upon the corporation he served and dramatically announced

work, it is rare that a self-respecting man feels himself called to this vocation. William J. Burns himself is credited with having said of the private detectives that "as a class, they are the biggest lot of blackmailing thieves that ever went unwhipped of justice," and a British investigator reporting to Scotland Yard upon the American industrial-espionage system made the statement, "There are detectives at the head of prominent agencies in the United States whose pictures adorn the rogues' galleries, men who have served time in various prisons for almost every crime in the calendar."[1]

Why employers pay good money for industrial espionage is difficult to understand. It seems unlikely that they are deceived by the representations, the advertisements, and literature of the detective agencies, which have a lot to say about "industrial harmony," "securing the good will of employees," and similar "subtle suggestions such as might be made by angels from heaven"—to use Roger Babson's language.[2] It must be that employers know the true character of espionage, although they are perhaps unacquainted with its ramifications and by-products. No doubt their resort to such methods is due to a great hatred and an unreasonable fear of labor unions, springing from a conviction that the management of the unions is criminal, and an acceptance of the philosophy that it takes a thief to catch a thief. Many employers who have long employed spies furnished by detective agencies are entirely satisfied with the services rendered and believe that through this means they have kept unions out of their plant. Yet it remains true, as Roger Babson says, that "any firm which has resort to hired spies thereby indicates the depths of inefficiency to which it has fallen."

And right here is one of the explanations of the bitterness of American labor disputes and the frequent resort to violence. The spy is the most hated, by workingmen, of all beings. When

that he would not act on the community labor board unless he could be sure that this corporation had nothing to do with the selection of the superintendent. Yet shortly after this occurrence, the president of this corporation wrote the provost marshal praising the splendid work in the interests of "industrial harmony" which the Sherman Service was performing in this plant!

[1] Howard, op. cit., pp. 111–112.

[2] This and the other quotations from Roger Babson in this and the next paragraph are taken from Babson's Labor Forecast, January, 1921.

he is discovered, he is certain to be attacked and his picture run in the rogues' galleries of labor journals. What organized workingmen believe about the spy system is almost incredible. They feel that spies are everywhere and that they have a hand in practically every union activity. Labor men are forever trying to discover whether their fellow officers in unions are spies, and they are never sure that they have got rid of all of them. Plus this suspicion, they entertain resentment not only against the spies and the detective agencies, but against the employers, who in the last analysis are responsible for their existence. This feeling of suspicion and resentment is a far more potent cause of violence than even the direct incitement to acts of lawlessness by the spies and strike guards furnished by detective agencies, of which there is considerable evidence. Again to quote Babson: "There is no surer way to breed unrest than to take on the services of these industrial detectives."

Organized labor would like to see detective agencies abolished or, at any rate, prohibited from engaging in industrial work. No state has gone thus far, but a number have in recent years enacted laws providing for state regulation. Of these, the laws of California, Michigan, and Wisconsin seem the most comprehensive.[1] All three require that detective agencies must have state licenses, to be issued on the character and competency of the applicants. In Michigan, a favorable recommendation from the police chief, and in Wisconsin from the fire and police commission of the

---

[1] California, Stats. 1927, c. 885; Michigan, Public Acts 1927, No. 383; Wisconsin, Stats. 1929, ss. 105.01–105.15 (enacted in 1925). In addition to state laws, there are numerous local ordinances licensing and to some extent regulating private detective agencies.

The Wisconsin law was sustained in Pinkerton v. Buech, 173 Wis. 433, 181 N. W. 125 (1921) and Pinkerton v. Wengert, 274 U. S. 712, 47 Sup. Ct. 573 (1927). Upon the constitutionality of laws regulating private detective agencies, see also Lehon v. City of Atlanta, 242 U. S. 53, 37 Sup. Ct. 70 (1916).

Besides the license laws, one other type of legislation has been devised to combat some of the evils of industrial espionage. Laws enacted in California (Stats. 1915, c. 65), Nevada (Acts 1915, c. 41), and Ohio (Laws 1917, p. 603) provide that employers shall give employees a hearing before discharging or disciplining them on the report of any "spotter" or private detective. A similar bill was held unconstitutional in an advisory opinion delivered by the Massachusetts Supreme Court, Opinion of the Justices, 220 Mass. 627, 108 N. E. 807 (1925). (*U. S. Labor Bull.* 186, p. 7.)

city where the agency is located, is a prerequisite, and in all three the issuing officer is vested with wide discretion and empowered to make independent investigations and to revoke licenses for a great variety of causes. Wisconsin requires the individual operatives, as well as the agencies by whom they are employed, to be licensed, and this, the most restrictive of such laws, has been sustained by the state and federal supreme courts. Yet this law has not solved the problem, although organized labor appears satisfied. Only a few individual operatives have applied for licenses, and while the Milwaukee fire and police commission has steadfastly refused to give a recommendation to any agency engaged in questionable industrial work, the largest and most aggressive of these, nevertheless, has procured a license by moving its office to a suburb in which the police authorities had no such scruples. The most serious defect appears to be that no provision is made for enforcement other than revocation of licenses after hearings on complaints, in which respect the California law is stronger, providing for a field investigator to run down violators. Under the best law, effective regulation of private detective agencies is difficult, but prohibition is out of the question, as it would be held unconstitutional.

In this connection, it is to be noted that a considerable number of great corporations have developed their own spy services.[1] These are part of the organization of many railroad and steel corporations and seem distinctly to be on the increase. While there is less danger of duplicity, the fundamental evils remain even when the spies are licensed and regulated. Workingmen resent being spied on, and, when labor troubles come, this feeling is likely to find active expression.

STRIKE BREAKERS AND STRIKE GUARDS

Besides supplying industrial spies, detective agencies furnish strike guards and assist employers in securing strike breakers.

---

[1] The author has been informed that one effect of the Wisconsin private detective-agency law has been the organization of their own spy services by many corporations which formerly contracted with detective agencies. A man who prior to this law operated an agency in Milwaukee which did extensive industrial work and who for this reason did not apply for a license (as he believed it useless for him to do so) claims that he has got around the new law by being placed on the pay rolls as an employee of a dozen corporations to manage and direct their spy services.

The term "strike breaker" is one applied loosely to all who work at plants against which strikes have been called. These may be men employed before the strike who remained loyal to the firm. More properly, strike breakers are new employees hired during the strike. If there is no violence or intimidation, employers often can get local men to take the place of strikers, particularly during periods of depression. There is, however, a certain stigma which attaches to strike breakers, even among unorganized workmen. This is powerfully stimulated by the action of pickets and strike sympathizers in calling these men "scabs," and by threats and fear of violence.

The net result is that employers frequently find it difficult to get enough men through their own efforts to take the place of the strikers. From this has arisen the service rendered by the detective agencies and employers' associations[1] of procuring strike breakers. These men are not employees of the detective agencies but are recruited by them, principally in the large cities. There are in these cities some professional strike breakers, and still larger numbers of men who are willing to take a strike job because they badly need work or are attracted by the higher pay which is always given strike breakers. These men are ordinarily not good workmen, and employers usually have no thought of keeping them after the trouble is over. They are hired to bring the strikers to terms, rather than to turn out work.

Between the strikers and the strike breakers there is naturally a most bitter feeling. The strikers look upon the strike breakers as men "who are taking the bread away from their children," while the strike breakers are made to feel that they are social outcasts and have reason to fear violence. In such an atmosphere there is always great danger of serious clashes. To prevent them, strike guards are regularly furnished by detective agencies as a part of their services when they contract to "handle" strikes or are recruited directly by great corporations.

The number of such guards is often very great. In the 1922 railroad shop crafts' strike, 53,831 extra guards were employed by 50 of the large railroad systems, which had a total of about

---

[1] Accounts of the services rendered by various employers' associations to their members in supplying strike breakers and strike guards are given in C. E. Bonnett, "Employers' Associations in the United States," 45–47, 74–80, 109–113, 246, The Macmillan Company, New York (1922).

250,000 men on strike.[1] Where strike breakers are procured through detective agencies, the ratio of strike guards to strike breakers is sometimes as low as three to one and seldom higher than five to one. Where state laws and local authorities permit, these guards are armed. Frequently, they secure commissions as special police or deputy sheriffs. When thus commissioned, they have all the powers of police officers but get their orders and pay from the detective agencies or corporations by whom they are employed.

Guards are employed not only during strikes but by some corporations at all times, in which case they are called "company guards" or "railroad police." The company-guard system, most widespread in the non-union coal fields, prevails also in the steel mills of Pennsylvania, on the railroads, and in numerous industrial plants. In West Virginia and Colorado, the company guards, at least formerly, constituted veritable private armies which, in the 1913–1914 strikes and the 1920 and 1922 mine marches, met the union miners in pitched battles. In West Virginia, these guards held commissions as sheriffs' deputies, although paid by the coal corporations. In Pennsylvania, a similar arrangement has existed under the term of "coal and iron police," the members of which receive their commissions from the governor but are privately selected, paid, and controlled. When Pennsylvania organized its state-police system, one of the arguments in its favor was that it would render unnecessary the many commissions to private guards but, in fact, the number of coal and iron police increased. When Gifford Pinchot became governor in 1923, there were no less than 5,830 commissions. In the great steel strike of 1919, 10,000 additional deputies were commissioned in Allegheny County alone. In 1931 Pinchot canceled all of the appointments, but the law under which the company guards in Pennsylvania have been given police powers remains, and new commissions may be issued at any time.[2] Nor is this practice of conferring police powers upon

---

[1] Statement of Judge Wilkerson in U. S. v. Railway Employees' Dept., A. F. of L., 290 Fed. 978 (1923).

[2] Upon the coal and iron police of Pennsylvania, the following brief accounts are valuable: Bruce Smith, "The State Police," pp. 33–34, The Macmillan Company, New York (1925); S. Adele Shaw, Closed Towns, etc., 43 *Survey* 58–64, 85–87, 92–93 (1919); Frank Butter and Robert Taylor,

strike and company guards confined to West Virginia and Pennsylvania. On the contrary, it seems to be widespread, although by no means universal.[1]

This practice has never been publicly defended and often strongly condemned.[2] The U. S. Coal Commission summarized

---

Coal and Iron Justice, 129 *Nation* 404–405 (1929); J. P. Shallow, The Private Police of Pennsylvania, 146 *Ann. Amer. Acad. Polit. Social Sci.* 55–62 (1929); *Baltimore Sun*, Nov. 17, 1927; *Toledo Union Leader*, Apr. 26, 1929.

In 1931, Governor Pinchot recommended that the coal and iron police be replaced by a force selected by the state but paid by the coal operators. This was not satisfactory to organized labor, which supported a bill prohibiting private police forces. The net result was that the legislature adjourned without taking any action on the subject.

[1] The author has noted accounts of the commissioning of private guards as deputy sheriffs in the following strikes outside of Pennsylvania and West Virginia:

1. American Railway Union strike (1894). Three to four thousand guards, supplied by a private detective agency and paid by the railroad companies, were commissioned as special deputies by the U. S. Marshal at Chicago under orders from Attorney-general Olney (W. R. Browne, "Altgeld of Illinois," pp. 146–147, Viking Press, New York [1924]).

2. Strike at the plant of the American Agricultural Chemical Co. at Roosevelt, N. J., 1915. Several hundred guards furnished by the Jerry O'Brien detective agency and paid by the chemical company were commissioned as deputy sheriffs and as such took part in a shooting affray in which two strikers were killed and seventeen wounded. Twenty-two of these deputies were then indicted for murder (unpublished report of Special Agents Brennan, O'Reagan, and Gill on their investigation of this difficulty to the U. S. Commission on Industrial Relations).

3. Strike against the Nekoosa-Edwards Paper Co. at Nekoosa, Wis., 1919. Guards furnished by a Chicago detective agency were commissioned as special marshals by the village president. Attorney-general, now Senator, John J. Blaine held this action to be a violation of the Wisconsin statutes (Madison *Capital Times*, Oct. 2, 1919).

4. Chicago carpenters' fight with the Citizens Committee to Enforce the Landis Award, 1922–1924. In Carpenters Union v. Citizens Committee, 244 Ill. App. 540 (1927), the court states that the Citizens Committee to Enforce the Landis Award organized a "protection department" in 1922, which employed several hundred guards. Between 130 and 135 guards were still employed in May, 1924. All these guards were given commissions as deputy sheriffs by the sheriff of Cook County—a practice severely scored by the court.

[2] Condemnation of this practice, among others, occurs in the final reports of the Anthracite Coal Commission (1903), the U. S. Commission on Industrial Relations (1915), and the U. S. Coal Commission (1923); also in the report of the Senate Committee on Education and Labor on its investigation of the steel strike of 1919.

the objections in this unanswerable sentence: "That a public official should be privately paid is indefensible." Some have gone further and have advocated the complete abolition of strike and company guards.[1] In support of such a position, it is urged that the private guard system amounts to a tolerance of private armies for industrial warfare. Policing is properly a function of government, and it is dangerous to vest private parties with this authority.

In opposition it can be truthfully said that the employment of private guards is ordinarily a defensive, not an offensive, move on part of employers. They employ guards because they expect attacks upon their employees and property in labor troubles and fear that they will not receive adequate police protection in such emergencies. That these fears are not groundless is undeniable. As long as this is true, private guards cannot well be prohibited. Further, it is difficult to draw the line between guards and watchmen. Watchmen practically everywhere have limited police authority on the premises and, in times of labor trouble, act virtually as guards. This is particularly true of railroad police, whose normal function is to prevent pilfering in railroad yards and terminals, but who become strike guards when labor difficulties arise.

But while the question of what ought to be done with the private guards presents complexities, it is certain that the guard system is a source of friction and of much abuse. It may be, as the author believes, that private policing cannot be prohibited until better public police protection is afforded, but no permanent solution can be thought of other than a really adequate public police system with a prohibition of all private policing.

STRIKE POLICING

Public police protection, if not the hub of the entire problem of law enforcement, is at least one of its most significant aspects. Inefficient policing encourages resort to violence, and police partisanship is a direct incentive to lawlessness. Many different methods and agencies for strike policing have been tried in

---

[1] This was the position taken in the report of the director of investigation of the U. S. Commission on Industrial Relations, in the final report of this commission (p. 152).

this country, none of them with entirely satisfactory results.[1]
Employers often have not received the protection to which they
are entitled, while workingmen have suffered from numerous
unjustified arrests.

In cities, the duty of keeping order in time of labor trouble in
the first instance falls upon the local police; in the country districts of most states, upon the sheriffs and their deputies. These
police authorities of the first instance have many times proved
both inefficient and partisan, although it must also be recorded
that there have been strikes—including some very great strikes—
in which there was little or no complaint of the police by either
side.

Policemen usually have no special training and no adequate
instructions for handling labor troubles. They are apt to regard
strikers as potential trouble makers, particularly if they are
foreigners or radicals; and such an attitude leads to needless
arrests and sometimes cruel treatment. Even more important
than the attitude of the individual policemen is that of the police
chiefs and of the mayors and councilmen. Almost inevitably,
the police reflect the prejudices of their superiors, and interference by them in strike policing is not uncommon. It has
frequently occurred that these executive officials have been
employees of the corporations involved in strikes, and, on the
other hand, there have been cases in which they were themselves
strikers.[2]

Another factor affecting the usefulness of the local police is
that usually no provision is made for any increase in the force
in emergencies, and in many communities the number of policemen is scarcely adequate for normal times. This is one reason

---

[1] A good summary of the American experience with strike policing is the
editorial on this subject in 6 *New Republic* 281–282 (1916).

[2] Fitch, in "The Causes of Industrial Unrest," p. 252, cites several Pennsylvania cities in which the principal officials during the steel strike of
1919 were employees of the steel companies. The opposite situation is
presented in Michaelson v. U. S., 266 U. S. 42, 45 Sup. Ct. 18 (1924), which
recites that the defendants in this case, who were strikers charged with
violation of an injunction issued in the railroad shop crafts' strike in 1922,
included the village president and the marshal of the village of North
Hudson, Wis. For another such illustration, relating to conditions in
Johnson County, Ky., in the coal strike of 1922, see the report of the U. S.
Coal Commission on Civil Liberties in the Coal Fields, *op. cit.*, pp. 173–174.

for the commissioning of private guards as special policemen in strike time—an evil quite as great as inadequate policing.

Everything that has been said regarding the local police in strikes applies equally to the sheriffs and sheriffs' deputies, upon whom falls the burden of strike policing in rural communities with, in some states, supplementary police powers in cities. The sheriffs and sheriffs' deputies are generally selected for political reasons and very frequently have had absolutely no training in police work. Again, the sheriffs face much the same problem as the police chiefs with regard to increasing their forces. They commonly have authority to commission as many deputies as they see fit, but usually only small funds with which to pay them, the result being that they oftentimes commission as deputies guards paid by the employers.[1]

Besides the local police and the sheriffs' deputies, ten states (Massachusetts, Connecticut, Pennsylvania, New York, Rhode Island, Michigan, Tennessee, West Virginia, New Jersey, and Oregon) have state-police forces, often called "state constabulary."[2] These forces are in normal times engaged principally in

---

[1] Even when the county pays the deputy sheriffs, they may be guards furnished by detective agencies. This occurred in the Calumet copper strike of 1913, in which more than fifty deputies were furnished by the Waddell Mahon Detective Agency (*Final Report, U. S. Commission on Industrial Relations*, p. 69).

[2] The years of the establishment of the state police systems and citations to the present laws are as follows:

Massachusetts (1865), G. L. 1922, c. 22, s. 3.

Connecticut (1903), G. S. 1918, ss. 2266–2303, amended by P. A. 1919, c. 297; P. A. 1921, c. 273; P. A. 1923, c. 202; P. A. 1925, c. 37; P. A. 1927, c. 580; P. A. 1929, c. 214.

Pennsylvania (1905), Stats. 1920, ss. 20112–20131, amended by P. L. 1921, p. 1061; P. L. 1925, p. 314; P. L. 1929, p. 414.

New York (1917), Laws 1928, c. 676.

Michigan (1919), P. A. 1921, No. 123.

Tennessee (1919), Ann. Code Suppl. 1926, ss. 6925a9 to 6925a18.

West Virginia (1919), Code 1923, c. 19.

New Jersey (1921), Laws 1921, c. 102, amended by Laws 1922, c. 271; Laws 1928, c. 218; and Laws 1929, c. 61.

Rhode Island (1925), Laws 1925, c. 588.

Oregon (1931), Laws 1931, c. 139.

Outside these ten states, state police forces were at one time maintained in Arizona, Colorado, Idaho, New Mexico, and Texas but have been abandoned. South Dakota has a state sheriff's department, but this is con-

patrolling the state highways and the rural communities. In times of strike, however, they are used in strike-police duties, supplementing the local police and the sheriffs' deputies.

Organized labor has very bitterly condemned the state police and their activities in strikes. This has been especially true of the Pennsylvania constabulary, to which labor has applied the term "cossacks" and made charges of every conceivable crime.[1] Yet in the 1927–1928 coal strike, Basil Manly, former director of research of the U. S. Commission on Industrial Relations and the joint chairman, representing labor, of the War Labor Board, reported that in Pennsylvania communities where the policing was done by state troopers, there was "a minimum of friction and violence," while in all places where the policing was done by coal and iron policemen employed by the coal companies, "there has been endless bitterness and brutality."[2] Organized labor in Pennsylvania, however, remains hostile to the state constabulary, although perhaps less violently so than in former years. In New York, at least some of the labor leaders have commended the state police, but this is exceptional. Wherever state-police bills have been proposed in states without such a force, organized labor has fought them with all the means in its power, and only Rhode Island and Oregon have passed such laws in the last decade, while two other states have repealed theirs.

Organized labor looks upon the state police as organized primarily to curb its efforts in labor disputes. The proponents of the system advance very different arguments, stressing the crime wave and the need for more efficient rural policing. In opposition, there also are arguments which have nothing to do with labor difficulties, particularly the expense involved and the

---

stituted of the sheriffs and their deputies, acting under the general direction of a state officer.

[1] Early complaints regarding the state police are summarized in the publication of the Pennsylvania State Federation of Labor, "The American Cossack" (1915). For later complaints, see W. Z. Foster, "The Great Steel Strike," pp. 119–139, Viking Press, New York (1920), and S. Adele Shaw, Closed Towns, etc., 43 *Survey* 58 (1919).

[2] Statement reprinted in *Congressional Record*, Feb. 1, 1928. In this connection, it is worthy of note that Miss Shaw in the article cited in the previous note, in which she sharply criticises the conduct of the state police in the steel strike of 1919, states that "in the Westinghouse strike of 1915, they behaved admirably."

interference with local home rule.   The principal opposition, however, comes from the labor unions.   Attempts to allay this opposition by the insertion of provisions restricting the activities of the state police in labor disputes[1] have been futile, no formula having been found which satisfies labor.

THE MILITARY IN STRIKES

When the police forces of the first instance fail to preserve law and order in strikes, it is customary for the governor to order out the militia.   This is usually done after the sheriff or other local authorities have declared that they are unable to handle the situation, but the governor may intervene without consulting anyone.   Under the constitutions of all states, the governor has authority to use the militia to suppress insurrections and to preserve law and order, and it is settled that his discretion in this respect is final.   No court will review his action either in proclaiming that a state of insurrection exists within a given region or in refusing to order out the militia when requested to do so.[2]

---

[1] New York, New Jersey, Connecticut, and Massachusetts all provide that the state police may be used to suppress riots only upon approval or direction of the governor.   New York and New Jersey further provide that the state police may be used in cities only when request is made by the mayor; and Massachusetts, that they may be used to suppress riots only if actual violence has occurred.   These several provisions are set forth in Bruce Smith: "The State Police," pp. 59–65, The Macmillan Company, New York (1925).

[2] In re Boyle, 6 Idaho 609, 57 Pac. 706 (1889); in re Moyer, 35 Col. 159, 85 Pac. 190 (1904); Moyer v. Peabody, 148 Fed. 870, 212 U. S. 78, 29 Sup. Ct. 235 (1909); State v. Brown, 71 W. Va. 519, 77 S. E. 243 (1913); ex parte Jones, 71 W. Va. 567, 77 S. E. 1029 (1913); Hatfield v. Graham, 73 W. Va. 759, 81 S. E. 533 (1914); ex parte McDonald, 49 Mont. 454, 143 Pac. 947 (1914); U. S. v. Adams, 26 F. (2nd) 141 (1928).

For more complete discussions of the law governing the use of the militia, see H. W. Ballentine, Martial Law, 12 Columbia Law Rev. 529–538 (1912), Military Dictatorship in California and West Virginia, 1 California Law Rev. 413–426 (1913), and Unconstitutional Claims of Military Authority, 24 Yale Law Jour. 189–216, and in 5 Jour. Criminal Law 718–743 (1915); W. G. Mathews, Martial Law in West Virginia, 29 W. Va. Bar Assoc. 16–40 (1913); and H. J. Hershey, Power and Authority of a Governor and Militia in Domestic Disturbances, 19 Law Notes 28–33 (1915).   Ballentine, who regards the existing state of the law governing the use of the militia in strikes to be very unsatisfactory, outlined his remedy in Qualified Martial Law, a Legislative Proposal, 14 Mich. Law Rev. 102–115, 197–213 (1916).

This authority has been exercised often, and the course pursued by the militia in strikes has been subject to much criticism. Labor's feeling toward the use of the militia in strikes formerly was so intense that many labor unions forbade their members to belong to the national guard, an edict which led to the enactment of laws making it an offense for anyone to endeavor to prevent any person by threats from joining the militia.[1] No unions at present prohibit membership in the national guard, and a considerable number of union men have in fact become members. Even now, however, the militia has a doubtful reputation with labor, and it generally resents the calling out of the guard during strikes.

One factor in this attitude is the effect which such action has upon public opinion. A proclamation by the governor that a state of insurrection exists and the sending of the militia to preserve order is looked upon by the public as a condemnation of the course of the strikers. When the guard is called out, the strike can be put down as lost. Further, the militia has often acted arbitrarily in strikes. Its powers are broad, and it is answerable to no one but the governor. A majority of the courts, where the question has arisen, has held that when the governor has proclaimed that a state of insurrection exists in a given region the military authorities may arrest and detain without trial any person they deem necessary. In some states, it has even been held that the governor may suspend the writ of habeas corpus during labor troubles, and that persons charged with violations of the criminal laws may be tried in military courts, although the civil courts are open and functioning. And while these doctrines have drawn vigorous dissents and are not accepted by all courts, even under the narrowest view, the militia has all of the authority of the civil police and the vague additional power to do anything necessary to preserve law and order.[2]

---

[1] An example of such a statute is s. 21.14, Wis. Stats. 1929.

[2] All of the cases cited in Note 46 sustain the right of the military authorities to hold any person without trial when they deem it necessary. *In re* Boyle, 6 Idaho 609, 57 Pac. 706 (1899), State v. Brown, 71 W. Va. 519, 77 S. E. 243 (1913); *ex parte* Jones, 71 W. Va. 567, 77 S. E. 1029 (1913), go further and hold that martial law may be enforced during strike troubles and the writ of habeas corpus suspended. In the latter case, there was a

This authority has not been exercised wisely in all cases.   In the Colorado strike troubles of 1903–1904 and 1913–1914,[1] the military authorities arrested scores of strikers and held some of them for months without trial and, in the earlier of these troubles, deported many of the strike leaders.   In but few strikes have the military authorities acted so arbitrarily, but they have often refused to allow picketing and strike meetings, although on the whole the record of the militia in labor troubles is better than that of any other emergency police force except the federal troops.

Militia officers have little training for police duties and are likely to be unsympathetic toward the strikers.[2]   Their powers are ill defined, and in most states no attempt has ever been made to formulate any rules to govern their course in strikes.   Some of the militia officers have assumed their function to be the suppression of the strike.[3]   A further difficulty at times is that the guardsmen are quartered on the employers' premises, if not fed and armed at their expense as well.   The militia has not always made a bad record in strikes, and it is the author's impression that in most cases the calling out of the guard was justified. But clearly the use of the militia to preserve law and order

vigorous dissent by Judge Robinson. *Ex parte* McDonald, 49 Mont. 454, 143 Pac. 947 (1914), is more liberal, holding that while military authorities have a right to arrest and detain persons whom they believe necessary to suppress an insurrection, the reasonableness of their action may be reviewed by the civil courts, and, further, that they have no right to try and punish an offender while the regular courts are functioning.   An even more advanced position is taken in the most recent case involving the militia in strikes, U. S. v. Adams, 26 F. (2nd) 141 (1928), in which a federal court held that a proclamation of the governor of Colorado that an insurrection existed in a stated county in which an I. W. W. strike was in progress did not give authority to the militia to arrest persons conducting a peaceful strike meeting.

[1] The course of the militia in this strike is recounted at length in George P. West's *Report on the Colorado Coal Strike* pp. 107–138, U. S. Commission on Industrial Relations, Washington (1915).

[2] In the Colorado coal strike of 1913–1914, as guardsmen who desired to be relieved from strike duty were allowed to go home, their places were taken by mine guards recruited in the strike zone (West, *op. cit.*, p. 110).

[3] A Colorado officer, who, according to labor's version, was principally responsible for the Ludlow massacre in 1914, expressed this attitude, "I am Jesus Christ, and my men on horseback are Jesus Christs, and we have got to be obeyed." (West, *op. cit.*, p. 125.)

should be reserved for emergencies and as a regular procedure is a most unsatisfactory method of strike policing.

The federal troops have not been called out nearly so often as the militia, and their reputation with labor is considerably better. Labor did resent the sending of the federal troops to Chicago in the Pullman strike of 1894 and has occasionally complained of their actions in other strikes,[1] but it welcomed their intervention in the Colorado strike of 1913–1914 and in the West Virginia mine troubles of 1919–1921. Manifestly, however, the U. S. Army cannot regularly assume the duties of strike policing.

INTERFERENCE WITH UNION ORGANIZATION

A phase of the problem of law enforcement which deserves special attention is that of interference with organizing campaigns and union meetings. This has been a cause of much complaint, by both radical and conservative unions, with illustrations from every part of the country. Such interference may be the work of company guards and mobs, in communities where there is much antilabor sentiment. Almost every year, cases have occurred somewhere in which union organizers were kidnaped and told to leave town or were tarred and feathered and deported. Industrial Workers of the World and members of other communistic labor organizations have most commonly been the victims of such mob violence, but organizers of "regular" unions have suffered similar treatment.[2]

---

[1] Most bitter complaints were made by labor regarding the role of the federal troops in the Coeur d'Alene, Ida., miners' strike in 1899, for an account of which see Prof. Edward Berman's *Labor Disputes and the President*, pp. 36–45 (1924). Labor also charged gross unfairness against the troops employed at Gary, Ind., under the command of General Leonard Wood, in the 1919 steel strike (Interchurch World Movement, *Report on the Steel Strike of* 1919, pp. 240–242 [1920]; W. Z. Foster, "The Great Steel Strike," pp. 170–172, Viking Press, New York [1920]).

[2] A recent instance is the kidnaping of Edward F. McGrady, legislative agent of the American Federation of Labor, and Alfred Hoffman, an organizer of the United Textile Workers, at Elizabethton, Tenn. These men were in April, 1929, seized by a mob at their hotels, carried to the state line, and told never to return. The attempted kidnapping of a third organizer at the same time was prevented only by his wife's pointing a pistol at the attackers (*New York Times*, Apr. 5, 1929).

Of most serious import is the frequent interference with union organizers and union meetings by public authorities. This again has affected both radical and conservative unions and has occurred in many different sections of the country. In the heyday of the I. W. W., before the World War, many western communities were involved in prolonged free-speech fights with this organization. These all began with the refusal of the local authorities to allow I. W. W. speakers to hold meetings within their borders. Such action was treated by the I. W. W. as a challenge, and its members then flocked to the city in question and got themselves thrown into jail by attempting to hold meetings, soon filling all the jails and attracting a vast amount of public attention. These tactics were successful in some cases, forcing the local authorities to lift their ban against the I. W. W.[1] In a report made to the U. S. Commission on Industrial Relations, such free-speech fights were recounted as occurring in the years 1908–1914 in twelve cities as far apart as Dayton and Los Angeles,[2] and several such conflicts transpired thereafter, including the one at Everett, Wash., which culminated in the killing of several people and the murder trial against I. W. W. leaders mentioned in the preceding chapter.[3] Since the World War, popular fear of the radical labor organization has abated, but there are still communities in which communists are not allowed to hold a meeting.

Conservative unions have at times been faced with similar interference with their meetings, especially during strikes. At Columbus, Ohio, the police chief's refusal in 1916 to allow union organizers to hold meetings and his banishment of some of their number from the city led to a formal protest from President Gompers of the American Federation of Labor.[4] In the steel strike of 1919, union meetings were interfered with practically

---

[1] For a good account of these tactics, see W. M. Short, How One Town Learned a Lesson in Free Speech, 35 *Survey* 106–108 (1915).

[2] *Report* of Special Agent Blaine F. Moore, Free Speech, Free Press, and Right of Assembly. Besides the two cities mentioned, Mr. Moore discussed I. W. W. free-speech fights in Kansas City, Aberdeen, Minot, Denver, Grand Junction, Spokane, Seattle, Portland, Fresno, Los Angeles, and San Diego.

[3] *Cf.* pp. 166–167.

[4] 23 *Amer. Federationist* 500, 564–573 (1916).

everywhere throughout the Pittsburgh district.[1] All outdoor meetings were prohibited by the sheriff of Allegheny County. Indoor meetings were prohibited at Duquesne, McKeesport, and other places, which provided by ordinance that no meetings might be held without permission of the mayor, who invariably refused his assent. The same situation has existed for many years in southern West Virginia, of which the U. S. Coal Commission in its report on Civil Liberties in the Coal Fields in 1923 said: "Whatever may be the legal phase, it is no doubt a fact that under present conditions, Logan, Mingo, and MacDowell Counties, W. Va., are closed to representatives of the miners' union, especially if they engage in union activities."[2]

Questions regarding the extent to which public authorities may interfere with union meetings have several times come before the courts, and the governing principles are fairly well settled. Meetings in the public streets, save upon permit from a local official such as the mayor or the police chief, may be prohibited,[3] the underlying idea being that the public streets are intended for traffic, not for meetings; and it is settled that meetings on private property may be prevented or broken up if there is imminent danger of a disturbance.[4]

---

[1] Upon the course of the public officials in the Pittsburgh district during the steel strike, see S. Adele Shaw, *op. cit.*, 43 *Survey* 58 (1919); U. S. *Sen. Rep.* 289 by the Committee on Education and Labor on the steel strike, 66th Cong., 1st Sess. (1919); "Public Opinion and the Steel Strike," by investigators for the Interchurch World Commission, Harcourt, Brace & Company (1920); and W. Z. Foster, "The Great Steel Strike," pp. 112–118, 188–189, Viking Press, New York (1920), and pp. 175–178 for similar actions at Youngstown, Ohio.

[2] *Sen. Doc.* 195, Part I, p. 173, 68th Cong., 1st Sess. (1925).

[3] Commonwealth v. Davis, 162 Mass. 510, 39 N. E. 113 (1895); Davis v. Massachusetts, 167 U. S. 43, 17 Sup. Ct. 731 (1897); Harwood v. Trembly, 97 N. J. L. 173, 116 Atl. 430 (1922); City of Duquesne v. Fincke, 269 Pa. 112, 112 Atl. 130 (1921); People *ex rel.* Doyle v. Atwell, 232 N. Y. 96, 133 N. E. 364 (1922).

It has also been held that a municipality may prohibit the distribution of literature on the public streets without a permit: Almassi v. City of Newark, 150 Atl. 217 (N. J. 1930).

[4] This is accepted even by Justices Holmes and Brandeis, who in Schenk v. U. S., 249 U. S. 47, 39 Sup. Ct. 247 (1919) and in Gitlow v. U. S., 286 U. S. 652, 45 Sup. Ct. 625 (1925), vigorously dissented from the view of the majority that seditious utterances may be punished although there is no imminent danger either of a disturbance or of overt acts against the government.

These general principles leave a great deal to the discretion of the police and local executive authorities. If they are so inclined, they can prevent union meetings or at least compel the unions to go into the courts at great expense to protect their rights.[1]

CONCLUSIONS

As the above brief treatment of some of the problems of law enforcement in labor disputes discloses, the existing situation is anything but satisfactory. Violence is exceedingly prevalent in the United States. Responsibility for this condition rests in part on the public officials, but employers, employees, and the general public all must bear some of the blame. Labor does not advocate violence but has comparatively seldom interested itself in law enforcement or offered suggestions for more adequate strike policing.[2] The responsibility of employers is not less, nor is their attitude essentially better. Employers shudder at the criminal leadership of some unions, while retaining thugs and criminals as industrial spies and company guards, and often fail to realize that interference with union meetings and the right of union organization is as a match to a fuse and of itself a lawless

---

[1] Injunctions to prevent interference with union or radical meetings were allowed in Central Labor Council v. Baker, at Portland, Ore., 45 *Survey* 847 (1921) and American Civil Liberties Union v. Nimmo, Bergen County, N. J., 1926 (*Chicago Tribune*, May 1, 1926; *Toledo Union-Leader*, May 7, 1926); and a similar injunction was secured on behalf of the Amalgamated Association of Street and Electric Railway Employees against city and police officers of Indianapolis from the Circuit Court of Marion County, Ind., in 1926 (*Toledo Union-Leader*, June 18, 1926). Such injunctions were denied in United Mine Workers v. Chafin, 286 Fed. 959 (1923), and Welsh v. Vinton Colliery Co., Cambria County, Pa., 5 *Law and Labor* 36 (1923).

Even in the case of communists, the holding of meetings does not of itself constitute unlawful assembly, nor are public officials warranted in preventing such meetings in fear that speakers will make seditious utterances, although such statements if made can be punished regardless of their effects: State v. Butterworth, 104 N. J. L. 579, 142 Atl. 57 (1928).

[2] There have, of course, been instances where labor has actively interested itself in law enforcement. For such a case, see the article Intelligent Unionism, 62 *New Republic* 141 (1930). Another recent illustration of such a wholesome attitude was the declaration of President Green at the 1930 convention of the American Federation of Labor that he and the Executive Committee of the Federation would use all of their power to drive racketeers out of labor unions.

act. The public's responsibility arises from its lack of understanding of the problem and its failure to provide adequate and impartial police services.

The fundamental difficulty is the atmosphere of bitterness which surrounds all our industrial conflicts. At best, these will ever be serious disturbances, but, when employers and employees blindly refuse to consider anything but their own rights and the public lines up with one side or the other, the difficulties are immensely increased. Improved conditions will only come when employers and employed will each recognize the rights of the other and when government becomes truly neutral.

Bibliographical Note

While there is a considerable literature upon special phases, there are few accounts dealing comprehensively with the problem of law enforcement in labor disputes. The best is John A. Fitch, "Causes of Industrial Unrest," Harper & Brothers, New York (1924), particularly Chaps. X, XII, and XIII. The recent book of Louis Adamic, "Dynamite," Viking Press, New York (1931), is a journalistic treatment of the subject for the general reader. A most excellent unpublished study is Howard B. Meyers, "The Policing of Labor Disputes in Chicago," a University of Chicago Ph. D. thesis of 1929; and another, John W. Scott, "The Policing of Nonurban Industry," another Chicago thesis of the same year.

Regarding the extent of violence, no impartial study has ever been made, but there are many accounts, principally emanating from employer sources, dealing with particular labor troubles. Among these, three reports issued by the Cleveland Chamber of Commerce made by its committee on labor disputes in 1915–1927 on Violence in Labor Disputes and the booklet "Law and Order in San Francisco—a Beginning" published by the San Francisco Chamber of Commerce in 1916, are better than the average.

Upon causes of violence, the most suggestive treatment is the report of the U. S. Coal Commission on "Civil Liberty in the Coal Fields," made in 1923, published in U. S. *Sen. Doc.* 195, Part I, pp. 161–180, 68th Cong., 2nd Sess. (1925). Another illuminating discussion is the chapter by Stuart Chase on Violence in Labor Conflicts in J. B. S. Hardman, "American Labor Dynamics in the Light of Post-War Developments," pp. 349–356, Harcourt, Brace & Company, New York (1928).

Industrial espionage has provoked many pamphlets and articles. By far the best is Sidney Howard, "The Labor Spy," 1924 ed., New Republic Publishing Co. A shorter general account is given in Fitch, *op. cit.*, pp. 171–185. Good discussions of the roles of spy and strike guard in particular strikes include George P. West, *Report on the Colorado Strike*, pp. 102–106 (1915); William Hard, America in Passaic, 22 *New Republic* 182–185 (1920); *Report on the Steel Strike of* 1919, pp. 221–224, Commission of Inquiry of the Interchurch World Movement (1920); Arthur Gleason, Industrial Democracy and Gunmen, in 25 *New Republic*, 318–319 (1921); Garyism in West Virginia,

28 *New Republic* 86–88 (1921); John W. Owens, Gunmen in West Virginia, 28 *New Republic* 90–92 (1921).   William L. Stoddard, Confessions of the Gunmen of Industry, 32 *Pearson's Mag.* 147–157 (1914) is essentially a labor account, and Jean Spielman, "The Stool Pigeon," American Publishing Co., Minneapolis (1923) and Frank Palmer, "Spies in Steel," Denver Labor Press (1928) are admittedly so.   Much valuable information appears also in H. B. Meyers, "The Policing of Labor Disputes in Chicago."

The problem of strike policing is dealt with in John A. Fitch, *op. cit.*, pp. 241–259, and in an editorial on this subject in 6 *New Republic* 281–282 (1916).

On the subject of the state police, the best book is Bruce Smith, "The State Police: Administration and Organization," The Macmillan Company, New York (1925).   Katherine Mayo, "Justice to All," Houghton Mifflin Co., Boston (1920) and "Mounted Justice," Houghton Mifflin Co., Boston (1922), gives a rosy picture of the Pennsylvania constabulary; "The American Cossacks," by the Pennsylvania State Federation of Labor (1915); William Z. Foster, "The Great Steel Strike," pp. 119–139 (1920), and John P. Guyer, *"Pennsylvania Cossacks,"* People's Publishing Co., Reading (1923), the labor view.   A comprehensive bibliography prepared by Margaret Mary Corcoran was published in 14 *Jour. Criminal Law and Criminology*, pp. 544–555 (1924).

For an account of the use of federal troops in strikes, see Edward Berman's "Labor Disputes and the President," pp. 20–23, 36–45, 59–60, 64–69, 90–92, 172–173, 185, 207–213 (1924).

The private guard system is briefly treated in John A. Fitch, *op. cit.*, pp. 253–259; George P. West, *Report on the Colorado Strike*, pp. 102–106 (1915); and Jeremiah P. Shallow, The Private Police of Pennsylvania, 146 *Ann. Amer. Acad. Polit. Social Sci.*, No. 235, pp. 55–62 (1929).

Interference with union organization by or on behalf of employers is presented in S. Adele Shaw, Closed Towns—Intimidation as It Is Practiced in the Pittsburgh Steel District—the Contrast in Ohio, 43 *Survey* 58–64, 85–86, 92–93 (1919); Foster, *op. cit.*, pp. 112–118, 175–178, 188–189; West, *op. cit.*, pp. 59–61; Fitch, *op. cit.*, pp. 164–167, 211–216; and Heber Blankenhorn, "The Strike for Union," Bureau of Industrial Research (1924).

CHAPTER X

RESTRICTIONS ON EMPLOYERS

Thus far, this book has dealt almost exclusively with the restrictions on labor in its struggles with capital. This chapter will consider restraints on employers and the methods employers use in fighting labor organizations.

EMPLOYERS' COMBINATIONS

Few cases involving the legality of employers' combinations have come up, but these have all sustained the right to combine against the demands of employees. Employers' associations are legal, precisely as trade unions are, *per se*, legal.[1] Employers may agree to operate under the open-shop plan and may bind themselves by penalties not to deal with labor unions. Such penalties are enforcible both at law and through injunctions.[2] Further, it has been held, in the only case raising this question, that unions may not combine to prevent employers from belonging to employers' associations.[3]

---

[1] Cote v. Murphy, 159 Pa. 420, 28 Atl. 190 (1894) and cases cited in Note 2 below.

[2] City Trust, etc., Co. v. Waldhauer, 47 Misc. 7, 95 N. Y. S. 222 (1905); United Hat Manufacturers v. Baird-Unteidt Co., 88 Conn. 332, 91 Atl. 373 (1914); State v. Employers of Labor, 102 Neb. 768, 169 N. W. 717, 170 N. W. 185 (1918); Middleton v. Stark, 2 *Law and Labor* 121 (Super. Ct. Wash. 1920); Dyer Bros., etc., v. Central Iron Works, 182 Cal. 588, 189 Pac. 445 (1921); Trade Press Publishing Co. v. Milwaukee Typographical Union, 180 Wis. 449, 193 N. W. 507 (1923); Audroff v. Building Trades Employers Assoc., 7 *Law and Labor* 178 (Ind. App. 1925).

Cases in which attempts to enforce such penalties failed but without involving the general question whether employers may agree not to employ union labor and bind themselves by forfeits to observe such agreements are McCord v. Thompson-Starrett Co., 129 App. Div. 130, 113 N. Y. S. 385 (1908), and American, etc., Assoc. v. Proser, 190 App. Div. 164, 179 N. Y. S. 207 (1919).

[3] Parker Paint and Wall Paper Co. v. Local Union, 87 W. Va. 631, 105 S. E. 911 (1921).

In the even fewer cases of lockouts, the counterpart of strikes, the right of the employers to lock out their employees has been sustained, without question or qualification.[1]

Combinations to boycott participated in by employers are governed by the same principles of law as are trade-union boycotts. Business boycotts have often been before the courts, and while there are some decisions, especially early cases, sustaining such boycotts, the majority have gone the other way.[2] Employers' boycotts (understanding by this term, boycotts not to affect business but to combat labor unions) have come up much more rarely and the decisions are less unanimous. The best view, however, seems to be that employers' boycotts are to be judged by the same standards as labor boycotts.[3]

---

[1] Sinsheimer v. United Garment Workers, 77 Hun. 215, 28 N. Y. S. 321 (1894); Cote v. Murphy, 159 Pa. 420, 28 Atl. 190 (1894); Atkins v. Fletcher, 65 N. J. Eq. 658, 55 Atl. 1074 (1903); City Trust, etc., Co. v. Waldhauer, 47 Misc. 7, 95 N. Y. S. 222 (1905); McCord v. Thompson-Starrett Co., 129 App. Div. 130, 113 N. Y. S. 385 (1908). In the last-mentioned case, it was held unlawful, by a divided court, for employers to agree not to employ members of a particular union, but their right to lock out their employees is assumed.

[2] The U. S. Supreme Court condemned a trade boycott as a conspiracy in Aikens v. Wis., 195 U. S. 194, 25 Sup. Ct. 3 (1904), and it has held such boycotts to constitute a violation of the antitrust laws in many cases, including Granada Lumber Co. v. Miss., 217 U. S. 433, 30 Sup. Ct. 535 (1910) and Eastern States Retail Lumber Assoc. v. U. S., 234 U. S. 600, 34 Sup. Ct. 951 (1915).

[3] The most important case involving an employers' boycott ever to come before the courts was the suit brought by the United States to enjoin the Industrial Association of San Francisco from boycotting material dealers who sold to builders dealing with the unions. This case was carried to the U. S. Supreme Court, but the only point decided was that the federal antitrust laws did not apply. (Industrial Assoc. of San Francisco v. U. S., 268 U. S. 64, 45 Sup. Ct. 403 [1925].)

Employers' boycotts were held lawful in Cote v. Murphy, 159 Pa. 420, 28 Atl. 190 (1894), Buchanan v. Kerr, 159 Pa. 433, 28 Atl. 195 (1894); Delaney v. Master Plumbers (2nd Jud. Dist. Ramsay Co., Minn., 1920; text in Frey, "The Labor Injunction," pp. 136–139). Such boycotts were held unlawful in Murray v. McGarigle, 69 Wis. 483 (1887); Carlson v. Carpenters Contractors Assoc., 305 Ill. 331, 137 N. E. 222 (1922); Brescia Construction Co. v. Stone Masons, 195 App. Div. 647, 187 N. Y. S. 77 (1921).

EMPLOYMENT OF STRIKE GUARDS

Employers have an undoubted right to operate their plants during strikes and are entitled to police protection in doing so. Failure to afford protection has been held a cause of action at common law against the municipality responsible, and there exist some statutory provisions to the same effect.[1]

In operating their plants, employers may employ either local men or strike breakers brought in from a distance. In a few instances, public authorities have sought to prevent the importation of strike breakers, but such action has been held unlawful wherever this question has come before the courts.[2] The only restriction upon employers is the statute of about a dozen states providing that in advertising for labor during strikes they must make mention of the existence of labor trouble.[3]

---

[1] A case in point is Pittsburgh, etc., R. Co. v. City of Chicago, 244 Ill. 220, 89 N. E. 1022 (1909). A statute to this effect is Wis. Stats. 1929, s. 66.07. In Butte Miners Union v. City of Butte, 58 Mont. 391, 194 Pac. 149 (1920), a city was held liable because a mob wrecked a labor-union hall.

[2] An early instance of such an attempt was the issuance of an injunction by Judge Skidmore at the request of the district attorney of Cherokee County, Kan., in 1898, prohibiting the Kansas and Texas Coal Co. from bringing negro strike breakers into the county. This state court order was countered by the issuance of an injunction by U. S. Judge Hook against the courts and officials of Cherokee County, prohibiting them from interfering with the bringing in of these strike breakers (*Kan. Labor Bur. Rept.*, pp. 340–341 (1898); pp. 460–465 (1889). Similarly, during the steel strike of 1919, Major Davis of Cleveland announced that, to prevent riots, the police would arrest as "suspicious characters" all strike breakers brought into the city. This led to a federal injunction enjoining the major and police chief from interfering with the strikers: American Steel and Wire Co. v. Davis, 261 Fed. 800 (1919). A similar injunction was issued by the New Jersey courts against the enforcement of a Jersey City ordinance prohibiting importation of strike breakers (Swift v. Hague, 2 *Law and Labor* 9 [1920]); and still another injunction by a federal court in Ohio (Mullins Body Corp. v. International Assoc., 3 *Law and Labor* 148 [1921]); and a New York court enjoined the enforcement of an order issued by the major of Schenectady directing the street-car company not to operate its lines during a strike (Schenectady R. Co. v. Whitmeyer, 121 Misc. 4, 199 N. Y. S. 827 [1923]).

When martial law has been declared, however, the military authorities can prevent the employment of strike breakers if they deem this necessary to the preservation of law and order, and they have taken such action in a number of cases.

[3] Laws to this effect are: Colorado, C. L. 1921, ss. 4156, 4157, 4159; Minnesota, Mason's Stats. 1927, ss. 10392–10393; California, Hillyer's

To protect the strike breakers, employers may hire strike guards, whose employment the states may regulate but may not prohibit.[1] Such regulation consists principally of what were

Cons. Suppl. 1921–1925, p. 3182; Nevada, R. L. 1912, ss. 1936–1938; Alaska, Acts 1913, c. 36; Montana, R. C. 1921, ss. 11220–11222; Oklahoma, R. L. 1910, ss. 3765, 3766, 3768; Oregon, Laws 1920, ss. 6795–6796; Tennessee, Code 1917, ss. 4338*a*, 4338*a*–2, 4338*a*–4; Wisconsin, Stats. 1929, s. 103.43; Maine, R. S. 1916, c. 49, ss. 7, 8; New Hampshire, Pub. Acts 1926, p. 683; Massachusetts, G. L. 1921, c. 149, ss. 22, 23.

All of these laws except those of the three New England states, besides penalizing failure to mention the existence of strikes, also prohibit all false representations to induce workmen to accept employment. New York (Gilbert's Penal Law, s. 950) prohibits false representation but not failure to mention the existence of strikes.

Laws of this character were held constitutional in Commonwealth v. Libbey, 216 Mass. 356, 103 N. E. 923 (1914) and Biersach and Neidermeyer Co. v. State, 177 Wis. 388, 188 N. W. 650 (1922). Such a law was held unconstitutional in Josma v. Western Steel Car and Foundry Co., 249 Ill. 508, 94 N. W. 945 (1911).

The enforcement of these laws has proved a difficult matter in situations where a labor union insists that a strike is in progress while the employer claims the strike has been defeated or never materialized. This difficulty led Maine and Massachusetts to amend their laws so as to provide for an official determination by the state board of arbitration, upon the request of either party, regarding the existence or non-existence of the claimed strike, while Wisconsin added a subsection defining when a strike should be regarded as being in existence.

Supplementing the laws discussed in this note is the very general practice of public employment offices of advising applicants of the existence of strikes in plants calling for help. This is required by the statutes of New York (Cons. Laws 1909, c. 36, ss. 66*g* and 66*h*), Ohio (G. C. 1921, s. 896–3), and Texas (C. S. 1928, art. 5221); and elsewhere is a rule of the employment offices. During the World War, the government employment offices conducted by the U. S. Department of Labor refused to supply help to employers involved in strikes, but it is now regarded as a sound public employment office practice to serve employers having strikes as well as other employers, but to insist that workmen referred to such employers be told of the existence of strikes.

[1] The common law on this point was stated by Judge Paxson in his charge to the grand jury investigating the Homestead riots in 1892: "The company had the undoubted right to protect its property. For this purpose, it could lawfully employ as many men as it saw proper and arm them if necessary." Much the same position was taken in *ex parte* Reilly, 2 *Law and Labor* 4 (1920), in which a Cleveland ordinance prohibiting the employment of unlicensed strike guards was held unconstitutional. On the other hand, the Washington Supreme Court held constitutional the Washington law (enacted in 1893, repealed in 1909) prohibiting the employment of *armed* guards: State v. Gohl, 46 Wash. 408, 90 Pac. 259 (1907).

called at the time of their enactment the "anti-Pinkerton" laws[1] and of statutes prescribing citizenship and residence within the county as qualifications for deputy sheriffs and police officers.[2] The anti-Pinkerton laws, dating from the nineties, penalize the importation of armed guards from other states. Some of these laws are so limited as to be practically meaningless, and none seems ever to have been made the basis for criminal prosecutions. The requirement of local residence for deputy sheriffs and special police is of greater practical importance; and still more significant are the recent decisions holding employers responsible for unlawful acts committed by guards in the performance of their duties.[3]

DISCRIMINATION AND BLACKLISTING

The right to lock out their employees and, still more, to employ strike breakers and strike guards is of great value to employers in times of acute labor trouble. No less important to them are other privileges resorted to in anticipation of trouble and directed

---

[1] The common type of anti-Pinkerton law is one prohibiting the importation of armed guards from another state. Such laws are in force in: Arkansas, C. and M. Digest 1921, s. 2793; Kentucky, Const., s. 225, Stats. 1922, s. 1376; Missouri, R. S. 1919, s. 3484; Montana, Const., art. 3, s. 31, R. C. 1921, s. 10925; Nebraska, C. S. 1922, s. 9723; South Carolina, Const., art. VIII, s. 9; Utah, Const., art. 12, s. 16; Wyoming, Const., art. 19. South Dakota had a similar law from 1893 to 1903.

More limited in their scope are the statutes of the following states, which prohibit the employment of armed guards only where the workmen guarded were procured through false representations or are transported under arms: Alaska, Acts 1913, c. 36; Colorado, C. L. 1921, s. 4158; Oklahoma, R. L. 1910, s. 3767; Tennessee, Code 1917, s. 4338a–3.

Texas has a statute (C. S. 1928, art. 5207) prohibiting non-residents from acting as armed guards, with a proviso which, perhaps, nullifies the act; Wisconsin (Stats. 1929, s. 348.472) has a somewhat indefinite law which seems to prohibit the employment of any armed guards; while Minnesota (Stats. 1927, s. 10501) prohibits anyone from maintaining an armed force for hire within the state.

[2] Among the laws to this effect are Arkansas, C. and M. Digest 1921, ss. 2790–2794; Illinois, R. S. 1927, c. 125, s. 27; Kentucky, Stats. 1922, s. 1376; Missouri, R. S. 1919, s. 3480; Nebraska, C. S. 1922, s. 9724; N. Y. Penal Code, s. 1845; Pennsylvania, Stats. 1920, s. 15791; West Virginia, Code 1923, c. 148, s. 169; Wisconsin, Stats. 1929, s. 66.11 (1). Massachusetts (G. L. 1921, c. 149, s. 176), Texas (Stats. 1928, art. 5207), and West Virginia (Code 1923, c. 148, s. 169) prohibit the employment of private guards who are not citizens.

[3] See Note 1, p. 173.

toward keeping out the union and the union agitator. These are, particularly, the refusal to employ union men, the black-listing of strikers and trouble makers, the establishment of company unions, and the binding of employees to individual non-union agreements.

The right of employers to discriminate against union men is undoubted. Twenty-two states at one time had laws which made it a criminal offense for employers to discharge or refuse to employ a workman for membership in any labor union, and the federal government included a similar provision applicable to the railroads of the country in the Erdman Act of 1898. Some of these laws are still to be found in the statute books, but all of them have been rendered valueless by decisions of the Supreme Courts of the United States and nearly a dozen states holding such legislation to be unconstitutional.[1] Confronted first with the earliest form of these laws prohibiting discrimination against union members under criminal penalties, the U. S. Supreme Court in the Adair Case in 1908 held that employers have a right to discharge workmen for any or no reason, including the fact that they belong to labor unions. In the Coppage case in 1915, it condemned also the type of antidiscrimination law which penalizes not mere discharge for union membership but coercion

[1] The decisions of the U. S. Supreme Court referred to are Adair v. U. S., 208 U. S. 161, 28 Sup. Ct. 277 (1908) and Coppage v. Kansas, 236 U. S. 1, 35 Sup. Ct. 240 (1915). State supreme court decisions holding antidiscrimination laws to be unconstitutional are State v. Julow, 129 Mo. 163, 31 S. W. 781 (1895); Gillespie v. People, 188 Ill. 176, 58 N. E. 1007 (1900); State v. Kreutzberg, 114 Wis. 530, 90 N. W. 1098 (1903); Coffeyville, etc., Co. v. Perry, 69 Kan. 297, 76 Pac. 848 (1904); People v. Marcus, 185 N. Y. 257, 77 N. E. 1073 (1906); State v. Daniels, 118 Minn. 155, 136 N. W. 584 (1912); Jackson v. Berger, 92 Ohio 130, 110 N. E. 732 (1915); Bemis v. State, 12 Okla. Crim. 114, 152 Pac. 456 (1915); People v. Western Union Telegraph Co., 70 Colo. 90, 198 Pac. 146 (1924). Other cases holding antidiscrimination laws to be unconstitutional are Commonwealth v. Clark, 14 Pac. Super. 435 (1900); Goldfield, etc., Co. v. Goldfield Miners Union, 159 Fed. 500 (1908); Montgomery v. Pacific Electric Railway Co., 293 Fed. 680 (1923).

Cases denying recovery to workmen discharged for union membership, which did not involve antidiscrimination statutes, include Platt v. Philadelphia and Railroad Co. (sic.), 65 Fed. 660 (1894); Flaccus v. Smith, 199 Pa. 128, 48 Atl. 894 (1901); McNatt v. Lawther, 223 S. W. 503 (Tex. Civ. App. 1920); San Antonio Fire Fighters v. Bell, 223 S. W. 506 (Tex. Civ. App. 1920).

to compel employees or prospective employees to give up their union connections. While in both cases the court was divided, these decisions have been accepted everywhere.

In theory, the law is quite different as to blacklisting. This is forbidden by general statutes in twenty-five states.[1] Supplementing these, six states penalize refusal by employers to give discharged employees on demand a truthful statement of the reasons for their discharge, and one state provides that the records of any association which furnished information about workmen affecting their employment shall be open to public inspection. All of these anti-blacklist statutes are believed to be constitutional.[2] Until quite recently, there was grave doubt

---

[1] General anti-blacklist laws are to be found in Alabama, Code 1928, s. 3451, 3455; Arizona, R. C. 1928, ss. 4881, 4882; Arkansas, C. and M. Digest 1921, s. 7135; California, Stats. 1929, Penal Code s. 653e; Colorado, A. S. 1928, ss. 461–468; Connecticut, G. S. 1918, s. 6360; Florida, G. L. 1927, ss. 6606–6610, 7773; Illinois, R. S. 1927, c. 38, s. 139 (conspiracy to blacklist); Indiana, A. S. 1926, ss. 9364, 9365 (held, in Wabash R. R. Co. v. Young, 162 Ind. 102, 69 N. E. 1003, not to apply to employees voluntarily quitting); Iowa, Code 1924, ss. 13253, 13254; Kansas, R. C. 1923, ss. 44–117, 44–118; Minnesota, Mason's Stats. 1927, s. 10378; Mississippi, Hemingway's Annot. Code 1927, s. 9271 (applies to telegraph and telephone companies only); Missouri, R. C. 1919, s. 3505; Montana, R. C. 1921, ss. 3093, 11219; Nevada, R. S. 1912, ss. 6779–6782; New Mexico, Stats. 1915, ss. 1803–1805; North Carolina, A. C. 1927, ss. 4477, 4478; North Dakota, C. L. 1913, s. 9446; Oklahoma, Stats. 1921, s. 7267; Oregon, Laws 1920, ss. 2179, 2180; Texas, C. S. 1928, Penal Code, c. IX, arts. 1613–1621; Utah, Const., art. 12, s. 19; art. 16, s. 4; C. L. 1917, ss. 3680, 3681; Virginia, A. C. 1924, s. 1817; Wisconsin, Stats. 1929, s. 343.682.

The following states now have laws requiring employers to give discharged employees a truthful statement of their reasons for discharge: Florida, G. L. 1927, ss. 6608–6610; Indiana, A. S. 1926, ss. 9350, 9351; Montana, R. C. 1921, ss. 3094, 11219; Nebraska, C. S. 1922, ss. 7666–7668; Ohio, G. C. 1920, s. 9012; Oklahoma, C. S. 1921, s. 7266. Georgia (Acts 1890–1891, p. 183) and Texas (P. C. 1916, s. 1190) formerly had such laws, but these are no longer in force. Connecticut (G. S. 1918, s. 6361) provides that the employment records of employers' associations shall be open to public inspection.

[2] General anti-blacklist laws were held constitutional in State v. Justus, 85 Minn. 279, 88 N. W. 759 (1902) and Joyce v. Great Nor. Ry. Co., 100 Minn. 225, 110 N. W. 975 (1907). Such a law was held unconstitutional in part in Wabash R. R. Co. v. Young, 162 Ind. 102, 69 N. E. 1003 (1904).

Laws requiring employers to give discharged employees statements of the reasons for discharge were held unconstitutional in Crall v. T. & O. C. R. Co., 7 Ohio Cir. Ct. 132 (1894); Wallace v. Ga., etc., R. R. Co.,

as to the laws requiring employers to give employees a statement of the reasons for discharge, but two well-reasoned decisions of the U. S. Supreme Court have probably settled that these laws, also, are valid. Apart from statutes, it is an actionable wrong for an employer or anyone else to procure the discharge or prevent the employment of a workman by false representations. Even when the statements made are truthful, the majority of cases hold that the person procuring the discharge is liable if he acted from malicious motives.[1]

---

94 Ga. 732, 22 S. E. 579 (1893); A. T. & S. F. R. Co. v. Brown, 80 Kan. 312, 102 Pac. 459 (1909); St. Louis S. W. R. Co. v. Griffin, 106 Tex. 477, 126 S. W. 703 (1914); and the following cases, while not involving directly the constitutionality of such statutes, are much to the same effect: Cleveland, etc., R. Co. v. Jenkins, 174 Ill. 398, 51 N. E. 811 (1898); McDonald v. Ill. Central R. Co., 187 Ill. 529, 58 N. E. 463 (1900); N. Y. C. & St. L. R. Co. v. Schaffer, 65 Ohio 414, 62 N. E. 1036 (1902). Such laws, however, were held constitutional by the U. S. Supreme Court in Prudential Insurance Co. of America v. Cheek, 259 U. S. 530, 42 Sup. Ct. 516 (1922); Chicago R. I. & Pac. R. Co. v. Perry, 259 U. S. 548, 42 Sup. Ct. 524 (1922). The Connecticut statute providing that employers' associations which give out information about workmen must allow public inspection of their records was held constitutional in State v. Lay, 86 Conn. 141, 84 Atl. 522 (1912).

[1] Cases holding the procuring of discharge by untruthful statements to be actionable include Lally v. Cantwell, 30 Mo. App. 524 (1889); Mo. Pac. R. Co. v. Behee, 2 Tex. Civ. App. 107, 21 S. W. 384 (1893); Hundley v. Louisville & N. R. Co., 105 Ky. 162, 48 S. W. 429 (1896); Blumenthal v. Shaw, 77 Fed. 954 (1897); Hollenbeck v. Ristine, 114 Iowa 358, 86 N. W. 377 (1901); Willner v. Silverman, 109 Md. 341, 71 Atl. 962 (1909); Rhodes v. Granby Cotton Mills, 87 S. C. 18, 68 S. E. 824 (1910); Seward v. Seaboard Air Line Railway, 159 N. C. 241, 75 S. E. 34 (1912); Hefferman v. Whittelsey, 126 Minn. 163, 148 N. W. 63 (1914); Scott v. Prudential Outfitting Co., 92 Misc. 195, 155, N. Y. S. 497 (1915); Kennedy v. Hub Manufacturing Co., 221 Mass. 136, 108 N. E. 932 (1915); Dick v. Nor. Pac. R. Co., 86 Wash. 211, 150 Pac. 8 (1915); Southern Finance Co. v. Foster, 19 Ala. App. 109, 95 S. 388 (1923); Joyce v. Great Nor. Ry. Co., 100 Minn. 225, 110 N. W. 975 (1907).

Among cases holding it unlawful to maliciously procure the discharge of workmen even when the statements made are truthful are Chipley v. Atkinson, 23 Fla. 206, 1 S. 934 (1887); Danneberg v. Ashley, 10 Ohio C. C. 558 (1894); Moran v. Dunphy, 177 Mass. 485, 59 N. E. 125 (1901); London Guarantee and Accident Co. v. Horn, 206 Ill. 493, 69 N. E. 526 (1904); Gibson v. Fidelity and Casualty Co., 232 Ill. 49, 83 N. E. 539 (1908); Illinois Steel Co. v. Brenshall, 141 Ill. App. 36 (1908); Huskie v. Griffin, 75 N. H. 345, 74 Atl. 595 (1909); Jones v. Leslie, 61 Wash. 107, 112 Pac. 81 (1910); Evans v. McKay, 212 S. W. 680 (Tex. Civ. App. 1919); U. S.

Despite the many statutes against blacklisting and the decisions at common law against maliciously procuring the discharge of a workman, there have been few cases in which persons blacklisted because they were strikers or union men have secured any redress. Only two successful criminal prosecutions for blacklisting are known, and there have been less than a dozen cases in which strikers or union men have recovered damages, with but one instance of an injunction issued against a blacklist. Nearly all of these cases are old and are greatly outnumbered by unsuccessful actions.[1] The explanation lies partly in the wording

---

Fidelity and Guaranty Co. v. Millonas, 206 Ala. 147, 89 S. 732 (1921). To the contrary, Raycroft v. Tayntor, 68 Vt. 219, 35 Atl. 53 (1896); Holder v. Cannon Manufacturing Co., 138 N. C. 308, 50 S. E. 681 (1905); Hilton v. Sheridan Coal Co., 297 Pac. 413 (Kan. 1931).

[1] In the unreported case, State v. Wallace, in the New Haven City Court in January, 1887, two officers of a manufacturing corporation were convicted for blacklisting and fined fifty dollars and costs, although "the judge apologised for finding the distinguished prisoners guilty." (A. M. Edwards, Labor Legislation of Connecticut, 8 *Amer. Econ. Assoc. Publ.* 164, 3rd ser. (1907); "Railroad Conductor," pp. 161–162 (1887).) The other successful criminal prosecution for blacklisting is the reported case of State v. Justus, 85 Minn. 279, 88 N. W. 759 (1902).

Successful damage suits for blacklisting are Mary Slattery v. American Crockery Co. at Trenton, N. J., in 1883 (one hundred dollars awarded the plaintiff: *Iron Molders Jour.* July 1, 1883); Mattison v. L. S. and M. S. Ry. Co. (sic), 3 Ohio Dec. 526 (Superior Com. Pl. 1895); Ketcham v. Chicago & N. W. R. Co. ($21,633.33 damages awarded in 1895 to a blacklisted Pullman striker: 33 *Amer. Law Rev.* 563; 21 *Arena* 273); Johnson v. Mo. Pac. R. Co. at Memphis, Tenn., 1896 ($1,500 damages awarded to a Pullman striker: 3 *Amer. Federationist* 19); Willett v. Jacksonville, etc., R. Co. ($1,700 damages awarded in 1896 in the U. S. Circuit Court of the Southern District of Florida: *U. S. Labor Bull.* 4, p. 437); Drummond v. Evansville & Terre Haute R. Co. ($3,500 damages awarded in 1896 in the Circuit Court, Knox County, Ind., to a Pullman striker: 3 *Amer. Federationist* 97); Rhodes v. Granby Cotton Mills, 87 S. C. 18, 68 S. E. 824 (1910); Johnson v. Oregon Stevedoring Co., 128 Ore. 121, 270 Pac. 772 (1928) ($4,500 damages awarded against an employers' association maintaining a hiring hall system. The Supreme Court of Oregon in the reported case held the cause of action to be good but allowed a new trial, which was not had up to October, 1929). Demurrers to suits for damages by blacklisted men were overruled in Anderson v. Shipowners Assoc., 272 U. S. 359, 47 Sup. Ct. 125 (1926) and in Goins v. Sargent, 196 N. C. 478, 146 S. E. 131 (1929), but to date no damages have been recovered in either case.

The only injunction ever issued against blacklisting was allowed in Milwaukee in 1914 in the case of Potter v. Mayer Boot and Shoe Co. This

of some of the anti-blacklist laws, but more in the difficulty of proving the charge. Some anti-blacklist laws prohibit only conspiracy to blacklist; others, "blacklisting," without any attempt to define the term, which perhaps restricts their scope to the circulation of lists of workmen not to be employed. Thirteen states have still more ineffectual laws, which, while prohibiting blacklists, expressly legalize the most prevalent method, providing that employers may give a truthful statement of the reasons for discharge to anyone making inquiry therefor.[1] On the other hand, there are some anti-blacklist laws which in minute detail prohibit every known form of blacklisting; yet these have proved little more valuable than the laws which in a backhanded way actually legalize this practice.[2]

With the best law, it is difficult to prove blacklisting. When a workman is discharged because he was reported to be a trouble

---

injunction was issued *ex parte* by a court commissioner, and before the hearings were completed the strike was settled. Injunctions against blacklisting were denied in Worthington v. Waring, 157 Mass. 421, 32 N. E. 744 (1892); Boyer v. Western Union Telegraph Co., 124 Fed. 246 (1903); Cornellier v. Haverhill Shoe Manufacturers Assoc., 221 Mass. 554, 109 N. E. 643 (1915) (overruling Worthington v. Waring but denying injunction because of plaintiff's "unclean hands"). Unsuccessful damage suits are much more numerous, including the following reported cases: Mo. Pac. R. Co. v. Richmond, 73 Tex. 568, 11 S. W. 555 (1889); Bradley v. Pierson, 148 Pa. 502, 24 Atl. 65 (1892); Cleveland, etc., R. Co. v. Jenkins, 174 Ill. 398, 51 N. E. 811 (1898); McDonald v. Ill. Central R. Co., 187 Ill. 529, 58 N. E. 463 (1900); Wabash R. R. Co. v. Young, 162 Ind. 102, 69 N. E. 1003 (1904); St. Louis S. W. R. Co. v. Hixon, 126 S. W. 338, 104 Tex. 267, 137 S. W. 343 (1911); Dick v. Nor. Pac. R. Co., 86 Wash. 211, 150 Pac. 8 (1915); Cleary v. Great Nor. Ry. Co., 147 Minn. 403, 180 N. W. 545 (1920).

[1] The Illinois law is an example of a statute prohibiting only "conspiracy" to blacklist, and the Connecticut law one that prohibits blacklisting without defining the term. The twelve states whose anti-blacklist laws expressly legalize giving out the reasons for discharge upon request therefor are California, Colorado, Connecticut, Florida, Indiana, Iowa, Kansas, Montana, Nevada, North Carolina, Texas, Virginia, and Wisconsin.

[2] Examples of extremely detailed laws are the Arizona general anti-blacklist law and the Oklahoma service-letter law. Like other statutes of this type, the latter law requires employers to give former employees a truthful statement of the reasons for their discharge; and then, to guard against such service letters being made a means of blacklisting, the law provides that they must not be written on water-marked paper or have any other identification mark which might convey additional information about the employee than that expressed in writing.

maker, he has no redress against the employer who discharged him, since employers may discharge for any or no reason. His only action lies against the person who reported him, but, unless the employer cooperates, he cannot prove his case. Without such cooperation, he cannot establish why he was discharged, nor who supplied the information used against him.

There have been a considerable number of instances in which workmen have recovered from persons who procured their discharge.[1] Many of these have been cases in which casualty-insurance companies insisted upon the discharge of workmen who would not settle accident claims on the insurer's terms; others have involved finance companies and other creditors who, through this means, sought to take vengeance for non-payment of a disputed debt. In such situations, the employer is likely to sympathize with the workman he discharged, particularly if he later learns that the representations made to him were false or unjustified. In any event, no sense of class loyalty prevents his disclosing the facts to the discharged workman.[2]

In cases where a workman is discharged as a union agitator, the situation is vastly different. The last employer is not in sympathy with the workman, and a certain clannishness operates to prevent such employer from disclosing facts which could be used against the former employer. Some other reason is usually given for the discharge than the true cause—union membership—and no explanation at all need be given. Even when the last employer states the true reason, the workman can seldom prove from whom he received this information. In this day, the old-fashioned blacklist is *passé*. Reports about union agitators are conveyed by telephone, letter, or word of mouth, through a central hiring hall, or the record system of an employers' association. As long as it is lawful for an employer to discharge or refuse to employ a workman for any reason, anti-blacklist laws

---

[1] See Note 1, p. 214, last paragraph.

[2] The point made, that the success of actions for maliciously procuring discharge depends upon the cooperation of the employer, is illustrated by the Wisconsin case, Johnson v. Aetna Life Insurance Co., 158 Wis. 56, 147 N. W. 32 (1914), in which, unlike the usual run of cases against casualty-insurance companies by workmen who claimed to have been discharged because they would not settle personal-injury cases, the court held for the insurance company, because the employer would not testify that he discharged the plaintiff at the instance of the insurance company.

and the common law right of recovery for maliciously procuring discharge are practically worthless to workmen blacklisted for union membership. Even if the courts should reverse themselves and permit recovery from employers for discriminating against union members (which is most unlikely), it would still be only very little easier to make out a case, since usually the true reason for discharge could not be proved.

Blacklists are always shrouded in secrecy. While labor charges that the practice is flourishing, the extent of blacklisting at the present time is not known. There are workmen in nearly every community who claim inability to get work in their crafts because they have been blacklisted, but positive proof is lacking.

Lists of workmen not to be employed are probably now circulated very little.[1] Blacklisting through the record systems of employers' associations is more common. Many employers' associations keep card records of all workmen employed by their members, giving their employment history, reasons for discharge, etc., including in many cases facts regarding union membership. Before hiring new employees, the members make inquiry from the association or, if they take on men without such prior investigation, notify it afterwards. From that office, they get the workman's previous record and, while not obligated to do so, are thereby enabled to discriminate against union members.

Industrial espionage serves the same purpose and probably is today the principal source of information on the union affiliation of employees. It both supplements and renders unnecessary the older methods of blacklisting, as do also "yellow-dog" contracts. These accomplish all of the purposes of blacklisting and escape the blacklist's ban by the courts.

COMPANY UNIONISM

The company union is another method of combating unionism which has gained great impetus in recent years.[2] A conserva-

[1] The extensive blacklisting of workmen who made themselves objectionable to the employers in the steel strike of 1919 is briefly discussed in *The Report on the Steel Strike of* 1919, Commission of Inquiry of the Interchurch World Movement, pp. 219–221. The use of the record system of the National Founders Association for blacklisting purposes is mentioned in C. E. Bonnett, "Employers Associations in the United States," p. 80, The Macmillan Company, New York (1922).

[2] Good accounts of the company union movement and its significance include William M. Leiserson's The Accomplishments and Significance of

tive estimate places the membership of company unions at not less than one-third that of all labor unions, with a membership in manufacturing industries exceeding that of the "regular" unions. This entire growth is a development of the last decade, during which period the labor unions lost heavily in membership, particularly in the industries where company unionism is strongest.

Company unions differ from one another in their purposes and detailed structure, but all of them are plant organizations; that is, they are confined to a particular plant or corporation, without affiliation with a national or other larger organization. All of them also, as the name implies, enjoy the peculiar favor of the employer. Many of them were organized by the company and are virtually controlled by it.

The right of employers to organize company unions and to proselytize their employees has been challenged in only one case. This was an injunction action commenced in 1927 by the railway clerks' union against a railroad company in Texas connected with the Southern Pacific system.[1] This suit was premised upon a provision in the railroad labor act to the effect that neither side might interfere with the right of the other to be represented in the adjustment of labor disputes by representatives of their own choice. This the company was charged with having violated by organizing a company union and exerting itself in every way possible to induce its employees to leave the railway clerks' union and join its union, proof of this allegation being made by a letter of one of the officers of the corporation. The trial court decided for the union and issued an injunction restraining the railroad company from compelling its clerks to

---

Employee Representation, 4 *Personnel* 71–137 (1928) and Employee Representation—a Warning to Both Employers and Unions, 13 *Proc. Acad. Polit. Sci.* 96–109 (1928); H. R. Seager's Company Unions v. Trade Unions, 13 *Amer. Econ. Rev.* 1–13 (1923); E. R. Burton's "Employee Representation," Williams & Wilkins Co., Baltimore (1926); Paul H. Gemmill's The Literature of Employe Representation, 42 *Quart. Jour. Econ.* 479–494 (1928).

[1] Brotherhood of Railway and Steamship Clerks v. Tex. & N. O. R. Co., 24 F. (2nd) 426 (1928); 25 F. (2nd) 873 (1928); 33 F. (2nd) 13 (1929); 281 U. S. 550, 50 Sup. Ct. 427 (1930). The significance of this case is discussed in Edward Berman, the Supreme Court Interprets the Railway Labor Act, 20 *Amer. Econ. Rev.* 619–639 (1930).

give up their membership in the regular union and to join the company union. This was followed by a contempt case and a finding that the company had violated the injunction; whereupon the court issued a mandatory order directing the dissolution of the company union. The Circuit Court of Appeals, in a two to one decision, upheld the trial court, and the U. S. Supreme Court in 1930 unanimously sustained this decision.

That workingmen have a right to be represented in negotiations over conditions of employment by representatives of their own choice has been often stated by the courts, apart from any statutory provisions such as figured in this case.[1] This would seem to condemn company-controlled unions and afford a basis for injunctions to prevent employers from coercing their employees to join such organizations in preference to labor unions. Workingmen being conceded the right to bargain collectively in the determination of the conditions of their employment, it follows that employers should not be permitted to control the selection of the employees' representatives. As the U. S. Supreme Court said in the railway clerks' case: "Such collective action would be a mockery if representation were made futile by interference with the freedom of choice." A company-controlled union is not only an anomaly but a most serious invasion of the fundamental rights of the workmen.

YELLOW-DOG CONTRACTS

Company unions are an anathema to organized labor; yellow-dog contracts, still more so. Particularly is this true of the leaders who regard the law governing yellow-dog contracts as the most grievous wrong the courts have ever committed against labor save perhaps injunctions, which are the means used to make these contracts effective.

This term has been applied to a considerable variety of individual agreements signed by workmen as a condition of employment.[2] The simplest form is a promise not to join a particular

---

[1] A good statement to this effect occurs in Thomas v. Cincinnati, etc., R. Co., 62 Fed. 803, at 817 (1894), a decision of William Howard Taft while a circuit judge of the United States.

[2] A considerable number of such agreements are set forth in "Conditions in the Coal Fields of Pennsylvania, West Virginia, and Ohio," hearings conducted by a subcommittee of the Senate Interstate Commerce Committee,

labor union or any union. A variation is an agreement not to
join a union while continuing in the employment, which amounts
to pretty much the same thing, but under some decisions allows
the signers to join in a strike called by the union against their
employer. Another type is a promise not to agitate for, or join
in, any strike; a third, not to do anything to interfere with the
employer's conduct of a non-union, or open, shop; and a fourth,
not to make any effort to change the employer's working rules.
Some of these contracts are limited as to time; others run for an
indefinite period. In all of them, the consideration for signing
is employment, but the employer invariably reserves the right
to discharge the employee at any time, either for any reason
that he sees fit, or for stated reasons, which include all of the
common causes of discharge.

Such individual non-union agreements were known in the
1880's, when they were called "iron-clad" contracts.[1] Not
until after the Hitchman Coal and Coke Co. case[2] in 1917, when
they began to be referred to as "yellow-dog" contracts, did
their use become widespread. In this case, the U. S. Supreme
Court approved of the issuance of an injunction prohibiting the
United Mine Workers from making any attempt to organize the
employees of the plaintiff coal corporation, who had signed
agreements not to join the union while they continued in employment.[3] Three judges dissented vigorously, but the decision at

Part VIII, pp. 2055–2056, 2090–2098, 2110–2113 (1928). Other illustrations occur in Cornelius Cochrane's Why Organized Labor Is Fighting
"Yellow-dog" Contracts, 15 *Amer. Labor Legis. Rev.* 227–232 (1925).
Most reported cases involving yellow-dog contracts quote the agreements
in litigation in full.

[1] "Iron-clad" contracts were used to break up the weavers' union at
Fall River, Mass., in 1875 (G. E. McNeill, "The Labor Movements—The
Problem of Today," pp. 224–225, A. M. Bridgman, Boston [1887]). They
were employed in the early eighties in the West Virginia coal fields (Norman
J. Ware, "The Labor Movement in the United States 1860–1895," p. 124,
D. Appleton & Company, New York [1929]); in 1883, by the Western
Union Telegraph Co. (*ibid.*, p. 129); and in the Hocking Valley, Ohio, coal
miners' strike in 1884–1885 (*John Swinton's Paper*, Mar. 1, 1885). Platt v.
Philadelphia & Reading R. Co., 65 Fed. 660 (1894) is the first court case
involving such a contract.

[2] Hitchman Coal and Coke Co. v. Mitchell, 245 U. S. 229, 38 Sup. Ct.
65.

[3] When this suit was instituted in 1907, the Hitchman Company did
not have signed agreements but had posted notices that it was operating

the time attracted little attention in labor circles. Employers' attorneys, however, appreciated the importance of the decision and suggested to their clients involved in, or fearing, labor troubles, the advisability of binding their employees by individual non-union agreements. Several such contracts were inaugurated within a year after this decision, leading to protests from labor and decisions of the War Labor Board directing the employers to abandon them.[1] When the war ended the authority of this board, yellow-dog contracts were adopted very widely, the years 1919–1922 being the period of their greatest expansion. In some cases, yellow-dog contracts instituted during strikes have since been abandoned, but the total number of plants operating under such contracts and the number of employees affected has been increasing steadily. A recent labor estimate is that 1,250-000 workingmen are now employed under yellow-dog contracts.[2] This is very likely an overstatement, but there are instances of such contracts in all parts of the country. Their use is general in the non-union coal fields of the eastern states, in the boot and shoe industry in New England, in the full-fashioned hosiery industry, and in several large street-car systems. In most other industries, there are only scattered examples, but more than one-half of all national unions have had encounters with the "yellow dog."

While the use of yellow-dog contracts did not become widespread until after the Hitchman Coal and Coke Co. decision, this was not the first time that such agreements came before the

---

on a non-union basis. Two months after the beginning of the suit, it instituted written contracts and thereafter required all new employees to sign the promise that they would not join the United Mine Workers while continuing in employment. None of the employees actually joined the union, but a number of them agreed to do so at a future date, when the union was ready to receive them. For a criticism of this decision, to the effect that the Supreme Court misconstrued the facts in this case, see the article Inducing Breach of Contract, by Francis B. Sayre, 36 *Harvard Law Rev.* 663 at 690–696 (1923).

[1] The leading case which came before the War Labor Board involving this question was that of the General Electric Co. at Pittsfield, Mass., in 1918. In that case and several others, the War Labor Board directed the employers to abandon all attempts to get their employees to sign non-union contracts and to cease discriminations against workmen for union membership. See *National War Labor Board Dockets* 19, 154, 1049.

[2] Estimate of Chester M. Wright, *Toledo Union Leader*, May 26, 1930.

courts. Prior to that decision, it had been determined that employers might require workers to sign non-union agreements as a condition of employment. This was settled in the cases cited in the section above on discrimination and blacklisting, particularly the decision of the U. S. Supreme Court in the Coppage case. That case and many of those which preceded it involved what are now called "yellow-dog" contracts, not merely discharges for union membership. In a strict sense, the only point decided in these cases was that legislatures could not make it a criminal offense for employers to require their employees to sign non-union agreements, but the reasoning and language therein were so broad that they may be said to hold such agreements lawful in all respects.

Treating yellow-dog contracts as lawful, however, was not sufficient to make them very useful to employers in combating labor unions. This established only that the employer was within his rights in insisting that his employees should sign such contracts and that he could sue them for any breach if he could prove damages. Such proof is most difficult, if not impossible; and, as a matter of fact, it has never occurred in the entire history of yellow-dog contracts that any employer has sued any workman for violating such a contract. Employees who sign non-union agreements may feel morally obligated to observe them, but for practical purposes, such contracts are not legally enforcible against the signers. It is as a restraint upon third parties—the labor unions and their organizers—that yellow-dog contracts are valuable to employers. In this respect, the Hitchman case went beyond the prior decisions involving the antidiscrimination laws. This case did not stop with holding yellow-dog contracts to be lawful but decided, further, that third parties may not persuade the employees to violate these contracts.

This conclusion was based upon the theory that it is an actionable wrong for third parties to induce a breach of contract. In its modern form, this doctrine dates from the middle of the nineteenth century and was originally applied only to contracts for unique personal services.[1] In course of time, it was extended

---

[1] The history of this doctrine is discussed by Francis B. Sayre, Inducing Breach of Contract, 36 *Harvard Law Rev.* 663–703 (1923).

to many other kinds of contracts,[1] including, in a few cases, employment contracts terminable at will.   With a single exception,[2] however, no court prior to the Hitchman decision had held that it had any application to individual non-union agreements.

When the U. S. Supreme Court took this step, yellow-dog contracts came into use all over the country.   With these came injunctions restraining unions from attempting to organize the employees who had signed these contracts.   To date, there have been at least sixty such injunctions (half of them reported). While this is less than 10 per cent of the total injunctions during this period, several of these writs were taken out by a large number of employers acting jointly.   These, moreover, have been the most extensive of all injunctions in their provisions and remain in effect so long as the complainants continue to use individual non-union agreements.   Injunctions based on yellow-dog contracts now block all attempts to organize the coal miners throughout West Virginia; and there are a considerable number of scattered mines and manufacturing plants elsewhere which are protected against efforts at organization by injunctions issued some years since, now dormant, but likely to be revived should organizers put in an appearance.[3]   A further cramping use of yellow-dog contracts is the practice of getting professional strike breakers temporarily employed during strikes to sign them so as to enable the employers to get injunctions prohibiting all picketing and all interference with the plaintiff corporation or its employees.

The law on yellow-dog contracts cannot be regarded as finally settled.   From the Hitchman case have sprung several different interpretations.   Standing alone, this case might be construed as prohibiting all attempts by unions to induce workmen to go on strike, but the Supreme Court, speaking through Chief Justice Taft in its unanimous decision in the American Steel Foundries case,[4] held this an incorrect construction.   In this

---

[1] Cases cited in Note 3, p. 32; also the list of cases in Appendices A and B to the article by Dean Charles E. Carpenter, Interference with Contract Relations, 41 *Harvard Law Rev.* 728–768, at 764–768 (1928).

[2] The Pennsylvania Supreme Court in Flaccus v. Smith, 199 Pa. 128, 48 Atl. 894 (1901), sixteen years before the Hitchman case, reached the same conclusion, but this decision attracted no attention.

[3] See Note 1, p. 94.

[4] American Steel Foundries v. Tri-city Central Trades Council, 257 U. S. 184, at 211, 42 Sup. Ct. 72 at 79 (1921).

latter case, the element of deception involved in the Hitchman case is stressed, the court specifically stating that the action of the union organizers in inducing the employees to agree to join the union while they continued in employment was alone sufficient to make their conduct illegal. Taking this cue, the Ohio Supreme Court in the La France case[1] construed the Hitchman decision as not forbidding a union to induce workmen who have signed non-union contracts to join the union in a strike. A similar interpretation was adopted by the U. S. Circuit Court of Appeals of the sixth circuit in the Red Jacket case,[2] which was the basis for the successful fight waged by organized labor against the confirmation of Judge John T. Parker's appointment to the U. S. Supreme Court. While approving injunctions prohibiting all attempts to induce miners who had signed individual non-union agreements to breach them, the Circuit Court of Appeals added the proviso that nothing therein should be construed to prevent efforts to persuade these workmen to join the union after the expiration of their contracts.

A much more liberal position has been taken by the New York Court of Appeals. Without dissenting from the Hitchman decision, this court in two cases held yellow-dog contracts of a familiar type, obligating employees not to join a labor union, running for no definite period, and without pretense of consideration except employment, to be so lacking in mutuality that they could not be regarded as contracts at all.[3] These decisions were handed down in cases of little intrinsic importance, but they determined the outcome of the most advertised yellow-dog contract case as yet to come before the courts.[4] This was a suit (1927–1928) by the Interborough Rapid Transit Co. of New York City against the American Federation of Labor, all its affiliated unions, and their members, to enjoin them from attempting to

---

[1] La France Electrical Construction and Supply Co. v. International Brotherhood Electrical Workers, 108 Ohio 61, 140 N. E. 899 (1923).

[2] International Organization United Mine Workers v. Red Jacket Consolidated Coal and Coke Co., 18 F. (2nd) 839 (1927). See also Gasaway v. Borderland Coal Corp., 278 Fed. 56 (1921) and Bittner v. West Virginia Pittsburgh Coal Co., 15 F. (2nd) 652 (1926), decided by the same court.

[3] Exchange Bakery and Restaurant v. Rifkin, 245 N. Y. 260, 157 N. E. 130 (1927); Interborough Rapid Transit Co. v. Lavin, 247 N. Y. 65, 159 N. E. 863 (1928).

[4] Interborough Rapid Transit Co. v. Green, 227 N. Y. S. 258 (1928).

persuade the employees of this company to join any labor union. This action was based on a skillfully drawn antiunion contract limited to two years and promising on part of the company that it would faithfully observe all terms of an agreement made with the company union, of which all of the employees were members. In this case, labor presented an extensive brief prepared by Prof. Herman J. Oliphant, which showed that despite the appearance of consideration the company in reality did not bind itself, and gave opinions from many leading students of labor problems condemning yellow-dog contracts as a social menace.[1] The trial judge denied the injunction, and the company failed to appeal, as the New York Court of Appeals had in the meantime rendered the decisions holding yellow-dog contracts to lack mutuality.

Elsewhere, the Hitchman decision has been broadly interpreted and even extended.[2] The Georgia Supreme Court has

---

[1] This brief, published by the Workers Education Bureau, New York City, in 1928, is the best presentation of the case against yellow-dog contracts.

[2] The Georgia case referred to is Callan v. Exposition Cotton Mills, 149 Ga. 119, 99 S. E. 300 (1919). The unreported Ohio cases sustaining contracts prohibiting all social intercourse with union men are John Douglas Co. v. Metal Polishers, and Shafer v. International Pattern Makers League, both in the Superior Court at Cincinnati, Ohio, in 1920, discussed in 2 *Law and Labor* 188. Injunctions prohibiting all interference where strike breakers had signed non-union contracts were allowed in Skolny v. Hillman, 114 Misc. 571, 187 N. Y. S. 706 (1921); Schwartz v. Hillman, 115 Misc. 61, 189 N. Y. S. 21 (1921); Floersheimer v. Schlesinger, 115 Misc. 9, 187 N. Y. S. 89 (1921); Ellis Co. v. McBride, Sussex Co., Mass., 3 *Law and Labor* 193 (1921); Borst v. Reid, Cuyahoga County, Ohio, 3 *Law and Labor* 99 (1921); Altman v. Schlesinger, 204 App. Div. 513, 198 N. Y. S. 128 (1923). Other cases, in addition to those cited in preceding notes, in which injunctions were allowed on the strength of yellow-dog contracts, reported in the official reports or in *Law and Labor*, are: Third Ave. R. Co. v. Shea, 109 Misc. 18, 179 N. Y. S. 43 (1919); National Equipment Co. v. Donovan, Hampden County, Mass., 1 *Law and Labor* 151 (1919); Cambridge Gaslight Co. v. Gilligan, 2 *Law and Labor* 241 (Mass. 1920); Plant v. Gould, Suffolk Co., Mass., 2 *Law and Labor* 276 (1920); Nashville Railway and Light Co. v. Lawson, 144 Tenn. 78, 229 S. W. 741 (1921); Springfield Foundry Co. v. Campbell, Hampden County, Mass., 3 *Law and Labor* 259 (1921); Boldt Construction Co. v. United Brotherhood, Cuyahoga County, Ohio, 3 *Law and Labor* 227 (1921); United Shoe Machinery Corp. v. Fitzgerald, 237 Mass. 537, 130 N. E. 86 (1921); Algonquin Coal Co. v. Lewis, 3 *Law and Labor* 255 (W. Va. 1921); Algoma Coal and Coke Co. v.

held that an implied contract exists where an employer posts a notice that his shop is non-union, although the employees sign no contracts, and that in such circumstance the employer is entitled to an injunction prohibiting attempts to organize. In two unreported Ohio cases, contracts were enforced obligating the employees not only to stay out of unions but also to have no social intercourse with union members; and a considerable

---

Lewis, MacDowell County, W. Va., 3 *Law and Labor* 257 (1921); McMichael v. Atlanta Envelope Co., 151 Ga. 776, 108 S. E. 226 (1921); Cyrus Currier & Sons v. International Molders Union, 93 N. J. Eq. 61, 115 Atl. 66 (1921); Rice, etc., Co. v. Willard, 242 Mass. 566, 136 N. E. 629 (1922); Moore Drop Forging Co. v. McCarthy, 243 Mass. 554, 137 N. E. 919 (1921); Trade Press Publishing Co. v. Milwaukee Typographical Union, 180 Wis. 449, 193 N. W. 507 (1923); Montgomery v. Pacific Electric Railway Co., 293 Fed. 680 (1923); Altizer v. United Mine Workers, and Anderson Coal Co., v. United Mine Workers, Logan County, W. Va., 5 *Law and Labor* 123 (1923); Vail Ballou Press v. Casey, 125 Misc. 689, 212 N. Y. S. 113 (1925); Kilby Manufacturing Co. v. Local 218, 5 *Law and Labor* 93 (1925); U. S. v. Armstrong, 18 F. (2nd) 371 (1927); U. S. Gypsum Co. v. Heslop, 39 F. (2nd) 228 (1930).

Besides the Ohio and New York cases discussed in the text, injunctions premised upon yellow-dog contracts were denied in Piermont v. Schlesinger, 196 App. Div. 658, 188 N. Y. S. 35 (1921), and in Lovinger & Schwartz Co. v. Joint Board, 7 *Law and Labor* 120 (1925): in the former case because there was no proof that the defendants knew that the employees had signed yellow-dog contracts, and in the latter because the workmen in question had previously signed contracts with the union obligating them not to enter into non-union agreements.

Such contracts have been resorted to by unions in a number of instances, to combat yellow-dog contracts, but without success except in this case. Even here, the court refused an injunction restraining the employer from interfering with the contracts with its members, although it also denied the injunction sought by the employer to prevent the union from persuading workmen who had signed yellow-dog contracts to repudiate the same. Other cases in which unions unsuccessfully sought injunctions to restrain employers from interfering with contracts signed by their members not to enter into any yellow-dog contracts are International Stereotypers, etc., Union 31 v. Meyer, Superior Ct., Hamilton, Ohio, September, 1923; Philadelphia Electrotypers, etc., Union 12 v. Bethlehem Plate Co., Ct. of Com. Pl., Philadelphia County, Pa., December, 1924; New England Wood Heel Co. v. Nolan, 167 N. E. 323 (Mass. 1929); Nolan v. Farmington Shoe Manufacturing Co., 25 F. (2nd) 906 (1928). This subject of contracts by unions to prevent their members from entering into yellow-dog contracts is discussed in an article by H. Sears, A New Legal Problem in the Relations of Capital and Labor, 74 *Univ. of Pa. Law Rev.* 523–551 (1926).

number of injunctions have been allowed against all picketing and persuasion on the strength of yellow-dog contracts signed by strike breakers.

While the courts in recent cases have shown a questioning attitude toward yellow-dog contracts, only the New York decisions go the whole way with labor. Decisions like those of Judge Parker in the Red Jacket case, allowing the persuasion of workmen to join unions after quitting employment, are regarded as of little value, inasmuch as a strike cannot be conducted successfully without much preliminary organization work, which under these decisions employers can prevent through requiring their employees to sign non-union agreements—hence, labor's demand for legislation to forbid the issuance of any injunctions in enforcement of yellow-dog contracts.

As early as 1925, the Ohio State Federation of Labor had presented to the legislature of that state a bill providing that agreements obligating workmen not to join a labor union should be unenforcible and should not be made the basis of injunction.[1] This has since been endorsed by the American Federation of Labor and introduced in many state legislatures and is included in the Norris antiinjunction bill introduced in Congress in 1930.[2] In 1929, Wisconsin[3] enacted this proposal into law, and Arizona, Colorado, Ohio, and Oregon followed suit in 1931. The theory of these acts is that, while it cannot be made a crime for employers to require their employees to sign yellow-dog contracts, such contracts may be made unenforcible. Whether this will stand the test of the courts remains to be determined. The Massachusetts Supreme Court, in an advisory opinion, and also the attorney-

---

[1] The Ohio anti-yellow-dog contract bill is quoted and discussed in articles by Cornelius Cochrane, Attacking the Yellow Dog in Labor Contracts, Why Organized Labor Is Fighting Yellow-dog Contracts, and Labor's Campaign against "Yellow-dog" Contracts Makes Notable Gains, published, respectively, in *Amer. Labor Legis. Rev.* Vol. 15, pp. 151–154 (1925); Vol. 15, pp. 227–232 (1925), and Vol. 17, pp. 142–145 (1927). The Wisconsin law is dealt with in an article by Joseph A. Padway, The Yellow-dog Contract Is Outlawed in Wisconsin, 36 *Amer. Federationist* 1356–1361 (1929).

[2] Bill S-2497, 71st Cong., 1st Sess. For a further discussion of this measure, see Chap. XII, *supra.*

[3] *Wisconsin Statutes* 1929, s. 103.46. The Indiana legislature passed an anti-yellow-dog contract bill in 1931, but this was vetoed.

general of Indiana held the A. F. of L. bill to be unconstitutional, but a strong case can be made out on the other side.[1]

This proposed legislation covers only agreements not to join unions, leaving untouched the types of contract in which workmen obligate themselves not to strike, not to interfere with the employer's conduct of an open shop, or not to agitate for changes in working rules. But labor believes that if it can get the present bills enacted into law and sustained by the courts, the dangers accompanying these contracts will be largely removed, and it sees a good chance of favorable action by both the legislatures and the courts.

The hope for passage arises from the belief that public opinion will condemn yellow-dog contracts once they are made an issue. Seldom has anyone tried to justify such contracts other than on strictly legal grounds. Both the War Labor Board and the U. S. Coal Commission regarded them as a source of irritation and as an unjustified interference with the rights of workingmen.[2] The term itself arouses an unfavorable reaction. Just as the slogans "open shop" and "American plan" have proved valuable assets to employers in their fights against labor, so the protest "yellow dog," with its implication of absolute control by the employer, is certain to help labor's cause in the opinion of the general public, which has never taken kindly to dictation by either employers or employees.

The hope that the courts will sustain legislation against injunctions to prevent efforts at organizing employees, who have signed agreements not to join a labor union, lies in the fact that the court has never given consideration to the social consequences of allowing such injunctions. In neither the Coppage nor the Hitchman case were these as much as mentioned in either the briefs or the oral arguments, but they are certain to be brought

---

[1] The Massachusetts decision is reported in *In re* Opinion of Justices, 171 N. E. 234 (1930).

It was reported in the newspapers that Circuit Judge Schinz in his decision in Rich & Vogel Shoe Co. v. Lew (Shoe Workers International Protective Union), Milwaukee County, 1930, held the Wisconsin law to be constitutional, but this was incorrect. This question was raised in a counter-injunction action brought by labor (Dunn v. Rich-Vogel Shoe Co.), but this case is still under advisement.

[2] *Report* of the U. S. Coal Commission, Civil Liberties in the Coal Fields, *Sen. Doc.* 195, Part I, p. 179, 68th Cong. 1st Sess.

to the court's attention in any attack upon the constitutionality of the model anti-yellow-dog contract bill or any similar measure.

Even leaders of thought among employers are not happy about yellow-dog contracts. After the Hitchman Coal and Coke Co. decision, the League for Industrial Rights advised employers to make individual agreements with their employees providing for a definite number of days' notice before quitting work. As early as 1920, however, it issued a warning against extending yellow-dog contracts too far, and this is still its position.[1] While it opposes anti-yellow-dog contract bills, it fears that public opinion will turn against the employers if this device is carried too far.

EQUALITY BEFORE THE LAW

At this point, a general appraisal of the restrictions on employers seems not amiss. Labor has often bitterly complained that the law favors the employers, that capital is free in industrial disputes to do what is prohibited to labor.

There is little to support this charge in statements of the law occurring in court decisions and statutes. No court has ever said that employers are entitled to any special privileges. The same tests of legality apply to combinations of capital as to combinations of labor. Theoretically, the lockout stands on the same footing as the strike, the employer's boycott as the trade-union boycott. The right of the employer to discriminate against workmen because of union membership is matched by the right of workingmen to refuse to labor for employers who will not recognize their union. The shop closed to the union man is paralleled by the closed union shop, and so on.

When the actual operation of the law is considered, a different picture appears. Employers gain a great advantage through the conspiracy doctrine, which differentiates acts of combinations from those of individuals. Labor suffers because it needs must act in combination and must do so openly. Employers have less need for combination and, being fewer in numbers, can much more easily disguise what they are doing. The net result is that labor is in fact far more restricted in its activities than capital, although in theory there is no discrimination.

---

[1] 2 *Law and Labor* 166, 188–192.

The same situation prevails with reference to many "equal" rights. The right of the employer to discriminate against union members has no real parallel in any right of labor. This right nullifies all anti-blacklist laws and makes it more difficult for unions to get a foothold in non-union industries. Yet labor has become quite reconciled to this disadvantage and today objects principally to the extension of this doctrine represented by injunctions to prevent unions from organizing employees who have signed yellow-dog contracts. These amount to giving employers the aid of the courts in fighting unions. Labor concedes that employers be privileged to keep out unions by their own efforts but regards it unfair for the courts to aid them in this purpose. This is the real issue involved in the controversy over yellow-dog contracts. Through issuing injunctions prohibiting unions from attempting to organize workmen who have signed yellow-dog contracts, the courts become parties to the efforts of antiunion employers to destroy the unions.

Yellow-dog contracts are a grave menace to organized labor, perhaps the most serious it has ever confronted. Should they become universal or very nearly so, the labor unions will be destroyed or driven into secrecy. But it is not so much this danger, which is yet remote, that incenses labor, as the flagrant violation of the neutrality of the courts. Labor and capital do not receive equal treatment while the law thus aligns the government with the non-union employer.

LABOR'S RESORT TO INJUNCTIONS

Labor's other leading grievance is the injunction. It insists that injunctions are used against workingmen as against no other class and that through this means employers unfairly secure the aid of the courts in fighting labor. These complaints were discussed in the chapter on the results of injunctions. Here, labor's own use of injunctions alone will be dealt with, which *Law and Labor* has emphasized in recent years to rebut the contention that equity serves only the employers.

The author has information regarding eighty-eight cases of injunctions sought by, or in behalf of, labor unions against employers or public officials, not counting applications for writs to prevent the unauthorized use of union labels and trade marks.[1]

---

[1] The author listed seventy-three such cases in an appendix to the article Labor's Resort to Injunctions, 39 *Yale Law Jour.* 374–387. Since this

The earliest of such cases occurred as long ago as 1892, but two-thirds of the entire number belong to the last decade.   In the last two years, they were one-fourth as numerous as the applications for injunctions by employers.

---

article was prepared, in the summer of 1929, fifteen additional cases have come to light:

74. U. S. v. Moore, 129 Fed. 630 (1904).   Injunction sought to prevent interference with union organizers denied on the ground that no federal question was involved.

75. Sheet Metal Workers Union 73 v. Building Contractors Assoc., Super. Ct. Cook County, Ill.   Injunction issued September, 1914, by Judge Dever, prohibiting lockout; dissolved on hearing as unwarranted upon the evidence.

76. Central Labor Council v. Baker.   Injunction allowed by Judge Morrow, Feb. 5, 1921, prohibiting the mayor and chief of police of Portland, Ore., from interfering with a labor-union meeting to be addressed by Lincoln Steffens, which the mayor had refused to permit (45 *Survey* 847 [1921]).

77. Sadowsky v. American Cloak and Suit Manufacturers Assoc., N. Y. County, N. Y. (1923) (listed in P. F. Brissenden and C. O. Swayzee's Injunctions in the New York Needle Trades, 44 *Polit. Sci. Quart.* 556 (1929).

78. Albert v. American Sheepskin Coat Co., Sup. Ct., N. Y. County (1928) (Brissenden and Swayzee, 45 *Polit. Sci. Quart.* 87).

79. Hillman v. Rozensweig, N. Y. County (1928) (Brissenden and Swayzee, *op. cit.*).

80. Hillman v. Sun Star Manufacturing Co., N. Y. County (1929) (Brissenden and Swayzee, *op. cit.*).

81. Actors Equity Assoc. v. Marshall, Sup. Ct., Los Angeles, July, 1929.   Injunction sought to prevent a union actor from appearing in a production with non-members in violation of a union rule (*Labor*, July 27, 1929).

82. Godfrey v. Ray, 124 S. 151 (1929).   Injunction on behalf of the boiler makers' local of New Orleans to restrain the superintendent of police from arresting an employee of this union hired to operate a free bus during the New Orleans street-car strike.   Injunction denied and decision of trial court affirmed by the Louisiana Supreme Court.

83. Henry v. Century Shoe Co., Super. Ct. Essex County Mass., 12 *Law and Labor* 7 (1929).   Injunction allowed to the United Shoe Workers Union of Lynn, Mass., against breach of a trade agreement by the plaintiff corporation.

84. Ribner v. Rasco Butter and Egg Co., 238 N. Y. S. 132 (1929). Injunction on behalf of the Retail Clerks Union, Local 338, prohibiting breach of a trade agreement by the defendants' employment of three men expelled from the union.

85. Upholsterers Union Local 76 v. Albee Parlor Suite Co., Sup. Ct. N. Y. C.   Injunction in March, 1930, by Judge Hatting, prohibiting breach of a trade agreement (37 *Amer. Federationist* 796–798).

In forty-three of these, injunctions were allowed, of which eleven were subsequently dissolved. Included among these are several which labor regarded as great triumphs, the most notable being the injunction procured by the Brotherhood of Railway Clerks against the Texas and New Orleans Railroad Co., discussed in the section on company unions in this chapter. In this case, as well as some others, labor not only won a legal victory but gained every objective sought. A study of these cases leads inevitably to the conclusion that it is no longer true, as the executive committee of the American Federation of Labor said in 1922, that "the use of injunctions by labor is a snare and a delusion." Particularly where employers threaten to breach

86. International Ladies Garment Workers Union v. Stein, Sup. Ct. N. Y. C. A joint action by the plaintiff union and the American Cloak and Suit Manufacturers Association to prevent the defendant employer from sending out materials to be manufactured in non-union shops in violation of a trade agreement between the union and the employers' association. Injunction allowed by Justice Frankenthaler, May 14, 1930 (*N. Y. Times*, May 15, 1930).

87. International Ladies Garment Workers Union Local 66 v. Advance Art Embroidery Workers, Sup. Ct., N. Y. C., Justice Ingraham. Injunction allowed prohibiting an employer from breaching a trade agreement (*N. Y. Times*, May 11, 1930).

88. Weber v. Nasser, 286 Pac. 1074 (Cal. App., 1930). Injunction allowed by Appellate Court, after being denied by the trial court, to a musicians' union of San Francisco, against theaters affiliated with the Allied Amusement Industry of San Francisco, prohibiting them from discharging their orchestras in violation of a trade agreement.

89. Dunn v. Rich-Vogel Shoe Co., Cir. Ct., Milwaukee County, Wis. (1930). Application for injunction by the Shoe Workers' Protective Union against the employer's alleged use of "yellow-dog" contracts, after the employer had applied for an injunction. Case heard but never decided.

90. Morin v. Structural Steel, Board of Trade. Suit for injunction and $3,500,000 damages brought in New York City by the International Structural Iron Workers' Union for alleged breach of a trade agreement. Preliminary injunction allowed, January, 1931 (*N. Y. Times*, Nov. 21, 1930, Jan. 4, 1931).

91. Garman v. Stukel, Superior Ct., Los Angeles, Judge Gates, December, 1930. Injunction allowed to the *Los Angeles Citizen*, a labor paper, restraining the police from arresting persons distributing copies of an issue of this paper which contains a notice of a boycott against an "unfair" theater. The police disregarded this injunction and the chief of police was cited for contempt. In January, 1931, the injunction was dissolved as unwarranted and the contempt action dismissed (13 *Law and Labor* 107; 6 *Legal Information Bull.* 51).

trade agreements, or public officials refuse to allow union meetings, is an appeal to the courts likely to prove profitable to labor. This is coming to be recognized not only by the radical unions, which have procured most of the labor injunctions to date, but by the A. F. of L. unions and their attorneys as well.

Despite everything, however, injunctions are still principally a weapon of the employers and likely to remain so. The 43 injunctions issued at labor's instance are to be weighed against 1,845 injunctions allowed employers. It is only in situations where the substantive law supports labor's contentions that it can make effective use of injunctions. In states where trade agreements are regarded as enforcible contracts, labor can get an injunction when employers propose to disregard the same, but labor cannot get injunctions against yellow-dog contracts and similar antiunion activities where these are lawful. With the substantive law as it stands, injunctions by labor against employers are certain to be far less significant than injunctions by employers against labor.

A similar observation is to be made with reference to another recent tendency in connection with injunctions; namely, to place restrictions upon employers in injunctions allowed against strikers.[1] In several recent cases in which employers sought injunctions, the courts granted their petition but in the same order also placed restrictions upon the employers. All these cases have been regarded by labor as akin to victories, but the restrictions actually imposed have interfered far more with labor's activities than with those of the employers.

Bibliographical Note

Brief general accounts of the legal restrictions on employers in industrial controversies occur in all treatises on the law of labor combinations. The best of these are John R. Commons and John B. Andrews, "Principles of Labor Legislation," 1927 ed., pp. 123–125, Harper & Brothers, New York; Felix Frankfurter and Nathan Greene, "The Labor Injunction," pp. 37–42, The Macmillan Company, New York (1930); and E. S. Oakes,

---

[1] Such restrictions occur in the injunction issued by Judge Gehrz to the David Adler & Sons Co. in the Milwaukee Circuit Court in May, 1928, and the injunction issued by Judge Schinz of the same court in Rich & Vogel Shoe Co. v. Shoe Workers Protective Union in June, 1930. An earlier illustration of such a double-barreled injunction is Great Northern Railway Co. v. Brosseau, 286 Fed. 414 (1923).

"Organized Labor and Industrial Conflicts," Chaps. 10, 14, 26, 28, and 31, Lawyers Cooperative Publishing Co., Rochester (1927).

Yellow-dog contracts have given rise to numerous discussions in recent years, of which the most comprehensive is the brief of the defendants in Interborough Rapid Transit Co. v. Green, published by the Workers' Education Bureau, New York City (1928). Another valuable source of information on this subject is the debate in the U. S. Senate in 1930 on the confirmation of Judge John T. Parker, reprinted in part in the booklet of the American Federation of Labor, "'Yellow-dog' Contracts: Menace to American Liberties" (1930). A most excellent study, still unpublished, is E. R. Burton, "Anti-union Employment Contracts," prepared in 1929 for the National Civic Federation. Articles dealing only with the legal phases of yellow-dog contracts are H. F. Carey and Herman Oliphant, The Present Status of the Hitchman Case, 29 *Columbia Law Rev.* 441–460 (1929); Francis B. Sayre, Inducing Breach of Contract, 36 *Harvard Law Rev.* 663–703 (1923); C. E. Carpenter, Interference with Contract Relations, 41 *Harvard Law Rev.* 728–768 (1928); Horace Stern, A New Legal Problem in the Relations of Capital and Labor, 74 *Univ. of Pa. Law Rev.* 523–551 (1926); A. Doskow, Statutes Outlawing Yellow-dog Contracts, 17 *Amer. Bar Assoc. Jour.* 516–518 (1931); Non-union Employment Contracts, 12 *Law and Labor* 99–101 (1930); The "Yellow-dog" Device as a Bar to the Union Organizer, 41 *Harvard Law Rev.* 770–774 (1928). Labor's position and its efforts to get relief from yellow-dog contracts through legislation are set forth by William Green, Yellow-dog Contracts, 37 *Amer. Federationist* 662–665 (1930); E. P. Donnelly, The Individual or "Yellow-dog" Contract, *Proc.* Conference of Social Work, pp. 346–351 (1926); Joseph A. Padway, The Yellow-dog Contract Is Outlawed in Wisconsin, 36 *Amer. Federationist* 1356–1361 (1929); Paul F. Coe, "Yellow Dog" Contracts, 38 *Amer. Federationist* 175 (1931); and in several articles by Cornelius Cochrane, *Amer. Labor Legis. Rev.* XV, 151–154, 227–232 (1925); XVII, 142–145 (1927); XX, 181–184 (1930). The social aspects are considered in the issue of the *Information Service* of the Department of Research and Education of the Federal Council of the Churches of Christ in America on The Use of Injunctions in Labor Disputes, Vol. IX, No. 10, pp. 2–4, and in the booklet of the American Federation of Labor "Yellow-dog Contracts Condemned by Experts" (1930). The author's views have been elaborated in an article Yellow-dog Contracts, 6 *Wis. Law Rev.* 21 (1931).

The use of injunctions by labor unions is considered in articles by L. D. Clark: Action by Employees to Enforce Collective Agreements, 15 *Monthly Labor Rev.* 891–897 (1922); Alpheus T. Mason, Organized Labor as Party Plaintiff in Injunction Cases, 30 *Columbia Law Rev.* 466–487 (1930); and E. E. Witte, Labor's Resort to Injunctions, 39 *Yale Law Jour.* 374–387 (1930).

CHAPTER XI

CONCILIATION AND ARBITRATION

Thus far, this study has dealt with the law governing labor disputes and its enforcement. Government has been disclosed as the agency which makes, interprets, and enforces the rules of the game—a combined referee and policeman. In this role, it lets the parties fight it out, banning only unfair tactics and methods deemed to be against the public interest. This is not, however, the sum total of the government's activities. In some countries, the functions of the peacemaker and judge now overshadow those of the rule maker and umpire. While this is not true in the United States, it is recognized even here that the adjustment of labor disputes is a matter of serious concern, in which the government must play an active part.

COURTS, LEGISLATURES, AND EXECUTIVES AS CONCILIATORS

The courts, the legislatures, and the executives all have had something to do with adjustment, as with law enforcement; but in this field they count for far less than the administrative adjustment agencies. Courts, through their decisions, affect the outcome of strikes and may be the determining factor, but they are concerned with the legal rights of the contending parties, not the merits of the dispute; with litigation, not adjustment. In rare instances, judges have performed the functions of mediators.[1] As a rule, resort to the courts makes adjustment more difficult. The effect of the court's action is to tip the scales to one side or the other, not to restore the balance. The courts are not adjust-

---

[1] A recent instance is Cassidy v. Building Trades Employers Assoc., a case in the Supreme Court in New York City in May, 1929, which grew out of a threatened lockout of all the building-trades workmen in the metropolis. Suit for an injunction was filed May 14 and hearings were begun on May 17. In the course of these hearings, it developed that there was a possibility for settlement, whereupon Judge Crane continued the case for ten days. Largely through his efforts, the parties reached an adjustment on May 22 and the suit for an injunction was withdrawn.

ment agencies and, constituted and equipped as they are, cannot serve efficiently in this capacity.[1]

Aside from enacting the legislation creating administrative adjustment agencies, Congress and the state legislatures have had even less to do with adjustment than the courts. In the last thirty years, Congress has through regular or special committees investigated many strikes, and state legislatures have done likewise. Any prolonged, bitter strike involving a large number of men is likely to be made the subject of a legislative investigation, which may have real value in educating both the legislators and the public but tends rather to widen than to heal the breach between the parties. It is doubtful whether there is a single instance of a settlement brought about or hastened through a legislative investigation.

Presidents and governors have been far more influential in the adjustment of labor troubles. The President of the United States has taken a hand in some thirty great strikes since the turn of the century, sometimes only to send federal troops but usually to endeavor to prevent or settle the dispute.[2] The greatest success was attained during the World War, when the President could virtually dictate to war industries. In peace time, he has had to rely largely upon public opinion to bring the hostile parties to agreement, but such is the prestige of his office that his suggestions have generally been accepted. Governors

---

[1] In one class of cases, the courts have had to act as arbitrators of labor disputes, where the receivers of bankrupt properties within control of the court have sought approval of their labor policies, in view of protests by the employees. In the nineties, when most of the railroads were in the hands of receivers, there were many such cases, but there have been only a few since. In most of the early cases at least, the courts held against the employees, upholding wage reductions and even discrimination against union members. While inviting the employees to bring their grievances to them, the courts took the position that their duty to the creditors and stockholders is paramount to their responsibility to the employees. Cases disclosing such an attitude include Frank v. D. R. G. R. Co., 23 Fed. 757 (1885); Thomas v. C. N. O. & T. P. R. R. Co., 62 Fed. 669 (1894); Booth v. Brown, 62 Fed. 794 (1894); and Platt v. P. & R. Co., 65 Fed. 660 (1894). A more liberal position was taken in Ames v. U. P. R., 62 Fed. 7 (1894), and in U. S. Trust Co. v. O. & St. L. R. Co., 63 Fed. 737 (1894).

[2] Edward Berman, "Labor Disputes and the President" (1924) is an excellent account of the President's intervention in labor disputes during the years 1894–1922.

likewise have often intervened in strikes, calling the parties into conference, proposing bases for settlement, ordering investigations, and giving out statements designed to muster public opinion behind their programs for adjustment. Their intervention has been less effective than that of the Presidents but has been helpful in some instances.[1]

It is inevitable that when great strikes occur, Presidents and governors take a hand. The inconvenience to the public and the menace to law and order which such disputes entail compel action by the executive; if not before, he needs must act when appealed to for military protection. In such a crisis, an executive worthy of the office will use his influence to end the trouble. His position gives him a leverage no one else possesses; as a minimum, he can always get the parties to confer—of itself an immense gain.

But while Presidents and governors can be, and often are, influential in the adjustment of labor disputes, their usefulness in this respect has distinct limitations. They are burdened with many other duties, are inexperienced in mediation, and usually have no technical knowledge of industry. Above all, they may act only in really serious disputes, as their intervention is effective largely because it is unusual. Adjustment must ordinarily be the work of administrative agencies created for the purpose. If these function efficiently, the executive will not often have to intervene, and, when he must act, he will be equipped with the information necessary to wise action.

ADJUSTMENT OF RAILROAD LABOR DISPUTES

Federal adjustment machinery is far more important today than that of the states, functioning in (1) disputes affecting interstate carriers and (2) disputes in other industries. As to

---

[1] Such a case, of which the author has personal knowledge, occurred in Wisconsin in 1920 in a strike against the Northern Paper Mills at Green Bay. Governor Philipp was appealed to by the sheriff and the mayor to call out the state militia. Uncertain whether the facts warranted sending the militia, the governor asked the industrial commission to advise him. The commission, believing that there was a possibility for settlement, called the parties together for a conference, and within twenty-four hours they had reached an agreement. Had the governor sent in the militia without investigation, the strike would probably have dragged on for weeks and further disturbances resulted.

the first, the powers of the federal government are exclusive and mandatory; in the second, wholly optional with the parties. For the former, the existing adjustment agencies are the railroad boards of adjustment and the federal Board of Mediation, while the latter is the work of the Conciliation Service of the U. S. Department of Labor.

The present method of dealing with railroad labor disputes dates from the railroad labor act of 1926, which has a long history.[1] This begins with the arbitration act of 1888, providing for voluntary and compulsory investigation—a law which in the ten years that it was in force was not once used. Next came the Erdman Act of 1898, providing for mediation and arbitration, which was applied only once up to 1906 but in the next seven years was frequently called into operation. This was followed by the Newlands Act of 1913, which differed from the prior law principally in that it set up a permanent, full-time Board of Mediation and Conciliation, while previously this work fell as an added duty upon the Commissioner of Labor and the chairman of the Interstate Commerce Commission (after 1911, any member of the Interstate Commerce Commission or the Commerce Court designated to act by the President). This act worked satisfactorily (as far as the general public was aware) for three years and then failed completely, a nation-wide railroad strike being averted only by a hurried act of Congress virtually granting the employees' demands.

This breakdown occurred because railroad labor had become distrustful of arbitration as a method of adjusting labor disputes. Under both the Erdman and Newlands acts, mediation was to be employed first, and, that failing, the government mediators were to try to get the parties to agree to arbitration. In that event, a special arbitration board was to be set up for each dispute, composed of one or two representatives of the railroads, the employees, and the public, with the public representatives selected by the partisan members or, if they disagreed (the usual case), by the government. Awards made by arbitration boards were binding, and, if disputes arose over their interpretation, the boards might be reassembled.

---

[1] Citations for the three acts referred to in this paragraph are: Arbitration Act of 1888, 25 Stats. 501; Erdman Act, 30 Stats. 424; Newlands Act, 38 Stats. 103.

From 1906 to 1916, only one small strike occurred on the railroads of the country. Three-fourths of all disputes which the railroads could not settle directly with their employees were adjusted by the federal mediators, and the rest were settled by arbitration.[1] However, when in 1916 the railroads refused to accede to the employees' demands for a basic eight-hour day and all attempts at mediation failed, the employees flatly refused to submit the dispute to arbitration, claiming that their experience with arbitration had been unsatisfactory.[2] The railroads were willing to arbitrate, but only if the question of certain established working rules which they deemed inimical were included in the arbitration, along with the employees' demands. The *impasse* thus created was not solved until three days before all railroad men of the country were to go on strike, when the President recommended to Congress the enactment of a law establishing a basic eight-hour day for all men engaged in the movement of trains, which was promptly done in the Adamson Act.[3]

In the next session, which began a few months later, President Wilson advocated the enactment of a law forbidding strikes on railroads until after investigation by a mediating and fact-finding board clothed with power to make public its findings and suggestions for settlement. Other bills proposed compulsory arbitration. These, as well as the President's plan, were strongly opposed by labor. Protracted hearings followed,[4] but,

---

[1] Official statistics indicate that forty-five cases were settled through mediation under the Erdman Act, while sixteen went to arbitration, but these involved almost as many employees. Under the Newlands Act, there were 22 arbitration cases and 109 mediation cases, the arbitration cases having the larger total number of employees. This board was not formally abolished until the passage of the Railroad Labor Act of 1926 but after 1917 functioned only in disputes on lines of one hundred miles or less in length; and after 1919 it did not act in a single case.

[2] Specifically, the railroad brotherhoods complained that the representatives of the public on the arbitration boards, who in practically all cases actually determined the issues, were unsympathetic toward labor and impractical in their decisions. Further, they complained that the railroads did not give effect to awards favorable to labor.

[3] 39 Stats. 721. This law was held constitutional in Wilson v. New, 243 U. S. 332, 37 Sup. Ct. 298 (1917).

[4] 64th Cong., 2nd Sess., Hearings on "Government Investigation of Railroad Labor Disputes," by the Senate Committee on Interstate Commerce; and Hearings on "Interstate Commerce on Railroads," by the

as this was the eve of America's entrance into the World War, which crowded all domestic questions into the background, the only railroad legislation enacted by this Congress was to empower the President to take over the operation of the railroads in the event of war.

Soon after, we were involved in war, and before long the President did take over the railroads, radically altering the relation of the railroad men to the government. New agencies were created by executive orders for the adjustment of disputes over wages and working conditions, introducing for the first time the principle of adjustment through bipartisan boards without neutral members. The railroad administration pursued liberal labor policies throughout, and no strikes or other serious friction resulted in the three years the railroads were operated by the government.

When, after the war, the railroads were returned to private ownership, wide differences developed in Congress over the policy to be pursued toward labor disputes. The Senate passed a bill providing for compulsory arbitration, but the statute finally enacted[1] fell a little short of that. It set up the Railroad Labor Board, composed of nine members all appointed by the President, three each to represent employers, employees, and the public. This board was vested with powers of mediation and investigation and was to publish findings and recommendations, which, however, were not binding on either party. In addition to the governmental agency, the Transportation Act of 1920 provided for bipartisan regional boards of adjustment, to which all disputes were to go in the first instance, confining the Railroad Labor Board to a practically appellate jurisdiction.

The Railroad Labor Board started with the great handicap that the law under which it functioned was passed over labor's opposition. To add to labor's grievances, only one of the three members appointed to represent it was nominated by the unions, so that the railroad men felt that they had only one of nine representatives on the board. Unfortunately also, the chairman of the board seems to have regarded it as one of his duties to

House Committee on Interstate Commerce. These hearings are a very important source of information upon the actual operation of the preceding railroad labor acts.

[1] 41 Stats. 456.

denounce the unreasonableness of the labor unions. In addition to these handicaps, the board was soon swamped with cases, due in large part to the failure of the railroads and their employees to set up regional adjustment boards, as the law contemplated. This threw thousands of minor cases upon the board, which had an inadequate staff to handle efficiently all these many matters. Unreasonable delays resulted, and some of the decisions of the board were extremely unpopular with the employees. In the controversy in 1922 over working rules in the railroad shops, the employees refused to accept the board's decision and went on strike. The strike ended in failure, but the board's prestige was not enhanced by the partisan attitude of the chairman and other members. Soon after, the Pennsylvania Railroad flouted another of the board's decisions, directing it to deal with the regular labor unions instead of its company-controlled union. As the board had no way of compelling the company to observe its decision, the unions applied to the courts for a mandatory injunction. The U. S. Supreme Court, however, held that, while the labor sections of the Transportation Act were constitutional, they provided for no stronger means of enforcement than public opinion.[1]

The Railroad Labor Board officiated in a surprisingly large number of disputes—nearly thirteen thousand in the first five years of its existence. Aside from the outlaw switchmen's strike in 1920 and the railroad shop crafts' strike in 1922, no great railroad strike occurred during the period of its existence. The majority of its decisions were in favor of labor, and most of them seem to have been faithfully put into operation; yet, for the reasons noted, the board was discredited from the beginning and more so after the shop crafts' strike. The railroad unions took an active part in the congressional elections of 1922 and pledged many of the successful candidates to a repeal of the labor sections of the Transportation Act, and thereafter their efforts to gain new legislation never ceased. Due to the railroad opposition, however, labor made little headway in Congress until in 1925 the carriers executed an "about face" and joined labor in conferences to draft a new measure. Out of these conferences

---

[1] Pa. R. R. System and Allied Lines Federation v. Pa. R. Co., 267 U. S. 203, 45 Sup. Ct. 307 (1925); Pa. System Board of Adjustment v. Pa. R. Co., 267 U. S. 219, 45 Sup. Ct. 312 (1925).

developed the railroad labor act of 1926,[1] the law now governing railroad labor disputes. This was a measure supported by both the railroads and the railroad unions and opposed only by the National Association of Manufacturers and its affiliated organizations.[2]

The central board which functions under this act is the Board of Mediation, not unlike the Board of Conciliation and Mediation under the Newlands Act, a full time, five-member board appointed by the President and composed wholly of men unconnected with either side. Its primary duty is to mediate and, failing in this, to urge arbitration. Arbitration having once been accepted, awards are binding, and injunctional orders may be issued by the courts to give them effect. A separate board is created for each dispute referred to arbitration, with representation of both sides and a neutral chairman (or two neutral members if the board has a total membership of six) selected by the Board of Mediation if the partisan members are unable to agree upon a choice.

Supplementing this central machinery, copied from the Newlands Act, are boards of adjustment not unlike those of the war period except that they are system, not national, boards. These are set up by agreements between the railroads and their employees, for either a single system or a group of lines. They are composed exclusively of representatives of the carriers and their employees, to be selected by each side free from all interference by the other. Besides these, there is provision for the creation in emergencies of special boards of investigation with fact-finding and publicity powers similar to those of the railroad labor board. These boards are to be named by the President upon recommendation of the Board of Mediation when in its opinion a serious interruption of interstate commerce is threatened. When such a board is organized, no strike or change of conditions may occur for sixty days.

---

[1] 44 Stats. 568.

[2] How this bill was prepared and put through Congress is interestingly told in Donald Richberg's "Tents of the Mighty," pp. 179–203, Willett, Clark & Colby, Chicago (1930) by the attorney for the railroad unions and the real author of this legislation. A briefer account occurs in the article by C. O. Fisher, The Railroad Labor Act: a Comparison and Appraisal, 17 *Amer. Econ. Rev.* 177–187 (1927), at 178–179.

This entire plan might be described as an attempt to divide the load which overwhelmed the Railroad Labor Board. Under it, the Board of Mediation is relieved from the great mass of minor disputes, and the functions of public investigation have been entirely taken away and entrusted to specially created tribunals set up during great emergencies. The essence of the plan, however, is something much further-reaching—self-government in industry—the underlying idea being that the railroads and their employees can best settle their own troubles and that government ought to intervene only when they fail. The greatest reliance is placed on the boards of adjustment, which have no public representatives. On the other hand, the Board of Mediation is made an exclusively public body and is confined to the single function of bringing the parties to agreement when direct negotiations between them have been proved fruitless. It does not pass upon the merits of the respective contentions. When arbitration or public investigation becomes necessary, special tribunals are created.

This act has now been in effect for four years and has apparently worked well. Only one small strike has occurred, and no bitterness has resulted from any settlement. While during the period of the Railroad Labor Board, the railroads and their employees seemingly were getting further and further apart, a *rapprochement* appears to have occurred under the new law. Conditions have been much more favorable than during the troubled years of readjustment when the Railroad Labor Board began operations, but even more important has been the fact that the new agencies started with the good will of both parties, which they still seemingly enjoy. The recent decision of the U. S. Supreme Court in the railroad clerks' injunction case discussed in Chap. X,[1] in which the U. S. Supreme Court held that under the Railroad Labor Act the railroads may not attempt to gain control of the labor representatives on the adjustment boards through the organization of company unions, has further strengthened this system of adjustment. While no one can predict what the future may bring, we seemingly now have the best method of dealing with railroad labor disputes yet devised.

---

[1] *Cf.* p. 219.

U. S. CONCILIATION SERVICE

Likewise concerned with the adjustment of labor disputes, but operating in another sphere, is the Conciliation Service of the U. S. Department of Labor. This service had its beginning in a section of the 1913 act creating the Department of Labor, which authorized the secretary of labor to appoint conciliators in labor disputes. For some time these conciliators were employees of the department with other duties, but very soon a separate bureau was organized for this work, which now has an appropriation of $210,000 per year and a staff of some seventy people.

The Conciliation Service operates in disputes over which the federal government has no mandatory jurisdiction. It ordinarily comes in only at the request of one of the parties to the dispute or of the state authorities. Its efforts are confined to mediation, which often includes, however, suggestions for settlement. These may or may not be made public, as seems most likely to bring about an agreement, but the Conciliation Service never expresses an opinion upon the merits of the dispute.

The Conciliation Service cannot compel either party even to confer with its representatives, not to mention accepting their suggestions or meeting with the opposing side. Yet it has been successful in a surprisingly large number of cases. Up to June 30, 1929, it functioned in a total of 9,048 trades disputes, in more than seventy-five per cent of which its efforts at mediation are reported to have brought about settlement.[1] This percentage may overstate the value of the Conciliation Service, since it is impossible to say whether settlement would have occurred except for its intervention, but the increasing effectiveness of its mediation cannot be denied. In the early years of the service, it was viewed with considerable suspicion by employers, apparently because many of the conciliators were former trade-union officials. This distrust seems to have vanished, and the Conciliation Service is today by far the most important agency of mediation in the country. To a very great extent it has taken over work formerly done by state arbitration boards, with their full consent. United States conciliators come into practically all large labor

---

[1] Statistics on the work of the Conciliation Service since its organization, with a brief discussion of its methods and policies, are given in the *Annual Report of the Secretary of Labor for the Fiscal Year Ended June* 30, 1929, pp. 23–27.

disputes occurring anywhere in the country and, once in the field, stay on the job as long as there is any prospect of bringing the parties together. The great area of the country and the frequent failure of either party to inform the Conciliation Service of pending disputes before they reach the strike stage (when adjustment is, of course, much more difficult) are distinct limitations, but altogether the Conciliation Service represents one of the most constructive activities for the preservation of industrial peace now operative in this country.

WAR-TIME LABOR DISPUTES

At this point, mention must be made of the many adjustment agencies set up by the federal government during the period of America's participation in the World War. Early in the war, many strikes occurred, a result of the disturbed industrial conditions and the rapidly rising cost of living. These led the U. S. Chamber of Commerce, many great employers' associations, a large section of the press, and leading public men to advocate the prohibition of all strikes.[1] New Hampshire passed such a law in 1917, and the Minnesota Public Safety Commission promulgated an order to the same effect in 1918.[2] Twelve states enacted compulsory work laws[3] requiring all able-bodied men outside the military service to be gainfully employed, and these were in some instances construed to apply to workmen on strike. Several injunctions were issued on the theory that strikes are

---

[1] Good presentations of this policy were Walter Drew, The Workman behind the Army, *Bull.* 44, Nat. Assoc. of Mfr. (1917); James A. Emery, Industrial Relations and National Defense, 17 *Amer. Industries* 15–16, March, 1917; and Factory and Trench Service Equally Important, 18 *Amer. Industries* 15, January, 1918; Charles Nagel, The Army of the Shops, 5 *Nation's Business* 25, November, 1917; the statement of the National Industrial Conference Board respecting the labor situation in *Monitor*, pp. 5–9, September, 1917; and the article Industrial Peace and the World Peace, 9 *Unpopular Review* 21–38 (1918).

[2] New Hampshire, Acts 1917, c. 146; 7 *Monthly Labor Rev.* 1438–1439 (1918).

[3] For a digest of these laws, see 7 *Monthly Labor Rev.* 1811–1812 (1918). Other articles discussing this development include 5 *Monthly Labor Rev.* 525–527 (1917), 6 *Monthly Labor Rev.* 1561–1562 (1918), and 18 *New Republic* 144–146 (1919). The Delaware law was held constitutional in State v. McClure, 30 Del. 265, 105 Atl. 712 (1919); the West Virginia law unconstitutional in *ex parte* Hudgins, 85 W. Va. 526, 103 S. E. 327 (1920).

unlawful in war time, and there were numerous instances of the arrest or molestation of union organizers and pickets by local officials and overzealous military authorities.

The national administration, however, adopted a radically different policy. Instead of trying to strong-arm labor, the government treated it as a partner in the conduct of the war, gave it representation on all war boards, and, instead of forbidding strikes, appealed for peace in industry. When the carpenters' union refused to submit a controversy affecting cantonment construction to arbitration, the President sent a scathing telegram to the union president, but the only extended journey which President Wilson made until after the armistice was to address the 1917 convention of the American Federation of Labor in praise of labor's cooperation. The fuel administrator refused to deal with anthracite miners who went on strike in violation of an agreement and against the advice of their national officers but granted them an increase after they returned to work. The Secretary of War ruled early that striking workmen did not lose their draft exemption or deferred classification, and the provost marshal later held that the "work-or-fight" order (an executive decree very similar to the state compulsory-work laws) could not be used against pickets.

The government's program had the same purpose as that of the employing interests who clamored for the legal prohibition of strikes. It sought to accomplish this not through repressive legislation but through recognition of labor's rights and redress of its grievances. It placed great reliance on agencies for conciliation and settlement,[1] and no less than thirteen new adjustment agencies were created. A separate board was set up for each of the larger governmentally operated industries (the railroads, ship building, cantonment construction, etc.), and a National War Labor Board was created for disputes in essential war industries outside of the jurisdiction of any special board. This was constituted of an equal number of representatives of employers and labor, with two joint chairmen, Former President Taft and Frank P. Walsh (later replaced by Basil Manly). This board—or, more

---

[1] The best account of the adjustment agencies of wartime is A.M. Bing's "Wartime Strikes and Their Adjustment," E. P. Dutton & Co., Inc., New York (1921).

accurately, its predecessor the War Labor Conference Board—
at the outset formulated a set of principles which it announced
would guide all its decisions. These included the adjustment of
all disputes without strikes or lockouts, the maintenance of the
status quo in open and closed shops, the right of workmen to
belong to labor unions without interference from employers, collective bargaining between employers and employees, the basic
eight-hour day, and several other similarly progressive policies.
Determinations by the board in all controversies submitted were
binding, but submission was nominally voluntary, conditional
upon the consent of both parties. The government, however,
stopped only at legal compulsion to induce both parties in essential war industries to submit their disputes to the board and to
abide by its decisions. Many of the contracts for war supplies
included a clause to this effect; and when the Western Union
refused to discontinue its practice of compelling employees to
sign antiunion agreements, as ordered by the War Labor Board,
the President secured from Congress the power to operate all
telegraph lines; and by executive order the Secretary of War
commandeered the plant of the Smith-Wesson Company for a
similar act of defiance. On the other side, he forced recalcitrant
machinists at Bridgeport, Conn., into line by threatening to
draft them if they went on strike.[1]

The National War Labor Board did not decide any cases until
June, 1918, but in the last months of the war it was a very
important factor in preserving industrial peace. Not a single
strike or lockout was undertaken in defiance of its awards until
after the armistice. In all, it acted in 1,251 cases and rendered
490 formal decisions. The other war-time adjustment agencies,
considered together, functioned quite as effectively in an even
greater number of disputes.

If the number of strikes alone is considered, the war-time
adjustment machinery will seem a failure. More strikes occurred
in 1917 than in any other year, while 1918 was exceeded in this
respect by only the two preceding and the two following years.
Many of the strikes, however, were outside war industries and

---

[1] In one instance, strikers were actually drafted. This occurred during
a strike in construction work at the Watertown, Mass., arsenal in November,
1917.

most of the remainder were small affairs[1] of short duration.   At no stage did strikes seriously embarrass the United States in the World War—which is more than can be said of most of the warring countries.

The government's policy was on the whole satisfactory to labor, but not to many employers.   During the war, the labor unions greatly increased their membership and gained a foothold in many industries from which they had been previously barred. Antiunion employers viewed this development with alarm and, once the war was over, returned to their old methods of fighting the unions, supplemented by the new device of the yellow-dog contract, made possible by the Hitchman Coal and Coke Company decision.[2]   Labor fought back vigorously, displaying an aggressive attitude likely neither to conciliate employers nor to gain public confidence.   The year 1919 was one of great strikes, with more workmen directly affected than in any other year.   The climax came in the strike of the bituminous-coal miners of the entire country called to begin Nov. 1, 1919.   This was a strike in violation of an unexpired agreement which provided for a wage scale that had become inequitable with the increased cost of living.   After the strike order had gone out, Attorney-general Palmer took out an injunction prohibiting the calling of a strike, and this was followed by contempt proceedings and criminal prosecutions against some of the strike leaders.[3]   This course was premised upon the Lever Act, a war-time measure which penalized conspiring to limit or restrict the production of war necessities. When this measure was under consideration, officials of the American Federation of Labor were assured by members of Congress and others standing high in the councils of the adminis-

---

[1] While the index number of strikes on the basis, 1916 = 100, was 117 in 1917 and 88 in 1918, the number of workingmen involved was only 77 and 78, respectively, in these years.

[2] *Cf.* pp. 221–222.

[3] The injunction action referred to was U. S. v. Hayes, before Judge Anderson in the U. S. District Court, District Indiana (*cf.* p. 118).   U. S. v. Armstrong, 265 Fed. 683 (1920) was a criminal prosecution growing out of the same difficulty.

This was not the only instance in which the Lever Act was invoked against strikers.   In the "outlaw" switchmen's strike of the next year, 41 of the leaders were indicted for alleged violations of this act (*Industrial News Survey*, Aug. 28, 1920).

tration that this provision would not be construed to apply to
strikers, so that the government's course in the coal strike
appeared to the trade unionists of the country in the light of a
"broken pledge."[1]   President Wilson, by arranging a settlement
after the injunction failed to mine coal, somewhat smoothed over
this misunderstanding, but thereafter labor was quite as ready to
scrap all the wartime industrial legislation as were the employers.

And by 1920, this was accomplished.   After the armistice, the
National War Labor Board wound up its old cases, was defied in
numerous instances by employers who felt that its awards were
pro union or too liberal, and went out of existence in August,
1919.   The several adjustment boards for governmentally controlled industries disappeared when the period of government
operation ceased.   Not a single war-time agency of adjustment
survived, and only on the railroads was anything set up to
replace them.

Feeble attempts were made to perpetuate the spirit of war-
time adjustment.   The President convened an industrial conference, which after prolonged discussion produced a report in
1920 favoring the works council form of labor organization and
recommending an elaborate adjustment machinery.[2]   Its apparent endorsement of shop ("company") unions drew labor's
opposition, and nothing came of the recommendations.   The
same fate befell diverse proposals for an industrial code, a statement of fundamental principles whose acceptance it was felt
would facilitate adjustment of those disputes it failed to forestall.[3]   When somewhat later (1923) another presidential body,
the U. S. Coal Commission, made numerous, apparently well-
considered recommendations for lessening industrial friction and

---

[1] Upon this point, see Samuel Gompers, The Broken Pledge, 27 *Amer.
Federationist* 41–50 (1920).

[2] These recommendations are reprinted in 10 *Monthly Labor Rev.* 863–865
(1920) and in A. R. Ellingwood and Whitney Coombs, "The Government
and Labor," pp. 279–281, McGraw-Hill Book Company, Inc., New York
(1926).

[3] The most comprehensive proposal of this kind introduced in Congress
was Senator Kenyon's bill S-3147 (67th Cong.) for the settlement of labor
disputes in coal mines.   For a complete statement of the importance of
an industrial code and a discussion of the principles which it should contain,
see W. J. Lauck and C. S. Watts, "The Industrial Code," Funk & Wagnalls
Company, New York (1920).

the bitterness of labor disputes in the coal fields, Congress did not even publish its report until two years later.

Thus ended the war-time experiments in labor adjustment. They were not carried over into peace time and have exerted little influence upon the development of methods of dealing with labor disputes, but as an object lesson they are distinctly worth study.

STATE CONCILIATION MACHINERY

State machinery for adjustment is older but far less important than the federal agencies for conciliation. The first law for conciliation in labor disputes was the Maryland law of 1878, and the first permanent boards of arbitration those of Massachusetts and New York created in 1886. By 1900, the majority of the states had some legislation on this subject, and thirteen had permanent boards. Today there is far less work being done by the state governments in this field than thirty years ago. A recent study of the expenditures of representative states for labor law administration[1] indicates that on a per capita wage-earner basis, less than one-third as much money was spent for conciliation and arbitration in 1927 as in 1899, without taking into account the reduced value of the dollar.

A detailed analysis of the existing state laws is not worth while, because so many of them are virtually dead letters.[2] Several states provide for a permanent arbitration board but actually have no such board. The latest directory issued by the U. S. Bureau of Labor Statistics lists nine independent state concilia-

---

[1] Study by Elizabeth S. Johnson, Expenditures for the Administration of Labor Legislation in the United States, summarized in 20 *Amer. Legislation Rev.* 174–180 (1930).

[2] A brief digest of the provisions of the state laws governing conciliation and arbitration in labor disputes is presented in 9 *Bloomfield's Labor Digest* 3193–3196 (1925). A more comprehensive analysis (no longer entirely accurate) is given in Carl H. Mote's "Industrial Arbitration," pp. 215–238, Bobbs-Merrill Company, Indianapolis (1916). G. E. Barnett and D. A. McCabe's "Mediation, Investigation, and Arbitration in Industrial Disputes," pp. 3–128, D. Appleton & Company, New York (1916), and T. T. Ko's Governmental Methods of Adjusting Labor Disputes in North America and Australasia, pp. 14–23, "Columbia University Studies in History, etc.," No. 271 (1926), are the best available accounts of the actual operation of these laws.

tion boards and four subordinate conciliation bureaus.[1]   In addition, the labor departments of about a half-dozen states which have no special division for this purpose claim to do some work in the mediation of labor disputes.   Of all states (not counting Colorado, which has a distinct type of conciliation legislation, to be discussed later), only Massachusetts, New York, and Pennsylvania are really active in this field, and in the first two, the total expenditures in 1928 were only $15,000 and $23,000 respectively, and in Pennsylvania probably less.

The Massachusetts Board of Conciliation, which is a subordinate board within the Department of Labor and Industries, functions principally as an agency for arbitration under trade agreements in the boot and shoe industry.   These include a provision for the settlement of all disputes concerning the interpretations by this board.   In addition, it operates to some extent as a mediation agency and has power to conduct public hearings to determine the responsibility for disputes but has seldom done so.   In New York, there is no board but a Division of Mediation and Arbitration in the Bureau of Industrial Relations of the Department of Labor, consisting of five mediators.   Unlike the Massachusetts board, this functions principally as a mediation agency.   Rarely do the members of the division act as arbitrators.   In 1928, the division intervened in 42 of the 131 strikes occurring in New York that year and effected settlements in fourteen cases.   The Pennsylvania Bureau of Industrial Relations in the Department of Labor and Industry functions along lines very similar to those of New York.   In no other state is there a single state employee devoting full time to mediation in

---

[1] The state conciliation and arbitration agencies listed by the U. S. Bureau of Labor Statistics are the following: Connecticut, State Board of Mediation and Arbitration; Maine, State Board of Arbitration and Conciliation; Massachusetts, Board of Conciliation and Arbitration in the Department of Labor and Industries; New Hampshire, State Board of Conciliation and Arbitration; New York, Division of Mediation and Arbitration in the Bureau of Industrial Relations of the Department of Labor; Oklahoma, State Board of Arbitration and Conciliation; Oregon, State Board of Conciliation; Pennsylvania, Bureau of Industrial Relations in the Department of Labor and Industry; Rhode Island, Board of Labor; South Carolina, Board of Conciliation and Arbitration; Texas, Industrial Commission; Washington, Division of Industrial Relations in the Dept. of Labor and Industries; Wisconsin, Board of Conciliation.

labor disputes. The state boards of conciliation and arbitration and some of the state labor departments are occasionally called upon by one side or the other to attempt settlement and on rare occasions intervene on their own initiative or under instructions from the governor. But, all told, the work of the state adjustment agencies must be put down as negligible.

COLORADO INDUSTRIAL DISPUTES ACT

Colorado has a different method of dealing with labor disputes from any other state. This is embodied in the industrial disputes investigation act of 1915, as amended in 1921 and 1923.[1] This law was modeled after the better-known Canadian industrial disputes investigation act and was a direct outgrowth of the bitter Colorado coal strike of 1913–1914. The act prohibits strikes and lockouts in industries affected with a public interest,[2] pending investigation and report by the Colorado Industrial Commission, the state labor department. The report is to be filed within thirty days after the employer or the employees notify the commission of an intended change in wages or working conditions. If the investigation is not completed by that time, no strike may occur until the report is actually made. In its report, the commission makes findings and offers recommendations for settlement, but these are not binding unless both parties have agreed in advance to abide by the award. In other cases, a strike or lockout may thereafter be undertaken, but picketing is not allowed. To make a change in working conditions without notifying the commission or to strike before it files its report is punishable by fine and imprisonment, and since 1921 the commission has been authorized to take out mandatory injunctions in cases of violations, under which strikers may be punished for contempt.

From 1915 to the end of 1928, the Industrial Commission acted in 1,395 controversies.[3] Strikes or lockouts occurred after

[1] Colo. Annot. Stats., 1930, s. 3472c–3472v.

[2] The limitation of the act to industries affected with a public interest was taken out by an amendment in 1921 but restored in 1923.

[3] The best account of the operation of the Colorado industrial disputes act is the article by Colston E. Warne and Merrill E. Gaddis, Eleven Years of Compulsory Investigation of Industrial Disputes in Colorado, 35 *Jour. Polit. Econ.* 657–683 (1927). Official accounts upon the operation of the law are to be found in the biennial reports of the Colorado Industrial

investigations in only 74 of these, and more than one-third of all disputes were settled without necessitating a formal award.

But these statistics, taken from official reports, convey too rosy a picture of the operation of this law. From 1916 to 1927, there was a total of 217 strikes in Colorado, according to the U. S. Bureau of Labor Statistics. The difference between this number and the seventy-four strikes which the reports of the commission list as occurring after findings and awards is not entirely accounted for by illegal strikes (as some were in industries to which the law does not apply), but a great many fall in this category. In most of these illegal strikes, the commission took no action of any kind, but from 1919 to 1922 it instituted a number of criminal prosecutions against the leaders.[1] When the national coal strike of 1919 loomed, the attorney-general of the state took out an injunction prohibiting the Colorado miners from striking in violation of the industrial disputes investigation act and in the course of this litigation won a final decision upholding this law as constitutional.[2] Again, in the butcher workmen's strike in 1921, the union men in the Denver packing plants were enjoined from taking part. This injunction was defied and the union president and thirty-three others were sentenced to jail for contempt.[3]

These occurrences made the industrial disputes investigation act an issue in the 1922 state election, labor demanding that the law be repealed. The candidate whom it supported won, and Governor Sweet, after a survey of the operation of the law by Dr. John R. Commons, recommended the repeal of all penal provisions except those making it the duty of both parties to report contemplated changes in conditions to the industrial commission. The legislature did not follow this recommendation, making no amendment except to restore the original provision limiting its operation to industries affected with a public

---

Commission, the latest of which (the tenth report) is for the biennium 1926–1928.

[1] Among the criminal prosecutions under this law are People v. Butler, 2 *Law and Labor* 279 (1920) and People v. Fontuccio, 73 Colo. 286, 215 Pac. 145 (1923).

[2] People v. United Mine Workers, 70 Colo. 269, 201 Pac. 54 (1921).

[3] This incident is discussed in George Lackland, Colorado Tries to Outlaw Strikes, 11 *Labor Age* 4–6 (1922) and in the *Report of the Executive Committee of American Federation of Labor*, pp. 38–39 (1922).

interest. Since 1922, there have been few strikes in Colorado, as elsewhere, and the acuteness of the issue has been accordingly lessened. The Colorado employers favor the law and the fact that it has survived all of labor's attacks would seem to attest to the support of the general public. Labor, though, is still strongly opposed; strikes have not been eliminated, and the value of the penal provisions is debatable.[1]

KANSAS COURT OF INDUSTRIAL RELATIONS

A more radical innovation was the Kansas Court of Industrial Relations, which functioned from 1920 to 1923,[2] in essence a scheme for compulsory arbitration applicable to the public utilities, coal, and the food and clothing industries.[3] In these industries strikes were altogether prohibited, as were picketing and boycotting. As a substitute for the right to strike, this statute set up a court of industrial relations to fix rates and conditions of employment in the industries to which it applied. The court numbered three members appointed by the governor and combined the functions of an arbitration body with those of the state labor department. Proceedings before the court could be started whenever a controversy loomed which threatened interruption of work, either on its own initiative or on petition of the employers, a labor union, a specified number of unorganized workmen, or a group of citizens. Decisions made after hearings and investigations were binding upon all parties. Individual workmen might refuse to continue at work under the conditions

---

[1] A complaint deserving special mention is that unreasonable delays have occurred in investigations. This appears to have been well founded in the early years of the law, no less than 172 days having elapsed before the completion of the commission's investigation in the Denver tailors' case in 1915. More recently, there have been few long delays and these are stated by the commission to have all been due to the failure of one or both parties to cooperate.

[2] South Carolina, Laws 1922, Act 589, provides for binding arbitration upon the request of either contending party in disputes affecting street-car lines in certain counties. This act is of limited application and apparently has never been invoked.

[3] Governor Allen contended that the policy of the Kansas act was not compulsory arbitration, but the settlement of industrial disputes by judicial processes. The only basis for this attempted distinction was that the Kansas act made no provision for representation of the contending parties, which clearly does not alter the fundamental character of the scheme.

fixed by the court, and employers might close their plants, but no strike or lockout could be undertaken. Violations were punishable as criminal offenses and could also be enjoined.

The industrial relations court act[1] was passed in consequence of the 1919 strike in the Kansas coal fields, largely by the votes of farmer members of the legislature over labor's bitter opposition, with the employers divided. Its champion was Gov. Henry J. Allen and its author, William L. Huggins, who was appointed the court's first chairman. This act was in actual operation for about three years, during which time its history was one of extended conflict with organized labor, particularly the Kansas district of the United Mine Workers. Soon after its passage, Alexander Howat, the district president, and August Dorchy, the vice president, defied the court by refusing to testify. For this defiance, they were ordered committed to jail but appealed. After the trial court issued this order, the coal miners went on strike, and the attorney-general of the state secured an injunction forbidding the strike. No serious consequences followed for some months, as the miners returned to work after a few days' lay-off, while the union sought to get a decision from the Kansas Supreme Court holding the act unconstitutional. Instead, this court late in 1920 held the act constitutional.[2] Thereupon, the union officers seem to have determined upon open defiance of the law. In February, 1921, in violation of a trade agreement and of the rules of the national organization of the United Mine Workers, Howat called a strike against a coal operator to compel the payment of a disputed claim of an individual workman for back wages. For calling this strike, Howat and the entire executive board of the district organization were found guilty of having violated the injunction secured in the preceding year by the attorney-general and sentenced to one year in jail. They

---

[1] Kansas Laws, Special Session, 1920, c. 29, amended by Laws 1921, c. 261. This statute is reprinted in Francis B. Sayre, "Cases on Labor Law," pp. 918–923 (1922), and in A. R. Ellingwood and Whitney Coombs, "The Government and Labor," pp. 282–291, McGraw-Hill Book Company, Inc., New York (1926).

[2] The decisions of the Kansas Supreme Court in the three contempt cases against Howat and Dorchy, all of which are entitled State v. Howat, are reported in 107 Kan. 423, 191 Pac. 585 (1920); 109 Kan. 376, 198 Pac. 686 (1921); 109 Kan. 779, 202 Pac. 72 (1921); and the decision of the U. S. Supreme Court in Howat v. Kansas, 258 U. S. 181, 42 Sup. Ct. 277 (1922).

were also indicted criminally under the industrial relations court act, found guilty by a jury, and sentenced to an additional six months in jail; and while these cases were pending, they defied the court by calling still another strike, for which they were again found guilty of contempt and fined. In all these cases, appeals were taken to the Kansas Supreme Court, which sustained the sentences, and from this court to the U. S. Supreme Court, on the theory that the Kansas act violated the federal constitution. The Supreme Court, however, held that this question could not be raised in contempt proceedings, and the union officials were sentenced to jail. In protest against these sentences, the miners engaged in a series of strikes which kept the Kansas coal fields in turmoil for many months. In the end the strikers were beaten, largely through the action of the national officers of the United Mine Workers in ousting Howat and his entire executive board for their violation of the union constitution, and supplying coal miners from other states to break the strike. This outcome greatly enhanced the prestige of the court but made it more hateful than ever to labor.

Practically everything else that the court did had the same effect.[1] Governor Allen and other protagonists of the court made much of the fact that most of the cases coming before it were started by employees, that the majority of its decisions were in favor of labor, and that no strikes occurred in violation of its awards. But this was only a part—the least significant—of the story. In all of the national strikes of these years—the switchmen's strike of 1920, the butcher workmen's strike of 1921, and the railroad shop crafts' strike and coal miners' strike of 1922—

---

[1] Besides the incidents which are discussed in the text, the Industrial Relations Court gained unfavorable publicity through the dismissal, late in 1921, of Miss Linna E. Brisette, in charge of its woman and child-labor department, which the women's organizations and others interested in the work of this department ascribed to the influence of the manufacturers' association and regarded as an assault upon the woman and child-labor laws. Further, Chairman Huggins soon got into a very serious conflict with Governor Allen and publicly stated that the governor was trying to use the court as a political football. To cap the climax, the court during the shop crafts' strike of 1922 arrested William Allen White, the most influential editor in the state and originally a supporter of the Industrial Relations Court Act, because he expressed sympathy with the striking railroad employees.

the Kansas members of the unions completely ignored the Industrial Relations Court and quit work along with their fellows in other states. In these strikes the court, without taking any effective action, did cause some pickets to be arrested, again arousing labor's ire.[1]

The court got into conflict with the employers[2] when the Charles Wolff Packing Co. refused to put into effect a decision of the court fixing wages and hours of labor in its packing plants. The court then sought a mandatory injunction to compel this company to observe its award. This the company backed by the Associated Industries of Kansas resisted, claiming the act to be unconstitutional in its application to the food and clothing industries. This plea was overruled by the Kansas Supreme Court, but the U. S. Supreme Court early in 1923 sustained the employers' contention and held the act unconstitutional in so far as it gave power to the Industrial Relations Court to fix wages in the packing industry.[3] Thereafter, the Industrial Relations Court modified its award, striking out the portion relating to wage rates, and was again sustained by the Kansas Supreme Court. The U. S. Supreme Court once more reversed the state decision, now declaring the entire scheme of compulsory arbitration to be unconstitutional for industries not peculiarly affected with a public interest.

---

[1] For the course of the Industrial Relations Court in these strikes, consult the articles by H. Feis, The Kansas Miners and the Kansas Court, 43 *Survey* 822 (1922) and The Kansas Court and the National Strik s, 44 *Survey* 372 (1922); also *Res arch Report* 67 of the National Industrial Conference Board, The Kansas Court of Industrial Relations, pp. 52–67 (1924).   State v. Personett, 114 Kan. 680, 220 Pac. 520 (1923) is a reported case involving the prosecution of a picket under the Industrial Relations Court Act during the shop crafts' strike.

[2] On the attitude of the Kansas manufacturers toward the Industrial Relations Court, see the *New York Times*, Feb. 25, 1922; for that of the national employers organizations, *Research Report* 67 of the National Industrial Conference Board, *op. cit.*, and the article State Regulation, 4 *Law and Labor* 55–56 (1922).

[3] The reported decisions in this case are Court of Industrial Relations v. Wolff Packing Co., 109 Kan. 629, 201 Pac. 418 (1921); 111 Kan. 501, 207 Pac. 806 (1921); Wolff Packing Co. v. Court of Industrial Relations, 262 U. S. 522, 43 Sup. Ct. 630 (1923); Court of Industrial Relations v. Wolff Packing Co., 114 Kan. 304, 219 Pac. 259 (1923); 114 Kan. 487, 227 Pac. 249 (1923); Wolff Packing Co. v. Court of Industrial Relations, 267 U. S. 552, 45 Sup. Ct. 441 (1924).

More than a year before this last decision, the Industrial Relations Court had ceased to function. In the election of 1922, it had been a leading political issue. The Republican platform praised it highly; the Democratic platform repudiated the entire act. Inconsistently, the voters elected a Democratic governor and an overwhelmingly Republican legislature. Governor Davis upon assuming office promptly pardoned Howat after he had served eight and one-half months in jail, recommended repeal of the law to the legislature, and, after the decision of the U. S. Supreme Court in the first Wolff Packing Co. case, called upon the members of the court to resign, promising to leave their positions vacant. The legislature refused to follow this recommendation and the members of the court did not resign, but its appropriations were reduced and in 1925 the Industrial Relations Court was replaced by the Public Service Commission. In 1922, it heard but few cases, and after 1923 none at all. No mention of the industrial relations court act occurs in any report of the Kansas Public Service Commission or its successor (in the labor field) the Commission of Labor and Industry.

The industrial relations court act, however, is still on the statute books, and some portions probably remain effective. The compulsory arbitration provisions have been held unconstitutional in their application to coal mining and the food and clothing industries but may be valid as to railroads and public utilities.[1] Further, as a matter of law, strikes are still prohibited not only on the railroads and on the public utilities, but

---

[1] The decisions of the U. S. Supreme Court holding unconstitutional the provisions of the Kansas act relating to the state determination of wages and conditions of labor in their application to coal mining and the food and clothing industries turned upon the point that these industries are not public utilities. This alone suggests that compulsory arbitration might be constitutional for public utilities, a view which is strengthened by language which occurs in the court's decision in Wilson v. New, 243 U. S. 332, 37 Sup. Ct. 298 (1917), in which it sustained the Adamson Act. For a complete discussion of the constitutionality of compulsory arbitration, in view of the decisions rendered in the cases growing out of the Kansas Industrial Relations Court Act, see the articles by S. P. Simpson, Constitutional Limitations on Compulsory Arbitration, 38 *Harvard Law Rev.* 753–792 (1925); William L. Huggins, What the Supreme Court Has Done to the Kansas Industrial Court Act, 11 *Amer. Bar Assoc. Jour.* 363–367 (1925); and Edward Berman, The Supreme Court and Compulsory Arbitration, 18 *Amer. Econ. Rev.* 19–44 (1928).

also in the three industries in which compulsory arbitration has been held to be unconstitutional. Whether this prohibition of strikes is valid is still undecided. This question was raised in the last two cases to come before the U. S. Supreme Court involving the Kansas Act, both of which were appeals from the conviction of Dorchy (along with Howat) on criminal charges for calling strikes in 1921 in defiance of the Industrial Relations Court.[1] This conviction was passed upon by the U. S. Supreme Court after it had held in the first Wolff Packing Co. case that the compulsory-arbitration feature of the law was unconstitutional as applied to meat packing, and the court now held that it was unconstitutional also as to coal mining. It did not, however, free Dorchy but instead sent the case back to the Kansas Supreme Court for determination whether the prohibition of strikes (under which the defendant was convicted) was severable from the unconstitutional provisions of the law providing for wage determinations. This was so held by the Kansas court; whereupon the case was once more brought to the U. S. Supreme Court. That Court, in the second Kansas v. Dorchy case, upheld the conviction but based its decision upon the fact that the particular strike for which the defendants were convicted was one unlawful at common law. Thus, it left open the question whether Kansas or any other state may prohibit strikes otherwise lawful, and this remains undetermined. The Kansas act, while now dormant, may at some future time again trouble labor.

ARBITRATION UNDER TRADE AGREEMENTS

This completes the discussion of governmental agencies for the adjustment of labor disputes in the United States. Proposals for adjustment machinery which have not been enacted into law will be considered in the next chapter, and questions of policy in Chap. XIII.

Brief mention should be made here of non-governmental adjustment agencies, particularly those set up under trade agreements. Few trade agreements in this country have provided machinery for the settlement of disputes arising over their

---

[1] The decisions discussed in this paragraph are reported in State v. Howat, 112 Kan. 235, 210 Pac. 352 (1921); Dorchy v. Kan., 264 U. S. 286, 44 Sup. Ct. 323 (1923); State v. Howat, 116 Kan. 412, 227 Pac. 752 (1923); Dorchy v. Kan., 272 U. S. 306, 47 Sup. Ct. 86 (1926).

interpretation. Now, however, there are a number of agreements which do provide such machinery. Examples are those in the boot and shoe industry in Massachusetts, the national agreement in the photo-engraving industry, and the adjustment machinery set up in many of the men's clothing markets. The first mentioned provide for the settlement of all disputes concerning their meaning by the state board of conciliation and arbitration. The second is the outstanding example in this country of the joint council system of adjustment, without outside intervention, and the third, of the employment of paid, permanent, neutral arbitrators.

The adjustment machinery in the men's clothing industry had its beginning in the agreement negotiated in 1910 by the Amalgamated Clothing Workers with Hart, Schaffner & Marx at Chicago and has since been extended to all clothing centers. Under it, there are shop committees, composed of an equal number of representatives of the two sides, which try to settle all controversies arising within the shop during the contract period. When they fail, the disputes go to trade or arbitration boards, with a neutral (called the "impartial chairman") in the controlling position, who is employed on a permanent basis and paid by both sides. This system has worked now for considerably more than a decade to the apparent satisfaction of employers and employees and not only has eliminated all serious strikes over the interpretation of trade agreements but has operated gradually to reduce the number of cases in which resort to arbitration has been necessary for the settlement of disputes.[1]

Arbitration under trade agreements represents the most successful voluntary arbitration in this country; and the reason is that it is confined to the judicial function of interpretation. In other arbitrations, the arbitrator is the law maker, not merely

---

[1] There are some variations in details in the adjustment machinery in the several clothing markets; for instance, in the smaller markets, it is customary to call in the impartial chairmen of other cities when disputes arise, instead of having a designated, permanent arbitrator. The essence of the system, however, is in all markets as described. For accounts of the arbitration machinery set up under trade agreements, see Solomon Blum, "Labor Economics," pp. 244–247, Henry Holt & Company, New York (1925); W. A. Leiserson, The Way to Industrial Peace, 2 *Amer. Rev.* 252–263 (1924); and J. H. Tufts, Judicial Law-making Exemplified in Industrial Arbitration, 21 *Columbia Law Rev.* 405–415 (1921).

the interpreter.   Here, the parties have agreed upon the rules
and governing principles, and the arbitrator has only the task of
applying them.   The system has profited greatly from having
arbitrators of tact and ability.   Added to this, the permanence
of their positions gives them a technical knowledge in industry
which no outsider called in for a single dispute can possibly have.
But more than all else, the success of the adjustment machinery
in this industry is attributable to its foundation principle,
self-government.

Bibliographical Note

The literature of conciliation and arbitration is very extensive.   Brief
accounts occur in all text books on labor problems and fuller discussions in
John R. Commons and John B. Andrews, "Principles of Labor Legislation,"
pp. 147–161, 184–187, Harper & Brothers, New York, 1926 ed., and in G. C.
Watkins, "Introduction to the Study of Labor Problems," pp. 415–430,
Thomas Y. Crowell Company, New York (1922).   A. R. Ellingwood and
Whitney Coombs, "The Government and Labor," pp. 264–345, McGraw-Hill
Book Company, Inc., New York (1926), reprints most of the important
statutes in this field and some other source material.   A comprehensive bib-
liography is the "List of References on Industrial Arbitration" (mimeo-
graphed) prepared in 1920 and 1922 by the Division of Bibliography of the
Library of Congress.

The best studies on the adjustment of railroad labor disputes or some
phase thereof are Clyde O. Fisher, Use of the Federal Power in the Settlement of Railway Labor Disputes, *Bull.* 303, U. S. Bureau of Labor Statistics,
1922; T. T. Ko, Governmental Methods of Adjusting Labor Disputes, pp.
54–102, "Columbia University Studies in History, etc.," No. 271 (1926); H.
D. Wolf, "The Railroad Labor Board," University of Chicago Press (1927);
Leifur Magnusson and Marguerite A. Gadsby, Federal Intervention in Railroad Disputes, in 11 *Monthly Labor Rev.* 26–43 (1920); Frank H. Dixon,
Functions and Policies of the Railroad Labor Board, 10 *Proc. Acad. Polit.
Sci. City of New York* 19–27 (1922); C. O. Fisher, The New Railway Labor
Act: A Comparison and an Appraisal, 17 *Amer. Econ. Rev.* 177–187 (1927);
and A. R. Ellingwood, The Railway Labor Act of 1926, 36 *Jour. Polit. Econ.*
53–82 (1928).   "The Compilation of Laws relating to Mediation, Conciliation, and Arbitration between Employers and Employees," published
by the Government Printing Office (latest edition, 1930) is a convenient
collection of all statutes which have been enacted in this field, and the
Congressional Hearings upon these measures an important source of
information on their actual operation.   Of these Congressional Hearings,
the most valuable are those in the 64th Congress, 2nd Session (1917) on
"Government Investigation of Railway Disputes," by the Senate Committee on Interstate Commerce, and "Interstate Commerce on Railroads,"
by the House Committee on Interstate and Foreign Commerce; and in the
69th Congress, 1st Session (1926), on "Railroad Labor Disputes," by the

House Committee. Railroad Labor Arbitrations, *Sen. Doc.* 493, 64th Cong., 1st Sess. (1916), compiled by W. Jett Lauck, is a valuable source upon the arbitrations under the Erdman and Newlands Acts. "Some References to Material on Arbitration of Disputes between Railroad Companies and Employees by Government Boards of Arbitration" (mimeographed), Bureau of Railway Economics, Washington (1921), is the best available special bibliography.

Joshua Bernhardt, "The Division of Conciliation: Its History, Activities, and Organization," Inst. for Governmental Research, Service Mon. U. S. Government No. 20 (1923); M. H. Wiseman, Keeping the Peace with Labor, 59 *Industrial Management* 179–183 (1920); and J. A. Moffitt, Conciliation in Labor Disputes, *Bull.* 455, U. S. Bureau of Labor Statistics, pp. 119–125 (1927), are good accounts of the work of the U. S. Conciliation Service. Charles G. Wood, "Reds and Lost Wages," Harper & Brothers, New York (1930), recites some experiences of an American mediator.

On the adjustment agencies of the wartime, the best general accounts are A. M. Bing, "War-time Strikes and Their Adjustment," E. P. Dutton & Company, Inc., New York (1921); G. C. Watkins, "Labor Problems and Labor Administration in the United States during the World War," University of Illinois (1919); Edward Berman, Labor Disputes and the President, "Columbia University Studies in History, etc.," No. 249, pp. 126–153 (1924); and Louis B. Wehle, The Adjustment of Labor Disputes in the United States during the War, 32 *Quart. Jour. Econ.* 122–141 (1917). Articles of merit upon particular agencies include W. E. Hotchkiss and H. R. Seager, The Ship Building Labor Adjustment Board, *Bull.* 283, U. S. Bur. of Labor Stat. (1921); the bulletin on The National War Labor Board, *Bull.* 287, U. S. Bur. of Labor Stat. (1921); John A. Fitch, The War Labor Board: A Wartime Experiment with Compulsory Arbitration, 42 *Survey* 192–195 (1919); R. B. Gregg, The National War Labor Board, 33 *Harvard Law Rev.* 39–63 (1919); B. M. Squires, The New York Harbor Wage Adjustment, 7 *Monthly Labor Rev.* 477–502 (1918); and the same author's The National Adjustment Commission, 29 *Jour. Polit. Econ.* 543–570 (1921). Important sources are the "Docket" of the War Labor Board, published in five volumes by the Bureau of Applied Economics (1920), the *Memorandum Report* of the secretary of the Board, Government Printing Office (1919); and the *Report of the Activities of the War Department in the Field of Industrial Relations during the War*, Government Printing Office (1919).

The work of state conciliation and arbitration boards and of state labor departments in this field is discussed at length in G. E. Barnett and D. A. McCabe, "Mediation, Investigation, and Arbitration in Industrial Disputes," 3–128, D. Appleton & Company, New York (1916), and in T. T. Ko, Governmental Methods of Adjusting Labor Disputes, "Columbia University Studies in History, etc.," No. 271 (1926). Carl H. Mote, "Industrial Arbitration," pp. 191–288, Bobbs-Merrill Company, Indianapolis (1916), and the article How the States Provide for Arbitration of Labor Disputes: A Digest of State Machinery, 9 *Bloomfield's Labor Digest* 3193–3196 (1925), present digests of the state laws. The compilation of "Mediation and Arbitration Laws of the United States," published in 1913 by the U. S.

Bureau of Labor Statistics, reproduces their full text as they stood at that time.

An impartial account of the Colorado industrial disputes investigation system is the study by Colston E. Warne and Merrill E. Gaddis, Eleven Years of Compulsory Investigation of Industrial Disputes in Colorado, 35 *Jour. Polit. Econ.* 657–683 (1927). A favorable presentation is W. I. Reilly, Industrial Relations Act of Colorado, *Bull.* 389, U. S. Bur. of Labor Stat., pp. 48–54 (1924). Attacks by labor men are Samuel Gompers, Benevolent Compulsion in Colorado, and Compulsory Service or Freedom— Which?, both in 23 *Amer. Federationist* 437–452 and 929–936 (1916), respectively; and George Lackland, Colorado Tries to Outlaw Strikes, 9 *Labor Age* 4–6 (1922).

The Kansas Court of Industrial Relations is presented in a favorable light in Henry J. Allen, "The Party of the Third Part: the Story of the Kansas Industrial Relations Court," Harper & Brothers, New York (1921); W. L. Huggins, "Labor and Democracy," The Macmillan Company, New York (1922); and state publication "The Kansas Court of Industrial Relations," State Printer (1921). "The Allen-Gompers Debate," E. P. Dutton & Company, Inc., New York (1920), is a debate on the merits of this law. Impartial accounts of value include Kansas Court of Industrial Relations, *Bull.* 322, U. S. Bur. of Labor Stat. (1923); The Kansas Court of Industrial Relations, *Research Rept.* 67, Nat. Industrial Conference Board (1924); Herbert Feis, Kansas Miners and the Kansas Court, The Kansas Court and the National Strikes, and The Kansas Court of Industrial Relations, Its Spokesmen, Its Records, 47 *Survey* 822–826, 867 (1922), 49 *Survey* 372–374 (1922) and 37 *Quart. Jour. Econ.* 705–733 (1923), respectively; J. S. Young, Industrial Courts; with Special Reference to the Kansas Experiment, *Minn. Law Rev.* IV, 483–512 (1920), V, 39–61, 185–215, 353–366 (1921); and Herbert Rabinowitz, The Kansas Industrial Court Act, 12 *Calif. Law Rev.* 1–16 (1923). A comprehensive bibliography, by Laura A. Thompson, is published in *Bull.* 322, U. S. Bur. of Labor Stat. 39–51 (1923).

CHAPTER XII

PROPOSALS FOR LEGISLATION

HISTORICAL INTRODUCTION

There has been ceaseless agitation, especially by labor leaders, for changes in law ever since the first cases growing out of labor disputes were decided early in the nineteenth century. The proposals advanced have differed at various times, but organized labor has always sought legislation to get away from court decisions regarded as unjust. In the earliest stage, extending into the nineties, its demand was for the "repeal of the conspiracy laws," by which was meant the governmental recognition of trade unions and the legalization of their activities, including strikes.[1] The only results of this long agitation were the enactment of a few laws declaring it legal for workmen to combine to improve their conditions and of a greater number of statutes allowing unions to incorporate. And while these laws were being won, a greater volume of legislation was enacted in a spirit of hostility to labor organizations, particularly anti-boycott and anti-intimidation laws. After 1890, however, little more was heard of this demand, not because labor had gained its objectives, but because more pressing problems arose—the injunction and the application of the Sherman Antitrust Act to labor unions. Relief from "the abuse of injunctions" and exemption from the anti-trust laws now became labor's foremost legislative demands and have held this status ever since. These two matters are, of course, not the same but have ever been closely identified in the thoughts of the union workmen and frequently combined in the same legislative measures.

---

[1] No complete account of labor's efforts to "repeal the conspiracy laws" and the resulting legislation has ever been written, but the subject is briefly discussed in Selig Perlman, "History of Trade Unionism in the United States," pp. 152–154, The Macmillan Company, New York (1922), and in E. E. Witte, Early American Labor Cases, 35 *Yale Law Journal* 825, at 829–831 (1926). See also the statutes cited in Felix Frankfurter and Nathan Greene, "The Labor Injunction," p. 137, Note 5, The Macmillan Company, New York (1930).

For present purposes, it is unnecessary to discuss in detail the provisions or the fate of the numerous antiinjunction bills introduced in Congress from 1895 to 1914.[1] There was one or more such bills to which organized labor gave its support in each session. None of these was enacted, but several won favorable reports, passed one house, and were defeated only by the device of unsatisfactory committee substitutes. This incensed the Federation of Labor and led it in the 1906 elections to seek to prevent the reelection of congressional leaders responsible for these rebuffs. This first non-partisan campaign "to reward labor's friends and punish its enemies" was unsuccessful, at least as regards Congressman Littlefield of Maine, the principal object of attack. Ever since, however, organized labor has pursued the same tactics in congressional elections.[2] In 1908, the Federation took the further step of expressing its preference for a presidential candidate, favoring Bryan, because Taft, as a United States Circuit judge, had issued some of the first labor injunctions. The virtual partnership of organized labor with the Democratic party continued through the congressional elections of 1910 and the Presidential election of 1912 and led to the enactment of the Clayton Act in 1914.

During the eighteen years preceding this culmination, organized labor several times altered its proposals.[3] It first cham-

---

[1] A brief analytical account of these proposals occurs in Felix Frankfurter and Nathan Greene, "The Labor Injunction," pp. 134–141, 154–160, The Macmillan Company, New York (1930). A more detailed account is the author's unpublished report made in June, 1914, to the Commission on Industrial Relations on History of the Antiinjunction Bills in Congress (Appendix A to the *Report* on Congressional Action upon the Reform of Trade Union Law), on file in the Wisconsin Historical Library.

[2] Upon the political activities of organized labor in the United States, see Mollie R. Carroll, "Labor and Politics: the Attitude of the American Federation of Labor toward Legislation and Politics," Univ. of Chicago Press (1923); William English Walling, "American Labor and American Democracy," Harper & Brothers, New York (1926); and Organized Labor in National Politics, *Editorial Research Report*, pp. 767–793 (Aug. 31, 1928).

[3] The bills referred to in this and the succeeding paragraph are the following:

Jury Trial Bill, 54th Cong.: The bill favored by the American Federation of Labor is printed in 2 *Amer. Federationist* 171 (1895). This bill appears not even to have been introduced, but another measure acceptable to labor, the Hill bill (S. 2984) passed the Senate. The House committee on the

pioned a bill providing for jury trial in contempt cases. Then, from 1900 to 1906, it supported a measure providing that no act of a combination in connection with a trades dispute should be deemed a crime or a violation of the antitrust laws nor be enjoined, unless such act were criminal if committed by a single individual. In 1906, it presented a new bill providing that

---

judiciary reported a substitute not satisfactory to labor, and no further action was taken on the bill.

A. F. of L. Bill, 1900–1906: This bill, drafted by Jackson Ralston, attorney for the Federation, was first introduced in the 56th Congress as the Ridgely-Thurston bill (H. R. 8917, and S. 4233). This bill was reported for passage in both houses but never came to a vote in either. In the 57th Congress, it was reintroduced as the Hoar-Grosvenor bill (S. 1118 and H. R. 11060), passed the House, but was defeated in the Senate through the introduction of a substitute (by the committee on the judiciary) which, President Gompers stated editorially, made this a "pro-injunction," instead of an antiinjunction, bill. This same measure was reintroduced in the 58th Congress as the Grosvenor bill (H. R. 89) and in the 59th Congress as the Little bill (H. R. 4445) but in neither Congress was it given a hearing in either house. A measure incorporating this bill and adding to its provisions against the issuance of *ex parte* temporary restraining orders and for jury trial in contempt cases, known as the Rodenberg bill (H. R. 17137) was strongly supported by the railroad brotherhoods in the 60th Congress, but failed.

The A. F. of L. Bill, 1906–1913: This bill, declaring the right to do business not to be property, originated with T. C. Spelling, a writer of text books on the law of equity. It was first offered in the 59th Congress as the Pearre bill (H. R. 18752) and was reintroduced in the 60th Congress by the same member as H. R. 94. In the 61st and 62nd Congresses, it was known as the "Wilson bill" (H. R. 25188 and H. R. 11032, respectively). It was again introduced in modified form in the 62nd Congress as the Bacon-Bartlett bill (H. R. 23189 and S. 6266) and was favorably reported by the Committee on Labor of the House, but too late to be voted on; and it was again offered by the same authors in the 63rd Congress as H. R. 1873 and S. 927.

The bill to prohibit the issuance of injunctions without notice favored by President Roosevelt was the Gilbert bill, H. R. 9328 of the 59th Congress. The bill championed by President Taft was the Moon bill of the 61st Congress (H. R. 21334). The injunction limitation bill passed by the House of Representatives in the 62nd Congress was the Clayton bill (H. R. 23635) and the contempt bill of the same session (H. R. 22591), also by Clayton. The bill to exempt labor organizations from the antitrust laws introduced at the instance of the American Federation of Labor in 1908 was the Wilson bill (H. R. 20854).

An important development in connection with the proposal to exempt labor unions from the antitrust laws not discussed in the text was the offering

injunctions might be issued only to protect property and that the right to continue business should not be deemed a property right.   This was the principal proposal of the American Federation of Labor until the enactment of the Clayton Act, but when the Supreme Court's decision in the Danbury hatters case created what was thought a crisis threatening the very existence of the unions, the Federation brought forward a companion measure exempting labor and farmer organizations from the antitrust laws.

Besides these bills, numerous other antiinjunction proposals were presented in Congress.   President Roosevelt urged the enactment of legislation on this subject in strongest terms in no less than five messages from 1906 to 1908, specifically urging a measure to prohibit the issuance of injunctions without notice. This bill was endorsed by the railroad brotherhoods but regarded as inadequate by the American Federation of Labor, and in the end nothing came of all of Roosevelt's messages.   During the Taft administration, there were dozens of bills on this subject. The President gave support to a measure which provided that temporary restraining orders issued *ex parte* should expire within seven days unless renewed after notice to the adverse party.   The Democrats offered bills specifying conduct which should not be enjoined and providing for jury trial in indirect contempt cases.   These were passed by the House in the 62nd Congress but got no further, no injunction legislation whatsoever being enacted.

THE CLAYTON ACT

The next Congress gave organized labor the Clayton Act.[1] Section 6 of this act exempted labor organizations *per se* and

---

of amendments each year, beginning in 1910, to the item in the annual sundry civil appropriation bill for the enforcement of the antitrust laws, which provided that none of the money appropriated should be used for prosecuting farmer or labor organizations.   This amendment passed both houses when first offered in the 60th Congress but was dropped from the bill by the conference committee at the request of President Taft.   It again passed both houses in the 61st Congress and this time was vetoed by the President.   It passed once more in the 62nd Congress and was signed by President Wilson.   For many years thereafter, it was a regular feature of these bills.

[1] 38 Stats. 730.

their lawful activities from the antitrust laws.[1] Sections 17 to 19 prescribed certain procedural requirements applicable to all injunction cases in the federal courts: *Ex parte* temporary restraining orders must be set for a hearing within ten days; all injunctions were to be specific; injunctional orders were to apply only to the parties named therein and others who with knowledge of their terms act in concert with the named parties; and a bond must be filed before the issuance of any such order. Section 20, applying only to labor cases, set forth a long list of acts, qualified by the frequent use of the words "lawful," "lawfully," and "peacefully," which should not be enjoined or held a violation of any federal law: among others, terminating employment, ceasing to patronize, persuading others to quit work or to refrain from purchasing, and picketing peacefully. Sections 21 to 25 provided for jury trial in cases of indirect contempt in which the charges were premised upon conduct involving a crime.

These sections were not organized labor's own proposals and as originally presented were not at all satisfactory to it.[2] Slight changes, however, caused the American Federation of Labor to give up its expressed intention to fight this bill on the floor and led President Gompers to hail Sec. 6 as "labor's Magna Charta" and Sec. 20 as "labor's Bill of Rights." Members of Congress disagreed on the meaning of these crucial sections, and the committee reports gave them a much narrower construction than did the labor leaders.[3] The language used in the act itself was scant, and capable of many different interpretations.

---

[1] For the history of this section and its subsequent construction, see Chap. IV (pp. 66–69).

[2] A concise account of the congressional history of the Clayton Act is given in Felix Frankfurter and Nathan Greene, "The Labor Injunction," pp. 139–144, 154–163, 182–186, The Macmillan Company, New York (1930). A more detailed history is the author's unpublished report to the United States Commission on Industrial Relations on The Labor Provisions of the Clayton Act (Appendix B to the *Report on Congressional Action on Trade Union Law*), October, 1914, on file in the Wisconsin Historical Library.

[3] The leading business and employers' organizations—the National Association of Manufacturers, the American Anti-boycott Association, the United States Chamber of Commerce, among others—described the labor provisions of the Clayton bill while pending as extremely radical and subversive but, once it was enacted, claimed that it made no change in the law. For an illustration of this change of position, contrast the "Memorandum relative to the Injunction Features of H. R. 15657," by Daniel Davenport, general counsel of the American Anti-boycott Association,

Inferior courts passed frequently on the labor sections of the Clayton Act in the years following its enactment, but it was not until 1921 that any cases involving their construction reached the U. S. Supreme Court.[1] Then in Duplex Printing Co. v. Deering,[2] the Supreme Court construed Secs. 6 and 20 as in effect "declaratory of what was the best practice always"; that is, as making no change in law.

With this decision died organized labor's high hopes of the Clayton Act; Secs. 6 and 20, on which it principally relied, were rendered all but meaningless; Secs. 17 to 19, relating to injunction procedure, admittedly did no more than to write into the statutes the practices previously followed by most courts; Secs. 21 to 25, providing for jury trial in certain contempt cases, were held constitutional in 1924,[3] after numerous inferior court decisions to the contrary. These jury trial provisions represent the only benefit to organized labor from the Clayton Act, and these, as pointed out in Chap. V, are of but limited application. Since the Clayton Act, there have been far more cases against unions under the federal antitrust laws than before.[4] Similarly, injunctions have steadily grown more drastic despite Sec. 20. Whether the Clayton Act was a gold brick or an example of poor draftsmanship is debatable, but the fact that it afforded labor no relief is so clear that no one now holds a different view.

STATE ANTIINJUNCTION LAWS

In the long years when the American Federation of Labor was trying to get Congress to restrict the issuance of injunctions by

---

presented to the House Committee on the Judiciary in April, 1914, with his article An Analysis of the Labor Section of the Clayton Antitrust Bill, 80 *Central Law Jour.* 46–55 (1915). For the author's interpretation of the labor sections of the Clayton Act while this measure was pending, see the article The Clayton Bill and Organized Labor, 33 *Survey* 360 (1914).

[1] An excellent discussion of the decisions construing the labor provisions of the Clayton Act, both in the inferior federal courts and in the Supreme Court occurs in Frankfurter and Greene, *op. cit.*, pp. 145–148, 163–176, 191–194.

[2] 254 U. S. 443, 41 Sup. Ct. 172. The Supreme Court's construction of the labor provisions of the Clayton Act was to some extent foreshadowed in Paine Lumber Co. v. Neal, 244 U. S. 459, 37 Sup. Ct. 718 (1917).

[3] Michaelson v. U. S., 266 U. S. 42, 45 Sup. Ct. 18.

[4] *Cf.* Chap. IV (pp. 69–70).

the federal courts, the state federations were fighting for similar legislation. Most of the bills sponsored by them failed, but a few were enacted into law even prior to the passage of the Clayton Act.[1] California in 1903 and Oklahoma in 1907 passed laws modeled after the American Federation of Labor injunction bill of 1900–1906, providing that acts which are not criminal when done by individuals shall not be enjoined when committed by combinations in furtherance of trades disputes. These laws are still on the statute books, but have had no appreciable effect on the issuance of injunctions in these states. Oklahoma by constitutional amendment in 1907 and Massachusetts by statute in 1911 provided for jury trial in contempt cases, but the Massachusetts law was subsequently held unconstitutional.[2] In 1913 and 1914, while the Clayton Act was pending in Congress, Arizona and Kansas enacted laws very similar to Secs. 17 and 20 of the Clayton Act, providing that *ex parte* temporary restraining orders must be set for a hearing within ten (seven in Kansas) days and enumerating a long list of acts which should never be enjoined. At the same time, Montana legislated that injunctions should be granted in labor disputes only under the same conditions as in other controversies; while Massachusetts in two laws provided that peaceful persuasion should not be enjoined[3]

---

[1] The laws referred to in this paragraph which are still in force are: California, Laws (Deering) 1923, Act 1605; Oklahoma (antiinjunction), Stats. 1921, s. 7261; Oklahoma (jury trial), Const., art. II, s. 25, and Rev. Laws 1909, s. 2229; Kansas, Rev. Stats. 1923, ss. 60–1104 to 60–1107; Massachusetts (peaceful persuasion), Gen. Laws 1921, c. 149, s. 24; and Montana, Codes 1921, s. 9242.8. The laws held unconstitutional were Arizona, Rev. Stats. 1913, s. 1464; Massachusetts (jury trial), Laws 1911, c. 339; and Massachusetts (definition of property), Laws 1914, c. 778.

[2] Walton Lunch Co. v. Kearney, 236 Mass. 310, 128 N. E. 429 (1920). Laws providing for jury trial in contempt cases were held unconstitutional earlier in Michigan, Mississippi, Missouri, North Carolina, Ohio, Oklahoma, and Virginia, but these laws were not enacted through labor's efforts. For citations to these laws and the decisions declaring them unconstitutional, see Frankfurter and Greene, *op. cit.*, p. 195 and Note 245.

[3] The peaceful persuasion law was held in Folsom Engraving Co. v. McNeil, 235 Mass. 269, 126 N. E. 479 (1920) and in United Shoe Machinery Co. v. Fitzgerald, 237 Mass. 537, 130 N. E. 86 (1921) not to prevent injunctions against efforts to persuade employees to join in strikes where the strikes were undertaken for an illegal purpose. The statute defining property so as to withdraw injunctive protection from the right to do business was held unconstitutional in Bogni v. Perotti, 224 Mass. 152, 112 N. E. 853 (1916).

and that the right to do business should not be protected by injunctions, the second of which was held unconstitutional, while the first was virtually destroyed by construction.

After passage of the Clayton Act, the American Federation of Labor interested itself in getting the state legislatures to enact similar legislation. In 1915, its executive council promulgated a model state antiinjunction bill. This declared unions to be lawful organizations and provided that no person should be indicted or prosecuted for any agreement or combination to improve working conditions. It also declared that the labor of a human being is not a commodity or article of commerce, provided that injunctions should be issued only to prevent irreparable injury to property, and defined property so as to exclude the right to do business. It, also, virtually copied Sec. 20 of the Clayton Act, enumerating lines of conduct which might not be enjoined or held illegal in any sort of action. From 1915 to 1919, this model state antiinjunction bill was introduced in nearly every state legislature, in many of them more than once. It was enacted into law in 1917 or 1919 in North Dakota, Oregon, Utah, Washington, and Wisconsin, and in part in Iowa and Minnesota.[1]

Nearly all the state antiinjunction laws are still in force, but the heart has been taken out of them by the decision of the U. S. Supreme Court in Truax v. Corrigan holding unconstitutional the Arizona act as construed by the state supreme court.[2] This act was a virtual copy of Sec. 20 of the Clayton Act, which the U. S. Supreme Court found unobjectionable. When the Arizona Supreme Court construed the state statute as prohibiting the issuance of injunctions in cases of mass picketing conducted without physical violence, however, the U. S. Supreme Court in a five-to-four decision held that this statute violated the equal-protection and due-process clauses of the fourteenth amendment. Taking their cue from this decision, the supreme courts of other

---

[1] The statutes referred to in this paragraph are now: Iowa, Code 1924, s. 9916; Minnesota, Stats. 1927, ss. 4256–57; North Dakota, Comp. Laws Suppl. 1925, ss. 7214a1 to 7214a3; Oregon, G. L. 1920, ss. 6815–17; Utah, C. L. 1917, ss. 3652–3; Washington, C. S. 1922, ss. 7611–13; Wisconsin, Stats. 1929, s. 133.07. The model state antiinjunction bill also passed the California legislature but was vetoed by the governor.

[2] Truax v. Corrigan, 257 U. S. 312, 42 Sup. Ct. 124 (1921), reversing 20 Ariz. 7, 176 Pac. 570 (1918).

states have construed their anti-injunction laws as the U. S. Supreme Court interpreted Sec. 20 of the Clayton Act; that is, as merely restating the law theretofore recognized.[1]

NEW PROPOSALS

The decisions of the U. S. Supreme Court in Duplex Printing Press Co. v. Deering and Truax v. Corrigan disillusioned organized labor as to the value of the Clayton Act and the model A. F. of L. state antiinjunction bill and compelled it to give thought to a new measure for relief. For some years, however, the executive council of the American Federation of Labor was uncertain what to recommend for congressional action, and it abandoned all thought of a model state antiinjunction bill.[2] It continued to condemn injunctions but did not give its endorsement to any of the many antiinjunction bills introduced in Congress.[3] In consequence, none of these measures was accorded even a hearing.

---

[1] For decisions thus narrowly construing the state antiinjunction laws, see Crane & Co. v. Snowden, 112 Kans. 217, 210 Pac. 475 (1922); Bull v. International Alliance, 119 Kans. 713, 241 Pac. 459 (1925); Heitkemper v. Central Labor Union, 99 Ore. 1, 192 Pac. 765 (1920); Greenfield v. Central Labor Council, 104 Ore. 236, 207 Pac. 186 (1922); Pacific Coast Coal Co. v. District 10, United Mine Workers, 122 Wash. 423, 210 Pac. 953 (1922); Pacific Typesetting Co. v. International Typographical Union, 125 Wash. 273, 216 Pac. 358 (1923); Monday Co. v. Automobile Workers, 171 Wis. 532, 177 N. W. 867 (1920). See also Ossey v. Retail Clerks, 326 Ill. 405, 158 N. E. 162 (1927) construing the Illinois antiinjunction law of 1925, discussed in the next section, and Campbell v. Motion Picture Operators, 2 *Law and Labor* 213 (1920), a Minnesota district-court decision.

[2] The executive council, in its report to the 1925 convention, stated that, due to differences in state constitutions, "no general form of antiinjunction legislation is possible for each and every state." In 1926, however, a so-called "model antiinjunction bill," said to have been recommended by the American Federation of Labor, was introduced in the New York legislature at the instance of the state federation (*N. Y. State Federation of Labor Bull.*, Apr. 3, 1926) but does not seem to have been presented in any other state and was abandoned in New York after but one reintroduction.

[3] Among the antiinjunction bills of the years 1921–1928 were the following:

68th Congress: S. 2760 (Shipstead), H. R. 3208 (Thomas), H. R. 5712 (La Guardia).

69th Congress: S. 711 (McKellar), S. 972 (Shipstead), S. 2760 (Shipstead), H. R. 479 (La Guardia), H. R. 3920 (Moore).

70th Congress: S. 1482 (Shipstead), S. 4202 (Blaine), H. R. 7759 (La Guardia), H. R. 10082 (La Guardia).

In the meantime, the American Federation of Labor was trying to decide on an antiinjunction bill which it could wholeheartedly support. The story of its efforts to work out such a bill is an interesting one, but too long to be told here in detail.[1] Suffice it to say that this subject received frequent attention from the executive council and that outside advice was freely sought. In disregard of this advice, the Federation in 1927 brought forward a bill of only a few lines, by which it hoped to solve the entire injunction question.[2] This measure, known as the "Shipstead bill," provided that no injunction should be issued by any federal court except to prevent irreparable injury to property and that nothing which is not tangible and transferable should be considered property. Hearings were held on this bill in February and March, 1928,[3] in which labor made a strong showing on the need for legislation to curb the abuse of injunctions, but only a weak case for the particular measure it advocated. This was assailed as both unsound and ineffective, not only by representatives of the employers' associations but by every lawyer with one exception who testified, including several attorneys for unions.

After these hearings, the subcommittee of the committee on the judiciary which conducted them, consisting of Senators Norris, Blaine, and Walsh (Montana), decided that the Shipstead bill would not do and invited several specialists[4] to assist in drafting a more adequate measure. Such a substitute was reported by the subcommittee to the full committee near the end of the first session of the 70th Congress (May, 1928), and was printed in the *Congressional Record* to elicit criticisms and suggestions. Following this, both great political parties in their

---

[1] A part of this story is told in H. L. Childs, "Labor and Capital in National Politics," pp. 268–270, Ohio State Univ. Press (1930). Further information can be found in the annual reports of the executive council and the discussions of the injunction question at the conventions of the American Federation of Labor.

[2] S. 1482, 70th Cong., 1st Sess.

[3] Hearings on "Limiting Scope of Injunctions in Labor Disputes," Senate Committee on Judiciary, 70th Cong., 1st Sess.

[4] In its report, the committee acknowledges assistance received from Felix Frankfurter, Herman Oliphant, Donald R. Richberg, Francis B. Sayre, and Edwin E. Witte.

1928 national platforms included a brief promise of legislation to curb the abuse of injunctions in labor disputes.

In the preparation of the subcommittee bill, the American Federation of Labor was not consulted, but it was hoped that it would approve this measure. In the 1928 convention, however, this bill was attacked as inadequate by Andrew Furuseth, veteran president of the seamen's union and the author of the Shipstead bill, with the result that the Federation endorsed the original bill instead of the subcommittee substitute. This action doomed all possibility of any antiinjunction legislation in the 70th Congress. Beyond one hearing upon the proposed committee substitute, no further action was taken on this subject until the 71st Congress convened in December, 1929.

While Congress was marking time, the American Federation of Labor, at the Toronto convention in the fall of 1929, reversed its position on the subcommittee bill after discussion of the question for more than a day. With but one dissenting vote—that of Furuseth—the Federation then went on record in endorsement of this bill, with but minor suggestions for amendment.

Shortly thereafter, the new Congress convened, but it was some months before any action was taken on antiinjunction legislation. In the spring of 1930, the subcommittee again brought forward its injunction-limitation bill,[1] with some, but by no means all, of the amendments suggested by the American Federation of Labor. A majority of the full committee on the judiciary was opposed to this bill and took the unprecedented course of asking the attorney-general for an opinion upon its constitutionality. Attorney-general Mitchell quite promptly advised the committee that under the statutes he could not give legal opinions to Congress. Thereupon, ten members of the committee, constituting a majority, made an adverse report on this bill, while the minority of seven members recommended its passage.[2]

In the short session of the 71st Congress from December, 1930, to March, 1931, no attempt was made to get action on this bill. Neither the congressional friends of the measure nor its labor supporters appear to have been anxious to force a vote, as passage by the Senate was doubtful and a majority of the members

[1] Committee substitute to S. 2497, 71st Cong., 2nd Sess.
[2] *Sen. Rep.* 1060, Parts I and II, 71st Cong., 2nd Sess.

of the House were definitely hostile.   There again seems to have
developed some doubt within the ranks of the labor leaders as to
the adequacy of the proposed bill.   On the last day of this Congress, Senator Shipstead presented as a Senate document an
argument against the Norris (subcommittee) bill by Winter S.
Martin, an attorney very close to the American Federation of
Labor.[1] In this document, a new bill was suggested, which,
while phrased differently, is strongly suggestive of the original
Shipstead bill.   This measure was not actually introduced in
Congress and it is not known how much support it has among
labor leaders.   The criticism of the Norris bill and the presentation of the new bill, however, suggest that there is still division
of opinion among labor leaders as to the precise form of the antiinjunction legislation desired and that it is not entirely certain
what bill labor will offer in the 72nd Congress, which will convene
in December, 1931.

That the American Federation of Labor will have an antiinjunction bill and make a determined effort to get favorable
action in this session of Congress, however, is undoubted.   That
this Congress is very much more likely to pass an antiinjunction
bill than the preceding Congress also is acknowledged by everybody.   Prior to the election of this Congress, the non-partisan
campaign committee of the American Federation of Labor
declared antiinjunction legislation to be its foremost demand and
sought to get all candidates to state their position on this question.   Definite pledges of support were given by a large percentage of the successful candidates.   A majority of the members
in each house are believed to be in favor of antiinjunction legislation and if labor and its congressional supporters can unite on
one measure it will probably pass.

PROVISIONS OF THE NORRIS BILL

While a new bill may be presented at the next session, the
antiinjunction bill which has the endorsement of the American
Federation of Labor and the support of most of the disinterested
students of the injunction problem is the bill of the subcommittee
of the Committee on the Judiciary of the 71st Congress, usually
called the "Norris bill."   This bill is the longest and certainly
the most detailed antiinjunction measure ever presented; yet it

---

[1] *Sen. Doc.* 327, 71st Cong., 3rd Sess.

does not purport to be a complete solution of all problems in the law of labor disputes but only a politically and constitutionally practical approach to the injunction question. It prescribes the conditions under which injunctions may be issued by the federal courts in cases involving or growing out of labor disputes, carefully defining these terms to include all controversies which in common usage are regarded as labor disputes. The conditions proposed relate to both jurisdiction and procedure and, while by no means a complete code governing labor injunctions, deal with more phases of the injunction problem than any previous bill.

The bill begins with a declaration of public policy which sets forth the intent of Congress in the enactment of this measure. Quoting, almost verbatim, language used by Chief Justice Taft in the American Steel Foundries case,[1] it is declared that under existing economic conditions, workmen must have full freedom of association. This is followed, logically, by the provision that agreements in which workmen bind themselves not to join or belong to a labor union shall not be enforced in the federal courts, either in law or in equity. This does not forbid yellow-dog contracts but prevents employers from securing injunctions from the federal courts on the strength of these so-called "contracts" to keep out the union.

Following this is an enumeration of acts in labor disputes which are not to be forbidden by any federal court. This list is in many respects similar to Sec. 20 of the Clayton Act (to which it is supplemental), but without the vitiating "lawful," "lawfully," etc. The acts enumerated include terminating relations of employment, belonging to labor unions, paying strike benefits, aiding strikers involved in legal proceedings, giving publicity to the existence of strikes, peacefully assembling, agreeing with others upon such course of action, persuading anyone without threat, fraud, or violence to commit these acts, and giving notice of intent to do them. The same rights are accorded throughout to employers as to workmen, and it is specifically provided that the doing in concert of the specified acts shall not be enjoined as a conspiracy. These provisions virtually limit injunctions to the prohibition of acts of violence and intimidation and are fol-

---

[1] American Steel Foundries v. Tri-city Central Trades Council, 257 U. S. 184, at 209, 42 Sup. Ct. 72, at 78 (1921).

lowed by the further restriction that labor unions and employers' associations and their officers and members shall be held liable for the unlawful acts of individuals only when there is clear proof of participation, authorization, or ratification.

The rest of the bill—the major part—deals with matters of procedure. Injunctions are to be issued only after notice to the adverse party and to the public officers charged with the duty of protecting the complainants' property. Witnesses are to be examined orally in court, with right of cross-examination and opportunity to present contrary evidence. Temporary restraining orders without notice are not absolutely barred but may be issued only after the court has orally examined the complainants' witnesses and found their testimony to be sufficient if sustained to warrant the issuance of an injunction. Further, such *ex parte* temporary restraining orders may remain in force only for a maximum of five days, but they may be replaced by a temporary injunction issued after a hearing. In all suits for injunctions, the court is required to make findings of fact and must find not only that unlawful acts have been committed or are threatened, that substantial injury will result to the complainant, and that he has no adequate remedy at law, but also that the police and the executive authorities have failed or are unable to furnish adequate protection and that, as to each item of relief sought, greater injury will be inflicted upon the complainants if no injunction is issued than will be suffered by the defendants from the allowance of such order. No injunction is to be issued to any employer who has failed to comply with any obligation of law involved in the dispute or who has neglected to make reasonable efforts to adjust the difficulty. No temporary restraining order or temporary injunction may be issued until the complainant furnishes an adequate bond to cover all costs and attorneys' fees of the defendants in the event that the final decision is against him, upon which bond recovery may be had in the principal action without necessitating a separate suit. The prohibitions in injunctions must be confined to the specific acts complained of and found by the court to have occurred or be imminent. To facilitate appeals, the trial court is required upon demand of either party to forthwith certify the entire record to the Circuit Court of Appeals for review, and in that court appeals in labor injunction cases are to have precedence over all other actions. In all indirect contempt cases, the defendants may demand trial by jury and, if the charges arise from an attack upon the character or conduct of the judge, may compel the calling in of another judge.

The legal theory upon which this entire bill is framed is that the inferior federal courts are creatures of Congress and that it, therefore, can limit their jurisdiction and regulate their procedure as it sees fit.[1] Attorneys for employers' associations have urged that this is unsound, but Congress has done so in other cases. The constitutionality of some of the specific provisions is more seriously in doubt, but none is clearly unconstitutional. Further, the bill provides that if any clause is held invalid, none of the other provisions shall be affected.

OTHER LABOR PROPOSALS

This is the only antiinjunction bill which has much support either in the ranks of labor or among specialists in this field. There are, however, a few dissenters who believe that an entirely different approach is necessary to end "government by injunctions." Two principal alternatives are proposed: (1) to confine injunctions to the protection of tangible and transferable property and (2) to modify the substantive law so as to legalize boycotts, sympathetic strikes, etc. The first is the modern form of the old idea that the entire use of injunctions in labor disputes rests upon treating expectancies—the right to do or continue business—as property.[2] This was Samuel Gompers' theory and that of other labor leaders of his generation. Some of his close associates still cling to this conception of the injunction problem (which was incorporated in the original Shipstead bill), but it has almost no support among lawyers. Even Winter S. Martin, the only lawyer who in the Senate hearings in 1928 defended this theory, while still clinging to its substance, now presents it in an entirely new garb.[3] Nor is this theory in its new form of statement likely to appeal more strongly to lawyer members.

---

[1] For a good presentation of this view, see the minority report on this bill, *House Rep.* 1060, 71st Cong., 1st Sess., Part II, pp. 8–9, and the cases cited therein; also, Frankfurter and Greene, *op. cit.*, pp. 208–210.

[2] For a longer discussion of this theory and its weaknesses, see pp. 105–106.

[3] *Sen. Doc.* 327, 71st Cong., 3rd Sess. Instead of declaring that expectancies are not property, Martin in this memorandum urges that the law

The second approach to the injunction question, that of attempting to secure a modification of the substantive law, has the support of a much larger number of able lawyers.[1] The advocates of this approach argue that the Norris bill will prove another great disappointment. They point out that it relates only to injunctions, leaving open the possibility of damage suits and criminal prosecutions, and that it does not prohibit injunctions against boycotts or remote sympathetic strikes. According to these critics of the Norris bill, we need legislation in this country to the effect that acts of combinations are to be tested by the same standards as acts of individuals. In behalf of this proposal, it is to be said that similar legislation has, from organized labor's point of view, proved most successful in England. In this country, however, state laws on this model have been almost valueless.[2] The fundamental difficulty with this approach is that legal theories presented in labor cases are rather the courts' justification for the decisions they reach than the true reasons for these decisions. If the conspiracy theory is legislated against, the emphasis is likely to shift to the alleged illegal means employed by strikers, or to some other theory, without any real

should state positively that under the thirteenth amendment every person has a right to dispose of his labor as he sees fit. Such a statute, Martin believes, would prevent the issuance of injunctions in labor disputes except for the protection of tangible property, since employers can have no property rights in the labor of any person not under contract to work for them. While differently stated, this is essentially the old labor view that injunctions in labor disputes can be eliminated if only the expectancies arising from "the right to do business" are declared not to be property.

[1] A good presentation of this view is Francis B. Sayre, Labor and the Courts, 39 *Yale Law Jour.* 682–705 (1930). See also the chapter by Prof. William G. Hale, Injunctions against Interference with Trade, etc., in Pomeroy's "Equitable Remedies" (supplement to Pomeroy's "Equity Jurisprudence," 1919 ed.), Vol. V, Chap. 18, pp. 4564–4629.

This was the essence of the antiinjunction bill championed by the American Federation of Labor from 1900 to 1906 and also the principal feature of the Rodenberg bill (H. R. 17137) supported by the railroad brotherhoods in the 59th Congress. After the Clayton Act proved a disappointment, this proposal was revived in a tentative model bill drafted for the American Federation of Labor (for text, see John P. Frey, "The Labor Injunction," pp. 100–101, Equity Publishing Co., Cincinnati (1922), which, with some additions, was introduced as H. R. 3208 (Thomas) in the 68th Congress, H. R. 3920 (Moore) in the 69th Congress, and H. R. 10082 (La Guardia) in the 70th Congress.

[2] *Cf.* p. 80.

gain to labor. To draft a bill along this line which cannot be evaded would seem to be practically impossible, and any effective measure would have little chance of being sustained. Prescribing the substantive law to be enforced in cases in the federal courts goes much further than regulation of the procedure and jurisdiction of these courts. The latter is pretty clearly within the power of Congress; the former, probably an invasion of the constitutional functions of the states.

Besides these two proposals, which are urged by some of labor's friends as substitutes for the pending antiinjunction bill, one other suggested congressional measure merits mention. This is the matter of exempting labor from the antitrust laws. No bill proposing such an exemption is now before Congress, but labor still unanimously demands relief from the antitrust laws. In recent years, however, its demand has not been that labor should be exempted, but that the antitrust laws ought to be repealed in their entirety.[1] Labor has not made any active campaign to effect this purpose, and most of its congressional friends want the antitrust laws to be strengthened, not repealed. But the American Federation of Labor is officially on record for the complete repeal of these laws and defends its position on the score that they have failed to restrain combinations of capital while they have seriously handicapped labor.

In the states, other legislative proposals have been advanced. Although the decade of the twenties was one of hesitation in state as well as in congressional antiinjunction legislation, some progress was made.[2] Wisconsin, in 1923, enacted a statute

---

[1] Resolutions to this effect were adopted by both the 1922 and 1923 conventions of the American Federation of Labor. For good statements of labor's present attitude toward the antitrust laws, see Matthew Woll, Organized Labor Demands Repeal of the Sherman Act, 147 *Ann. Amer. Acad.* 185–188 (1930) and John P. Frey, The Double Standard in Applying the Sherman Act, 18 *Amer. Labor Legis. Rev.* 302–308 (1928).

[2] The laws referred to in this paragraph are the following: Wisconsin, Stats. 1929, ss. 133.07 (2) and 103.46; Illinois, Laws 1925, p. 378; New Jersey, Laws 1926, c. 207, Laws 1925, c. 169; Minnesota, Laws 1929, c. 260; N. Y., Laws 1930, c. 378.

The Illinois law was passed upon by the state supreme court in Ossey v. Retail Clerks, 326 Ill. 405, 158 N. E. 162 (1927), the court stating that this law was practically identical with Sec. 20 of the Clayton Act and holding, on the strength of the construction given to this latter act by the U. S. Supreme Court, that it does not legalize mass picketing. The similar New

requiring jury trial in all contempt cases and prohibiting the
issuance of injunctions in labor controversies until after a hearing
on at least forty-eight hours' notice to the adverse party, and in
1929 enacted the first statute directed against yellow-dog contracts.   Illinois passed a law in 1925 similar to Sec. 20 of the
Clayton Act, omitting "lawfully" but retaining "peaceably" and
avoiding all reference to boycotts.   New Jersey passed much the
same law in 1926 and a year earlier provided that contempt cases
shall be tried before another judge than the one who issued the
injunction and in the court's discretion may be tried before a
jury.   Minnesota, in 1929, prohibited the issuance of injunctions
without notice, with a proviso allowing *ex parte* temporary
restraining orders to be issued when necessary to prevent violence.
New York, in 1930, as a culmination of more than a decade of
bitter struggles in the legislature over antiinjunction bills, provided that no injunction of any kind shall be issued without
notice, leaving it to the courts to determine what notice shall be
given in any particular case.   Most of these measures were com-
promises not entirely satisfactory to labor, but all were heralded
as great victories.

In 1931, a new drive for state antiinjunction legislation was
begun.   A model state bill, very similar to the Norris bill in
Congress, was drafted by Attorney Nathan Greene (coauthor of
Frankfurter and Greene, "The Labor Injunction") and officially endorsed by a Committee on Labor Injunctions organized
by the National Civil Liberties Union and composed of many
leaders of liberal opinion.   This model bill or portions thereof
were introduced in most of the legislatures in session this year.
Only Wisconsin enacted the model bill *in toto*, but four states
have passed anti-yellow-dog contract laws.

EMPLOYERS' PROPOSALS

Throughout the entire history of the law of labor combinations
and labor disputes, labor has demanded change, while the
employers have been satisfied in the main with the existing
situation.   They have spent far less effort to win legislation than

---

Jersey law was held in Gevas v. Greek Restaurant Workers Club, 99 N. J. E.
770, 134 Atl. 309 (1926), to have no application where no strike exists.
The other statutes referred to in this note have not been passed upon by
courts of final jurisdiction.

to defeat proposals by labor. At all times, however, employers have made some legislative demands of their own,[1] particularly when the tide of popular approval has flowed against labor. The riots during the great railway strike of 1877 led to the enactment in many states of laws declaring interference with the operation of railroads and all resort to intimidation in labor disputes to be criminal. The Haymarket riot and the many boycotts of 1886 were followed by several anticonspiracy and antiboycott laws. But the most extensive efforts ever made by employers to gain legislation in this field followed the World War. In 1919, the League for Industrial Rights promulgated two model proposed statutes: one, a bill providing that unincorporated associations might be sued in their common name; the other, a measure declaring certain strikes and lockouts to constitute "unwarranted industrial warfare."[2] These included strikes of government employees and, perhaps, of employers of contractors doing government work, strikes in violation of trade agreements and arbitration awards, strikes undertaken without first presenting demands to the employer, and all strikes not of direct benefit to the participants. In such "unwarranted industrial warfare," the taking of strike votes, the paying of strike benefits, persuasion of anyone to participate, picketing, and all similar methods of carrying on the dispute were forbidden, and both the government and private parties injured were authorized to take action in law or equity to prevent the commission of any of these acts. From 1919 to 1923, these two bills were introduced in many state legislatures, and modifications, especially proposals to prohibit government employees from belonging to unions or going on strike, in even a larger number of states. A few states

---

[1] The first law enacted in this country dealing specifically with labor disputes—the La Salle black law of 1863 of Illinois (Public Laws 1863, p. 70)—was an employers' measure.

[2] On these two bills, see the booklet "Two Proposed Statutes Advocated by the League for Industrial Rights and Supporting Memorandum," published by the League in 1919. These bills were foreshadowed in "Some Recommendations Submitted to the United States Commission on Industrial Relations," by the American Anti-boycott Association (1919) and in the "Proposed Legislation on Public Policy and Industrial Warfare Submitted to the Industrial Conference," also by the League for Industrial Rights in 1919.

enacted laws incorporating some of these proposals.[1] Alabama
provided that unincorporated associations may be sued, Texas
prohibited attempts to keep employees of common carriers from
working (later this statue was held unconstitutional); Nebraska
enacted an antipicketing law, and Utah, an antiintimidation
statute. Everywhere else, the model bills of the League for
Industrial Rights and their adaptations were defeated and,
since 1923, although not abandoned, have received no real
consideration.

Other proposals for restrictions upon union activities put forward during the World War and the years immediately following
fared considerably better. During this period, nearly half of the
states enacted antisyndicalism laws, aimed at the revolutionary
labor unions but regarded with some suspicion by the "regular"
unions. From these years date the majority of the state police
systems, which organized labor has always bitterly opposed.
Finally, there was strong sentiment for compulsory arbitration,
culminating in the Kansas Industrial Relations Court Act and
the Railroad Labor Board Act, both of 1920. Compulsory
arbitration was not then, nor ever, an employers' program, but
many employers were receptive toward this program and some
of them actively in its favor, particularly for public utilities.

Compulsory arbitration has now been held unconstitutional
except possibly in its application to public utilities. Recent
state police bills have generally included provisions restricting
the use of the state constabulary in labor troubles, despite which
organized labor has relentlessly and successfully fought these
measures. Proposals to make unions suable and to prohibit
strikes of government employees still have strong support, but
not enough to carry them over labor's opposition. For the
present, labor is so much the under dog in the industrial struggle
that there is little prospect of further legislative restrictions upon
labor combinations in the near future; but when the tide turns,
these and other employers' proposals are likely again to receive
serious consideration.

---

[1] The statutes referred to in the next sentence are: Alabama, Code 1928,
ss. 5723–28; Texas, Acts 1920, 4th C. S., c. 5; Nebraska, C. L., ss. 9752–54;
and Utah, Laws 1923, c. 93. A bill allowing unincorporated unions to be
sued in their common name also passed the Massachusetts legislature but
was defeated in a popular referendum in 1922.

GOVERNMENTAL AND PRIVATE INQUIRIES

In concluding this survey of proposals for changes in the existing law governing labor disputes, note should be taken of suggestions made by governmental commissions and private organizations such as the American Bar Association, the Federal Council of the Churches of Christ in America, and the National Civic Federation. The most comprehensive of these were made in the several final reports of the U. S. Commission on Industrial Relations in 1915.[1] The Clayton Act had only recently been enacted and had not yet been construed, so that, despite doubts as to the value of its labor provisions, little was said in these reports about injunctions or the application of the antitrust laws to labor organizations, but they made many suggestions for legislation upon other phases of the law of labor disputes. The members split upon the central proposal in the majority report for the creation of state and federal industrial commissions to enforce all labor laws, with broad fact-finding and order-making powers, but were in agreement on the need for legislation to safeguard workmen in the exercise of their constitutional rights during labor troubles. All of the several reports advocated the strict regulation of private detective agencies, the formulation of a definite code governing the use and powers of the militia in strikes, the prohibition of the employment of armed guards, and the recognition of the right of workingmen to associate for their own advancement. Nothing came of any of these proposals, nor of numerous others along much the same line in the report of the director of investigation. The suggestions made, however, are still distinctly worth consideration. The next similar body created to consider the policy which the government ought to pursue in labor disputes, the President's Industrial Conference of 1919–1920, adopted a very different course. This conference avoided all controversial questions and reached a unanimous conclusion,[2] in which it suggested the establishment of regional

---

[1] The final report of the Commission on Industrial Relations was published separately by the Government Printing Office in 1915 and was included in Vol. I of the *Final Report and Testimony of the Commission on Industrial Relations*, published as *Sen. Doc.* 415, 64th Cong., 1st Sess.

[2] The report of the President's Industrial Conference was published by the Government Printing Office in 1920. The recommendations therein are reprinted in 10 *Monthly Labor Rev.* 863–870 (1920) and in A. R. Elling-

boards of inquiry and a national industrial tribunal for the adjustment of labor disputes, and endorsed the principle of collective bargaining, without specifying whether this should be carried on through company unions or labor unions.   These recommendations pleased neither the employers nor the unions and mustered no support in Congress.

The U. S. Coal Commission, in its report in 1923,[1] opposed compulsory arbitration and the legal enforcibility of trade agreements.   It recommended legislation to curb industrial espionage and the private guard system and appealed to employers to abandon attempts to prevent union organization and to the miners' union to cooperate with the operators, instead of continually fighting them.   As has proved true with all federal study commissions, no legislation followed this report, but it takes high rank as an impartial analysis of the causes of industrial unrest, not only in coal mining but in industry at large.

Since 1923, there has been no similar governmental commission on industrial unrest, but there have been several inquiries by private organizations.[2]   Of these, the most novel suggestion was

---

wood and Whitney Coombs, "The Government and Labor," pp. 279–281, McGraw-Hill Book Company, Inc., New York (1926).   A good contemporary criticism of this report is Felix Frankfurter, The President's Industrial Conference, 22 *New Republic* 179–182 (1920).

[1] The report of the U. S. Coal Commission, in five parts, was published in 1925 as *Sen. Doc.* 195, 68th Cong., 2nd Sess., Part I of which is devoted to the principal findings and recommendations.

[2] Besides the Bar Association committee inquiry discussed in the text, the following other studies should be noted in this connection:

1. The report of the Department of Research and Education of the Federal Council of the Churches of Christ in America on The Use of Injunctions in Labor Disputes, published in the *Information Service* of this organization, Vol. IX, No. 10, March 8, 1930.   This report recommends extensive changes both in the substantive law and in the procedure in injunction cases, which, while not going so far as labor desires on some points, in the main supports its contentions.

2. The still uncompleted study of the antitrust laws by the committee on the Study of Antitrust Legislation of the Industrial Inquiry Commission of the National Civic Federation, some of whose probable conclusions are foreshadowed in the article by its chairman, Wheeler P. Bloodgood, The Effects of the Administration of the Antitrust Laws upon Labor and Services, 147 *Ann. Amer. Acad.* 111–116 (1930).

3. The completed but still unpublished report on "Antiunion Employment Contracts," prepared by E. R. Burton, director of study for a com-

that of the subcommittee on federal industrial legislation of the committee on commerce of the American Bar Association in 1927–1928.[1] For many years, this committee had on its agenda the subject of compulsory arbitration but did nothing with it until, in 1927, it declared the compulsory arbitration of industrial disputes to be out of the question in view of the decisions of the U. S. Supreme Court. At the same time, it suggested a study of the advisability of extending the machinery of commercial arbitration to industrial disputes and invited the American Federation of Labor to appoint a committee to confer with its subcommittee on this subject. This was done, and after some conferences, the bar association committee, through its chairman Julius Henry Cohen, announced plans early in 1928 for a tentative federal bill and held extensive hearings participated in by the foremost leaders of the labor and employers' organizations of the country. This bill made two principal proposals: (1) the extension of the federal commercial arbitration law to voluntary industrial arbitrations so as to make them legally enforcible and (2) the creation of a federal industrial council composed of representatives of the employers' associations, the labor unions, the farmers' organizations, the bar association, and the Secretaries of Commerce and Labor, to study continuously conditions in industry likely to result in strikes and to make recommendations for their avoidance and, upon the request of the President or of the Congress, to investigate particular strikes. At the hearings held upon this proposed bill, only William Z. Foster, representing radical labor, voiced opposition, and the American Bar Association in its 1928 convention strongly endorsed the proposal and instructed its committee to take steps to have this measure introduced in Congress. At the American Federation of Labor convention,

---

mittee of the Industrial Inquiry Commission of the National Civic Federation.

4. The report on injunctions in labor disputes made in January, 1931, by James W. Gerard to the Commission on Industrial Inquiry of the National Civic Federation. This endorses the Norris bill, denounces yellow-dog contracts, and advocates the application of the rule of reason to cases under the antitrust laws growing out of labor disputes.

[1] On the work of this committee and its proposed bill, see 53 *Proc. Amer. Bar Assoc.* 110–113, 343–373 (1928); 14 *Amer. Bar Assoc. Jour.* 166–168 (1928); 54 *Proc. Amer. Bar Assoc.* 105–106, 314–315 (1929); *A. F. of L. Weekly News Service*, Apr. 12, 1929.

no action was taken on the proposed bill, the executive committee merely expressing satisfaction that the American Bar Association had come out against compulsory arbitration.   Some months later, the committee decided that it could not support the feature making arbitration awards legally enforcible.   Since then, the American Bar Association in its 1929 and 1930 conventions has reaffirmed its support of the proposal, but it has not been introduced in Congress and no one in particular seems to be interested in the measure.

Bibliographical Note

The best account of the history of the attempts to change the substantive and procedural law of labor disputes by legislation is the chapter on Legislation Affecting Labor Injunctions in Felix Frankfurter and Nathan Greene, "The Labor Injunction," Chap. IV., The Macmillan Company, New York (1930).   W. G. Merritt, "The Struggle for Industrial Liberty," pp. 33–54, League for Industrial Rights (1922), is a similar review from an antiunion point of view.   Good articles dealing with the legislation enacted are J. P. Chamberlain, The Legislature and Labor Injunctions, 11 *Amer. Bar Assoc. Jour.* 815–817 (1925), and Paul Donovan, Legislation Affecting Labor Injunctions, 16 *Amer. Bar Assoc. Jour.* 561–563 (1930).   The article Constitutional Status of Antiinjunction Legislation, 29 *Monthly Labor Rev.* 380–385 (1929) is an analysis of state antiinjunction laws and their interpretation.   The most important source materials for further historical studies in this field are the numerous Congressional hearings on proposed antiinjunction bills which are listed in the "Select List of References on Boycotts and Injunctions in Labor Disputes," published by the Library of Congress in 1911 and in Laura A. Thompson, Injunctions in Labor Disputes: Select List of Recent References, 27 *Monthly Labor Rev.* 631–650 (1928).

On the injunction-limitation bill now under consideration in Congress, the majority and minority reports, published as *Sen. Rep.* 1060 (2 parts), 71st Cong., 2nd Sess., are the official statements of the case against and for this measure, stressing constitutionality.   The briefs of William Green and Walter Gordon Merritt in the number of the *Information Service*, Vol. IX, No. 10 (Mar. 8, 1930) of the Department of Research and Education of the Federal Council of the Churches of Christ in America on The Use of Injunctions in Labor Disputes are excellent non-legal presentations of the opposite points of view.   The concluding chapter in Frankfurter and Greene, "The Labor Injunction" and the article on Congressional Power over the Labor Injunction by the same authors, 31 *Columbia Law Rev.* 385–415 (1931), are longer arguments in support of the Norris bill; the Statement in Opposition to Substitute Shipstead Antiinjunction Bill presented to the Senate Committee on the Judiciary in 1930 by James A. Emery, counsel of the National Manufacturers Association, and Thomas J. Norton, Further Light on Pending Antiinjunction Measure, 17 *Amer. Bar Assoc. Jour.* 59–62 (1930), elaborations of the case against this measure;

and U. S. *Sen. Doc.* 327, 71st Cong., 3rd Sess., Injunctions in Labor Disputes, a criticism of this measure by an advocate of the original Shipstead bill.

The new model state antiinjunction bill, with a supporting argument, has been published (January, 1931) by the National Committee on Labor Injunctions (100 Fifth Ave., New York City).

References to the principal sources of information on employers' proposals for legislation and those of federal study commissions and the American Bar Association are given in notes on pp. 283–287.

CHAPTER XIII

FUTURE POLICIES

As the preceding chapter abundantly illustrates, large sections of the American public are demanding changes in the existing methods of dealing with labor disputes. The organized workingmen believe the courts to be unfair, want labor injunctions abolished, and seek complete freedom for the unions to effect their purposes by all peaceful means. Employers have fewer complaints and ask far less legislation, yet they are dissatisfied with the inadequate police protection accorded their property and employees and the difficulties encountered in collecting damages for losses sustained through unlawful acts committed during labor disputes. The public knows little about the problem, but all students of industrial relations, as well as most men in public life, know that the present situation is far from satisfactory, despite the great decrease in the number of strikes in the last decade.

Injunctions and yellow-dog contracts have become important political questions, which, it would seem, must be decided in the near future. But these are only acute phases of a much larger problem; the growing distrust of the courts, the frequent lawlessness in labor disputes, the bitter struggles over the issue of unionization, and numerous other manifestations of unrest all point to the need for a well-defined, comprehensive public policy toward labor disputes.

Widely divergent views may be honestly and intelligently maintained on what this policy ought to be. It is with some hesitation that the author presents in this chapter his own views, not as the last words to be said on this subject, but, at any rate, as conclusions arrived at independently after years of study. To him, it has always seemed that the purpose of social study should be more than analysis and description; that it should aim at appraisal and improvement. So, he feels that his readers are entitled to know what he has to suggest for improving the unsatisfactory conditions which now exist.

PUBLIC POLICY TOWARD LABOR ORGANIZATIONS

What policy the government should pursue in labor disputes seems to the author to turn principally upon the desirability of labor unions. Throughout this study, it has been assumed that these organizations are socially useful and should be given a fair opportunity to effect their purposes. This is in accord with what the courts have repeatedly declared to be the law of the country. Court decisions abound in declarations that not only have workingmen a right to combine to improve their conditions, but that their doing so is desirable. Labor unions have long enjoyed in American law and legislation the status not only of lawful, but of favored, organizations[1]—favored because it is recognized that only through acting in combination can workingmen deal on terms of equality with their employers.[2] The modern corporation laws allow capital to combine freely; to preserve equality, a like right must be accorded to labor.

Labor unions exist primarily for the advancement of their members; and the wage differential which they enjoy over the unorganized workingmen attests their value in this respect. But the unions benefit not only their members but all industrial workers. The labor legislation of which they have been the principal champions has been far more necessary to the unorgan-

---

[1] For citations to laws according privileges to labor unions, see the footnote on this subject in United Mine Workers v. Coronado Coal and Coke Co., 257 U. S. 344 at 386, 42 Sup. Ct. 570 at 574 (1922).

[2] An excellent statement to this effect occurs in the unanimous opinion of the U. S. Supreme Court in American Steel Foundries v. Tri-city Central Trades Council, 257 U. S. 184 at 209, 42 Sup. Ct. 72 at 78 (1921), written by Chief Justice Taft:

"They (the labor unions) were organized out of the necessities of the situation. A single employee was helpless in dealing with an employer. He was dependent ordinarily on his daily wage for the maintenance of himself and family. If the employer refused to pay him the wages that he thought fair, he was nevertheless unable to leave the employ, and to resist arbitrary and unfair treatment. Union was essential to give laborers opportunity to deal on equality with their employer . . . The right to combine for such a lawful purpose has in many years not been denied by any court. The strike became a lawful instrument in a lawful economic struggle or competition between employers and employes as to the share or division between them of the joint product of labor and capital. To render their combination at all effective, employees must make their combination extend beyond one shop."

ized than the organized. The existence of unions has been a
powerful stimulus to the non-union employers to grant their
employees higher wages and some voice in the determination of
the conditions of their employment.

Labor unions are of benefit also to the general public, of which
wage earners constitute an important element. The payment
of high wages is recognized by numerous progressive business
men to be essential to good business. Improved conditions of
labor are a first step toward a more intelligent citizenship. By
compelling employers and the public to give more attention to
the human side of industry, labor unions have helped to bring
about more satisfactory industrial relations and, as one writer
has put it, "kicked society ahead."[1]

Nor have unions outlived their day of usefulness. The existing industrial depression, with its unemployment and wage
reductions, demonstrates that conditions for the industrial
workers are far from ideal. Even in the preceding period of
great prosperity, the workingmen were not nearly so well off as
represented. The acquisition of stock by wage earners failed to
usher in the much heralded "second industrial revolution,"
which was to identify the interests of the workingmen with those
of their employers. There has long been, is now, and probably
will always be conflict over the distribution of the products of
industry. The individual laborer is, if anything, even more
handicapped today in bargaining with employers than he was
formerly. Company unions and shop committees cannot take
the place of labor unions. Only unions organized on a national
basis, free from all domination by employers, are able to bargain
on terms of equality. The traditional American policy of regarding labor organizations as both lawful and desirable is as sound
today as it ever was and should serve as the starting point in any
well-considered program for dealing with labor disputes. This
policy has the unanimous endorsement of all courts of final
jurisdiction and of public men of all shades of opinion.[2] Beyond
this, there is disagreement.

---

[1] G. H. PHELPS, "Our Biggest Customer," p. 39, Boni & Liveright,
New York (1929).

[2] There has been some agitation for legislation to prohibit public employees
from belonging to any union affiliated with an organization sanctioning the
strike—by which is meant the American Federation of Labor. No law to

TRADE-UNION ACTIVITIES

Trade unions, though regarded as lawful and useful organizations, are restricted at many points. Decisions which dwell at length upon the right to combine and the desirability of doing so conclude with condemning the means which the workmen employ to make their combination effective.[1] The tendency of decisions has been more and more restrictive: many types of strikes and the great majority of all boycotts held unlawful, picketing confined within narrow limits, and even persuasion enjoined.

These decisions are based upon legal theories which are plausible but far from conclusive.[2] All of them are essentially subjective, and the judges' decisions must needs turn upon their conception of the social desirability of the workingmen's conduct and the merits of their demands. The issues raised by labor disputes cannot be solved by abstract theories or logical syllogisms. As a first step toward reform, all of the theories invoked in labor cases might well be discarded[3] or treated as inapplicable, and the questions presented decided upon the basis of economic facts.

Opinions will differ as to what activities of labor organizations should, as a matter of social policy, be held legal. The contention of the spokesmen for organized labor, that workingmen have

---

this effect, however, has been passed in any state, and only a specious argument can be presented in support of such a policy. The teachers', firemen's, and other public employees' unions never resort to strikes and have no provisions in their constitutions for strikes. To say that these unions shall not affiliate with the American Federation of Labor because other unions affiliated with this organization make use of the strike is little short of ridiculous.

[1] This attitude toward labor unions was aptly expressed in Dooley's (Finley Peter Dunn's) essay on the open shop:

"'But,' said Mr. Hennessey, 'these open shop min ye menshun say they are f'r unions iv properly conducted.'

"'Shure,' said Mr. Dooley, 'iv properly conducted. An' there we are. An' how would they have thim conducted? No strikes, no rules, no contracts, no scales, hardly iny wages, an' dam few mimbers.'"

[2] *Cf.* Chap. III.

[3] The author would discard the restraint-of-trade theory along with the conspiracy theory, the just-cause theory, etc. The antitrust laws may serve a useful purpose in the business field but have no proper place in labor controversies. Labor unions are not trusts and should not be treated as such. Their activities should be judged by their social effects, not on the basis of incidental restraint of trade which they may involve.

an absolute and natural right to strike and to boycott, is only
another abstract theory which leads to all kinds of difficulties.
The American public is not prepared to approve general strikes,
strikes of policemen, or strikes for purposes of extortion.   As a
matter of fact, only a few such strikes have ever occurred in this
country, and debates over whether they should be permitted are
largely theoretical.   Of much greater practical importance are
the questions of the legality of strikes for union recognition, for
the discharge of non-union workmen, against non-union materials,
and in aid of fellow workmen.   These present the really crucial
issues in the substantive law: the purpose of strengthening the
union as a justification for strikes and the extent to which workmen not directly interested may become participants.

As to unionization, it would seem to follow that, if it is necessary and desirable for workingmen to combine, it is legitimate
for them to seek to strengthen their organization.   Only a strong
union can bargain effectively or hope to win and maintain for its
members the higher wages, shorter hours, and better conditions
of labor which all cases hold are the proper objectives of labor
organizations.   Strengthening the union is, therefore, an absolutely indispensable preliminary.   For this reason, the New York
position, that strikes for union recognition and the closed shop
are legal, seems preferable to that of Massachusetts, which
regards all such strikes as attempts to maliciously injure the non-
union workmen.

The extent to which members of unions may aid fellow unionists depends upon the social desirability of labor unions.   If
strong unions are desirable, it will not do to say that unionists
must be strangers to their fellows.   Workingmen have no less a
legitimate interest outside of their particular shop and craft than
a midwestern manufacturer in the freight rates enjoyed by an
eastern competitor.   Defeat of the union in one plant makes it
more difficult for the employees in a similar establishment to
maintain the union conditions they enjoy.   Similarly, workmen
in one craft are vitally interested in the wages and conditions of
the workmen in an allied craft.   The problem is one of drawing
a line which will recognize the legitimate interests of workingmen
in disputes directly affecting fellow workmen and yet not sanction the general strike.   The pending federal injunction-limitation bill proposes to draw this line so as to allow sympathetic

action wherever the workmen involved are engaged in the same industry, trade, craft, or occupation; who work for the same employer, or belong to the same national union. This seems to the author to mark fairly the line of legitimate interests, but whether this precise demarcation is accepted or not, the condemnation of every type of sympathetic action is utterly inconsistent with the acceptance of labor unions as socially desirable.

Picketing and boycotting are the other two activities of labor combinations which have come frequently before the courts. With regard to the law of picketing, the controlling principle stated in the American Steel Foundries case[1] cannot be improved upon. Persuasion is legitimate, intimidation unlawful; and the dividing line depends upon the facts in each case. This is a sound principle, but it does not automatically decide whether picketing should be permitted in a particular situation. To answer this question fairly involves careful study of all surrounding facts—which precludes the prohibition of picketing on *ex parte* representations of the employer, without hearing or investigation. It also precludes sanctioning everything that goes by the name of picketing. Mob demonstrations and violence are not fair methods of combat although they may be called "picketing." On the other hand, slavish adherence to the rule of one picket per gate, which many courts have adopted since the American Steel Foundries case, often denies strikers a fair opportunity to present their case to new and prospective employees. What is needed is an appreciation on part of police officers and judges that picketing has a legitimate purpose and when organized and controlled can be made to serve the cause of law and order. The precise number of pickets is far less significant than the way the picketing is conducted. Wide leeway seems warranted as long as the pickets conduct themselves peacefully, but when they are guilty of acts of violence all picketing may properly be prohibited.

A similar policy is suggested for parades and meetings. It is reasonable to require a permit for meetings and parades in congested public streets, but no discrimination should be made on the basis of the opinions of persons applying for permits. Strikers

---

[1] American Steel Foundries v. Tri-city Central Trades Council, 257 U. S. 184, 42 Sup. Ct. 72 (1921).

and radicals have the same right to present their views as anyone else. No public official should have the right to censor meetings in advance, nor to break up any meeting unless unlawful acts are advocated or a disturbance results for which the speakers are responsible. To suppress free speech makes martyrs of intended victims and spreads their doctrines. "With effervescing opinions, as with the not yet forgotten champagnes, the quickest way to let them get flat is to let them get exposed to the air."[1]

With regard to boycotting, the author believes the present condemnation of all boycotts to be utterly illogical. This amounts to making a scarecrow out of the word "boycott"— making it synonymous with coercion and intimidation. In actual fact, most labor boycotts are conducted solely by informing union members and sympathizers that an employer is having difficulties with organized labor. Whether this should be permitted is much the same question as that involved in the sympathetic strike, namely, the extent to which persons not direct participants in a dispute may assist those immediately concerned. That sympathizers may assist strikers financially is granted by everyone, yet the strikers are forbidden to ask the sympathizers not to purchase the goods of the employer against whom their strike is directed. This not only denies the strikers a peaceful method of combat but is akin to a fraud upon the union sympathizers. By continuing to buy the goods of the employer in question, they help to defeat the strikers whom they wish to help. In fairness to such "outsiders," it ought to be lawful to advise them that the employer is "unfair," by which is meant that he is having difficulties with organized labor. But whether or not the law is thus changed is far less important to

---

[1] Quoted from a communication by Justice Holmes to the Harvard Liberal Club, Jan. 12, 1920.

The policy here advocated is the one which has long been followed in Great Britain. Hyde Park in London is virtually a free meeting place furnished at public expense to speakers of a radical stripe of opinion, and no public official presumes to censor what is said by anyone unless he advocates the immediate commission of a crime. This policy has resulted in far less trouble with the extreme radicals than our American cities have encountered in trying to prevent meetings of communists and radical laborites. By action of the Mayor and city council of Detroit in March, 1931, the city hall steps were made the Hyde Park of this American city.

the labor unions than is the legal status of strikes and picketing, as there are relatively few employers who can be successfully boycotted.

The views presented in this section regarding desirable changes in the law relating to union activities are premised upon the proposition that if unions are legalized they should be given a fair opportunity to accomplish their purposes. It is this consideration which leads the author to advocate that the substantive law of labor combinations be liberalized so as to allow workingmen a practically free hand in carrying on disputes with employers, barring only fraud, intimidation, and violence.

Like other fundamental policies, the one here advocated is admittedly difficult of application in some situations. The qualification that the combination must not resort to fraud, intimidation, or violence requires careful study of the concrete facts in each case and manifestly leaves a great deal to the individual judge. For this reason, there is little hope that the changes advocated can be brought about by enacting appropriate legislation. It is difficult to state any controlling principles so precisely that they cannot be evaded and to define the conduct which is to be regarded as lawful so exactly as to fit all situations which arise. The courts, moreover, have the final word as to constitutionality and are not likely to sustain any policies or actions which they do not approve. There may be some value in legislation dealing with the substantive law of labor disputes as an expression of public opinion, but in the last analysis the substantive law depends more upon the courts than upon the legislators. We may as well frankly face the fact that the bulk of the law is made by the courts[1]—that the social point of view of the judges, particularly of the judges of courts of final jurisdiction, is the most important factor in the decisions in labor cases, which means that the liberalization of the substantive law is largely a matter of educating or selecting the judges.

The situation is by no means hopeless. While more and more restrictions have been placed upon union activities, there are numerous liberals among the judges. There are relatively far more judges than members of the bar who regard labor problems

---

[1] Upon this point, see Donald R. Richberg, "Tents of the Mighty," pp. 169–173, Willett, Clark & Colby, Chicago (1930).

realistically and sympathetically, and a hopeful sign is that most of the legal writers who have discussed this subject have advocated greater freedom to labor combinations. If all judges could be made to realize that labor disputes present social problems that cannot be settled by rules of logic alone, the greatest obstacle to a more liberal substantive law would be removed.

LABOR INJUNCTIONS

There are greater possibilities for effective legislation in the procedural than in the substantive law. The most acute problem in the law of labor disputes is that of "the abuse of injunctions," which has reference principally to the use of injunctions to prevent or break strikes. There is much more likelihood of preventing such abuse through procedural changes than through legislation dealing with the substantive law, primarily because procedural changes are more apt to stand the test of constitutionality.

The author sees little justification for injunctions in labor disputes. Some have undoubtedly cleared the atmosphere, prevented trouble, or hastened adjustment. More have made no particular difference. By and large, however, injunctions have not only seriously handicapped the workingmen against whom they were directed but have added greatly to the bitterness of labor disputes. As measures for the protection of property and the preservation of law and order, they have generally proved worthless. Worst of all, their frequent employment in labor disputes has lowered the prestige of the courts and tended to destroy the confidence of the workingmen in their government.

The author would go as far as any labor leader in "abolishing" injunctions but sees no simple formula for doing so. Legislation providing that no injunctions shall be issued in labor disputes (or that the courts shall not have jurisdiction to issue such injunctions) stands no chance of passage and if passed would be held unconstitutional. Nor does the formula that injunctions shall be issued only for the protection of property, which shall not include the right to do business, solve the problem. Such a formula would prevent the issuance of injunctions in many situations not connected with labor disputes where their use is beneficial and probably would have little effect upon their use in contests between employers and employees,[1] even if it should be held constitutional. Similarly, exemption from the antitrust laws is not sufficient, as the great majority of injunctions are not premised upon the antitrust laws.

The injunction problem cannot be solved by the meaninglessly vague phrases of a Clayton Act. Needed above all else in legislation are provisions so definite that they must either be given effect or held unconstitutional. Constitutionality cannot be guaranteed for any proposal on this subject, but meritorious things can be done which have an even chance of being sustained.

The pending Norris injunction-limitation bill seems to the author to meet these tests. This is by no means a radical measure. It will not do away with all injunctions in labor disputes and does not affect damage suits and criminal prosecutions.[2] It promises, however, to check the most serious abuses and will make resort to injunctions less frequent and profitable.

The changes proposed in this bill do not all relate to matters of procedure. Yellow-dog contracts are made unenforcible in the federal courts. A statutory rule is inserted to govern the responsibility of the officers and members of labor unions and employers' associations for unlawful acts claimed to have been committed in their behalf. A long list of acts is enumerated which are not to be enjoined by any federal court. This list

---

[1] *Cf.* pp. 105–106.

In connection with this and other "cure-all" proposals for dealing with labor injunctions, the observation of Dean Roscoe Pound of the Harvard Law School is apropos:

"Labor has much to complain of in the way in which injunctions have been developed by American courts in labor litigation. But it has been fortunate that the legislative remedies which labor leaders have urged to meet the bad features of this development have mostly failed of enactment. For the greater part, they were fraught with possibilities to the remedial processes of courts of equity rather than with possibilities of relief from abuse of the preventive jurisdiction of the courts in labor litigation." (Address at the Hanover Conference of the Social Science Research Council, Aug. 29, 1927.)

[2] An exception to this statement must be made as to Secs. 2 and 6. The former provides that yellow-dog contracts shall not afford any basis for either *legal or equitable* relief in the federal courts, while the latter lays down a rule for determining responsibility for unlawful acts committed in behalf of a union or of an employers' association which applies to all kinds of legal actions, not merely to injunctions.

includes all normal union activities and peaceful picketing and striking (except remote sympathetic strikes), but not boycotting (because it was feared that the inclusion of a provision legalizing boycotting might doom the entire bill).

Strong arguments can be made in support of all these proposed changes in the substantive law. The author, however, places more faith in the procedural sections which follow. These again are not extreme. In fact, many are but statements of principles long recognized as sound in other fields of equity. Others are novel but are justified by the special situation presented in labor controversies, where time means everything and there is no possibility of preserving the *status quo*. All requirements are eminently fair and do not bar the use of injunctions when resort to this extraordinary remedy is really necessary.

This bill will curb the serious abuse of the issuance of injunctions without hearings. It does not prohibit *ex parte* temporary restraining orders altogether[1] but provides that they shall be void after five days.[2] In all subsequent stages of the proceedings, both parties are allowed to present testimony and to cross-examine the adverse witnesses, eliminating the present practice of conducting preliminary hearings (preceding temporary injunctions) on the pleadings and affidavit testimony alone.

No less important are the safeguards against the issuance of injunctions on insufficient proof. These have been detailed in the preceding chapter and need not again be enumerated. Particularly important are the requirements that all testimony must be taken in open court and that the judge must make findings of fact.

---

[1] Until 1872, the federal statutes did provide that no injunction shall be issued "in any case without reasonable notice to the adverse party" (1 Statutes-at-Large 333–335). Not until this late date was the issuance of *ex parte* temporary restraining orders authorized by statute, although some such orders seem to have been issued earlier.

[2] This differs from the corresponding provision in the Clayton Act, which merely provides that *ex parte* temporary restraining orders shall be set for a hearing within ten days and shall terminate at the end of this period unless renewed. This operates so that the average length of time elapsing before a decision is reached upon the propriety of continuing *ex parte* temporary restraining orders is nearer thirty than ten days (see p. 92). The Norris bill does not allow *ex parte* temporary restraining orders to be renewed at all and they automatically terminate at the end of five days.

Other safeguards relate to bonds and appeals. It is made easier to sue on bonds, and appeals are facilitated. If this bill is enacted, it should be possible in many cases to get a review of an injunction while the dispute is still in progress.

More radical are the provisions relating to contempts. Where the contempt charges are premised upon criticisms of the judge uttered outside of the court room, the defendants may demand trial before another judge, and in all cases of indirect contempt the defendants are allowed (at their request) a trial by jury.[1] These go the full length of labor's demands on these points, but they are responsive to a widespread public demand and will go far to allay criticism of the courts. Despite all the nice distinctions that may be drawn between contempts and crimes, no layman will ever understand why the constitutional guarantee of a jury trial to persons accused of crime does not apply to men who may be sentenced to jail for contempt. Nor does the right of trial by jury undermine the authority of the courts. The power to inflict summary punishment for contempt was a comparatively late innovation in Anglo-Saxon law. For hundreds of years, contempts were punished precisely as are other crimes, and this is still the usual procedure in England.[2] It is not necessary for the courts to violate Anglo-Saxon concepts of what constitutes a fair trial to enforce their orders.

Collectively, the several provisions of this bill deal in a practical manner with all the principal abuses of injunctions. If enacted into law and sustained by the courts, there is every reason to believe that injunctions will cease to be much of a problem in labor controversies.

If organized labor will give the Norris bill its united support, it should be possible to enact this measure in the 72nd (present) Congress, barring a Presidential veto. The attitude which the

---

[1] At present, under the provisions of the Clayton Act, jury trial is allowed only where the conduct upon which the contempt charges are premised is forbidden by the criminal laws and even then is not granted where the government is a party to the injunction.

[2] Michaelson v. U. S., 266 U. S. 42 at 67, 45 Sup. Ct. 18 at 20 (1924), and references cited. See also Felix Frankfurter and J. M. Landis, Power of Congress over Procedure in Criminal Contempts in "Inferior" Federal Courts, 37 *Harvard Law Rev.* 1010–1113 (1924) and John C. Fox, "The History of Contempt of Court," The Clarendon Press, Oxford (1927).

courts will take is more problematical, but the prospect is not hopeless. The basic theory of the Norris bill, that Congress has authority to prescribe the jurisdiction of the inferior federal courts, seems firmly established. The other fundamental assumption, that rules may be prescribed for the conduct of labor injunction cases different from those applicable to other injunction cases, also seems sound. Language in the decision of the Supreme Court in Truax v. Corrigan[1] suggests that precisely the same rules must be applied in labor cases as in other controversies, but this can hardly be the court's final conclusion. Special procedural rules are now in force for patent cases, which assuredly do not require special treatment more than do labor cases. The use of injunctions in labor disputes presents situations and problems which arise in no other controversies. The principles of justice are the same in all cases, but variations must be made in the procedure in differing situations unless grave injustice is to result.

The Norris bill is a congressional measure and will affect only the federal courts. Most labor injunctions are issued by the state, not the federal, courts. To solve the injunction problem, hence, requires state as well as federal legislation. In most states, the trial courts, unlike their status in the federal system, are constitutional creations, subject only to a limited control by the legislature. For this reason it is probably more difficult to draft a constitutional state antiinjunction law than a federal bill. The new model state bill drafted by Mr. Greene is well done, indeed, but will have to be adapted to the constitution and statutes of each state. State antiinjunction legislation will necessarily be a slow process, but the time seems ripe for procedural reforms at least. The pending federal bill is crucial. If this passes, is sustained, and proves effective, similar legislation by the states may confidently be expected.

RIGHTS OF EMPLOYERS

Any sound public policy should take into consideration the rights and interests of employers no less than those of employees. To insure fair play, employers and employees should be placed upon an absolute equality before the law.

---

[1] 157 U. S. 312, 42 Sup. Ct. 124 (1921).

Employers, for all practical purposes, now enjoy complete freedom of combination in their dealings with employees. This extends not merely to the organization of corporations and employers' associations, but to the methods used by them to combat labor combinations. They can deal with unions or not, as they see fit. In times of trouble, they have a free hand to employ strike breakers and strike guards. They are privileged to discharge or refuse to employ workmen because of union membership and, to all practical intents and purposes, can with immunity resort to the blacklist if they so choose.[1]

With these rights, the author has no quarrel. He believes in complete freedom of combination for both employers and employees. Employers should not be compelled to deal with labor unions but should be allowed to resist their demands by all peaceful means. Were employers forbidden to employ strike breakers, there would be far less violence in labor disputes, but such a law would place the employers at the mercy of the labor unions. Ideally, policing should be exclusively a governmental function, but while employers are not afforded adequate protection for their property and employees in labor troubles they must have the right of self-protection. Bad as are private guards, if the state does not provide protection there is no alternative.

The author also believes that employers should have the right to deal with plant unions in preference to labor unions; but they should not be allowed to use the former to destroy the latter. A company union is an anomaly. Not only, as the U. S. Supreme Court has said, can there be no real bargaining when the company controls the representatives on both sides of the table, but any attempt to force such a situation upon its employees is an invasion of their right to combine for their own advancement and to be represented in negotiations with their employers by men of their own choice. There may be a justification for genuine shop committees and shop unions, but the company-controlled union is a social menace.

This position on yellow-dog contracts and company unions[2]

---

[1] *Cf.* pp. 211–218.

[2] The author's position on company-controlled unions is in accord with the decision of the Supreme Court in Texas and New Orleans R. R. Co. v.

may be regarded as narrowing the rights of employers, but neither of these is necessary to give them a fair opportunity to protect their interests. Without being enabled to use these devices to enlist the aid of the courts in efforts to destroy the labor unions, employers are fully able to cope with these organizations, even with the restrictions on injunctions and the changes in the substantive law advocated in this chapter.

Much is to be said for changes in law to enable employers to sue unincorporated labor unions for unlawful acts committed in their behalf.[1] With the substantive law as it now stands and the uncertainties of agency law as applied in labor cases, however, such a step would unfairly embarrass the unions. Allowing them to be sued freely would expose them to numerous legal attacks by their own members and make it possible for employers to tie up their funds whenever they were so inclined. Until the substantive law is made fair to organized labor, it would be a mistake to help employers to sue unions.

LAW AND ORDER

The real grievance of employers is not against the present laws so much as their lack of enforcement. More adequate police protection would benefit them vastly more than an easier method of suing unions. In no respect is the present situation more unsatisfactory and improvement more urgently necessary.

And here there are no wide differences of opinion or irreconcilable clashes of interest. Everyone is agreed that law and order must be preserved in labor disputes, that the calling of a strike

---

Brotherhood of Railroad and Steamship Clerks, 281 U. S. 550, 50 Sup. Ct. 427 (1930). While this turned upon a special statute, the language used by the court is broad enough to condemn all company-controlled unions.

[1] It has been suggested that allowing employers to sue labor unions freely would solve the injunction problem, as employers would not then be able to plead that injunctions should be allowed because they would otherwise sustain irreparable losses. This argument overlooks the fact that the employers' claim that the threatened losses are irreparable is not based primarily upon the fact that the unions cannot be sued. Rather, it rests upon the proposition that no amount of damages can compensate a going business for unlawful interruption and that such damages are not capable of definite determination. In states where unions can be sued in their common name, injunctions are allowed just as frequently as in the states where this cannot be done.

affords no excuse for a disregard of the criminal law by either party, that violence by labor hurts rather than helps its cause, and that it is the function of government to protect life and property. "That state and local government has not risen to the level of the average idea of justice in America which has not the will and the power to preserve the life and property of its citizens."[1]

That the government has often failed in this primary duty is undeniable. No method of strike policing has given general satisfaction. The attitude of the government seriously affects the outcome of labor disputes, but its course is frequently partisan, feeble, unintelligent, and provocative.

As a first step toward better law enforcement, responsibility should be placed upon the executive officials. They alone have adequate authority and means to preserve the peace. Reliance upon injunctions for this purpose is absurd.[2] The courts cannot supervise the policing of strikes; it is both unfair and futile to rely upon them for law enforcement. As long as this policy is continued, so long will executive officials, who alone can cope with the problem, dodge their responsibility.

With responsibility in the proper place must go a truly neutral attitude on the part of the law-enforcing authorities. The public officials responsible for law and order should not be concerned with the merits or the outcome of the dispute, but solely with the preservation of the public peace. Only if they are truly neutral will they be able to keep the confidence of both sides and control of the situation.

These are the first essentials for better law enforcement in labor disputes. Legislation is less important but can be helpful, particularly in removing some of the complicating factors. Employers probably cannot be forbidden to employ private guards, but the practice of commissioning guards as special police or sheriffs' deputies can be stopped. Industrial espionage cannot be completely prohibited, but private detective agencies can be strictly regulated and men with criminal records barred from acting as either guards or detectives. A drastic licensing law,

---

[1] Report of the U. S. Coal Commission on Civil Liberties in the Coal Fields, published in *Sen. Doc.* 195, Part I, pp. 161–180, at 180, 68th Cong., 2nd Sess.

[2] *Cf.* pp. 111–117.

applying to both the detective agencies and the individual operatives, with adequate provisions for enforcement, ought to be
enacted by every state and the federal government (for agencies
doing an interstate business). Something can also be done
better to protect workingmen in the exercise of their civil rights
during strikes. Police officers can and should be instructed to
treat strikers as they do other citizens. A complete code governing the exercise of martial law should be formulated. Strikers
and union organizers denied civil rights by either public officers
or mobs can be given a right of action against the community in
which such lawless acts occur, precisely as property owners now
have a right under the statutes of many states to recover damages
for losses sustained through mob violence.[1]

On the other side, more adequate strike policing is imperative.
This requires backbone on the part of executive officials, and an
increase in the police forces in times of emergency. Violence
must not be tolerated; life and property must be protected at all
costs. The situation requires not more law but more law
enforcement.

Governmental action, however, cannot solve the entire problem. Employers, employees, and the general public bear
responsibility for the existing unsatisfactory situation no less
than do public officials. There is needed above all a recognition
on each side of the rights of the other. The cause of organized
labor is hurt more by lawlessness than anything else. A realization of this should lead it to adopt a constructive program for
and take an active interest in law enforcement. Employers, on
their part, should realize that spies and guards breed trouble and
that interference with the civil rights of anyone, even a radical
organizer, is a lawless act no less serious than the destruction of
property. And the general public needs to be educated to
holding the executive officials responsible for law enforcement
and backing them up when they do their duty.

ADJUSTMENT OF LABOR DISPUTES

While the preservation of law and order is the primary duty
of the government, its interest in labor disputes cannot end there.

---

[1] This was suggested by Dr. John R. Commons in his majority report
of the U. S. Commission on Industrial Relations in 1915 but has not been
enacted into law anywhere.

Labor disputes are not an unmixed evil, and certainly not the most serious of present-day industrial problems. Yet it is unquestionably in the public interest that their number should be reduced to a minimum and that those occurring should be settled as promptly as possible.

This does not lead inevitably to compulsory arbitration. The limited experience this country has had with compulsory arbitration has been wholly unfavorable. Not only is compulsory arbitration unconstitutional, except possibly in its application to public services and public utilities, but it will not work under the conditions now existing in the United States. Neither the organized employers nor the organized employees want compulsory arbitration, and, without at least tacit acceptance by both parties, no system of adjustment can possibly be successful. In the absence of a generally accepted industrial code, compulsory arbitration is necessarily not a judicial but a law-making procedure—and law making by the arbitrary *fiat* of outsiders often poorly informed regarding the points at issue and the practices of industry.

The prohibition of strikes pending compulsory investigation is but a step removed from compulsory arbitration. It is likewise strongly opposed by organized labor and unpopular among employers but has the merit that it gives the government notice of pending labor troubles before they reach the breaking point.[1] The underlying assumption that public opinion, when informed regarding the merits of the dispute, will force the party at fault to yield, however, has proven unsound. Public hearings are sometimes helpful; more often, they result in further estrangement.

American experience indicates that the most successful adjustment machinery is that allowing a maximum of self-government. The best results are secured when the parties themselves make the rules and arbitration is confined to the application of these rules. This does not mean a hands-off policy. The govern-

---

[1] This can be made a requirement of a mediation law, without powers of either compulsory arbitration or compulsory investigation. It can be provided that every union official and every employer having knowledge of any contemplated demand or change in conditions likely to lead to a strike shall give prompt notice thereof to the state department in charge of mediation in labor disputes, and failure to give such notice can be made punishable by a fine, without forbidding or penalizing the strike itself.

ment has its responsibility in bringing the parties together and, if they so desire, may well give legal force to their agreements. It may properly set up machinery for voluntary arbitration, to which the parties may appeal if they cannot reach an agreement. In strikes which cause great suffering to the public, the entire executive power of the government must needs be exerted to bring about an adjustment.

A permanent, impartial mediation service is essential to any sound governmental policy toward labor disputes, particularly in this country, where the majority of employers still refuse to deal with labor unions. Mediation is a most difficult function. There are few mediators who can keep the good will of both employers and employees for years. To do so, mediators must be truly non-partisan and concerned only with effecting a settlement. Mediation and arbitration cannot be combined in the same officials, as the arbitrator must pass upon the merits of the dispute—an approach that is fatal in mediation.

Arbitration is still more difficult in the absence of a code of industrial law which the arbitrator can apply. Where it involves something more than the interpretation of agreements, it is far less likely to result in a satisfactory adjustment than where the parties themselves reach a settlement, but it does work in some cases, and it is desirable that there should be machinery for arbitration when other methods fail.

With all its difficulties, adjustment is the aspect of governmental activity in labor disputes which needs to be stressed above others. If when labor disputes occur, emphasis were placed upon adjustment rather than suppression, their seriousness could be greatly mitigated. Instead of applying for injunctions, employers would do well to call in government mediators and, still better, to confer with their own employees about a settlement. Far more important than the determination of the party at fault is the restoration of peace.

Permanent full-time adjustment machinery can be set up only by the federal government and the larger industrial states. Part-time and amateur mediation is very likely to prove wasted effort. Under existing conditions, the federal government must carry the bulk of the work of adjustment. The smaller states, at least, will do well to confine themselves to reporting difficulties promptly to the federal agencies and helping the federal mediators to gain an entrée. Most valuable of all is the adjustment machinery set up by employers and employees on an industry basis. This should have the endorsement of public opinion and be encouraged and promoted by government.

PREVENTION OF LABOR DISPUTES

The fundamental purpose of any program for dealing with labor disputes should be the promotion of industrial peace and social justice. Of these two, the latter is the more important. The peace of the graveyard is not ideal for industry; but war unfortunately does not always, nor even generally, result in greater justice. Industrial strife causes untold suffering, creates intense bitterness, and endangers the public peace. While not wholly without compensations, the final balance is probably a net social loss.

To many, industrial disputes seem an anachronism. Individual wrongs are now righted by judicial process, not by wager of battle. Industrial disputes, it is urged, should be dealt with similarly. Let disputes be settled either by the existing courts or specially constituted tribunals and strikes be prohibited or surrounded with so many restrictions that they cannot possibly be successful.[1] This analogy between industrial disputes and ordinary controversies, the author believes fallacious. Industrial disputes grow out of mass movements, not individual differences. They involve profound social issues, centering around the fundamental problem of the distribution of the joint products of industry. These cannot be settled by the *ipse dixit* of any tribunal, but only by the slow and uncertain process of democracy. Since there is no law to apply or interpret, courts and judicial processes, so well constituted and adapted for the settlement of ordinary legal controversies, are peculiarly inept for the determination of the merits of industrial disputes.

The policy of wide freedom for both employers and employees to work out their own destinies is advocated in this chapter in the belief that it will result in a minimum of industrial friction. Making strikes unlawful does not prevent their occurrence. They are results, not causes. To suppress them is to deal with

[1] A good presentation of this argument is H. W. Ballentine, Evolution of Legal Remedies as a Substitute for Violence and Strikes, 69 *Ann. Amer. Acad.* 140–149 (1917).

the symptoms without remedying industrial ills.   The decisions holding strikes for many purposes to be unlawful have had little or no effect upon the frequency of such strikes; injunctions, instead of promoting peace, have increased the tension in industrial disputes.   Likewise, the outlawing of the labor unions is not the solution.   Where employers recognize the unions, there is far less bitterness in labor controversies than where they obstinately refuse to accord their employees the same right to act in combination they claim for themselves.

The author does not advocate that government compel employers to deal with the labor unions.   Rather, he favors the policy of complete freedom to both sides, with strict neutrality on the part of the government.   Instead of having the courts or other public officials pass upon the merits of disputes, the author advocates confining the role of government to the preservation of law and order and efforts at adjustment.   Such a policy, he believes, will result in better law enforcement and fewer strikes— certainly in less resentment against the government and distrust of the courts.

This, however, is only the beginning.   Many industrial disputes develop out of industrial wrongs; most of the rest, out of the gradual advance of the toilers to a higher plane of economic well-being.   It is here that the influence of government is most important.   Many of the causes of industrial disputes can be eliminated by an intelligent social policy, reinforced by legislation.   Attention to the fighting of industrial wrongs will accomplish more towards the elimination of industrial disputes than any policy of suppression.

Bibliographical Note

Practically every extended account of the present law governing labor disputes (outside of law textbooks) concludes with a general appraisal and suggestions for changes.   The following, among others, have the general point of view taken in this chapter: John R. Commons and John B. Andrews, "Principles of Labor Legislation," pp. 98–135, Harper & Brothers, New York (1927 ed.); Solomon Blum, "Labor Economics," pp. 120–145, 268–291, Henry Holt & Company, New York (1925); Felix Frankfurter and Nathan Greene, "The Labor Injunction," The Macmillan Company, New York (1930); R. L. Hoxie, "Trade Unionism in the United States," pp. 211–253, D. Appleton & Company, New York (1923 ed.); and John A. Fitch, "The Causes of Industrial Unrest," pp. 101–139, 351–419, Harper & Brothers, New York (1924).   Shorter articles which reflect the same philosophy include J. W. Bryan, Proper Bounds for the Use of the Injunction in Labor Disputes, 36 *Ann. Amer. Acad. Polit. Social Sci.* 288–301 (1910); John A. Fitch, Government Coercion in Labor Disputes, 90 *Ann. Amer. Acad. Polit. Social Sci.* 74–82 (1920); Rev. J. A. Ryan, Labor and the Law, 6 *Catholic Charities Rev.* 11–15 (1922); and William A. Leiserson, War and Peace in the Industrial World, 1 *Amer. Rev.* 17–30 (1923).

Articles contending that the present law is satisfactory in all material respects are less numerous. This view is presented best in the editorials in *Law and Labor* (published monthly by the League for Industrial Rights, New York City) and in the "Recommendations by the American Anti-boycott Association," pp. 12–16 (1915); M. T. Quigg, Function of the Law in Relation between Employers and Employees, 9 *Amer. Bar. Assoc. Jour.* 795–801 (1923); and G. E. Newlin, Proposed Limitations upon Federal Courts, 15 *Amer. Bar Assoc. Jour.* 401–403 (1929).

The labor point of view appears in John P. Frey, "The Labor Injunction," Equity Publishing Co., Cincinnati (1922), and in the numerous editorials and articles on injunctions and related questions in the *American Federationist.*

The pros and cons of unionism have given rise to much controversial literature. Good presentations of the case for labor unions are William Green, "Modern Trade Unionism," American Federation of Labor (1925); M. L. Cooke, Some Observations on Workers' Organizations, 36 *Amer. Federationist* 23–35 (1929); Louis Stark, Are Labor Unions Destructive? Prospects for Industrial Peace, 154 *Outlook* 325–328, 357–358 (1930); and the collection of endorsements of unionism by prominent public men in the U. S. Senate Hearings on "Limiting Injunctions," pp. 98, 101–106, 70th Cong., 1st Sess., Committee on the Judiciary (1928). Attacks on unions occur in many of the publications of the National Association of Manufacturers, of which the leaflet "Evidence for the Open Shop" (1927) is the best, as well as in *Law and Labor, The Shop Review,* and other organs of employers' associations, and in many articles that can readily be located through the "Readers' Guide to Periodical Literature." The subject is discussed in all textbooks on labor problems and in several books devoted exclusively to trade unionism. Of these, R. L. Hoxie, "Trade Unionism in the United States," 3rd ed., D. Appleton & Company, New York (1923) deserves special mention, while C. E. Bonnett, "Employers' Associations in the United States," The Macmillan Company, New York (1922) is the only extended account of the organization and functions of employers' associations.

APPENDIX A

FOREIGN EXPERIENCE

Every civilized country has had some experience with labor disputes and has some legislation on the subject. Economic and political conditions in other countries differ so greatly from the situation in the United States that it is difficult to draw conclusions from foreign experience that are worth much as a guide for future American policy. This experience, however, has been so extensive and varied as to be of interest on its own account and deserves some consideration in connection with our American problems.

THE BRITISH POLICY OF FREEDOM OF COMBINATION

The common law which plays such a large part in the present American law of labor combinations was derived from England. The British law today, however, differs in many fundamental respects from that of the United States. It is mainly statutory and much more definite than the American law. The abstract legal theories upon which the American law is premised have all been discarded in England. Full freedom of combination is accorded to both sides, with specific restrictions of long standing designed to eliminate all intimidation and more recent limitations prohibiting certain specified kinds of strikes. All other strikes, as well as boycotts and blacklists, are lawful. Labor injunctions are practically unknown; there is no law of yellow-dog contracts, no antitrust act applied to labor combinations. Neither unions nor employers' associations are held legally responsible for unlawful acts committed in their behalf. With this wider freedom goes strict law enforcement. For apparent collective responsibility, England has substituted genuine individual responsibility.

Back of this present status is an interesting history,[1] which begins with a diametrically opposite policy from that now pur-

---

[1] Brief accounts of the development of the law are included in every treatise on British trade union law. Longer histories are H. R. Hedges

sued. Both at common law and by statutes, all combinations of workingmen were in the eighteenth century declared to be criminal conspiracies. This policy was materially modified by the Combinations Acts of 1824 and 1825, which repealed the prior anticombination laws and expressly declared it to be legal for workingmen to combine to fix their wages and hours of labor but penalized intimidation and molestation. These laws by no means conferred complete freedom of combination; on the contrary, numerous trade union leaders were in the next decades convicted on criminal charges of conspiracy for ordinary trade-union activities and some of them deported to the Australian penal colony. Strikes to procure the discharge of non-union workmen, and even peaceful picketing, were held criminal offenses. The trade unions themselves were regarded as extra-legal organizations and denied all right to sue in the courts, even for the protection of their funds.

Parliament enacted various laws to give the trade unions a better status, which culminated in the Trade Union Acts of 1871 and 1876 and the Conspiracy and Protection of Property Act of 1875.[1] The Trade Union Acts not only legalized the unions but gave them all of the advantages of incorporation without any of the disadvantages. By merely registering, they were given the right to sue in their common name but for thirty years thereafter were believed not to be subject to suit. The Conspiracy and Protection of Property Act[2] was intended to sweep away the common-law doctrine of conspiracy in its application to labor disputes. It expressly provided that "an agreement, or

---

and A. Winterbottam, "The Legal History of Trade Unionism in England," Longmans, Green and Co., New York (1930) and J. Wallace Bryan, Development of the English Law of Conspiracy, "John Hopkins University Studies," Vol. XXVII, 247–290 (1909), which comes down only to the passage of the British Trades Disputes Act.

[1] 34 and 35 Vic. c. 31; 39 and 40 Vic. c. 22; 38 and 39 Vic. c. 86.

[2] This act was preceded by the Criminal Law Amendment Act of 1859, which declared peaceful persuasion of workmen to abstain from working for a given employer, and also picketing for this purpose, to be legal. This was followed by the Criminal Law Amendment Act of 1871, which repealed the prior combination laws and in lieu thereof specifically enumerated conduct in labor disputes which should be deemed not to be unlawful. Both of these acts, however, were construed by the courts as having made no essential change in the common law of conspiracy as theretofore interpreted.

combination, by two or more persons to do, or procure to be done, any act in contemplation or furtherance of a trade dispute between employers and workmen shall not be indictable as a conspiracy, if such act committed by one person would not be punishable as a crime." For the common-law doctrine of conspiracy, it substituted specific prohibitions against certain offensive conduct in labor disputes, such as violence, intimidation, the persistent following of some other person from place to place, and picketing except for purposes other than "peacefully obtaining or communicating information." It also declared criminal the breach of employment contracts with knowledge that such breach will endanger human life, expose valuable property to destruction, or deprive a municipality of gas or water; and it provided that strikers should still be liable to prosecution for rioting, unlawful assembly, breach of the peace, and sedition, if guilty of these offenses.

In several decisions of trial and intermediate courts in the next decades, the Conspiracy and Protection of Property Act was narrowly construed, but not until 1901 did the unions deem it necessary to ask for any new legislation. Two decisions rendered by the House of Lords in this year created consternation in the union ranks. Quinn v. Leathem[1] held that workingmen acting in combination with intent to injure another were civilly liable despite the Conspiracy and Protection of Property Act; and the Taff-Vale case[2] decided that trade unions might be sued and their funds taken for damages caused by their unlawful acts. The trade unions in alarm demanded remedial legislation and this became an important issue in the election of 1905. The Liberal government which came into power brought in a bill which went only halfway on the most important issue in question, that of the liability of the unions for damages. So many of its supporters, however, had pledged their votes to the complete exemption of unions from all actions in tort that the government withdrew its first bill and in 1906 presented and secured the passage of the British Trades Disputes Act.[3]

---

[1] [1901] A. C. 495.

[2] Taff-Vale Railway Co. v. Amalgamated Society of Railway Servants [1901] A. C. 426.

[3] 6 Edw. VII c. 47.

This act is still in effect and, although it has since been supplemented by more restrictive legislation, remains the principal law governing labor disputes in England. It provides that no act done by a combination of either employers or workingmen in contemplation or furtherance of a trade dispute shall give rise to either civil or criminal liability unless the act if done by one person would be actionable. It expressly legalizes peaceful picketing and peaceful persuasion, retaining, however, the enumeration of specific unlawful actions in labor disputes included in the Conspiracy and Protection of Property Act. Further, it provides that no action shall be maintained in a trade dispute for persuasion to break contracts (which bars all possibility of using individual non-union contracts as a basis for prohibiting efforts at union organization). Finally, it declares that no trade union, employers' association, nor agents or members of either may be sued in tort for unlawful acts alleged to have been committed in behalf of the union or association.

In the twenty-five years that this act has been in force, it has been less liberally interpreted than the trade unions desired,[1] but no decision has destroyed its essential provisions. These, however, have been to some extent modified by the Trade Disputes and Trade Union Act of 1927,[2] which was passed,

---

[1] Soon after the passage of the Trades Disputes Act, the House of Lords held that threat of a strike by union officers when the union has not expressly authorized the calling of a strike is not an act "in contemplation or furtherance of a trades dispute" (Conway v. Wade [1909] A. C. 506). Lower court decisions have even more narrowly construed this provision and the related clause, "by or on behalf of a trades union." The section legalizing peaceful picketing has been construed not to legalize mass picketing, meetings on public highways, or trespass on private property. That the trades unions were not entirely satisfied with the state of the law even as it stood prior to the Trade Disputes and Trade Union Act of 1927 is brought out clearly in the article The Right to Strike, published in the *Monthly Circular of the Labor Research Department*, pp. 269–272, December, 1925.

[2] 17 and 18 Geo. V. c. 22. The Trade Union Act of 1913 (2 and 3 Geo. V c. 30) was another important statute to the trade unions but affected their political rather than their industrial activities. This act was preceded by a decision of the House of Lords that trade unions might not use their funds for political purposes (Osborne v. Amalgamated Society of Railway Servants [1910] A. C. 87). In the Trade Union Act of 1913, unions were permitted to make expenditures for political purposes, but only when so authorized by a referendum vote of their members and with the further

following the general strike of 1926, over the determined opposition of the trade unions. This act, besides imposing restrictions on the use of union funds for political purposes, modified the Trades Disputes Act by declaring certain strikes to be illegal, namely, strikes "designed or calculated to coerce the government either directly or by inflicting hardship upon the community" and all strikes for any "object other than or in addition to the furtherance of a trades dispute." This clearly renders illegal a general strike and perhaps any sympathetic strike, although this is not certain. This act also placed further restrictions upon picketing, declaring illegal all picketing conducted in such a manner as to cause "a reasonable apprehension of injury" to the non-union workmen. It also provides that civil servants (government employees) may not belong to, or be affiliated with, unions which have any members outside the government service.

This entire act is very objectionable to the trade unions, which ever since its passage have demanded its repeal. The Labour Party promised such a repeal measure in the general election of 1929 and in 1930 brought in a Trades Disputes Bill to redeem this pledge. In this, a sympathetic strike was declared to be lawful, but a revolutionary or political strike unlawful. The restriction against affiliation by unions of government employees with the general labor movement was entirely repealed and it was provided that no person should be held guilty of the crime of intimidation merely for doing or stating that he intends to do something which he may lawfully do (*e.g.*, threaten to strike). This bill met strenuous opposition[1] not only from the

---

proviso that any member might refuse to allow any part of his dues to be used for such a purpose by giving notice to this effect to his union. This "contracting out" section was strongly objected to by the Labour Party, in whose behalf all political expenditures of British trade unions are made, but the Trade Disputes and Trade Union Act of 1927 went even further, prohibiting the use of dues of any union member for political purposes who has not in writing authorized such use. The Trade Disputes Bill of 1930 of the present Labour Government proposed the repeal of the entire "contracting out" provision, substituting therefor permission to trade unions to use their funds for political purposes whenever a majority of the members vote in favor of such action.

[1] Much of the opposition arose over the provision, mentioned in the preceding note, repealing all restrictions upon the use of union funds for political purposes when a majority of the members have authorized such use.

Conservatives but from the Liberal allies of the government and was amended in committee so as to be no longer acceptable to the trade unions, whereupon the government withdrew the measure and the law remains as modified by the Trade Disputes and Trade Union Act of 1927.

Even with this 1927 act, the British policy is essentially one of full freedom of combination for both employers and employees. The rights of the contending parties in labor disputes and the restrictions applicable to them are all prescribed quite definitely in statutes. Neither the fact of combination nor the motives of those combining have any weight in determining the legality of acts in labor disputes. Compared with the United States, there are few restrictions and relatively few legal actions. All strikes, with exceptions specified in the Trade Disputes and Trade Union Act of 1927, are lawful. So is peaceful picketing, but with definite restrictions designed to keep it peaceful. The British law differs from the American law most radically in that no action is allowed to be brought against unions for wrongful acts alleged to have been committed in their behalf. The British policy is to hold responsible the individuals who commit these acts, but not the union nor members unconcerned with these acts.

Wide freedom for both employers and employees is accompanied by strict law enforcement. There is little violence in labor disputes in England, and those guilty of acts of violence are usually apprehended and convicted. There are no private detective agencies engaged in industrial work and even the employment of strike breakers is rare.

Great Britain is also the country in which voluntary arbitration has been most fully developed.[1] In many industries,

---

[1] Good general accounts of British legislation and experience in the adjustment of labor disputes are: Lord Amulree, "Industrial Arbitration in Great Britain," Oxford University Press, New York (1929) and the article Conciliation and Arbitration in Great Britain, 1 *Inter. Labour Rev.* 91–109 (1921). The industrial court and its operation are dealt with in Sir William Mackenzie, "The Industrial Court: Practice and Procedure," Butterworth, London (1923) and The British Industrial Court, 3 *Inter. Labour Rev.* 41–50 (1921); Sir Lynden McCassey, The Industrial Courts Act, 1919, 2 *Jour. Comparative Legislation* 3d ser., 72–76 (1920); and in the article Industrial Court of Great Britain, 27 *Monthly Labor Rev.* 102–105 (1928). Sir George Askwith, "Industrial Problems and Disputes," John Murray,

bipartisan adjustment boards set up under trade agreements have been in continuous existence for nearly fifty years. Since the Conciliation Act of 1896, the government has also taken an active part in this work of adjustment. Prior to the World War, it had no permanent arbitrators (although resort to arbitrators selected especially for the particular dispute was frequent) but did have government mediators of a high caliber, who made this their life work and enjoyed the confidence alike of the employers and the trade unions. During the World War, England resorted to compulsory arbitration in essential war industries, with indifferent success.[1] As soon as the war was

London (1920) is an autobiographical sketch of the experiences and impressions of England's greatest mediator, which throws much light upon the problems and difficulties of industrial mediation and arbitration, not only in England but in all countries.

[1] A permanent arbitration tribunal, known as the "Committee on Production," was established early in 1915 for the engineering and shipbuilding trades. Soon thereafter the government negotiated an agreement with the trade union leaders calling for the adjustment without strikes of all disputes affecting essential war industries. In the Munitions of War Act of 1915, this agreement was given statutory form, strikes being prohibited in all munition industries under penalties of both fine and imprisonment.

In the early months of the war, prior to the advent of compulsory arbitration, there were very few strikes. Thereafter they increased but for several years remained below the prewar level. Most of the war-time strikes, moreover, were of short duration and in only a few cases did the government take any action against the strikers, instead usually conceding their demands. As the war progressed, strikes greatly increased and industrial unrest became menacing. A governmental Commission of Inquiry into Industrial Unrest reported as one of the principal causes the system of compulsory arbitration, particularly because of the long delays in adjustment which it entailed. A further source of trouble was the tendency of the system of compulsory arbitration to undermine the influence of the more conservative national trade union leaders, who endeavored faithfully to comply with the law while irresponsible local leaders who disregarded its provisions gained the confidence of the workers through unauthorized strikes, which nearly always accomplished their purpose. As soon as the war was over, compulsory arbitration was abandoned and has not since been seriously urged by any person of prominence in England.

For a more complete discussion of the British war-time experience with arbitration, see Matthew B. Hammond, British Labor Conditions and Legislation during the War, "Preliminary Economic Studies of the War No. 14," of the Carnegie Endowment for International Peace (1919), especially Chaps. 5 and 9; Milton Moses, Compulsory Arbitration in Great Britain during the War, 26 *Jour. Polit. Econ.* 882–900 (1918); and Industrial

ended, the compulsory features were scrapped, with the approval of both employers and employees, and a permanent arbitration tribunal established, known as the "Industrial Court." Resort to this court, which still exists, is wholly voluntary but it has functioned in several thousand cases. There also still exist efficient government mediators, and many disputes not settled through direct negotiations between the parties are referred to special arbitrators selected for the occasion. Very important in the British adjustment machinery remain the arbitration boards set up voluntarily by trade unions and employers, to which have been added as a postwar development joint industrial councils in a considerable number of industries, which, while established primarily for other purposes, operate to minimize industrial strife. Encouragement of such voluntary adjustment machinery is a well-defined governmental policy. The only compulsory feature in the entire system is the power of the government to investigate any dispute, but this power has been exercised very sparingly.

Since the British Trades Disputes Act was passed, England has had many strikes—since the close of the World War, relatively more than the United States. Superficially, a strong case can be made against the entire British policy of dealing with labor disputes. On the other side, it can be contended with much force that the many strikes have been due rather to the serious economic situation in England than to its labor policy. The war-time experience with compulsion was as distasteful to the employers as to the trade unions, and there appears to be little sentiment among British employers for the abandonment of the policy of allowing wide latitude in labor disputes to both sides for a fair fight. Even in the Trade Disputes and Trade Union Act of 1927, the complete immunity of trade unions from lawsuits, which to Americans seems the most extreme feature of British law, was left untouched, as were the clauses of the Trades Disputes Act to the effect that neither the fact of combination nor

---

Unrest in Great Britain, U. S. Bur. of Labor Stat. *Bull.* 237 (1917), which gives the text of the report of the Commission of Inquiry into Industrial Unrest. The *Report of Proceedings under the Conciliation Act and of Arbitration under the Munitions of War Acts,* 1914–1918 (White Paper 185 of 1919, by the British Ministry of Labour) is the official record of all conciliation and arbitration proceedings during this period.

the motive of those combining should have any effect upon the legality of behavior. British employers complain of the privileges which the trade unions enjoy, but trade unionism seems to be so firmly established that not even the employers wish to see the unions seriously weakened.

THE AUSTRALASIAN SYSTEM OF COMPULSORY ARBITRATION

At the other extreme from the British policy is the Australasian system of compulsory arbitration.[1] This was instituted by New Zealand in 1894, followed by New South Wales in 1901, West Australia in 1902, the Australian Commonwealth (federal government) in 1904, and South Australia and Queensland in 1912. All of these acts are still in effect but have been frequently amended. Of all Australian states, only Tasmania and Victoria are without compulsory-arbitration laws, and these two have wage boards functioning in many respects like arbitration courts, but without prohibition of strikes.

The compulsory-arbitration systems of Australasian states differ in details; no attempt will here be made to present other than their main features. All set up permanent arbitration courts for the settlement of industrial disputes. Resort to these courts is compulsory in specified classes of cases and their decisions are binding. Not all strikes, however, are prohibited. In New Zealand, only in the public utilities and certain other essential industries are strikes absolutely forbidden; in other industries, unregistered unions may call strikes but if they do so cannot avail themselves of the arbitration machinery. In New South Wales, under its most recent arbitration law, enacted in 1918, strikes are prohibited only in the government service, railroads, public utilities, and industries in which arbitration awards are in effect, and in all disputes where less than fourteen days' notice of intent to strike is given. Queensland prohibits strikes only if undertaken without a referendum vote of the union members. The Australian Commonwealth law prohibits all strikes extending into two or more provinces, but no prosecutions for violations may be brought until approved by the arbitration court.

---

[1] For references to books and articles dealing with compulsory arbitration in Australia and New Zealand, see the bibliographical note at the end of this Appendix.

Supplementing the permanent arbitration courts, New Zealand has courts of conciliation to which disputes must be brought before the arbitration court will take cognizance of them. In the Australian Commonwealth act, the arbitration court is empowered to create "boards of reference," composed of representatives of both sides, to which any dispute may be referred; and the law of Western Australia provides for advisors, known as "assessors," to assist the court. These agencies bring the employers and the employees together and endeavor to influence them to agree without necessity of resort to arbitration. In the arbitration courts themselves conciliation is often attempted and many adjustments are made without necessity of formal decisions.

Most of the Australian states having compulsory-arbitration laws establish tribunals consisting of a single judge. These judges hold office practically for life and appear generally to be men of the highest caliber. Awards are enforcible both by the courts and by the executive branch of the government, and drastic penalties apply against strikes in defiance of awards.

Contradictory claims are made regarding the success of the Australasian policy of compulsory arbitration, which are difficult to appraise at this distance. Some facts, however, are indisputable. The majority of the people of the several Australasian states are strongly favorable to compulsory arbitration. Employers and the unions have both at times demanded repeal or drastic modification[1] and subsequently reversed their attitude. At present, the labor unions appear to be more strongly favorable, but the employers as a group can hardly be said to oppose it. The 1929 Australian Commonwealth election was fought out

---

[1] The I. W. W. and other syndicalist unions have at all times been strongly opposed to compulsory arbitration. These unions were very strong in New Zealand for some years preceding the World War and more recently have figured prominently in Australian strikes.

For hostile criticisms of compulsory arbitration by Australasian employers, see Henry Brodhead, "State Regulation of Labour and Labour Disputes in New Zealand," Christchurch, N. Z. (1908); J. MacGregor, "Industrial Arbitration in New Zealand," Dunedin, N. Z. (1911); Sir Charles G. Wade, "Australia: Problems and Prospects," Clarendon Press, Oxford (1919); Stanley Morrison, Adventures in Class Government, 11 *Law and Labor* 201–207 (1929); and the letter of H. E. Guy, 10 *Law and Labor* 36 (1928).

over the issue of the abolition of the Commonwealth Court of Arbitration and the turning over of its functions to the states, which was favored by the Conservatives. The Labour Party, favoring the continuance of the court, won an overwhelming victory on this issue, but earlier the voters rejected a proposed constitutional amendment to give the Commonwealth government exclusive control over all labor problems.

While supported by public opinion, compulsory arbitration has not operated to prevent all strikes. For twelve years following the enactment of the New Zealand law, there was not a single strike, and this country was heralded as "the land without strikes." Since then strikes have occurred each year, becoming most numerous in the second decade of the century. In Australia there have been many strikes at all times since compulsory arbitration was inaugurated, with peaks in 1916 and 1917, 1920 and 1921, and 1924–1929. Relative to population, Australia has had far more strikes than either the United States or England.[1] The conclusion of practically every person who has studied the Australian system, however, is that the arbitration machinery, although it has not prevented strikes, has tended to reduce their bitterness and duration.

Many of the strikes in both New Zealand and Australia have been illegal strikes, in direct violation of the compulsory-arbitration acts. The penal provisions of these laws have been enforced only infrequently and spasmodically. The recent tendency appears to emphasize conciliation rather than arbitration; certainly, more disputes are adjusted through direct negotiations between the parties than through either mediation or arbitration.

Compulsory arbitration in Australia has functioned under a condition of strong organization on both sides. As was stated by former Premier William M. Hughes: "For practical purposes, there are practically no non-unionists in Australia."[2] Compulsory arbitration has doubtless had a tendency to strengthen the

---

[1] In 1927, there were 441 strikes in Australia, involving above 200,000 working people, in a total population of 7,000,000. In the same year, there were 734 strikes in the United States and not quite 350,000 people directly affected, in a population of 120,000,000.

[2] Address at the banquet of the National Manufacturers Association as reported in the *Proceedings of the N. A. M.* 1924, p. 235. In New Zealand, the unions have never been nearly so strong, and J. B. Condliffe in Experiments in State Control in New Zealand, 9 *Inter. Labour Rev.* 334–360 (1924),

unions.   Only labor organizations (not individual employees) can bring cases before the arbitration tribunals.   In their awards, the arbitration courts have seldom accorded preference to unions but, as stated by former Chief Justice Higgins of the Commonwealth Arbitration Court, the entire system "is based on unionism.   Indeed, without unions it is hard to conceive how arbitration could be worked."[1]

CANADIAN INDUSTRIAL DISPUTES INVESTIGATION ACT

The Canadian way of dealing with labor disputes[2] might be described as a "middle of the road" program between the British hands-off policy and the Australasian system of compulsory arbitration.   Canada does not prohibit strikes but in some essential industries penalizes strikes and wage changes until after an investigation by a specially created tribunal.

The Canadian Industrial Disputes Act dates from 1907[3] and was the outgrowth of prolonged strikes causing great public inconvenience in the coal fields of western Canada.   This original act remained in force with only minor amendments until 1925, when the Privy Council of England (the final authority in the interpretation of the British North America Act, the fundamental law of Canada) held that this act went beyond the powers of the Dominion government.   Soon thereafter an amending act[4] was passed which confined the operation of the law to labor disputes within the scope of the powers of the Dominion government, but with the provision that the provinces might by appropriate enabling legislation bring under this act all disputes occurring within their territorial boundaries and to which the original law would have been applicable.

---

argues that this is to be ascribed to the compulsory arbitration law which has "taken the steel out of the unions."

[1] H. B. HIGGINS, "A New Province for Law and Order," p. 15, Archibald Constable & Co., Ltd., London (1922).

[2] For reference to the literature on the Canadian Industrial Disputes Act, see the bibliographical note at the end of this Appendix.

[3] The original act was frequently called the "Lemieux Act" after the Minister of Labour in office when it was enacted.   Its reputed author was W. L. Mackenzie King, then the Assistant Minister of Labour and more recently Premier of Canada.

[4] Acts 1925, c. 14.   The entire law as now in force is c. 112 R. S. C. 1927 and is obtainable in pamphlet form from the Ministry of Labour, Ottawa.

The 1907 law applied to all disputes affecting mines, railroads, or public utilities and, by agreement of the employers and the employees affected, might be extended to any other disputes or industries. During the World War, the act was by orders in council extended to all industries deemed essential to the conduct of the war. The 1925 (present) act applies outside the four provinces mentioned hereafter only to disputes affecting navigation, interprovincial railroad transportation, or businesses conducted by aliens, foreign corporations, or corporations operating under a Dominion (as distinguished from a provincial) charter. Six provinces—British Columbia, Saskatchewan, Manitoba, Alberta, Nova Scotia, and New Brunswick—have through appropriate enabling acts extended the scope of the law to include all disputes affecting mines, railroads, or public utilities occurring within these provinces.[1]

In the industries to which the Canadian act applies, strikes and lockouts are forbidden until after investigation by a board of inquiry. Under the 1925 act, any general change in wage rates within these industries is similarly prohibited without prior investigation. Boards of inquiry are set up on the petition of either the employers or employees, but only if deemed advisable by the Minister of Labour. A separate board is created for each controversy, but the same persons have been appointed as public representatives on many different boards. All boards are composed of a representative of the employers and another of the employees selected by the contending parties, and a third member nominated by the other two or selected by the Minister of Labour if the other two cannot agree. The boards of inquiry are to be set up within thirty days after petition therefor, but in numerous instances considerable delay has occurred and not infrequently the application for a board has been rejected by the Minister of Labour.

The boards of inquiry have complete testimonial powers and are charged with the duty of investigating all phases of the dis-

---

[1] Besides the Industrial Disputes Investigation Act, the Canadian Department of Labour administers a conciliation law. This is applicable to industries to which the Industrial Disputes Investigation Act does not apply. This conciliation service operates on a strictly voluntary basis and confines its efforts to mediation, the service corresponding very closely to the mediation service of the U. S. Department of Labor.

pute and making a public report on the merits of the controversy, with recommendations for settlement.   After publication of the report, both parties are free to accept or disregard the recommendations made and may thereafter lawfully proceed with their strike or wage reduction.   The theory of the system is that the public, which is such a heavy sufferer from labor disputes, is entitled to know all essential facts bearing upon the merits of the controversy and that when the public is fully informed neither party will wish to proceed in defiance of the recommendations of the board of inquiry.

This original theory has been considerably altered in actual practice.   The Canadian boards of inquiry now are more concerned with getting the parties to reach a mutually satisfactory settlement than with publicly determining which side is in the wrong.   Only when efforts at mediation fail do the boards make formal findings and recommendations.

Canada, like other countries, has failed to eliminate strikes. The number of strikes after findings and recommendations by boards of inquiry has been small.   Up to 1925, there occurred only 44 such strikes, constituting 9 per cent of all the cases in which boards of inquiry were created.   There have been far more illegal strikes, that is, strikes without requesting or awaiting a board of inquiry.   In contrast with 44 legal strikes, there were in these first eighteen years of the operation of the law 472 illegal strikes;[1] but even this number is relatively small compared with strikes in the United States, England, or Australasia. Prosecutions for illegal strikes have been fewer even than in Australasia, and there have been none at all in recent years.

Beyond question, the Industrial Disputes Investigation Act is quite popular.   Most of the trade unionists are members of international unions affiliated with the American Federation of Labor, the Canadian Trades and Labor Congress being composed exclusively of the Canadian locals of such international unions. The American Federation of Labor, under the leadership of Samuel Gompers, was strongly opposed to the Canadian Industrial Disputes Investigation Act at the time of its enactment, regarding it as a denatured form of compulsory arbitration. Under this leadership, most of the Canadian unionists were at

---

[1] SELEKMAN, BEN M., "Postponing Strikes: A Study of the Canadian Industrial Disputes Act," Russell Sage Foundation, New York (1927).

first very hostile to the law and some of them have remained so to this day.   This is particularly true of the United Mine Workers of America, whose Canadian districts and locals have often boldly defied the act.   Other unions—for instance, the railroad telegraphers—have always been favorable to the law.   The Canadian Trades and Labor Congress declared for the repeal of the act in 1912 and again in 1916 but reversed its position after the World War, endorsing the law but suggesting some amendments.   The principal amendment sought was to prohibit wage reductions until after investigation, just as strikes were prohibited, and this amendment was incorporated in the new act of 1925.   At present, the great majority of the Canadian union members seem to be well satisfied with it, as are the employers as well.   The law is particularly favorable to weak unions.   A union in a given establishment or industry too weak to conduct a successful strike may request the creation of a board of inquiry. Very generally, the creation of such a board results in the employees' getting at least some of their demands, which enhances the prestige of the union.   Strong unions are handicapped by their inability to call strikes until after investigation, which prevents their availing themselves of the most opportune time to strike; yet, with a few exceptions, the Canadian unions are now in favor of the system of compulsory investigation.

OTHER COUNTRIES

England, Australia, New Zealand, and Canada are the countries whose institutions and general legal systems are most like those of the United States; for this reason, the major part of this brief discussion of foreign experience in dealing with labor disputes is devoted to them.   For other countries, only a few general facts will be given to develop what appear to be the principal tendencies in dealing with labor disputes abroad.[1]

---

[1] The best brief account for American readers on the law governing labor combinations and labor disputes in foreign countries is the article by Jean Nicod, Freedom of Association and Trade Unionism: an Introductory Survey, 9 *Inter. Labour Rev.* 467–480 (1924), which was reprinted in 7 *Law and Labor* 38–43 (1925).   Volume I of the very comprehensive five-volume world-wide survey "Freedom of Association," published by the International Labour Office in 1927–1930, is a comparative summary which gives all essential facts regarding the laws governing labor combinations and labor disputes in all countries.

Everywhere in continental Europe, the law of labor disputes is statutory, but with a wide discretion vested in administrative officials. The regular courts have practically nothing to do with strikes or any other phase of industrial conflict. Nor do the special labor courts which exist in many of these countries deal with labor disputes, but rather with controversies between employers and individual workmen growing out of the employment relation. A clean-cut distinction is made between such individual controversies and collective labor disputes, and special machinery set up to deal with the latter.

In most of these countries, trade unionism developed later than in England or the United States; not until after our Civil War were workmen permitted to combine. Today labor unions are lawful in all countries and are relatively much stronger in Germany and some other countries than in the United States. Throughout Europe trade unions are required to register and are subject to some degree of governmental control.[1] In return, the unions are recognized as the representatives of both the organized and unorganized workmen of their respective crafts, being permitted to bring suits on behalf of these workmen in the courts and to act for them in all matters pending before administrative tribunals.

The right to strike is restricted to some extent in every country, most of these restrictions having been developed since the World War. Turkey prohibits all strikes; Rumania, strikes in plants employing more than ten employees and all strikes affecting government service, transportation, mining, public utilities, or meat packing. Hungary prohibits strikes in the government service or against public utilities and permits strikes in other industries only after conciliation has failed. Italy under Mussolini has what appears to an outsider to be a system of compulsory arbitration applicable to all industries. Norway also has a system of compulsory arbitration, which dates back to 1916 but applies only to disputes concerning the interpretation of trade agreements and disputes which the crown deems dangerous.

---

[1] This is most extensive in Italy, which has virtual compulsory trade unionism, but under strict government control. See G. Arias, Trade Union Reform in Italy, 14 *Inter. Labour Rev.* 345–356 (1926); and G. E. Modigliana, Compulsory Trade Unionism, 6 *Labour Monthly* 68–71 (1927).

Denmark similarly has a permanent arbitration court with power to interpret and enforce trade agreements and since 1921 has prohibited strikes in disputes which the public conciliator declares to be of public importance. France prohibits strikes in government service, which includes the government railways. Germany has written into its republican constitution an express right of association but in its statutes gives the government wide powers to prevent or terminate strikes imperilling the safety of the nation.

The tendency to place restrictions upon the right to strike has gone hand in hand with the establishment of machinery for adjustment. Denmark and Norway have established permanent courts of arbitration, and in practically all other European countries there is an extensive conciliation machinery, which is perhaps most fully developed in Germany.[1] There are in Germany 103 permanent conciliation committees, each operating within a definite territorial area and constituted of representatives of the employers and employees, with an impartial chairman appointed by the Minister of Labor. Alongside these are sixteen district conciliation officers, also appointed by the Minister of Labor. On the petition of either party or on their own motion, the conciliation committees take cognizance of any industrial dispute which develops within their districts. At the first stage, the neutral chairman of the conciliation committee attempts to mediate the difficulty. If no settlement is reached, the entire conciliation committee is convened which, after hearing both parties, renders a decision outlining a basis for settlement. These decisions are not binding unless accepted by both parties, or declared binding by the district conciliation officer on appeal of either party or the conciliation committee. This provision for binding awards without approval of both parties was introduced in the German law to give the government power to prevent disputes threatening the safety of the nation and has been frequently exercised, even in relatively unimportant disputes. There is much opposition to this feature of the German arbitration system,

---

[1] Good accounts of the German adjustment machinery are the articles by Dr. Fritz Sitzler, The Compulsory Adjustment of Industrial Disputes in Germany, 12 *Inter. Labour Rev.* 457–466 (1925); and William T. Ham, The German System of Arbitration, 39 *Jour. Polit. Econ.* 1–24 (1931).

particularly among employers.[1] At a national conference on this subject called by the government in 1928, demand was made that the system of binding awards be abandoned, but this recommendation has not been adopted to date.

Belgium and other European countries have somewhat similar conciliation machinery, but without the feature of making binding awards over the objection of one of the parties to the dispute. The first emphasis everywhere is upon a mutually satisfactory settlement, to which end considerable pressure is exerted by the government. Agreements when reached are treated as binding contracts, and breaches make the party guilty of such violations liable in damages to the injured party. In Denmark and Germany damages have quite often been recovered by employers from trade unions because they violated trade agreements or binding awards, and the unions have, similarly, been allowed damages against employers. Several of the European countries forbid the making of individual contracts in contravention of collective agreements which affect the industry. In Germany and Austria, agreements made between a majority of the employers in a given industry and their employees may be extended by order of the government throughout the entire industry and when so extended are binding alike upon the signatory parties and other employers and employees in the industry. Questions regarding the interpretation of agreements are settled by the courts and strikes over such questions forbidden in all three of the Scandinavian countries.

In addition to the formal conciliation machinery, several of the continental countries have since the World War developed voluntary works councils and similar plant organizations which, while not primarily concerned with the adjustment of disputes, undoubtedly are designed to remove causes of friction. Austria, Germany, Norway, and Czechoslovakia all have laws making it mandatory for medium-sized and large manufacturing and commercial establishments to have works councils composed of representatives of the management and elected delegates of the

---

[1] ALBRECHT, GERHARD, Die Reformbedürftigkeit des Schlicttungswesens, 129 *Jahrb. f. Nationalökon. u. Stat.* 833–852 (1928); Walther Weddingen, Angewandte Theorie der Schlichtung, 130 *Jahrb. f. Nationalökon. u. Stat.* 339–392 (1929).

employees.[1]   While these councils have perhaps not fulfilled the
high hopes which were expressed when they were established in the
years immediately following the war, they are still required in all
of these countries and seem to be functioning satisfactorily in
preventing minor differences arising within the plant from becoming causes of strikes.

Non-European countries, not being so well developed indus-
trially, have had a much less extensive experience in the matter
of dealing with labor disputes.   Several of the non-European
countries, however, have in recent years enacted legislation
reflecting the tendencies operative in Europe.   Colombia has
since 1920 had a system of compulsory arbitration for transportation and public-utility services and the nationally owned mines.
Bolivia prohibits strikes of government employees and requires
one week's notice before strikes may be undertaken on railroads
or public utilities and five days' notice of other strikes.   Similarly
some of the Mexican states require ten days' notice of contemplated strikes on railroads and other public utilities.   The
federal government of the Union of South Africa has prohibited
strikes on railroads and all public utilities, and the Transvaal has
since 1909 had a compulsory investigation act modeled after the
Canadian law.   Japan, in contrast, liberalized its laws in 1927
to permit strikes without restrictions but at the same time provided for special conciliation boards in all disputes.

Bibliographical Note

An exhaustive world-wide survey of the laws governing trade unions and
labor disputes is the five-volume study of the International Labour Office

[1] For a brief summary of the compulsory works council laws, see Works
Councils in Foreign Countries, 4 *Law and Labor* 265–267 (1922).

In addition to its system of works councils, Germany, France, and
Czechoslovakia have national economic councils and Austria district
chambers of labor, representing employers and employees and functioning
to advise the government and the national parliament in industrial matters.

In England a Parliamentary commission, popularly known as the
"Whitley Commission," strongly endorsed the works council idea and also
the creation of joint industrial councils bringing together management
and employees on an industry basis.   England, however, never made the
works councils mandatory and, while numerous works councils and also
joint industrial councils were established, these have never become so
general as in the central European countries.   Numerous joint industrial
councils exist also in Belgium

on Freedom of Association, *Studies and Reports*, Ser. *A*, Nos. 28–32 (1927–1930), the first volume of which is a comparative analysis. A briefer summary of this monumental study is Jean Nicod, Freedom of Association and Trade Unionism: an Introductory Survey, 9 *Inter. Labour Rev.* 467–480 (1924), which is reprinted in 7 *Law and Labor* 38–43 (1925). For developments since these *Reports* on Freedom of Association were issued, the "Legislative Series" of the International Labour Office, in which are reprinted all important labor laws and administrative orders in all countries since 1920, and its annual "International Survey of Legal Decisions on Labour Law," issued since 1926 and now covering England, France, Germany, Italy, and the United States, should be consulted. For secondary accounts of these developments, the *International Labour Review*, issued monthly by the International Labour Office, Geneva, Switzerland, is invaluable.

The International Labour Office has also published a brief one-volume study on "The Conciliation and Arbitration of Industrial Disputes—an International Survey" (1927). Much the same ground is covered in three articles in the *International Labour Review* on The Conciliation and Arbitration of Industrial Disputes, 14 *Inter. Labour Rev.* 640–659, 833–860 (1926), 15 *Inter. Labour Rev.* 78–97 (1927).

On the British law, there are numerous legal treatises, among others: Sir Henry H. Slesser, "The Law Relating to Trade Unions," Labour Publishing Co., London (1921); Sir Henry H. Slesser and Arthur Henderson, Jr., "Industrial Law," Benn, London (1924); Arthur Henderson, Jr., "Trade Unions and the Law," Benn, London (1927); Sir Cyril Asquith, "Trade Union Law for Laymen," Cassell, London (1927); E. P. Hewitt, "Trade Unions and the Law," Solicitors' Law Stationery Soc., London (1927); W. M. Geldart, "The Present Law of Trade Disputes and Trade Unions," Milford, London (1914); and John H. Greenwood, "A Handbook of Industrial Law," University of London Press, London (1916).

On the more recent developments in the British law, the following articles may be consulted: H. A. Millis, British Trade Disputes and Trade Union Acts, 36 *Jour. Polit. Econ.* 305–329 (1928); Alpheus T. Mason, The British Trades Disputes Act of 1927, 22 *Amer. Polit. Sci. Rev.* 143–153 (1928); Ramsey Muir, "Trade Unionism and the Trade Union Bill, with an Appendix on the Legal Position of Trade Unions by W. A. Jowitt," Williams & Norgate, London (1927); Arthur Henderson, Jr., The Trade Disputes and Trade Union Act, 1927, 8 *Labour Monthly* 157–160 (1929); W. A. Robson, The Future of Trade Union Law, 1 *Polit. Quart.* 86–103 (1930); and Arthur Henderson, Jr., An Analysis of the Trade Disputes and Trade Unions (Amendment) Bill, 1931, 9 *Labour Mag.* 390–392 (1931).

References to the British industrial arbitration machinery, its history, and functioning are given in the footnote on p. 318, and references to the war-time experiment with compulsory arbitration, in the footnote on p. 319.

The Australasian system of compulsory arbitration has provoked a wealth of literature. The principal American accounts are Henry D. Lloyd, "A Country without Strikes," Doubleday, Page & Company, Garden City (1900), now interesting only as a curiosity; E. S. Furniss and L. R. Guild,

"Labor Problems," pp. 441–529, Houghton Mifflin Company, Boston (1925); John R. Commons and John B. Andrews, "Principles of Labor Legislation," pp. 164–180, Harper & Brothers, New York (1927); M. B. Hammond, The Australian System of Compulsory Arbitration, 7 *Proc. Acad. of Polit. Sci. in the City of N. Y.* 19–30 (1917); Clarence Northcutt, "Australian Social Development," pp. 117–144 (1918); T. T. Ko, Governmental Methods of Adjusting Labor Disputes in North America and Australia, pp. 127–199, "Columbia Univ. Studies in History" No. 271, New York (1926); National Industrial Conference Board, "Arbitration and Wage Fixing in Australia" (1918) and "Conciliation and Arbitration in New Zealand" (1919); and George Beeby (former Minister of Labor of New South Wales), The Australian System of Dealing with Labor Disputes, 42 *Survey* 399–401 (1919). Among many noteworthy accounts of the Australian system published abroad are Henry B. Higgins, "A New Province for Law and Order," Constable, London (1922); W. P. Reeves, "State Experiments in Australia and New Zealand," Allen & Unwin, London (1924); Mary T. Rankin, "Arbitration and Conciliation in Australasia," Allen & Unwin, London (1916); Jethro Brown, Industrial Courts in Australia, 2 *Jour. Comparative Legis.* 3d ser., 169–188 (1920); Dorothy M. Sells, The Development of State Wage Regulation in Australia and New Zealand, 10 *Inter. Labour Rev.* 607–629, 779–799, 962–1004 (1924); Sir John Findlay, Industrial Peace in New Zealand, 4 *Inter. Labour Rev.* 32–46 (1921); Thomas W. McCawley, Industrial Arbitration in Queensland, 5 *Inter. Labour Rev.* 385–409 (1922); J. B. Condliffe, Experiments in State Control in New Zealand, 9 *Inter. Labour Rev.* 334–360 (1924); O. de R. Foenander, The New Conciliation and Arbitration Act in Australia, 19 *Inter. Labour Rev.* 151–174 (1929); F. A. W. Gisborne, Arbitration in Australia, 241 *Edinburgh Rev.* 230–247 (1925); W. H. Crocker, Industrial Arbitration in New Zealand, 4 *Econ. Rev.* 227–238 (1928); and George Anderson, The Commonwealth Conciliation and Arbitration Act, 1928, 4 *Econ. Rev.* 279–301 (1928). The decisions of the Australian Commonwealth Arbitration Court are regularly published under the title *Commonwealth Arbitration Reports.*

The Canadian Industrial Disputes Investigation Act received much attention from research students in this country prior to the World War, but far less since. Among the more important studies are Ben M. Selekman, "Postponing Strikes," Russell Sage Foundation, New York (1927); B. M. Squires, Operation of the Industrial Disputes Investigation Act of Canada, *Bull.* U. S. Bur. of Labor Stat. 233 (1918); Margaret Mackintosh, "Government Intervention in Labour Disputes in Canada," Queen's University, Kingston, Canada (1924); also published as a supplement to the *Canadian Labour Gazette* March, 1925; G. R. Askwith, "The Industrial Disputes Investigation Act of Canada," British Blue Book Cd. 6603 (1913); T. T. Ko, Governmental Methods of Adjusting Labor Disputes in North America and Australia, pp. 103–126, "Columbia Univ. Studies in History," No. 271, New York, (1926); National Industrial Conference Board, "The Canadian Industrial Disputes Investigation Act," The Board, Boston, (1918); R. M. MacIver, Arbitration and Conciliation in Canada, 107 *Ann. Amer. Acad. of Polit. and Social Sci.* 294–298 (1923); C. E. Dankert, The Canadian Industrial Disputes Act, 36 *Jour. Polit. Econ.* 141–164 (1928); and J. F. Plant, Methods of Adjusting Industrial Disputes in Canada, 30 *Canadian Labour Gazette* 647–651 (1930).   Reports of all proceedings under the Canadian Industrial Disputes Investigation Act are published currently in the *Canadian Labour Gazette* and are incorporated in annual reports published as an appendix to the *Report* of the (Canadian) Department of Labour.

On the laws of other countries, the best sources of information for Americans are the *Reports* of the International Labour Office on Freedom of Association and the Conciliation and Arbitration of Industrial Disputes noted earlier in this bibliographical note.   Other accounts in English include:

France: J. H. Romanes, The Law of Trade Unions in France, 36 *Juridical Rev.* 339–349 (1924); A. Boissard, The Legal Position of Public Servants in France, 12 *Inter. Labour Rev.* 317–345 (1925).

Germany: Dr. Fritz Sitzler, The Law of Collective Bargaining in Germany, 6 *Inter. Labour Rev.* 511–526 (1922); Emil Frankel, How Germany Settles Industrial Disputes, 17 *Monthly Labour Rev.* 578–587 (1923); Dr. Fritz Sitzler, The Compulsory Adjustment of Industrial Disputes in Germany, 12 *Inter. Labour Rev.* 457–466 (1925); William T. Ham, The German System of Arbitration, 39 *Jour. Polit. Econ.* 1–24 (1931).

Italy: H. E. Giuseppe Bottai, Trade Organization in Italy under the Act and Regulations on Collective Relations in Connection with Employment, 15 *Inter. Labour Rev.* 815–827 (1927); Gino Arias, Trade Union Reform in Italy, 14 *Inter. Labour Rev.* 345–356 (1926).

Belgium: Conciliation and Arbitration Boards in Belgium, 27 *Canadian Labour Gazette* 1158, November, 1927.

Scandinavian Countries: Compulsory Arbitration in Swedish Labor Disputes, *Swedish-American Trade Jour.*, pp. 224–226, July, 1928; Compulsory Arbitration in Norway, 15 *Monthly Labour Rev.* 211–213, August, 1922.

Russia: Labour Disputes in Soviet Russia, 14 *Inter. Labour Rev.* 262–268 (1926); N. S. Timacheff, Conciliation Procedure in Soviet Russia, 22 *Inter. Labour Rev.* 209–220 (1930).

Japan: The New Japanese Act on the Conciliation of Labour Disputes, 15 *Inter. Labour Rev.* 257–271 (1927).

APPENDIX B

EX PARTE TEMPORARY RESTRAINING ORDERS DISSOLVED OR MODIFIED AFTER A HEARING

Federal:

Union Pacific R. Co. v. Reuf, 120 Fed. 102 (1902).

Wabash R. R. Co. v. Hannahan, 121 Fed. 563 (1903).

Omaha, etc., Transfer Co. v. Teamsters, Dist. Neb. 1903 (*Omaha Bee*, May 8, 1903).

Kemmerer v. Haggerty, 139 Fed. 693 (1905).

Allis-Chalmers Co. v. Iron Molders' Union, Dist. Wis., June 16, 1906. Dissolved July 14, 1906. (Supplemental bill later and new injunction issued.)

Pope Motor Car Co. v. Keegan, 150 Fed. 148 (1906).

Barnes v. Berry, 157 Fed. 813 (1908) (after trial).

Delaware, etc., R. R. Co. v. Switchmen's Union, 158 Fed. 541 (1908).

Baltimore & Ohio R. R. Co. v. Machinists, W. D. Pa. (Judge Yound), 1909 (*Machinists Jour.*, p. 1085, November, 1909).

Ill. Central R. Co. v. Machinists, S. D. Ill., Oct. 11, 1911. Modified Nov. 6, 1911. (Testimony of Frank Comerford in U. S. Commission on Industrial Relations: *Final Report and Testimony* (64th Cong., 1st Sess., *Sen. Doc.* 415), X, 9931).

Aluminum Castings Co. v. Iron Molders' Union, 197 Fed. 221 (1912).

Paine Lumber Co. v. Neal, 212 Fed. 259 (1913) (after trial).

Irving v. Neal, 209 Fed. 471 (1913) (after trial).

Quincy Show Case Works v. Carpenters' Local 1366, S. D. Ill. (Judge Humphrey), June 11, 1913. Modified Sept. 27, 1913.

Duplex Printing Press Co. v. Deering, S. D. N. Y., Apr. 30, 1914. Dissolved after trial in 247 Fed. 192 (1917) (subsequently restored on appeal).

U. S. Mortgage & Trust Co. v. Colgan, Dist. Ind., 1915. (*Motorman and Conductor*, p. 91, March 1916.)

Hamilton v. Garretson, Dist. Neb., Aug. 30, 1916. Dissolved Sept. 2, 1916.

King v. Weiss & Lesh Manufacturing Co., Sept. 9, 1919. Modified Sept. 20, 1919. (Frankfurter and Greene, "The Labor Injunction," Appendix I.)

Kinloch Telephone Co. v. Local Union 2,265 Fed. 312 (1920). (Frankfurter and Greene, "The Labor Injunction," p. 237.)

Buyer v. Guillan, S. D. N. Y. 1920 (*Industrial News Survey*, Aug. 28, 1920.) (Revived on appeal.)

Silverstein v. Local 280, Sept. 8, 1921. Dissolved Nov. 22, 1921. Decision affirmed in 284 Fed. 833.

Mitchell Bros. v. International Ladies' Garment Workers, N. D. Ill., Aug. 1923. (*Chicago Herald Examiner*, Aug. 26, 1923.)

Western Union Telegraph Co. v. International Brotherhood of Electrical Workers, N. D. Ill., 1924. (6 *Law and Labor* 209.)

Howe v. United Mine Workers of America, Dist. Ind., May 1925. (*N. Y. Times*, May 10, 20, 1925.)

Columbus Heating and Ventilating Co. v. Pittsburgh Building Trades Council, 17 F. (2nd) 806 (1926).

Barker Painting Co. v. Local 734. Brotherhood of Painters, Dist. N. J., 1926. (8 *Law and Labor*, 183.)

Pittsburgh Coal Co. v. Cinque, S. D. Ohio, June, 1927. (*Chicago Tribune*, June 17, 25, 1927.)

United Brotherhood of Miners v. United Mine Workers of America, District 13, S. D. Ia., Dec. 13, 1927. Dissolved January, 1928.

Detroit Tile and Mosaic Co. v. Mason Contractors, E. D. Mich., March, 1929. Dissolved Feb. 21, 1930.

California:

Pierce v. Stablemen's Union, Sup. Ct., San Francisco (Judge Murasby) Aug. 2, 1905. (*San Francisco Chronicle*, Aug. 3, 1905.)

Overland Publishing Co. v. San Francisco Typographical Union 21, 1921. (*Amer. Photo-engraver*, June, 1921.)

Colorado:

Davis Iron Works v. Machinists Local 47, Dist. Ct., Denver (Judge Jackson) 1898. (*Machinists' Jour.*, p. 751, January, 1899.)

Colorado Amusement Co. v. Denver Trades' Assembly, 1899. (*Colorado Bureau of Labor Rept.*, pp. 189–190, 1899–1900.)

Connecticut:

Master Builders' Assoc. v. Bricklayers, etc., Union, Sup. Ct., Bridgeport (Judge Gager) July, 1906. Dissolved Oct. 12, 1906. (*N. Y. Times*, Oct. 13, 1906.)

Florida:

Jetton-Dekle Lumber Co. v. Mattier, 53 Fla. 569, 43 So. 590 (1907).

Illinois:

Frazer & Chalmers v. Iron Molders' Union, Cir. Ct., Cook County (Judge Hancey), August, 1899.

Efting v. Waitresses Union, Cir. Ct., Cook County, June 29, 1914. (Materially modified July 1914.)

Sheet Metal Workers' Union 73 v. Architectural Iron League, Cir. Ct., Cook County, 1914.

American Hide and Leather Co. v. Tannery Workers' Local 15051, Sup. Ct., Cook County (Judge Baldwin), June, 1916.

Anderson & Lind Mfg. Co. v. Carpenters, 199 App. 330 (1916).

R. R. Donnelly & Sons Co. v. Chicago Typographical Union 16, Sup. Ct., Cook County, 1923. (5 *Law and Labor* 334.)

Indiana:

Anderson v. Indianapolis Drop Forging Co., 1903. (*Machinists' Jour.*, p. 139, February, 1903.)

Shafer Saddlery Co. v. Amerine, Cir. Ct., Adams County, July 13, 1914. Dissolved July 30, 1914.

Union Sanitary Manufacturing Co. v. Iron Molders, Hamilton County (Judge Kent), 1917. (*Inter. Molders' Jour.*, p. 430, June, 1917.)

Iowa:

Morrell Packing Co. v. Butcher Workmen, Wapello County (Judge Anderson), 1921. (*Federated Press Bull.*, Jan. 14, 1922.)

Kentucky:

St. Bernard Coal Co. v. United Mine Workers of America, Cir. Ct., Hopkins County, 1901. (*Louisville Courier-Jour.*, May 11, 1901.)

Massachusetts:

Brine Transportation Co. v. Teamsters, 1902. (*Boston Jour.*, Mar. 1, 1902.)

Waldberg Brewing Co. v. Ward, Suffolk County, 1904. (*Mass. Labor Bull.* 70, pp. 134–135.)

National Blank Book Co. v. Hoffman, Hampden County, 1907. (*Mass. Labor Bull.* 70, p. 146.)

Macullar-Parker Co. v. United Garment Workers, Sup. Ct., Suffolk County, 1913. (*Mass. Labor Bull.* 117, p. 227.)

Michigan:

Michigan Chair Co. v. Furniture Workers, at Grand Rapids (Judge McDonald), May 17, 1911. Modified June 6, 1911. (*Grand Rapids Herald*, May 18, June 6, 1911.)

Baltic Mining Co. v. Western Federation of Miners, Cir. Ct., Houghton County, September, 1913. (Restored by the Michigan Sup. Ct. in 177 Mich. 632.)

Mack v. Watrous, Cir. Ct., Wayne County (Judges Hosmer and Collingwood), Dec. 15, 1915. Modified after trial, May, 1916.

Prange v. Trades and Labor Council, Cir. Ct., Kent County, Aug. 11, 1916. Dissolved January, 1917. (*A. F. of L. Weekly News Letter*, Jan. 27, 1917.)

Roller Foundry Co. v. International Molders' Union 378, Cir. Ct., Bay City (Judge Houghton), February, 1917.

Minnesota:

Grant Construction Co. v. St. Paul Building Trades Council, Dist. Ct., Ramsay County, 2nd Judicial District, May 10, 1916. Dissolved June 27, 1916. (Decision affirmed by Minn. Sup. Ct. in 136 Minn. 167.)

Mississippi:

Curphey & Mundy v. Terrell, 39 S. 477 (1905).

Missouri:

Gast Bank Note, etc., Co., v. Fennimore Assoc., 79 Mo. App. 612 (1899).

Hughes v. Motion Picture Operators' Union 170, Cir. Ct., Division 3, Jackson County, 1916.

Nebraska:

State v. Employers' of Labor, Dist. Ct., Douglas County, June 18, 1917. Modified Aug. 11, 1917.

New Jersey:

Frank v. Herold, 63 N. J. Eq. 443, 52 Atl. 152 (1901).   (*New York World,* July 2, 1901.)

Atkins v. Fletcher Co., 65 N. J. Eq. 658, 55 Atl. 1077 (1903).

Allman v. Carpenters, 79 N. J. Eq. 150, 81 Atl. 116 (1910).

Forstmann & H. Co. v. United Front Committee, 133 Atl. 202 (1926).

New York:

Rogers v. Evarts, 17 N. Y. S. 264 (1891).

Sleicher v. Grogan, 59 N. Y. S. 1065 (1899).

Reform Club v. Laborers', etc., Society, 60 N. Y. S. 388 (1899).

Payne v. Waddell, Sup. Ct. at Elmira, 1899.   (*Machinists' Jour.,* p. 751, December, 1899.)

Krebs v. Rosenstein, 66 N. Y. S. 42 (1900).

Levy v. Rosenstein, 66 N. Y. S. 101 (1901).

Master Horseshoers' Protective Assoc. v. Quinlivan, 82 N. Y. S. 288 (1903) (restored on appeal).

Everards' Breweries v. Local 59 United Brewery Workers, N. Y. C., 1903. (3 *N. Y. Labor Bull.* 145.)

Searle Manufacturing Co. v. Terry, 106 N. Y. S. 438 (1905).

Butterick Publishing Co. v. Typographical Union, 100 N. Y. S. 292 (1906). Dissolved May 5, 1906.

Slingerland v. Albany Typographical Union, Apr. 28, 1906. (*Typographical Jour.,* p. 61, July, 1906.)

Russell v. Stampers' Union, 107 N. Y. S. 303 (1907).

Fell v. Berry, 108 N. Y. S. 669 (1908).

Hogle Co. v. Mulvaney, Sup. Ct., Kings County. Issued February, 1912. Dissolved May 9, 1912.

Woolf & Schulhof v. Amalgamated Ladies' Garment Cutters' Assoc., Local 10, New York City, Supt. Ct. (Judge Guy), September, 1916. (*Ladies Garment Cutter,* Sept. 30, 1916.)

Seubert v. Reiff, 164 N. Y. S. 522 (1917).

Rogers-Peet Co. v. Hillman, Sup. Ct., New York County, 1919. (45 *Polit. Sci. Quart.* 90.)

Michaels v. Hillman, 181 N. Y. S. 195 (1921).

International Paper Co. v. Clifton, Sup. Ct., Niagara County, September, 1921.

Wood Mowing and Reaping Machine Co. v. Toohey, 114 Misc. 185, 186 N. Y. S. 95 (1921).

J. Friedman Co. v. Amalgamated Clothing Workers, 188 N. Y. S. 879 (1921).

Bonwit v. Schlesinger, 4 *Law and Labor* 130 (1922).

Katz & Ogush v. Jewelry Workers' Union 1, New York County, 1922. (*N. Y. Times*, Nov. 8, 1922.)

Segenfeld v. Friedman, 193 N. Y. S. 128 (1923).

Berg Auto Trunk Specialty Co. v. Wiener, 200 N. Y. S. 745 (1923).

Maisel v. Sigman, 205 N. Y. S. 807 (1924).

Bellin v. Millinery Workers, 216 N. Y. S. 68 (1926).

Public Baking Co. v. Stern, 215 N. Y. S. 537 (1926).

Interborough Rapid Transit Co. v. Green, 227 N. Y. S. 258 (1928).

Faddis v. Wilson, New York City (Justice Levy), Jan. 31, 1929. Dissolved by Justice Bijur, Feb. 7, 1929. (*N. Y. Times*, Feb. 1, 8, 1929.)

Carlstrom Bros. v. Brotherhood of Painters, Dist. Council 28, Queens County (Justice Humphrey), October, 1929. (*N. Y. State Feder. of Labor Bull.*, Nov. 9, 1929.)

Ohio:

Perkins v. Rogg, 11 Ohio Dec. Reprints 585 (1892).

Standard Tube, etc., Co. v. International Union, 7 Ohio N. P. 87 (1899).

Niles Tool Works v. Webster, at Hamilton (Judge Fisher), July, 1901. (*Cincinnati Enquirer*, July 12, 1901.)

Morgan Engineering Co. v. Nichols, 13 Ohio S. & C. P. Dec. 614 (1906).

Menjon v. Waiters' Union, Cuyahoga County, 1906. (*Cleveland Citizen*, Nov. 3, 1906.)

Jeffrey Manufacturing Co. v. Iron Molders' Union, Ct. of Comm. Pleas, Franklin County, 1906. (*Iron Molders' Jour.*, p. 728, October, 1906.)

Taylor-Boggis Co. v. Iron Molders' Union, Comm. Pleas, Cuyahoga County, 1916. (*Inter. Molders' Jour.*, p. 893, October, 1916; pp. 961–963, November, 1916; pp. 445–446, June, 1917.)

La France, etc., Co. v. International Brotherhood, 3 *Law and Labor* 280 (1921).

Oklahoma:

Electric Planing Mill v. Chickasha Trades' Council, 15th Judicial Cir., 1910.

Pennsylvania:

McKeesport, etc., Ice Co. v. Journeymen's Horseshoers Union, 37 *Pitts. Law Jour.*, n. s. 55 (1906).

Morris Run Coal Co. v. Guy, 14 Pa. Dist. 600 (1905).

Vermont:

International Paper Co. v. Bellows Falls Local 5, Windham County, Feb. 15, 1922. Modifi d Apr. 7, 1922.

Virginia:

Waddey Co. v. Typographical Union, Chancery Ct., Richmond, Oct. 21, 1905. Dissolved Nov. 23, 1905. Decision affirmed in 105 Va. 188, 53 S. E. 273 (1906).

Washington:

Lloyd Transfer Co. v. International Brotherhood of Teamsters; Fortune v. International Brotherhood, Seattle Drayage and Storage Co. v. International Brotherhood, Super. Ct., Kings County, August, 1913. Materially modified Oct. 18, 1923.

Commercial Binding and Printing Co. v. Tacoma Typographical Union, Sup. Ct., Pierce County, May 21, 1914. Dissolved June, 1914. Decision affirmed in 85 Wash. 234, 147 Pac. 1143 (1915).

Wisconsin:

Weyenberg Shoe Co. v. Local 41 United Shoe Workers, Milwaukee County, February, 1914. (*Milwaukee Jour.*, Feb. 20, 22, 1914.)

Harsh-Edmonds Shoe Co. v. Oldham, Milwaukee County, February, 1914. (*Milwaukee Jour.*, Feb. 19–22, 1914.)

Nekoosa-Edwards Paper Co. v. Nekoosa Council, Cir. Ct., Wood County, (Judge Park), October, 1919. (*Grand Rapids* [Wis.] *Daily Leader*, Aug. 7, 8, Oct. 13, 1919.)

Oshkosh Trunk Co. v. Leather Workers, Winnebago County, 1920. (*Oshkosh Daily Northwestern*, Sept. 3, 1920.)

Hamilton-Beach Manufacturing Co. v. Special Machinists, Local 767, Racine County, 1921. (*Racine Times-Call*, Jan. 17, 1921.)

Trade Press Publishing Co. v. Milwaukee Typographical Union, Cir. Ct., Milwaukee County, 1921.

Polacheck v. Amalgamated Clothing Workers, Milwaukee County, March, 1923. (*Documentary History of the Amalgamated Clothing Workers*, 1920–1922, p. xxxiv.)

APPENDIX C

DECISIONS OF TRIAL COURTS IN LABOR INJUNCTION CASES REVERSED UPON APPEAL

I. *Injunctions Dissolved or Modified upon the Defendants' Appeal.*

Arthur v. Oakes, 63 Fed. 310 (1894).

Kemmerer v. Haggerty, 139 Fed. 693 (1905).

Iron Molders' Union v. Allis-Chalmers Co., 166 Fed. 45 (1908).

Corcoran v. National Telephone Co., 175 Fed. 761 (1909).

Bittner v. West Virginia-Pittsburgh Coal Co., 214 Fed. 716 (1914).

Hill v. Eagle Glass Manufacturing Co., 219 Fed. 719 (1915).

Hitchman Coal and Coke Co. v. Mitchell, 214 Fed. 685 (1917). (Reversed in 245 U. S. 229.)

Tri-city Central Trades Council v. American Steel Foundries, 238 Fed. 728 (1917).

Mahon v. Guaranty Trust and Safe Deposit Co., 239 Fed. 266 (1917).

Niles-Bement-Pond Co. v. Iron Molders, 258 Fed. 408 (1918).

Davis v. Henry, 266 Fed. 261 (1920).

Buyer v. Guillan, 271 Fed. 65 (1921).

Gable v. Vonnegut Machinery Co. 273 Fed. 66 (1921).

Gasaway v. Borderland Coal Corp., 275 Fed. 871 (1921).

Keeney v. Borderland Coal Corp., 282 Fed. 269 (1922).

Dwyer v. Alpha Pocahontas Coal Co.; Willis Branch Coal Co. v. Keeney; Dry Branch Coal Co. v. Keeney; Nelson Fuel Co. v. Keeney; Aetna-Sewell Smokeless Coal Co. v. Dwyer; all 282 Fed. 270 (1922).

United Mine Workers v. Lievale Coal Co., 285 Fed. 32 (1922).

Danville Local Union v. Danville Brick Co., 283 Fed. 909 (1922).

Foss v. Portland Terminal Co., 287 Fed. 33 (1923).

Carbon Fuel Co. v. International Organization, 288 Fed. 1020 (1923).

National Assoc. Window Glass Workers v. U. S., 263 U. S. 403, 44 Sup. Ct. 148 (1923).

United Leather Workers v. Herkert & Meisel Trunk Co., 265 U. S. 457, 44 Sup. Ct. 623 (1924).

Bittner v. West Virginia-Pittsburgh Coal Co., 15 F. (2nd) 652 (1926).

Goldberg-Bowen Co. v. Stablemen's Union, 149 Cal. 429, 86 Pac. 806 (1906).

Parkinson Co. v. Building Trades Council, 154 Cal. 581, 98 Pac. 1027 (1908).

Crescent Feather Co. v. United Upholsterers, 153 Cal. 433, 95 Pac. 871 (1908).

Pierce v. Stablemen's Union, 156 Cal. 70, 103 Pac. 324 (1909).

Southern California Iron and Steel Co. v. Amal. Assoc., 186 Cal. 604, 200 Pac. 1 (1921).

Jones v. Van Winkle General, etc., Co., 131 Ga. 336, 62 S. E., 236 (1908).

Burgess v. Ga. F. & A. R. Co., 148 Ga. 415, 96 S. E. 864 (1918).

Burgess v. Ga. F. & A. R. Co., 148 Ga. 417, 96 S. E. 865 (1918).

Robinson v. Hotel and Restaurant Employees, 35 Ida. 418, 207 Pac. 132 (1922).

Shaughnessy v. Jordan, 184 Ind. 499, 111 N. E. 622 (1916).

Diamond Block Coal Co. v. United Mine Workers, 188 Ky. 477, 222 S. W. 1079 (1920).

International Pocketbook Workers v. Orlove, 148 Atl. 826 (Md. 1930).

Pickett v. Walsh, 192 Mass. 572, 78 N. E. 753 (1906).

Hotel and Railroad News Co. v. Leventhal, 243 Mass. 317, 137 N. E. 534 (1922).

Escanaba Manufacturing Co. v. Trades and Labor Council, 160 Mich. 656, 125 N. W. 709 (1910).

Gray v. Building Trades Council, 191 Minn. 171, 97 N. W. 663 (1903).

Minnesota Stove Co. v. Cavanaugh, 131 Minn. 458, 155 N. W. 638 (1915).

Marx, etc., Clothing Co. v. Watson, 168 Mo. 133, 675 W. 391 (1902).

New Jersey Painting Co. v. Local 26, 96 N. J. Eq. 632, 126 Atl. 399 (1924).

Sinsheimer v. United Garment Workers, 28 N. Y. S. 321 (1894).

Sun Printing, etc., Co. v. Delaney, 48 App. Div. 623, 62 N. Y. S. 750 (1900).

Mills v. U. S. Printing Co., 99 App. Div. 605, 91 N. Y. S. 185 (1904).

Kissam v. U. S. Printing Co., 199 N. Y. 76, 92 N. E. 214 (1910).

Grassi Construction Co. v. Bennett, 174 App. Div. 244, 160 N. Y. S. 279 (1916).

Bossert v. Dhuy, 221 N. Y. 342, 117 N. E. 582 (1917).

Albro J. Newton Co. v. Erickson, 221 N. Y. 632, 117 N. E. 1059 (1917).

Reardon v. Caton, 189 App. Div. 501, 178 N. Y. S. 713 (1919).

Piermont v. Schlessinger, 196 App. Div., 658, 188 N. Y. S. 35 (1912).

A. L. Reed Co. v. Whiteman, 238 N. Y. 545, 144 N. E. 885 (1924).

Wilson & Adams Co. v. Pearce, 218 App. Div. 865, 219 N. Y. S. 940 (1926).

Federal Hats, Inc., v. Golden, 226 N. Y. S. 747 (1927).

Exchange Bakery and Restaurant, Inc., v. Riffkin, 245 N. Y. 260, 157 N. E. 130 (1927).

Interborough Rapid Transit Co. v. Lavin, 247 N. Y. 65, 159 N. E. 863 (1928).

Nann v. Raimist, 174 N. E. 690 (N. Y. 1931).

Smith v. Bricklayers', etc., Union, 2 *Law and Labor* 43 (Ohio App. 1919).

McManus-Troup Co. v. International Typographical Union, 7 *Law and Labor* 22 (Ohio App. 1924).

Greenfield v. Central Labor Council, 104 Ore. 259, 192 Pac. 783, 207 Pac. 168 (1922).

Crouch v. Central Labor Council, 293 Pac. 729 (Ore. 1930).

Rhodes Bros. Co. v. Musicians, 37 R. I. 281, 92 Atl. 641 (1915).

Adler Co. v. Magglio, 228 N. W. 123 (Wis. 1930).

II. *Successful Appeals by Complainants.*

Eagle Glass and Manufacturing Co. v. Rowe, 245 U. S. 275, 38 Sup. Ct. 80 (1917).

Duplex Printing Press Co. v. Deering, 254 U. S. 443, 41 Sup. Ct. 172 (1921).

Buyer v. Guillan, 271 Fed. 65 (1921).

Kinloch Telephone Co. v. Local Union 2, 275 Fed. 241 (1921).

Truax v. Corrigan, 257 U. S. 312, 42 Sup. Ct. 124 (1921).

Staudte & Rueckholdt Manufacturing Co. v. Carpenters, 12 F. (2nd) 867 (1926).

Aeolian Co. v. Fischer, 40 F. (2nd) 189 (1930).

Hardie-Tynes Manufacturing Co. v. Cruse, 189 Ala. 66, 66 So. 657 (1914).

Patterson Glass Co. v. Thomas, 41 Cal. App. 559, 183 Pac. 190 (1919).

Rosenberg v. Retail Clerks, 39 Cal. App. 67, 177 Pac. 864 (1918).

Henrici Co. v. Alexander, 198 Ill. App. 568 (1916).

Scofes v. Helmar, 153 N. E. 802 (Ind. 1926).

Beck v. Railway Teamsters, 118 Mich. 497, 77 N. W. 13 (1898).

Ideal Manufacturing Co. v. Wayne Circuit Judge, 139 Mich. 92, 102 N. W. 372 (1905).

Baltic Mining Co. v. Houghton Circuit Judge, 177 Mich. 632, 144 N. W. 209 (1913).

Hughes v. K. C. Motion Picture Operators, 282 Mo. 304, 221 S. W. 95 (1920).

Master Horseshoers v. Quinlivan, 83 App. Div. 459, 82 N. Y. S. 288 (1903).

Altman v. Schlesinger, 204 App. Div. 513, 198 N. Y. S. 128 (1923).

Yablonowitz v. Korn, 205 App. Div. 440, 199 N. Y. S. 769 (1923).

Arnheim, Inc., v. Hillman, 198 App. Div. 88, 189 N. Y. S. 369 (1926).

Daitch & Co. v. Retail, etc., Clerks' Union, 218 App. Div. 80, 217 N. Y. S. 817 (1927).

Rentner v. Sigman, 216 App. Div. 407, 215 N. Y. S. 323 (1926).

Carnation Photoplay, Inc., v. Basson, 215 N. Y. S. 824 (1926).

Citizens Co. v. Asheville Typographical Union, 187 N. C. 42, 121 S. E. 31 (1924).

Asheville Times Co. v. Asheville Typographical Union, 187 N. C. 157, 121 S. E. 37 (1924).

McGinnis v. Raleigh Typographical Union, 182 N. C. 770, 108 S. E. 728 (1921).

Kilby Mfg. Co. v. Local 218, 5 *Law and Labor*, 93 (Ohio App. 1922).

Wick China Co. v. Brown, 164 Pa. 449, 30 Atl. 261 (1894).

O'Neil v. Behanna, 182 Pa. 236, 37 Atl. 843 (1897).

Nashville R. & L. Co. v. Lawson, 144 Tenn. 78, 229 S. W. 741 (1921).

Webb v. Cooks, etc., Union, 205 S. W. 465 (Tex. Civ. App., 1918).

Commercial Binding, etc., Co. v. Tacoma Typographical Union, 85 Wash. 234, 147 Pac. 1143 (1915).

St. Germain v. Bakery, etc., Workers' Union, 97 Wash. 282, 166 Pac. 665 (1917).

Baasch v. Cooks' Union, 99 Wash. 378, 169 Pac. 843 (1918).

Pacific Coast Coal Co. v. District 10, United Mine Workers, 122 Wash. 423, 210 Pac. 953 (1922).

Danz v. American Federation of Musicians, 133 Wash. 186, 233 Pac. 630 (1925).

APPENDIX D

SUCCESSFUL DAMAGE SUITS AGAINST LABOR UNIONS OR THEIR MEMBERS FOR ACTS COMMITTED IN BEHALF OF THE UNION

I. *Cases in Which Final Judgments Were Rendered or Settlements Made Out of Court.*

Carew v. Rutherford, 106 Mass. 1 (1871). Judgment never paid as a new strike compelled plaintiff to forego collection. (*Amer. Workman*, Aug. 19, 1871.)

Webber v. Barry, 66 Mich. 127, 33 N. W. 289 (1887).

Parker v. Bricklayers' Union, 10 Ohio Dec. Reprint 458 (1889).

People *ex rel.* Deverell v. Musical Mutual Protective Union, 118 N. Y. 101 (1889). (Incorporated union.)

Moores v. Bricklayers' Union, 10 Ohio Dec. Reprint 665 (1890).

Mersheim v. Musical Mutual Protective Union, 8 N. Y. S. 702 (1890). (Incorporated union.)

Toledo, Ann Arbor R. R. Co. v. Arthur (president, Brotherhood Locomotive Engineers). Two thousand five hundred dollars damages paid at close of Ann Arbor strike in 1893. (*Amer. Federationist*, pp. 54–56, January, 1895.)

Connell v. Stalker, 20 Misc. 423, 45 N. Y. S. 1048 (1897).

Curran v. Galen, 152 N. Y. 33, 46 N. E. 297 (1897).

Hess v. San Francisco Typographical Union, Sup. Ct., San Francisco, 1898. Award of $1,200 damages to non-unionist. (Lucile Eaves, "History of California Labor Legislation," pp. 397–403, Univ. of California Press [1910].)

Berdnerick v. Manhattan Shirt-Ironers' Assoc., Dist. Ct. Passaic, N. J., 1902. One hundred dollars damages awarded to union member wrongfully expelled. (*N. Y. World*, Nov. 22, 1902.)

Berry v. Donovan, 188 Mass. 353, 74 N. E. 603 (1905).

Fuerst v. Musical Mutual Protective Union, 95 N. Y. S. 155 (1905). (Incorporated union.)

F. R. Patch Manufacturing Co. v. Protection Lodge, 77 Vt. 294, 60 Atl. 74 (1905); F. R. Patch Manufacturing Co. v. Capeless, 79 Vt. 1, 63 Atl. 938 (1906).

Schneider v. Local Union 60, 116 La. 270, 40 So. 700 (1905).

Thompson v. Grand International Brotherhood, 41 Tex. Civ. App. 176, 91 S. W. 834 (1905); St. Louis S. W. R. Co. v. Thompson, 102 Tex. 89, 113 S. W. 144 (1908); 192 S. W. 1095 (1917).

March v. Bricklayers' Union, 79 Conn. 7, 63 Atl. 291 (1906).

Purvis v. United Brotherhood, 214 Pa. 348, 63 Atl. 585 (1906).

Brennan v. United Hatters, 73 N. J. L. 729, 65 Atl. 165 (1906).

Schultz v. Dressen, Racine Co., Wis., 1906. Action against Racine Trades and Labor Council and about one hundred individuals by master baker declared unfair. (*Milwaukee Sentinel*, Aug. 29, 1906.)

Loewe v. Lawlor, 148 Fed. 924 (1907); 208 U. S. 274, 28 Sup. Ct. 301 (1908); 187 Fed. 552 (1911); 223 U. S. 729 (1912); 209 Fed. 712 (1913); 235 U. S. 522, 35 Sup. Ct. 170 (1915).

Wyeman v. Deady, 79 Conn. 414, 65 Atl. 129 (1906).

Aberthaw Construction Co. v. Cameron, 194 Mass. 208, 80 N. E. 478 (1907).

Campbell v. Johnson, 167 Fed. 102 (1909).

J. B. Honor & Co. v. Longshoremen's Union of New Orleans. One thousand two hundred dollars damages awarded in 1909 for breach of trade agreement. (*Birmingham Labor Advocate*, Feb. 5, 1909.) (Union probably incorporated.)

Jones v. Maher, 116 N. Y. S. 180 (1909); 125 N. Y. S. 1126 (1911).

Blanchard v. Newark Dist. Council, 77 N. J. L. 389, 71 Atl. 1131 (1909).

Ruddy v. United Assoc., 79 N. J. L. 388, 75 Atl. 742 (1910).

Folsom v. Lewis, 208 Mass. 336, 94 N. E. 316 (1911).

De Minico v. Craig, 207 Mass. 593, 94 N. E. 317 (1911).

Hanson v. Innis, 211 Mass. 301, 97 N. E. 756 (1912).

Sutton v. Workmeister, 164 Ill. App. 105 (1912).

Berry Foundry Co. v. International Molders' Union, 177 Mo. App. 84, 164 S. W. 245 (1914).

United Mine Workers v. Cromer, 159 Ky. 605, 167 S. W. 891 (1914).

Burnham v. Dowd, 214 Mass. 351, 104 N. E. 841 (1914).

Fairbanks v. McDonald, 219 Mass. 291, 106 N. E. 1000 (1914).

Auburn Draying Co. v. Wardell, 178 App. Div. 270, 165 N. Y. 469 (1917); 227 N. Y. 1, 124 N. E. 97 (1919).

Dowd v. United Mine Workers of America, 235 Fed. 1 (1916), 242 U. S. 653 (1917); Coronado Coal Co. v. United Mine Workers of America, 258 Fed. 829 (1919); United Mine Workers of America v. Coronado Coal Co., 259 U. S. 344, 42 Sup. Ct. 570 (1922); Finley v. United Mine Workers of America, 300 Fed. 972 (1924); United Mine Workers of America v. Coronado Coal Co., 268 U. S. 295, 45 Sup. Ct. 551 (1925).

Cisco v. Looper, 236 Fed. 336 (1916).

Robinson v. Dahm, 94 Misc. 729, 159 N. Y. S. 1053 (1916).

Mukijian v. Tracey, Sup. Ct., Essex County, Mass. Two hundred dollars damages and costs to non-unionist in suit against Lasters' Union 1 of Lynn. (*Mass. Labor Bull.* 117, p. 208.)

Shinsky v. Tracey, 226 Mass. 21, 114 N. E. 957 (1917).

Harvey v. Chapman, 226 Mass. 191, 115 N. E. 304 (1917).

Clarkson v. Laiblan, 202 Mo. App. 682, 216 S. W. 1029 (1919). See 161 S. W. 660 and 664 for earlier phases of this case.

Sander v. Amalgamated Clothing Workers, 1 *Law and Labor* 4 (Mass., January, 1919).

Nederlansch, etc., v. Stevedores, etc., Society, 265 Fed. 397 (1920). (Incorporated union.)

Langenberg Hat Co. v. United Cloth Hat and Cap Makers, 226 Fed. 127 (1920). Final outcome reported in 11 *Monthly Labor Rev.* 195 (1920).

Godin v. Niebuhr, 236 Mass. 350, 128 N. E. 406 (1920).

Sister v. Du Bourg, 3 *Law and Labor* 70 (N. Y. 1921).

Jackson v. Brown, 3 *Law and Labor* 53 (Mass. 1921).

Stenzel v. Cavanaugh, 189 N. Y. S. 883 (1921).

Meyer v. Local 26, International Ladies Garment Workers Union, 3 *Law and Labor*, 247 (Ohio Comm. Pleas, 1921).

Pacific Typesetting Co. v. International Typographical Union, 125 Wash. 273, 216 Pac. 358 (1923).

R. & W. Hat Shop v. Sculley, 98 Conn. 1, 118 Atl. 55 (1922).

Geo. T. McLauthlin Co. v. McDonald, 4 *Law and Labor* 288 (Mass. 1922).

Southern Illinois Coal Co. v. United Mine Workers of America 12, U. S. Dist. Ct., S. D. Ill., 1922. Settled by purchase of property of complainants. (6 *Law and Labor* 295.)

Grand International Brotherhood of Locomotive Engineers v. Green, 210 Ala. 496, 98 So. 569 (1923).

Local Union 65 v. McNalty, 7 F. (2nd) 100 (1925).

Culberson v. United Brotherhood of Carpenters and Joiners; Baldridge v. Same; Wunrath v. Same, Sup. Ct., City and County of San Francisco, 1926. Damage suits by non-unionists who were assaulted during the San Francisco carpenters' strike in 1926. Settled out of court by payment to the plaintiffs of five thousand, one thousand, and eight hundred dollars respectively. (Information from Paul Eitel, director industrial relations, Industrial Assoc. of San Francisco.)

Mullen v. Seegers, 220 Mo. App. 847, 294 S. W. 745 (1927).

Colsen v. Furriers' Union, Sup. Ct., N. Y. C. Twenty-five thousand dollars damages awarded in uncontested suit to non-unionist, 1926. (*N. Y. Times*, Sept. 2, 1926.)

Alden Bros. v. Dunn, 264 Mass. 355, 162 N. E. 773 (1928).

Bricklayers, Masons and Plasterers' International Union v. Seymour Ruff & Co., 154 Atl. 52 (Md. 1931).

Decorative Stone Co. v. Building Trades' Council, U. S. Dist. Ct., S. D. N. Y. (1931).

II. *Cases in Which Unions or Their Members Were Held Liable but in Which the Case Was Remanded for Further Proceedings.*

Walker v. Cronin, 107 Mass. 555 (1871).

Old Dominion S. S. Co. v. McKenna, 30 Fed. 48 (1887).

Luecke v. Clothing Cutters, 77 Md. 396, 26 Atl. 505 (1893). (Incorporated union.)

Perkins v. Pendleton, 90 Me. 166, 38 Atl. 96 (1897).

O'Neill v. Behanna, 182 Pa. 236, 37 Atl. 843 (1897).

Thacker Coal and Coke Co. v. Burke, 59 W. Va. 253, 53 S. E. 161 (1906).

Carter v. Oster, 134 Mo. App. 146, 112 S. W. 995 (1908).

Bausbach v. Rieff, 237 Pac. 482, 85 Atl. 762 (1912); 244 Pa. 559, 91 Atl. 224 (1914).

Connors v. Connolly, 86 Conn. 641, 86 Atl. 600 (1913).

Powers v. Journeymen Bricklayers' Union, 130 Tenn. 643, 172 S. W. 284 (1914).

New England Cement Gun Co. v. McGivern, 218 Mass. 198, 105 N. E. 885 (1914).

Max Ams Machine Co. v. International Assoc. of Machinists, 92 Conn. 297, 102 Atl. 706 (1917).

Michaels v. Hillman, 112 Misc. 395, 183 N. Y. S. 195 (1920).

Brescia Construction Co. v. Stone Mason Contractors, 195 App. Div. 647, 187 N. Y. S. 77 (1921).

Order of Railway Conductors v. Jones, 78 Colo. 80, 239 Pac. 882 (1925).

INDEX

A

Absolute-rights theory, 59–60
Adair case, 212
Adamson Act, 240
Adjustment methods, appraisal of, 306–309
  in continental countries, 328–331
  in Great Britain, 318–320
Affidavits in injunction cases, 86–88, 92
Agency law applied to unions, 144–148
American Bar Association, recommendations on legislation, 287–288
American Railway Union strike, 121
American Steel Foundries case, 35–36, 54
Antiinjunction legislation and proposals, 265–289
Anti-syndicalism laws, 12–13, 79
Antitrust laws, 61–74, 77
  proposals to repeal, 281
Appeals, cases reversed on, list of, 341–344
Arbitration, Australasian system, 321–324
  and conciliation, 236–264
  suggestions on, 306–309
  (*See also* Conciliation.)
  in Great Britain, 318–320
  Kansas Act, 255–260
  proposals for compulsory arbitration in United States, 9
  under trade agreements, 260–262
Arrests, 152–159

B

Bedford Cut Stone Co. case, 72–73, 117
Bibliography (*See* end of each chapter).
Blacklisting, 213–218
Bonds in injunction cases, 91
Boycotts, employers', 208
  injunctions against, 119–120
  law of, 38–43
  state laws against, 78
  suggestions on law, 296–297
British policy toward unions, 313–321
British Trades Disputes Act, 316–318
Bucks' Stove and Range Co. case, 41, 43, 119

C

Canadian Industrial Disputes Investigation Act, 324–327
Clayton Act, 66–74
  history of, 268–270
Closed shop, 23–26
Coal and iron police, 192–193
Colorado Industrial Disputes Act, 253–255
Company guards, 190–192
  police powers of, 192–194
  restrictions on, 209–211
Company unions, 5
  law of, 218–220
Complaints and answers in injunction cases, 85–88
Conciliation, and arbitration, 236–264

349